STUDY GUIDE

PARKIN

MACROECONOMICS

FIFTH EDITION

MARK RUSH
University of Florida

Addison-Wesley
An imprint of Addison Wesley Longman, Inc.

Reading, Massachusetts ◆ Menlo Park, California ◆ New York
Harlow, England ◆ Don Mills, Ontario ◆ Sydney
Mexico City ◆ Madrid ◆ Amsterdam

ISBN 0-201-63787-1
1 2 3 4 5 6 7 8 9 10 - CRS - 03020100

HOW TO EARN AN A!

■ Introduction

My experience has taught me that what students want most from a study guide is help in mastering course material in order to do well on examinations. I have developed this *Study Guide* to respond specifically to that demand. Using this *Study Guide* alone, however, is not enough to guarantee that you will do well in your course. In order to help you overcome the problems and difficulties that most students encounter, I have some general advice on how to study, as well as some specific advice on how best to use this *Study Guide*.

Economics requires a different style of thinking than what you may encounter in other courses. Economists make extensive use of assumptions to break down complex problems into simple, analytically manageable parts. This analytical style, while ultimately not more demanding than the styles of thinking in other disciplines, feels unfamiliar to most students and requires practice. As a result, it is not as easy to do well in economics on the basis of your raw intelligence and high-school knowledge as it is in many other courses. Many students who come to my office are frustrated and puzzled by the fact that they are getting A's and B's in their other courses but only a C or worse in economics. They have not recognized that economics is different and requires practice. In order to avoid a frustrating visit to your instructor after your first test, I suggest you do the following.

◆ *Don't rely solely on your high-school economics.* If you took high-school economics, you have seen the material on supply and demand which your instructor will lecture on in the first few weeks. Don't be lulled into feeling that the course will be easy. Your high-school knowledge of economic concepts will be very useful, but it will not be enough to guarantee high scores on exams. Your college or university instructors will demand much more detailed knowledge of concepts and ask you to apply them in new circumstances.

◆ *Keep up with the course material on a weekly basis.* Skim the appropriate chapter in the textbook *before* your instructor lectures on it. In this initial reading, don't worry about details or arguments you can't quite follow — just try to get a general understanding of the basic concepts and issues. You may be amazed at how your instructor's ability to teach improves when you come to class prepared. As soon as your instructor has finished covering a chapter, complete the corresponding *Study Guide* chapter. Avoid cramming the day before or even just the week before an exam. Because economics requires practice, cramming is an almost certain recipe for failure.

◆ *Keep a good set of lecture notes.* Good lecture notes are vital for focusing your studying. Your instructor will only lecture on a subset of topics from the textbook. The topics your instructor covers in a lecture should usually be given priority when studying. Also give priority to studying the figures and graphs covered in the lecture.

Instructors do differ in their emphasis on lecture notes and the textbook, so ask early on in the course which is *more* important in reviewing for exams — lecture notes or the textbook. If your instructor answers that both are important, then ask the following, typical economic question: which will be more beneficial — spending an extra hour re-reading your lecture notes or an extra hour re-reading the textbook? This question assumes that you have read each textbook chapter twice (once before lecture for a general understanding, and then later for a thorough understanding); that you have prepared a good set of lecture notes; and that you have worked through all of the problems in the appropriate *Study Guide* chapters. By applying this style of analysis to the problem of efficiently allocating your study time, you are already beginning to think like an economist!

◆ *Use your instructor and/or teaching assistants for help.* When you have questions or problems with course material, come to the office to ask questions. Remember, you are paying for your education and instructors are there to help you learn. I am often amazed at how few students come to see me during office hours. Don't be shy. The personal contact that comes from one-on-one tutoring is professionally gratifying for instructors as well as (hopefully) beneficial for you.

◆ *Form a study group.* A very useful way to motivate your studying and to learn economics is to discuss the course material and problems with other students. Explaining the answer to a question *out loud* is a very effective way of discovering how well you understand the question. When you answer a question only in your head, you often skip steps in the chain of reasoning without realizing it. When you are forced to explain your reasoning aloud, gaps and mistakes quickly appear, and you (with your fellow group members) can quickly correct your reasoning. The "You're the Teacher" questions in the *Study Guide* and the Review questions at the end of each textbook chapter are extremely good study group material. You might also get together *after* having worked the *Study Guide* problems, but *before* looking at the answers, and help each other solve unsolved problems. You may also find it useful to participate in the on-line, E-mail discussion located on the Internet at ParkinSt@AW.COM.

◆ *Work old exams.* One of the most effective ways of studying is to work through exams your instructor has given in previous years. Old exams give you a feel for the style of question your instructor may ask, and give you the opportunity to get used to time pressure if you force yourself to do the exam in the allotted time. Studying from old exams is not cheating, as long as you have obtained a copy of the exam legally. Some institutions keep old exams in the library, others in the department. Students who have previously taken the course are usually a good source as well. Remember, though, that old exams are a useful study aid only if you use them to *understand* the reasoning behind each question. If you simply memorize answers in the hopes that your instructor will repeat the identical question, you are likely to fail. From year to year, instructors routinely change the questions or change the numerical values for similar questions.

◆ *Use Economics in Action.* This is state-of-the-art interactive software for IBM-compatible computers. It is an integrated tutorial, graphing, demonstration, and testing program that covers all the main themes in the textbook using three modes. The tutorial mode places you in an economics-related job situation and leads you through assignments that reveal and explore economic concepts and principles. The free mode allows you to interact with economic models by changing parameters and observing the effects on graphs. The quiz mode gives you graphical or data-related multiple-choice questions. When you select an answer, you are given a detailed explanation (and graphical illustration) of why your answer is right or wrong. All software modes are closely integrated with the textbook.

■ Using Your *Study Guide*

You should only attempt to complete a chapter in the *Study Guide* after you have read the corresponding textbook chapter and listened to your instructor lecture on the material. Each *Study Guide* chapter contains the following sections.

Key Concepts. This first section is a short summary, in point form, of all key definitions, concepts and material from the textbook chapter. Key terms from the textbook appear in bold. Each term in bold is in the glossary of the textbook. This first section is designed to focus you quickly and precisely on the core material that you *must* master. It is an excellent study aid for the night before an exam. Think of it as crib notes that will serve as a final check of the key concepts you have studied.

Helpful Hints. When you encounter difficulty in mastering concepts or techniques, you will not be alone. Many students find certain concepts difficult and often make the same kinds of mistakes. I have taught over 17,000 students the principles of economics and I have seen these common mistakes often enough to have learned how to help students avoid them. The hints point out these mistakes and offer tips to avoid them. The hints focus on the most important concepts, equations, and techniques for problem solving. They also review crucial graphs that appear on every instructor's exams. I hope that this section will be very useful, because instructors always ask exam questions designed to test these possible mistakes in your understanding.

Self-Test. This will be one of the most useful sections of the *Study Guide*. The questions are designed to give you practice and to test skills and techniques you must master to do well on exams.

There are plenty of multiple-choice type of questions and other types of questions in the Self-Test, each with a specific pedagogical purpose. Indeed, this book contains over 825 multiple choice questions in total! Before I describe the four parts of the Self-Test section, here are some general tips that apply to all parts.

Use a pencil to write your answers in the *Study Guide* so you have neat, complete pages from which to study. Draw graphs wherever they are applicable. Some questions will ask explicitly for graphs; many others will not but will require a chain of reasoning that involves shifts of curves on a graph. *Always draw the graph.* Don't try to work through the reasoning in your head — you are much more likely to make mistakes that way. Whenever you draw a graph, even in the margins of the *Study Guide,* label the axes. You may think that you can keep the labels in your head, but you will be confronting many different graphs with many different variables on the axes. Avoid confusion and label. As an added incentive, remember that on exams where graphs are required, instructors will deduct points for unlabelled axes.

Do the Self-Test questions as if they were real exam questions, which means do them *without looking at the answers.* This is the single most important tip I can give you about effectively using the *Study Guide* to improve your exam performance. Struggling for the answers to questions that you find difficult is one of the most effective ways to learn. The adage — no pain, no gain — applies well to studying. You will learn the most from right answers you had to struggle for and from your wrong answers and mistakes. Only after you have attempted all the questions should you look at the answers. When you finally do check the answers, be sure to understand where you went wrong and why the right answer is correct.

There are many questions in each chapter, and it will take you somewhere between two and six hours to answer all of them. If you get tired (or bored), don't burn yourself out by trying to work through all of the questions in one sitting. Consider breaking up your Self-Test over two (or more) study sessions.

The four parts of the Self-Test section are:

True/False/Uncertain and Explain. These questions test basic knowledge of concepts and your ability to apply the concepts. Some of the questions challenge your understanding, to see if you can identify mistakes in statements using basic concepts. These questions will identify gaps in your knowledge and are useful to answer out loud in a study group.

When answering, identify each statement as *true, false,* or whether you are *uncertain* because the statement may be true or false depending on circumstances or assumptions. Explain your answer in one sentence in the space underneath each question.

Multiple-Choice. These more difficult questions test your analytical abilities by asking you to apply concepts to new situations, manipulate information and solve numerical and graphical problems.

This is the most frequently used type of exam question, and the Self-Test contains many of them.

Read each question and all four choices carefully before you answer. Many of the choices will be plausible and will differ only slightly. You must choose the one *best* answer. A useful strategy in working these questions is first to eliminate any obviously wrong choices and then to focus on the remaining alternatives. Don't get frustrated or think that you are dim if you can't immediately see the correct answer. These questions are designed to make you work to find the correct choice.

Short Answer. Each chapter contains several Short Answer questions. Some are straightforward questions about basic concepts. They can generally be answered in a few sentences or, at most, in one paragraph. Others are problems. The best way to learn to do economics is to do problems. Problems are also the second-most popular type of exam question — practice them as much as possible!

You're the Teacher. Each chapter contains from one to three questions that either cover very broad issues or errors that are all too common among students. These questions may be the most valuable you will encounter for use in your study group. Take turns by pretending that you are the teacher and answer the questions for the rest of your group. Who knows, you may like this process so much that you actually do become a professor at a university teaching economics!

Answers. The Self-Test is followed by answers to all questions. Unlike other study guides on the market, I have included complete answers because I believe that reading complete answers will help you master the material ... and that's what this *Study Guide* is all about! But do *not* look at an answer until you have attempted a question. When you do finally look, use the answers to understand where you went wrong and why the right answer is correct.

As you work through the material, you'll find that the true/false and multiple choice questions, as well as their answers, are identified by a heading from the textbook. If you find that you are missing a lot of questions from one particular section, it is time to head back to the textbook and bone up on this material! In other words, *use* the textbook and this study guide to pull the A you want to earn!

Chapter Quiz. The last page in each chapter contains another 10 multiple questions covering the material in the chapter. These are questions that I and other instructors have included on our exams. Because these questions have been written by several instructors, they differ in style from the others in the chapter and are thus a very good tool to be sure that you grasp the material. You can use the questions immediately after you finish each chapter, or else you can hoard them to help you prepare when exam time rolls around. In either case, the answers are given at the back of the book.

Part Overview Problem. Every few chapters, at the end of each of the parts of the textbook, you will find a special problem (and answer). These multi-part problems draw on material from the part you have just concluded and are similar to the "Reading Between the Lines" sections in your textbook. There is also a self-test that contains four multiple choice questions drawn from each chapter in the section. The questions are in order, with the first four from the first chapter in the section, the second four from the second chapter, and so forth. If you miss several questions from one chapter, you'll know to spend more time on that chapter when preparing for your exam. These multiple choice questions are written in a different style than those in the chapter because instructors have different ways of writing questions. By encountering different styles, you will be better prepared for *your* test.

Final Exams. At the end of the *Study Guide* are two multiple choice final exams and answers. These are final exams that I have used in my class at the University of Florida. You should use them to help you study for the final exam in your class.

If you effectively combine the use of the textbook, the *Study Guide, Economics in Action,* and all other course resources, you will be well prepared for exams. You will also have developed analytical skills and powers of reasoning that will benefit you throughout your life and in whatever career you choose.

■ Your Future and Economics

After your class is concluded, you may well wonder about economics as a major. The last essay in this *Study Guide*, written by Robert Whaples, helps examine your future by discussing whether economics is the major for

you. I invite you to read this chapter and consider the information in it. Economics is a major with a bright future so I think you'll be interested in this important chapter.

■ Final Comments

I have tried to make the *Study Guide* as helpful and useful as possible. Undoubtedly I have made some mistakes; mistakes that you may see. If you find any, I, and succeeding generations of students, would be grateful if you could point them out to me. At the end of my class at the University of Florida, when I ask my students for their advice, I point out to them that this advice won't help them at all because they have just completed the class. But, comments they make will influence how future students are taught. Thus, just as they owe a debt of gratitude for the comments and suggestions that I received from students before them, so too will students after them owe them an (unpaid and unpayable) debt. You are in the same situation. If you have questions, suggestions, or simply comments, let me know. My address is on the next page, or you can reach me via E-mail at either ParkinEd@AW.COM or else directly at RUSH@DALE.CBA.UFL.EDU. Your input probably won't benefit you directly, but it will benefit following generations. And, if you give me permission, I will note your name and school in following editions so that any younger siblings (or, years down the road, maybe even your children!) will see your name and offer up thanks.

To date, students who have uncovered errors and to whom we all owe a debt of gratitude include:

♦ Jeanie Callen at the University of Minnesota-Twin Cities.

♦ Brian Mulligan at the University of Florida

♦ Patrick Lusby at the University of Florida

♦ Jonathan Baskind at the University of Florida

♦ Breina Polk at Cook College at Rutgers University

♦ Ethan Schulman at the University of Iowa

♦ Adrian Garza at the University of Iowa

♦ Curtis Hazel at the University of North Florida

♦ Zhang Zili at American University

♦ Valerie Stewart at the University of Georgia

♦ Rob Bleeker at The Ohio State University

♦ Katherine Hamilton at the University of Florida

♦ Dennis Spinks at The Ohio State University

♦ Debbie McGuffie at the University of Florida

I owe Avi J. Cohen, of York University, and Harvey B. King, of University of Regina. Their superb study guide for the Canadian edition of Michael Parkin's book was the basis for this study guide. This book uses many of their chapter summaries, helpful hints, and questions. Much of what is good about the book is a direct reflection of their work.

Robert Whaples of Wake Forest University wrote the section of the *Study Guide* dealing with majoring in economics. He also checked an edition of the manuscript for errors and provided questions that I use in this edition. Robert is a superb economist and this book is by far the better for this fact! Another brilliant teacher, Carol Dole of University of North Carolina at Charlotte, also supplied questions that I use with this edition. I think it fair to say that the clever questions are the work of Carol and Robert. For a previous edition, Andrew Foshee of McNeese State University checked the entire manuscript for accuracy. I wish I could report that he found none... but such reporting would be dishonest. He found many errors and I think I adopted each suggestion he made.

Deb Kiernan at Addison Wesley Longman played a key role coordinating my work; her cheerful voice at the other end of the phone was a truly motivating factor. How anyone can be so chipper at all hours of the day is a marvel... and also somewhat obscene. I also owe Lena Buonanno a debt for keeping track of the suggestions made about how to improve previous editions of the *Study Guide*. Without her efforts, I would have worked a lot less (so, why am I thanking her?) but the *Study Guide* would be the poorer (oh yeah, that's why I'm thanking her!).

I need to thank Michael Parkin and Robin Bade. Michael has written such a superior book that it was easy to be enthusiastic about writing the *Study Guide* to accompany it. Moreover, both Michael and Robin have played a hands on role in creating this *Study Guide* and have made suggestions that vastly improved the *Study Guide*.

I want to thank my family: Susan, Tommy, Bobby, and Kathryn, who, respectively: allowed me to work all hours on this book; helped me master the intricacies of FTPing computer files; let me postpone riding bicycles with him until after the book was concluded; and would run into my typing room to share her new discoveries. Thanks a lot!

Finally, I want to thank Nerf and Pearl who sat at my feet and next to the computer in a box (and occasionally meowed) while I typed.

Mark Rush
Economics Department
University of Florida
Gainesville, Florida 32611
May, 1999.

Table of Contents

Preface	How to Earn An A!	iii
Chapter 1	What is Economics?	1
Chapter 2	Making and Using Graphs	11
Chapter 3	The Economic Problem	25

■ Part Review 1 — **43**

| Chapter 4 | Demand and Supply | 49 |

■ Part Review 2 — **67**

Chapter 5	A First Look at Macroeconomics	71
Chapter 6	Measuring GDP, Economic Growth, and Inflation	81
Chapter 7	Measuring Employment and Unemployment	93
Chapter 8	Aggregate Supply and Aggregate Demand	103

■ Part Review 3 — **119**

Chapter 9	The Economy at Full Employment	125
Chapter 10	Capital, Investment, and Saving	137
Chapter 11	Economic Growth	151

■ Part Review 4 — **165**

Chapter 12	Expenditure Multipliers	171
Chapter 13	Fiscal Policy	187
Chapter 14	Money	201
Chapter 15	Monetary Policy	215
Chapter 16	Inflation	229

■ Part Review 5 — **243**

| Chapter 17 | The Business Cycle | 249 |
| Chapter 18 | Macroeconomic Policy Challenges | 261 |

■ Part Review 6 — **277**

| Chapter 19 | Trading With the World | 283 |
| Chapter 20 | International Finance | 299 |

■ Part Review 7 — **313**

Practice Final Exams		319
Answers to the Chapter Quizzes		327
Conclusion	Should You Major in Economics?	329

Chapter 1

WHAT IS ECONOMICS?

A Definition of Economics

The fundamental economic problem is scarcity. Because the available resources are never enough to satisfy everyone's wants, choices are necessary.

Economics is the science of choice; it explains the choices we make and how the choices we make help us cope with scarcity.

Big Economic Questions

Economic choices can be summarized by five big questions:

♦ **What** goods and services are produced and in **what** quantities?

♦ **How** are goods and services produced?

♦ **When** are goods and services produced?

♦ **Where** are goods and services produced?

♦ **Who** consumes the goods and services produced?

Big Ideas of Economics

♦ A choice involves a *tradeoff*, that is, something is given up to get something else. The *opportunity cost* of a choice is the highest valued alternative foregone. Opportunity cost is not all the alternatives foregone, but is the highest valued alternative foregone.

♦ Choices are made in small steps, which means choices are made at the margin, and choices are in-
fluenced by incentives. When making choices, people compare the *additional* cost — the marginal cost — of an action to the *additional* benefit — the marginal benefit — of the action. Changes in marginal cost and/or changes in marginal benefit affect the decisions made.

♦ Voluntary exchange makes *both* buyers and sellers better off, and markets are an efficient way to organize such an exchange. Both the buyer and seller of a product must be made better off from a transaction, or the transaction will not take place.

♦ The market does not always work efficiently, so sometimes government action is necessary to overcome market failure and lead to a more efficient use of resources.

♦ For the economy as a whole, expenditure equals income equals the value of production.

♦ Living standards improve when production per person increases.

♦ Inflation occurs when the quantity of money increases faster than the production of goods and services.

♦ Unemployment can result from market failure but some unemployment is productive and can improve the nation's productivity.

What Economists Do

Economics is divided into two branches, microeconomics, the study of individual firms, individual consumers, and individual markets, and macroeconomics, the study of national and global economies and the factors that shape them.

Economists distinguish between:

♦ Positive statements — statements about what is. These can be shown to be true or false through observation and measurement.

♦ Normative statements — statements about what ought to be. These are matters of opinion.

Economic science is a collection of positive statements that are consistent with the real world. Economic science uses three steps to progress:

♦ Observation and measurement — economists observe and record economic data.

♦ Model building — an economic model contains simplified descriptions of the economic event under study that include only the factors considered most important.

♦ Testing — a model is tested to determine how well its predictions correspond with the real world.

When developing models and theories, economists use the idea of *ceteris paribus*, which is Latin for "other things being equal", to focus on the effect of one particular factor.

In the development of theories and models, two pitfalls are possible:

♦ Fallacy of composition — the assertion that what is true for a part must be true for the whole, or what is true for the whole must be true for each of the parts.

♦ *Post hoc* fallacy — the assertion that one event caused another because the first occurred before the other.

Helpful Hints

1. **CHOICES AND INCENTIVES :** The basic assumption made by economists about human behavior is that people try to make themselves as well off as possible. As a result, people respond to changed incentives by changing their decisions. The key idea is that an individual compares the additional (or "marginal") benefits from taking an action to the additional (or "marginal") costs of the action. If the marginal benefits from the action exceed the marginal costs, taking the action makes the person better off, so economists assume that the person takes the action. Conversely, if the marginal bene-

fits fall short of the marginal costs, economists assume that the action is not taken.

The key aspect of this analysis is that only the *additional* benefits and costs — not the *total* benefits and costs of the action — are considered. Only the additional benefits and additional costs are relevant because they are the ones that the person will enjoy and pay if the action is undertaken. Keeping straight the distinction between additional benefits and costs versus total benefits and costs is a vital part of economics, particularly of microeconomics.

2. **MODELS AND SIMPLIFICATION :** In attempting to understand how and why something works (for example, an airplane or an economy), we can use description or we can use theory. A description is a list of facts about something. But it does not tell us which facts are essential for understanding how an airplane works (the shape of the wings) and which facts are less important (the color of the paint). Scientists use theory to abstract from the complex descriptive facts of the real world and focus only on those elements essential for understanding. These essential elements are fashioned into models — highly simplified representations of the real world.

Economic models are how economic theory is cast. Economic models focus on the essential forces (such as competition) operating in the economy, while abstracting from less important forces (such as whims or advertising). In a real sense, models are like maps, which are useful precisely because they abstract from real world detail. A map that reproduced all the details of the real world (street lights, traffic signs, electric wires) would be useless. A useful map offers a simplified view, which is carefully selected according to the purpose of the map. A useful theory is similar: It gives guidance and insight into how the immensely complicated real world functions and reacts to changes.

3. **WHAT'S COMING UP :** Because of its introductory nature, this chapter covers a lot of ground. The following chapters are more focused. They examine specific topics to help fill in the details that are sketched in this overview. After you complete your course, you will find it enlightening and fun to return to this chapter and quickly read through it again. You will be amazed at how much you have learned and at the understanding that your course has given you into how the world functions!

Questions

■ True/False/Uncertain and Explain

A Definition of Economics

1. Scarcity is a problem only for the poor.

Big Economic Questions

2. Answering the question "What goods are produced?" automatically answers another question, "Where are goods produced?"

3. An example of the "how" question is: "How does the nation decide who gets the goods and services that are produced?"

Big Ideas of Economics

4. Because resources are limited, people must learn to make decisions with no opportunity costs.

5. The opportunity cost of buying a slice of pizza for $2 rather than a burrito for $2 is the burrito and not the $2 that was spent on the pizza.

6. Voluntary exchange always makes the seller better off but may or may not make the buyer better off.

7. All unemployment is harmful.

What Economists Do

8. Macroeconomics studies the factors that change total employment and income.

9. A positive statement is about what is; a normative statement is about what will be.

10. The idea of *ceteris paribus* is used whenever a *post hoc* fallacy is being discussed.

■ Multiple Choice

A Definition of Economics

1. The fact that wants cannot be fully satisfied with available resources is called the problem of
   a. opportunity cost.
   b. scarcity.
   c. what to produce.
   d. for whom to produce.

2. The issue of scarcity exists
   a. only in the past but not anymore.
   b. only in very poor economies.
   c. in all economies.
   d. now and in the past, but will be eliminated at some point in the future because of economic growth.

3. Scarcity can be eliminated through
   a. competition.
   b. markets.
   c. voluntary exchange.
   d. none of the above because scarcity cannot be eliminated.

Big Economic Questions

4. Which of the following is NOT one of the five big economic questions?
   a. What goods and services are produced?
   b. How are goods and services produced?
   c. When are goods and services produced?
   d. Why are goods and services produced?

5. The question, "Should personal computers or mainframe computers be produced?" is an example of the
   a. "what" question.
   b. "how" question.
   c. "where" question.
   d. "who" question.

6. An example of a "where" question is
   a. "Will buses or subways be produced?"
   b. "Will professional football players or video game programmers be paid more?"
   c. "Will the local Taco Bell be open or closed at 2 A.M.?"
   d. "Will rice be grown in Kansas or California?"

7. People have different amounts of income. This observation is directly related to which of the five big economic questions?
   a. The "what" question.
   b. The "how" question.
   c. The "where" question.
   d. The "who" question.

Big Ideas of Economics

8. When the government chooses to use resources to build a dam, these resources are no longer available to build a highway. This choice illustrates the concept of
   a. a market.
   b. macroeconomics.
   c. opportunity cost.
   d. marginal benefits.

9. From 9 to 10 A.M., Fred can sleep in, go to his economics lecture, or play tennis. Suppose that Fred decides to go to the lecture but thinks that, if he hadn't, he would otherwise have slept in. The opportunity cost of attending the lecture is
   a. sleeping in *and* playing tennis.
   b. playing tennis.
   c. sleeping in.
   d. one hour of time.

10. To make a choice, an individual
    a. ignores any opportunity cost if the marginal benefit from the action is high enough.
    b. will choose to use his or her scarce resources only if there is a very large total benefit from so doing.
    c. compares the marginal cost of the choice to the marginal benefit.
    d. makes the choice with the smallest opportunity cost.

11. Which of the following is <u>NOT</u> necessarily a cause of market failure?
    a. When a single producer controls the market.
    b. When producers do not take account of costs they inflict on others.
    c. When the price of a product rises so that fewer people buy it.
    d. When a good, such as national defense, must be consumed by everyone equally.

What Economists Do

12. Which of the following is a microeconomic topic?
    a. The reasons why Kathy buys less orange juice.
    b. The reasons for a decline in average prices.
    c. The cause of an increase in total production.
    d. The effect of a government budget deficit.

13. A positive statement is
    a. about what ought to be.
    b. about what is.
    c. always true.
    d. one that does not use the *ceteris paribus* clause.

14. Which of the following is a positive statement?
    a. The government must lower the price of a pizza so that more students can afford to buy it.
    b. The best level of taxation is zero percent because then people get to keep everything they earn.
    c. My economics class should last for two terms because it is my favorite class.
    d. An increase in college tuition will cause fewer students to apply to college.

15. An economic model includes
    a. only normative statements.
    b. no use of *ceteris paribus*.
    c. all known facts about a situation.
    d. only details considered essential.

16. The Latin term *ceteris paribus* means
    a. "false unless proven true."
    b. "other things the same."
    c. "after this, then because of this."
    d. "not correct, even though it is logical."

17. One student from a class of 30 can walk easily through a door. Assuming that all 30 students simultaneously therefore can walk easily through the same door is an example of the
    a. opportunity cost fallacy.
    b. fallacy of composition
    c. fallacy of substitution.
    d. *post hoc* fallacy.

18. The *post hoc* fallacy is the
    a. assertion that what is true for a part of the whole must be true for the whole.
    b. claim that one event caused another because the one event came first.
    c. use of *ceteris paribus* in order to study the impact of one factor.
    d. claim that the timing of two events has nothing to do with which event caused the other.

■ Short Answer Problems

1. "In the future, as our technology advances even further, eventually we will whip scarcity. In the high-tech future, scarcity will be gone." Do you agree or disagree with this claim? Explain your answer and what scarcity is. Also, why does the existence of scarcity require choices?

2. Ashley, Doug, and Mei-Lin are planning to travel from New York to Boston. The trip takes one hour by airplane and five hours by train. The air fare is $200 and train fare is $120. They all have to take time off from work while traveling. Ashley earns $10 per hour in her job, Doug $20 per hour, and Mei-Lin $24 per hour.

   Calculate the opportunity cost in terms of dollars of air and train travel for each person. If each wants to travel at the lowest possible opportunity cost, how will each of them travel to Boston?

3. "Education is a basic right. Just as kindergarten through 12th grade education is free, so, too, should a college education be free and guaranteed to every American." This statement can be analyzed by using the economic concepts discussed in this chapter to answer the following questions.

   a. What would be the opportunity cost of providing a free college education for everyone?

   b. Is providing this education free from the perspective of society as a whole?

4. Indicate whether each of the following statements is positive or normative. If it is normative, rewrite it so that it becomes positive. If it is positive, rewrite it so that it becomes normative.

   a. The government ought to slow the rate at which the amount of money increases in order to lower the inflation rate.

   b. Government imposition of a tax on tobacco products will decrease their consumption.

   c. Health care costs should be lower so that poorer people can afford quality health care.

5. In sciences such as chemistry, controlled experiments play a key role. How does that relate to economists' use of *ceteris paribus*?

■ You're the Teacher

1. Your friend asks, "Does everything have an opportunity cost?" Your friend has hit upon a very good question; provide an equally good answer!

2. "Economic theories are useless because the models on which they are based are totally unrealistic. They leave out so many descriptive details about the real world, they can't possibly be useful for understanding how the economy works." So says your skeptical friend. You'd like to keep your friend in your economics class so that you two can study together. Defend the fact that economic theories are much simpler than reality and help your friend realize that time spent studying economic theories is time well spent!

Answers

■ True/False Answers

A Definition of Economics

1. **F** Scarcity exists because people's wants exceed their ability to meet those wants, and this fact of life is true for *any* person, rich or poor.

Big Economic Questions

2. **F** Almost always, goods and services can be produced at many different locations, so the "where" question must be answered separately from the "what" question.

3. **F** The "how" question asks, "How are goods and services produced?"

Big Ideas of Economics

4. **F** Every choice has an opportunity cost.

5. **T** The opportunity cost is the burrito that was foregone in order to buy the pizza.

6. **F** Voluntary exchange must make *both* the buyer and the seller better off or else they would not engage in the transaction.

7. **F** Some unemployment is productive because it helps allocate workers to their best jobs.

What Economists Do

8. **T** Macroeconomics studies the entire economy; microeconomics studies separate parts of the economy.

9. **F** Although a positive statement is, indeed, about what is, a normative statement tells what policies should be followed.

10. **F** *Ceteris paribus*, Latin for "other things being equal", is used in order to focus on the effect from a change in one factor alone.

■ Multiple Choice Answers

A Definition of Economics

1. **b** Scarcity refers to the observation that wants are unlimited but that the resources available to satisfy these wants are limited.

2. **c** Scarcity is the fundamental economic problem that will exist forever in all economies.

3. **d** Scarcity is the universal condition in which wants always exceed the resources available.

Big Economic Questions

4. **d** "Why" is not one of the five big economic questions.

5. **a** The "what" question asks in part, "What goods and services are produced?"

6. **d** The "where" questions asks, "Where are goods and services produced?" In this case, it is the choice whether rice will be produced in California or Kansas.

7. **d** People with high incomes will get more goods and services than those with low incomes.

Big Ideas of Economics

8. **c** Because the resources are used to build a dam, the opportunity of using them to build a highway is foregone.

9. **c** The opportunity cost of an action is the (single) best alternative foregone by taking the action.

10. **c** Comparing marginal cost and marginal benefit is an important technique, especially in microeconomics.

11. **c** Rising prices allocate more benefits to sellers and fewer to buyers, but they do not necessarily indicate market failure.

What Economists Do

12. **a** Kathy is an individual consumer, so the reasons why she reduces her purchases of orange juice is a microeconomic topic.

13. **b** Positive statements describe how the world operates.

14. **d** This statement is the only one that tries to describe how the world actually works; all the others are normative statements that describe a policy that should be pursued.

15. **d** By including only essential details, economic models are vastly simpler than reality.

16. **b** *Ceteris paribus* is the economic equivalent of a controlled experiment: Its use allows us to determine the effect from each factor alone even though many factors may play a role in affecting a variable.

17. **b** In this case, the fallacy of composition is arguing that what is true for a part must necessarily be true for the whole.

18. **b** The usual *post hoc* fallacy is to claim that one event caused another because the first event occurred before the second.

■ Answers to Short Answer Problems

1. This claim is incorrect. Scarcity will always exist. Scarcity occurs because people's wants are unlimited, but the resources available to satisfy these wants are finite. As a result, not all of everyone's wants can be satisfied; the goods and services that are needed to meet all the wants are simply unavailable. For instance, think about the number of people who want to spend all winter skiing on uncrowded slopes. Regardless of the level of technology, there simply are not enough ski slopes available to allow everyone who wants to spend all winter skiing in near isolation to do so. Uncrowded ski slopes are scarce and will remain so forever. Thus technology can never eliminate scarcity.

   At its most basic level, scarcity is a problem of essentially infinite wants and limited resources. Because not all the goods and services wanted can be produced, choices must be made about which wants will be satisfied and which wants will be disappointed.

TABLE **1.1**

Short Answer Problem 2

Traveler		Train	Plane
Ashley			
(a)	Fare	$120	$200
(b)	Opportunity cost of travel time at $10 per hour	50	10
	Total cost	$170	$210
Doug			
(a)	Fare	$120	$200
(b)	Opportunity cost of travel time at $20 per hour	100	20
	Total cost	$220	$220·
Mei-Lin			
(a)	Fare	$120	$200
(b)	Opportunity cost of travel time at $24 per hour	120	24
	Total cost	$240	$224

2. The main point in this question is that the total opportunity cost of travel includes *both* the value of the travel time and the train or air fare. Thus for Ashley the opportunity cost of traveling by train is the fare she gives up, $120, plus the use of the time she foregoes, which has a value of $50. Hence for

Ashley, the opportunity cost of traveling by train is $170. All the total opportunity costs of train and air travel for Ashley, Doug, and Mei-Lin are calculated in Table 1.1. Based on the calculations in Table 1.1, Ashley will take the train, Mei-Lin will take the plane, and Doug might take either.

3. a. Even though a college education may be offered without charge ("free"), opportunity costs still exist. The opportunity cost of providing such education is the highest valued alternative use of the resources used to construct the necessary universities and the highest valued alternative use of the resources (including human resources) used in the operation of the schools.

   b. Providing a "free" college education is hardly free from the perspective of society. The resources used in this endeavor would no longer be available for other activities. For instance, the resources used to construct a new college cannot be used to construct a hospital to provide better health care. Additionally, the time and effort spent by the faculty, staff, and students operating and attending colleges has a substantial opportunity cost, namely, that these individuals cannot participate fully in other sectors of the economy. These examples show that providing a "free" college education to everyone is not free to society!

4. a. This statement is normative. A positive statement is: "If the government slowed the rate at which the amount of money increases, the inflation rate would fall."

   b. This statement is positive. A normative statement is: "The government should tax tobacco products in order to decrease their consumption."

   c. This statement is normative. A positive statement is: "If health care costs were lower, more poor people would receive health care."

5. Chemists can check the predictions of a model by conducting controlled experiments and observing the outcomes. For instance, when determining the effect of temperature on a particular reaction, chemists can ensure that, between different experiments, *only* the temperature changes. Everything else is held constant. Economists usually cannot perform such controlled experiments and instead must change one variable at a time in a model and compare the results. This approach involves the use

of *ceteris paribus*, wherein only one factor is allowed to change. Additionally, economists' models can be tested only against variations in data that occur naturally in the economy. Thus, economists face more difficult and less precise model building and testing than is possible for the controlled experiments of chemists and other scientists.

■ You're the Teacher

1. "Virtually everything has an opportunity cost. People sometimes say that viewing a beautiful sunset or using sand from the middle of the Sahara Desert have no opportunity costs. But that isn't strictly true. Viewing the sunset has an opportunity cost in terms of the time spent watching it. The time could have been utilized in some other activity and, whatever the next highest valued opportunity might have been, that is the opportunity cost of watching the sunset. Similarly, making use of sand from the Sahara also must have some opportunity cost, be it the time spent in gathering the sand or the resources spent in gathering it. Thus from the widest of perspectives, the answer is: Yes, everything does have an opportunity cost."

2. "Economic theories are like maps, which are useful precisely because they abstract from real world detail. A useful map offers a simplified view, which is carefully selected according to the purpose of the map. No map maker would claim that the world is as simple (or as flat) as the map, and economists do not claim that the real economy is as simple as their theories. What economists do claim is that their theories isolate the effects of real forces operating in the economy, yield predictions that can be tested against real-world data, and result in predictions that often are correct.

"I've got a book here that my parents gave to me by Milton Friedman, a Nobel Prize winner in Economics. Here's what he says on this topic: 'A theory or its 'assumptions' cannot possibly be thoroughly 'realistic' in the immediate descriptive sense.... A completely 'realistic' theory of the wheat market would have to include not only the conditions directly underlying the supply and demand for wheat but also the kind of coins or credit instruments used to make exchanges; the personal characteristics of wheat-traders such as the color of each trader's hair and eyes, … the number of members of his family, their characteristics, … the kind of soil on which the wheat was grown, … the weather prevailing during the growing season; … and so on indefinitely. Any attempt to move very far in achieving this kind of 'realism' is certain to render a theory utterly useless.'

"I think Friedman makes a lot of sense in what he says. It seems to me that theories have to be simple in order to be powerful and so I don't see anything wrong with the fact that economic theories leave out a bunch of trivial details."

From Milton Friedman, "The Methodology of Positive Economics," in *Essays in Positive Economics.* (Chicago: University of Chicago Press, 1953), 32.

Chapter Quiz

1. The most fundamental economic problem is
   a. reducing unemployment.
   b. health and health care.
   c. scarcity.
   d. decreasing the inflation rate.

2. When the economy produces fireworks for sale at the Fourth of July, it most directly is answering the _____ question.
   a. what
   b. when
   c. where
   d. how

3. When doctors have an average income that exceeds $250,000, the economy most directly is answering the _____ question.
   a. what
   b. how
   c. when
   d. who

4. Opportunity cost is
   a. zero for services, because services do not last for very long, and positive for goods, because goods are long lasting.
   b. paid by society not by an individual.
   c. the highest-valued alternative foregone by making a choice.
   d. all the alternatives foregone by making a choice.

5. Markets coordinate individual decisions chiefly through
   a. government edicts.
   b. firms planning what they will produce.
   c. advertisements.
   d. price adjustments.

6. Market failure occurs
   a. when one producer controls the market.
   b. whenever the price rises but not when it falls.
   c. whenever the price falls but not when it rises.
   d. whenever the price rises or falls.

7. Studying how an individual firm decides to set its price is primarily a concern of
   a. normative economics.
   b. macroeconomics.
   c. microeconomics.
   d. all economists.

8. Which of the following is a macroeconomic topic?
   a. Why has the price of a personal computer fallen over time?
   b. How does a rise in the price of cheese affect the pizza market?
   c. What factors determine the nation's inflation rate?
   d. How does a consumer decide how many tacos to consume?

9. In economics, positive statements
   a. are only about facts that economists are certain (are "positive") are true.
   b. tell what policy the government ought to follow.
   c. depend on value judgments.
   d. in principle, can be tested to determine if they are true or false.

10. The fallacy of composition is the (false) statement
    a. that theory is necessary to better understand the real world.
    b. that models can be normative in nature without any positive conclusions.
    c. that people's free will makes predicting their behavior futile.
    d. that what is true for the whole must necessarily be true for the part.

The answers for this Chapter Quiz are on page 327

MAKING AND USING GRAPHS

Key Concepts

■ Graphing Data

Graphs represent quantity as a distance on a line. On a graph, the horizontal line is the *x-axis*, the vertical line is the *y-axis*, and the intersection of the two lines is the *origin*.

The three main types of economic graphs are:

♦ **Scatter diagrams** — show the relationship between two variables, one measured on the *x*-axis and the other on the *y*-axis. Such a relationship indicates how the variables are *correlated*, not whether one variable *causes* the other.

♦ **Time-series graphs** — demonstrate the relationship between time (measured on the *x*-axis) and other variable(s) (measured on the *y*-axis). Time-series graphs reveal the variable's level, direction of change, speed of change, and **trend**, which is its general tendency to rise or fall.

♦ **Cross-section graphs** — show the values for different groups of a variable at a point in time.

Graphs can be misleading when they stretch, squeeze, or break the measurement scale to exaggerate or understate the magnitude of the variation of the variables.

■ Graphs Used in Economic Models

The four important relationships between variables are:

♦ **Positive relationship (direct relationship)** — the variables move together in the same direction, as illustrated in Figure 2.1. The relationship is upward-sloping, so the slope is a positive number.

♦ **Negative relationship (inverse relationship)** — the variables move in opposite directions, as shown in Figure 2.2. The relationship is downward-sloping and so the slope is a negative number.

FIGURE **2.1**
A Positive Relationship

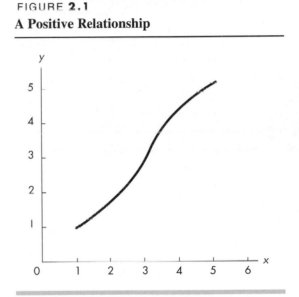

FIGURE **2.2**
A Negative Relationship

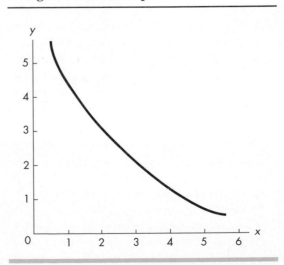

♦ **Maximum or minimum** — the relationship reaches a maximum or a minimum point, then changes direction. Figure 2.3 shows a minimum.

♦ **Unrelated** — the variables are not related so that, when one variable changes, the other is unaffected. The graph is either a vertical or horizontal straight line, as illustrated in Figure 2.4.

Graphs are used to help illustrate **economic models**, which are simplified descriptions of the economy or a part of the economy.

■ The Slope of a Relationship

The slope of a relationship is the change in the value of the variable on the y-axis divided by the change in the value of the variable on the x-axis. The formula for slope is $\Delta y/\Delta x$, with Δ meaning "change in."

A straight line (or linear relationship) has a constant slope. A curved line has a varying slope, which can be calculated two ways:

♦ **Slope at a point** — by drawing the straight line tangent to the curve at that point and then calculating the slope of the line.

♦ **Slope across an arc** — by drawing a straight line across the two points on the curve and then calculating the slope of the line.

■ Graphing Relationships Among More Than Two Variables

Relationships between more than two variables can be graphed by holding constant the values of all the variables except two (the *ceteris paribus* assumption, that is, "other things remaining the same") and then graphing the relationship between the two with, *ceteris paribus*, only the variables being studied changing. When one of the variables not illustrated in the figure changes, the entire relationship between the two that have been graphed shifts.

Helpful Hints

1. **IMPORTANCE OF GRAPHS AND GRAPHICAL ANALYSIS :** Economists almost always use graphs to present relationships between variables. This fact should not "scare" you nor give you pause.

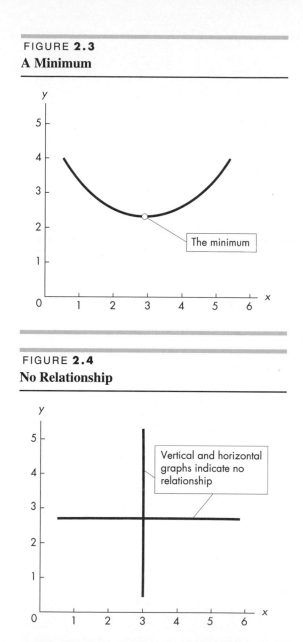

FIGURE 2.3
A Minimum

FIGURE 2.4
No Relationship

Economists do so because graphs *simplify* the analysis. All the key concepts you need to master are presented in this chapter. If your experience with graphical analysis is limited, this chapter is crucial to your ability to readily understand economic analysis. However, if you are experienced in constructing and using graphs, this chapter may be "old hat." Even so, you should skim the chapter and work through the questions in this *Study Guide.*

2. **CALCULATING THE SLOPE :** Often the slopes of various relationships are important. Usually what is key is the sign of the slope — whether the slope is positive or negative — rather than the actual value of the slope. An easy way to remember the formula for slope is to think of it as the "rise over the run," a saying used by carpenters and others. As illustrated in Figure 2.5, the *rise* is the change in the variable measured on the vertical axis, or in terms of symbols, Δy. The *run* is the change in the variable measured on the horizontal axis, or Δx. This "rise over the run" formula also makes it easy to remember whether the slope is positive or negative. If the rise is actually a drop, as shown in Figure 2.5, then the slope is negative because when the variable measured on the horizontal axis increases, the variable measured on the vertical axis decreases. However, if the rise actually is an increase, then the slope is positive. In this case, an increase in the variable measured on the *x*-axis is associated with an increase in the variable measured on the *y*-axis.

Questions

■ True/False/Uncertain and Explain

Graphing Data

1. The origin is the point where a graph starts.

2. A graph showing a positive relationship between stock prices and the nation's production means that an increase in stock prices causes an increase in production.

3. In Figure 2.6 the value of *y* decreased between 1994 and 1995.

4. In Figure 2.6 the value of *y* increased most rapidly between 1997 and 1998.

5. Figure 2.6 shows a trend with *y* increasing, generally speaking.

6. A cross-section graph compares the values of different groups of a variable at a single point in time.

Graphs Used in Economic Models

7. If the graph of the relationship between two variables slopes upward to the right, the relationship between the variables is positive.

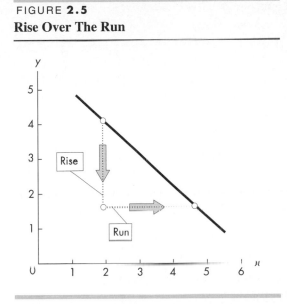

FIGURE **2.5**
Rise Over The Run

FIGURE **2.6**
True/False/Uncertain Questions 3, 4, 5

8. If the relationship between *y* (measured on the vertical axis) and *x* (measured on the horizontal axis) is one in which *y* reaches a maximum, the slope of the relationship must be negative before and positive after the maximum.

9. To the left of a minimum point, the slope is negative; to the right, the slope is positive.

10. Graphing things that are unrelated on one diagram is <u>NOT</u> possible.

The Slope of a Relationship

11. It is possible for the graph of a positive relationship to have a slope that becomes smaller when moving rightward along the graph.

12. The slope of a straight line is calculated by dividing the change in the value of the variable measured on the horizontal axis by the change in the value of the variable measured on the vertical axis.

13. For a straight line, if a large change in *y* is associated with a small change in *x*, the line is steep.

14. The slope of a curved line is <u>NOT</u> constant.

15. The slope of a curved line at a point equals the slope of a line tangent to the curved line at the point.

Graphing Relationships Among More Than Two Variables

16. *Ceteris paribus* means "everything else changes."

17. The amount of corn a farmer grows depends on its price and the amount of rainfall. The curve showing the relationship between the price of a bushel of corn and the quantity grown is the same curve regardless of the amount of rainfall.

■ **Multiple Choice**

Graphing Data

1. Demonstrating how an economic variable changes from one year to the next is best illustrated by a
   a. one-variable graph.
   b. time-series graph.
   c. linear graph.
   d. cross-section graph.

2. You notice that, when the inflation rate increases, the interest rate also tends to increase. This fact indicates that
   a. there may be false causality between inflation and the interest rate.
   b. higher inflation rates must cause higher interest rates.
   c. a scatter diagram of the inflation rate and the interest rate will show a positive relationship.
   d. a cross-section graph of the inflation rate and the interest rate will show a positive relationship.

3. Which type of graph can mislead?
   a. A time-series graph.
   b. A cross-section graph.
   c. A scatter diagram.
   d. *Any* type of graph might mislead.

4. You hypothesize that more natural gas is sold in the Northeast when winters are colder. Which of the following possibilities would best reveal if your belief is correct?
   a. A time-series diagram showing the amount of natural gas sold in the Northeast during the last 30 years.
   b. A time-series diagram showing the average temperature in the Northeast during the last 30 years.
   c. A scatter-diagram plotting the average temperature in the Northeast against the amount of natural gas sold.
   d. A trend diagram that plots the trend in natural gas sales over the last 30 years against the average temperature in the Northeast 30 years ago and this year.

5. You believe that the total amount of goods produced in the United States has generally increased. In a time-series graph illustrating the total amount produced, you expect to find
   a. an upward trend.
   b. no relationship between time and the amount of goods produced.
   c. an inverse relationship between time and the amount of goods produced.
   d. a linear relationship.

Graphs Used in Economic Models

6. If variables *x* and *y* move up and down together, they are
   a. positively related.
   b. negative related.
   c. unrelated.
   d. trend related.

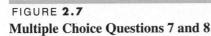

FIGURE **2.7**

Multiple Choice Questions 7 and 8

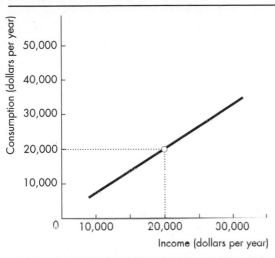

FIGURE **2.8**

Multiple Choice Question 10

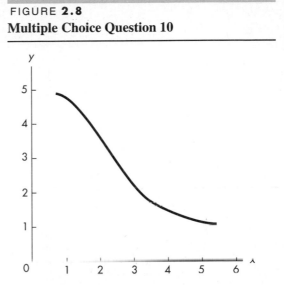

7. In Figure 2.7 when income equals $20,000, what does consumption equal?

   a. $0

   b. $10,000

   c. $20,000

   d. Impossible to tell

8. The relationship between income and consumption illustrated in Figure 2.7 is

   a. positive and linear.

   b. positive and nonlinear.

   c. negative and linear.

   d. negative and nonlinear

9. The term "direct relationship" means the same as

   a. correlation.

   b. trend.

   c. positive relationship.

   d. negative relationship.

10. Figure 2.8 shows

   a. a positive relationship.

   b. a time-series relationship.

   c. a negative relationship.

   d. no relationship between the variables.

11. The relationship between two variables, x and y, is a vertical line. Thus x and y are

   a. positively correlated.

   b. negatively correlated.

   c. not related.

   d. falsely related.

The Slope of a Relationship

12. The slope of a negative relationship is

   a. negative.

   b. undefined.

   c. positive to the right of the maximum point and negative to the left.

   d. constant as long as the relationship is nonlinear.

13. A linear relationship

   a. always has a maximum.

   b. always has a constant slope.

   c. always slopes up to the right.

   d. never has a constant slope.

FIGURE **2.9**
Multiple Choice Questions 14 and 15

FIGURE **2.9**
Multiple Choice Questions 14 and 15

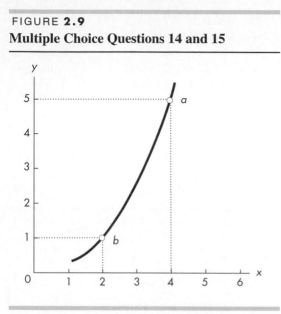

FIGURE **2.10**
Multiple Choice Questions 16 and 17

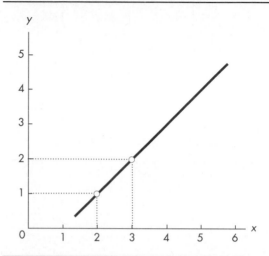

14. The relationship between x and y in Figure 2.9 is
    a. positive with an increasing slope.
    b. positive with a decreasing slope.
    c. negative with an increasing slope.
    d. negative with a decreasing slope.

15. In Figure 2.9 the slope across the arc between points a and b equals
    a. 5.
    b. 4.
    c. 2.
    d. 1.

16. In Figure 2.10, between $x = 2$ and $x = 3$, what is the slope of the line?
    a. 1
    b. −1
    c. 2
    d. 3

17. In Figure 2.10 how does the slope of the line between $x = 4$ and $x = 5$ compare with the slope between $x = 2$ and $x = 3$?
    a. The slope is greater between $x = 4$ and $x = 5$.
    b. The slope is greater between $x = 2$ and $x = 3$.
    c. The slope is the same.
    d. The slope is not comparable.

Graphing Relationships Among More Than Two Variables

18. In Figure 2.11 x is
    a. positively related to y and negatively related to z.
    b. positively related to both y and z.
    c. negatively related to y and positively related to z.
    d. negatively related to both y and z.

FIGURE **2.11**
Multiple Choice Questions 18, 19, 20

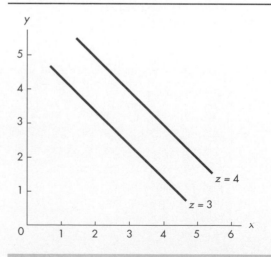

19. In Figure 2.11, *ceteris paribus*, an increase in x is associated with

    a. an increase in y.
    b. a decrease in y.
    c. an increase in z.
    d. a decrease in z.

20. In Figure 2.11 an increase in z causes a

    a. movement up along one of the lines showing the relationship between x and y.
    b. movement down along one of the lines showing the relationship between x and y.
    c. shift rightward in the line showing the relationship between x and y.
    d. shift leftward in the line showing the relationship between x and y.

■ Short Answer Problems

1. a. The data in Table 2.1 show the unemployment rate in the United States between 1976 and 1998. Draw a time-series graph of these data.

    b. When was the unemployment rate the highest?

TABLE **2.2**

Short Answer Problem 2

x	y
1	2
2	4
3	6
4	8
5	7
6	6

2. a. Use the data in Table 2.2 to graph the relationship between x and y.

    b. Over what range of values for x is this relationship positive? Over what range is it negative?

    c. Calculate the slope between $x = 1$ and $x = 2$.

    d. Calculate the slope between $x = 5$ and $x = 6$.

    e. What relationships do your answers to parts c and d have to your answer for part b?

3. a. In Figure 2.12, use the tangent line in the figure to calculate the slope at point b.

    b. Compute the slope across the arc between points b and a.

    c. Calculate the slope across the arc between points c and b.

TABLE **2.1**

Short Answer Problem 1

Year	Unemployment rate
1976	7.7
1977	7.1
1978	6.1
1979	5.8
1980	7.1
1981	7.6
1982	9.7
1983	9.6
1984	7.5
1985	7.2
1986	7.0
1987	6.2
1988	5.5
1989	5.3
1990	5.5
1991	6.7
1992	7.4
1993	6.8
1994	6.1
1995	5.6
1996	5.4
1997	5.6
1998	5.0

FIGURE **2.12**

Short Answer Problem 3

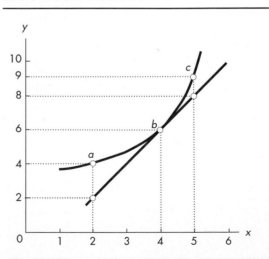

4. Can a curve have a positive but decreasing slope? If so, draw an example.

5. a. Bobby says that he buys fewer compact discs when the price of a compact disc is higher. Bobby also says that he will buy more compact discs after he graduates and his income is higher. Is the relationship between the number of compact discs Bobby buys and the price positive or negative? Is the relationship between Bobby's income and the number of compact discs positive or negative?

   b. Table 2.3 shows the number of compact discs Bobby buys in a month at different prices when his income is low and when his income is high. On a diagram with price on the vertical axis and the quantity purchased on the horizontal axis, plot the relationship between the number of discs purchased and the price when Bobby's income is low.

   c. On the same diagram, draw the relationship between the number of discs purchased and the price when Bobby's income is high.

   d. Does an increase in Bobby's income cause the relationship between the price of a compact disc and the number purchased to shift rightward or leftward?

TABLE **2.3**

Short Answer Problem 5

Price (dollars per compact disc)	Quantity of compact discs purchased, low income	Quantity of compact discs purchased, high income
$11	5	6
12	4	5
13	3	4
14	1	3
15	0	2

■ **You're the Teacher**

1. "Hey, I thought this was an *economics* class, not a *math* class. Where's the economics? All I've seen so far is math!" Reassure your friend by explaining why the concentration in this chapter is on mathematics rather than economics.

2. "I don't understand why we need to learn all about graphs. Instead of this, why can't we just use numbers? If there is any sort of relationship we need to see, we can see it easier using numbers instead of all these complicated graphs!" Explain why graphs are useful when studying economics.

3. "There must be a relationship between the direction a curve is sloping, what its slope is, and whether the curve shows a positive or negative relationship between two variables. But I can't see the tie. Is there one? And what is it?" Help this student by answering the questions posed.

Answers

■ True/False Answers

Graphing Data

1. **F** The origin is where the horizontal and vertical axis start, *not* where the graph starts.

2. **F** The graph shows a correlation between stock prices and production, but that does not necessarily mean that an increase in stock prices causes the increase in production.

3. **T** According to the figure, y decreased from about 12 to about 10.

4. **F** Between 1990 and 1991, y rose the most.

5. **T** As the figure makes clear, there has been an upward trend in y. Note how the time-series graph made answering the last questions easy.

6. **T** This is the definition of a cross-section graph.

Graphs Used in Economic Models

7. **T** If the graph slopes upward to the right, then an increase in the variable measured along the horizontal axis is associated with an increase in the variable measured on the vertical axis.

8. **F** As Figure 2.13 illustrates, before the maximum is reached, the relationship must be positive;

FIGURE **2.13**
True/False/Uncertain Question 8

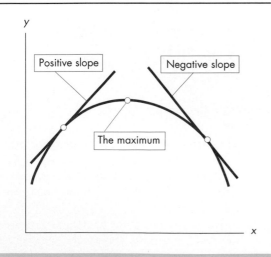

after the maximum is attained, the relationship must be negative.

9. **T** To verify this answer, flip Figure 2.13 upside down. Note that to the left of the minimum the line is falling, so its slope is negative; to the right the line is rising, so its slope is positive.

10. **F** If two unrelated variables are graphed on the same diagram, the "relationship" between the two is either a vertical or a horizontal straight line.

The Slope of a Relationship

11. **T** Figure 2.14 shows a positive relationship whose slope decreases when moving rightward along it from point *a* to point *b*.

FIGURE **2.14**
True/False/Uncertain Question 11

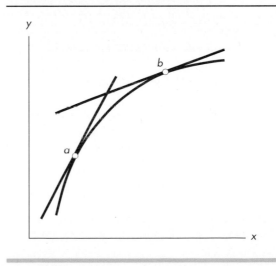

12. **F** Just the reverse is true: Divide the change in the variable on the *vertical* axis by the change in the variable on the *horizontal* axis.

13. **T** The definition of slope is $\Delta y/\Delta x$. Thus, if a large change in y (the numerator) is associated with a small change in x (the denominator), the slope is relatively large, indicating that the line is relatively steep.

14. **T** Only the slope of a straight line is constant.

15. **T** This question tells precisely how to calculate the slope at a point on a curved line.

Graphing Relationships Among More Than Two Variables

16. **F** *Ceteris paribus* means that only the variables being studied change; all other variables do not change.

17. **F** For different amounts of rainfall, there are different curves showing the relationship between the price of a bushel of corn and the quantity that is grown.

■ Multiple Choice Answers

Graphing Data

1. **b** A time-series graph illustrates how the variable changes over time.

2. **c** A positive correlation between inflation rates and interest rates is reflected in a scatter diagram as a positive relationship; that is, the dots would tend to cluster along a line that slopes upward to the right.

3. **d** Any type of graph can be misleading.

4. **c** A scatter diagram will show the correlation between temperature and natural gas sales.

5. **a** The upward trend indicates a general increase in production over time.

Graphs Used in Economic Models

6. **a** In this case, an increase (or decrease) in x is associated with an increase (or decrease) in y, so the variables are positively related.

7. **c** Figure 2.7 shows that when income is $20,000 a year, then consumption is also $20,000 a year.

8. **a** The relationship is positive (higher income is related to higher consumption) and is linear.

9. **c** The term "positive relationship" means the same as "direct relationship."

10. **c** As x increases, y decreases; thus the relationship between x and y is negative.

11. **c** Figure 2.15 demonstrates that the change in y from 2 to 3 has no effect on x — it remains equal to 3.

The Slope of a Relationship

12. **a** A negative relationship has a negative slope; a positive relationship has a positive slope.

13. **b** A straight line — that is, a linear relationship — has a constant slope whereas nonlinear relation-

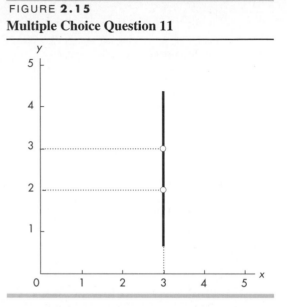

FIGURE **2.15**
Multiple Choice Question 11

ships have slopes that vary. Thus the slope of a straight line is the same anywhere on the line.

14. **a** The slope is positive and, because the line is becoming steeper, the slope is increasing.

15. **c** The slope between the two points equals the change in the vertical distance (the "rise") divided by the change in the horizontal distance (the "run"), that is, $(5-1)/(4-2)=2$.

16. **a** The slope equals the change in the variable measured along the vertical axis divided by the change in the variable measured along the horizontal axis, or $(2-1)/(3-2)=1$.

17. **c** The figure shows a straight line. The slope of a straight line is constant, so the slope between $x = 4$ and $x = 5$ is the same as the slope between $x = 2$ and $x = 3$.

Graphing Relationships Among More Than Two Variables

18. **c** The curves showing the relationship between x and y demonstrate that x and y are negatively related. For any value of y, an increase in z is associated with a higher value for x, so x and z are positively related.

19. **b** Moving along one of the lines showing the relationship between x and y (say, the line with $z = 3$) shows that as x increases, y decreases.

20. **c** The higher value of z shifts the entire relationship between x and y rightward.

■ Answers to Short Answer Problems

FIGURE **2.16**

Short Answer Problem 1

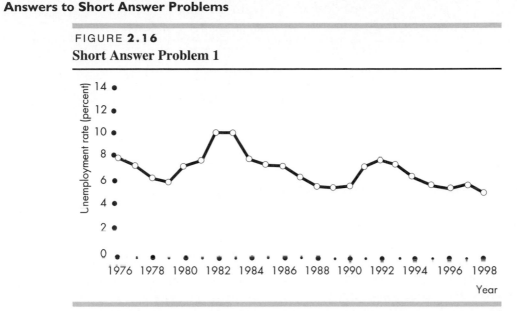

1. a. Figure 2.16 shows the time series of unemployment rates in the United States.

    b. The unemployment rate was the highest in 1982, when it equaled 9.7 percent.

FIGURE **2.17**

Short Answer Problem 2

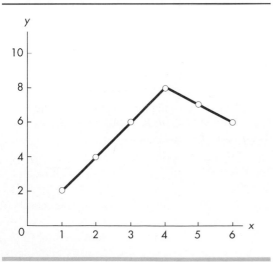

2. a. The relationship between x and y is illustrated in Figure 2.17.

    b. The relationship between x and y changes when x is 4. The relationship is positive between $x = 1$

and $x = 4$. Between $x = 4$ and $x = 6$, the relationship is negative.

    c. The slope equals $\Delta y/\Delta x$ or, in this case between $x = 1$ and $x = 2$, the slope is $(2 - 4)/(1 - 2) = 2$.

    d. Between $x = 5$ and $x = 6$, the slope is equal to $(7 - 6)/(5 - 6) = -1$.

    e. Over the range of values where the relationship between x and y is positive — from $x = 1$ to $x = 4$ — the slope is positive. Over the range where the relationship between x and y is negative — from $x = 4$ to $x = 6$ — the slope is negative. Thus positive relationships have positive slopes, and negative relationships have negative slopes.

3. a. The slope is $(8-2)/(5-2) = 2$.

    b. The slope is $(6-4)/(4-2) = 1$.

    c. The slope is $(9-6)/(5-4) = 3$.

4. Yes, a curve can have a positive, decreasing slope. Figure 2.18 (on the next page) illustrates such a relationship. In it, at relatively low values of x the slope is quite steep, indicating a high value for the slope. But as x increases, the curve becomes flatter, which means that the slope decreases. (To verify these statements, draw the tangent lines at points a and b and then compare their slopes.) This figure points out that there is a major difference between the value of a curve at some point, that is, what y equals, and what the curve's slope is at that point!

FIGURE **2.18**
Short Answer Problem 4

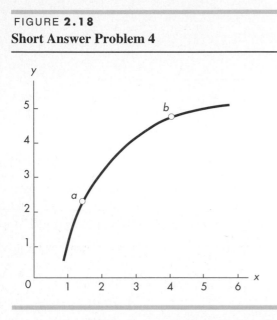

FIGURE **2.19**
Short Answer Problem 5

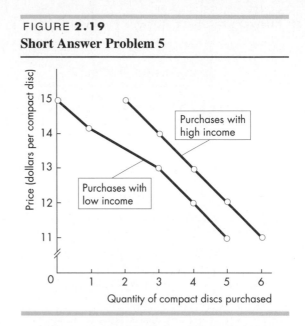

5. a. Because Bobby buys more compact discs when their price is lower, the relationship between the number of compact discs Bobby buys and the price is negative. Similarly, the relationship between Bobby's income and the number of compact discs he buys is positive.

  b. Figure 2.19 illustrates the relationship between the price of a compact disc and the number Bobby buys when his income is low.

  c. Also illustrated in Figure 2.19 is the relationship between the number of compact discs Bobby buys and their price when Bobby's income is high.

  d. An increase in Bobby's income shifts the relationship between the price of a compact disc and the number Bobby buys rightward.

■ **You're the Teacher**

1. "This *is* an economics class. But understanding some simple graphing ideas makes economics a lot easier to learn. Learning about graphing for its own sake is not important in this class; what is important is learning about graphing to help with the economics that we'll take up in the next chapter. So look at this chapter as a resource. Whether you already knew everything in it before you looked at it or even if everything in it was brand new, anytime you get confused by something dealing with a tech-

nical point on a graph, you can look back at this chapter for help. So, chill out; we'll get to the economics in the next chapter!"

2. "Graphs make understanding economics and the relationships between economic variables easier in three ways. First, graphs are extremely useful in showing the relationship between two economic variables. Imagine trying to determine the relationship between the interest rate and inflation rate if all we had was a bunch of numbers showing the interest rate and inflation rate each year for the past 30 years. We'd have 60 numbers; good luck in trying to eyeball a relationship from them! Second, graphs can help us more easily understand what an economic theory is trying to explain because they allow us to see quickly how two variables are related. By showing us the general relationship, we can be assured that any conclusions we reach don't depend on the numbers that we decided to use. Finally, graphs sometimes show us a result we might not have otherwise noticed. If all we had were numbers, we could easily become lost trying to keep track of them. Graphs make our work easier, and for this reason we need to know how to use them!"

3. "The connection between the direction a line slopes, its slope, and whether the relationship is positive or negative is easy — once you see it! Take a look at Figure 2.20. In this figure, the line slopes upward to the right. The slope of this line is positive: An in-

FIGURE **2.20**
You're the Teacher Question 3

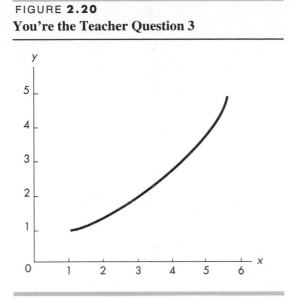

FIGURE **2.21**
You're the Teacher Question 3

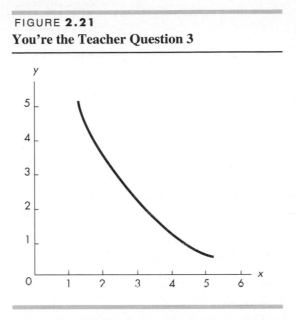

crease in x is associated with an increase in y. Because increases in x are related to increases in y, the graph shows a positive relationship between x and y.

Now look at Figure 2.21. Here the line slopes downward to the right. The slope of this line is negative: An increase in x is related to a decrease in y. Because x and y are inversely related, the relationship shown in Figure 2.21 is negative.

So, look: Positive relationships have positive slopes and negative relationships have negative slopes!

We can summarize these results for you so that you'll always be able to remember them by putting them all together:

Direction of line		Sign of slope		Type of relationship
Upward to the right	⇔	Positive	⇔	Positive
Downward to the right	⇔	Negative	⇔	Negative

This summary should help you keep everything straight. Things should be easier now"

Chapter Quiz

1. The vertical scale line of a graph is called the
   a. origin.
   b. scalar.
   c. *y*-axis.
   d. *x*-axis.

2. On a time-series graph, time is usually shown
   a. as a triangular area.
   b. as a rectangle.
   c. along the horizontal axis.
   d. at the origin.

3. A time-series diagram of the price of a purse between 1985 and 1999 has a downward trend. Hence the price of a purse
   a. is higher in 1985 than in 1999.
   b. is higher in 1999 than in 1985.
   c. definitely has fallen each year.
   d. None of the above.

4. A scatter diagram between two variables has a negative slope. Hence an increase in the variable measured on the vertical axis is associated with _____ the variable measured on the horizontal axis.
   a. an increase in
   b. no change in
   c. a decrease in
   d. no *consistent* change in

5. A graph shows the number of males and females majoring in economics in 1999. The kind of graph used to show this data would be
   a. a scatter diagram.
   b. a time-series graph.
   c. a cross-section graph.
   d. a Venn diagram.

6. Which of the following is true regarding a trend?
   a. Only a cross section graph shows trends.
   b. Both cross section and time-series graphs show trends.
   c. Only a time-series graph shows a trend.
   d. Both time-series graphs and scatter plots show trends.

7. As a point on a graph moves upward and leftward, the value of its *x*-coordinate _____ and the value of its *y*-coordinate _____.
   a. rises; rises
   b. rises; falls
   c. falls; rises
   d. falls; falls

8. The slope of a line equals the
   a. change in *y* plus the change in *x*.
   b. change in *y* minus the change in *x*.
   c. change in *y* times the change in *x*.
   d. change in *y* divided by the change in *x*.

9. As a curve approaches a minimum, its slope will be
   a. positive before the minimum and negative after the minimum.
   b. negative before the minimum and positive after the minimum.
   c. remain constant on either side of the minimum.
   d. change, but in no consistent way from one curve to the next.

10. If the change in *y* equals 10 and the change in *x* equals –5,
    a. the slope of the curve is positive.
    b. the slope of the curve is negative.
    c. the curve must be a straight line.
    d. the slope cannot be calculated without more information.

The answers for this Chapter Quiz are on page 327

Chapter 3

THE ECONOMIC PROBLEM

Resources and Wants

Scarcity occurs whenever there are insufficient resources to satisfy everyone's wants. Wants are unlimited, so scarcity is always present. **Economics** studies the choices people make to cope with scarcity.

The four categories of resources are:

♦ **Labor** — the time and effort people devote to producing goods and services.

♦ **Land** — inputs from nature, such as water, minerals, land, and so on.

♦ **Capital** — goods, such as buildings and dams, that are used to produce other products. **Human capital** is the knowledge and skills that people possess that are used to help produce goods and services.

♦ **Entrepreneurship** — the resource that directs how land, labor, and capital will be used to produce goods and services.

Resources, Production Possibilities, and Opportunity Cost

Production is limited by the amount of resources available. The **production possibility frontier** (*PPF*):

♦ is the boundary between unattainable and attainable production possibilities, with the attainable points being those on and within the *PPF*.

♦ shows maximum combinations of goods and services that can be produced with given resources and technology.

FIGURE 3.1
A *PPF* with Increasing Opportunity Costs

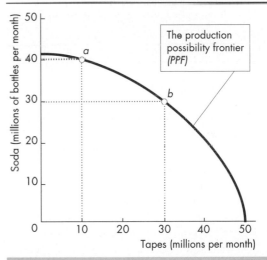

A *PPF* is illustrated in Figure 3.1. This figure shows two characteristics in common to all production possibility frontiers:

♦ Production points inside and on the *PPF* are attainable. Points beyond the *PPF* are not attainable.

♦ Production points on the *PPF* achieve **production efficiency** because when moving between two points on the *PPF*, more of one good can be obtained only by producing less of the other good. Production points inside the *PPF* are *inefficient*, with misallocated or unused resources.

Moving between points *on* the *PPF* involves a **tradeoff** because something must be lost to get more of something else. The **opportunity cost** of an action is the highest-valued alternative foregone. In Figure 3.1, the opportunity cost of obtaining 20 million more tapes by moving from point *a* to point *b* is the 10 million bottles of soda that are foregone. Opportunity cost is a ratio, the decrease in the production of one good divided by the increase in the production of another good.

When resources are not equally productive in producing different goods and services, the *PPF* has increasing opportunity costs and bows outward, as illustrated in Figure 3.1. As more and more tapes are produced, the opportunity cost of a tape increases.

■ Using Resources Efficiently

♦ **Marginal cost** of a good is the opportunity cost of producing *one* more unit of a product. Because of increasing opportunity cost, along a production possibility frontier the marginal cost of an additional unit of a product increases as more is produced. Thus the marginal cost curve — illustrated in Figure 3.2 — slopes upward.

♦ **Marginal benefit** from a product is the benefit a person obtains from consuming one more unit of a good. Marginal benefit is measured as the maximum amount someone is willing to pay for another unit of the product. The marginal benefit from additional units of a product decreases, so the marginal benefit curve — illustrated in Figure 3.2 — slopes downward.

Resources are used **efficiently** when the goods valued most highly are produced. Efficient use of resources occurs when the marginal benefit from another unit of a product equals the marginal cost. In Figure 3.2 producing 30 million tapes means the efficient quantity of resources are allocated to the production of tapes.

■ Economic Growth

Economic growth occurs when the *PPF* shifts out. The faster it shifts, the more rapid is economic growth.

♦ **Technological change** is the development of new goods or new ways to produce goods. **Capital accumulation** is the growth of the capital stock. Both shift the *PPF* outward and are causes of economic growth.

♦ The opportunity cost of economic growth is today's foregone production and consumption.

♦ Nations that devote more resources to capital accumulation grow more rapidly.

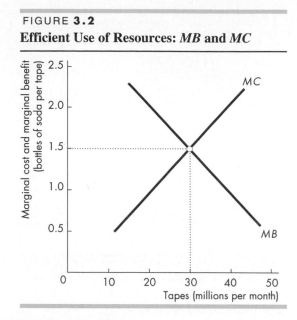

FIGURE **3.2**
Efficient Use of Resources: *MB* and *MC*

■ Gains from Trade

♦ An individual has a **comparative advantage** in producing a good if he or she can produce it at a lower opportunity cost than anyone else.

♦ Comparative advantage differs from absolute advantage. **Absolute advantage** occurs when a person can produce more of *both* goods than the other person can.

Specialization according to comparative advantage and trading for other goods creates gains from trade because such specialization and exchange allows consumption (not production) at points outside the *PPF*.

♦ **Dynamic comparative advantage** occurs when production involves substantial **learning-by-doing**.

■ The Market Economy

Property rights and markets have evolved to help reap the gains from specialization.

♦ **Property rights** are social arrangements that set the terms of the ownership, use, and disposal of resources, goods, and services.

♦ A **market** is any arrangement that allows buyers and sellers to do business with each other. Markets pool information into a price, which signals buyers and sellers about the actions they should take.

♦ **Goods markets** are where goods and services are bought and sold; **resource markets** are where productive resources are bought and sold.

Helpful Hints

1. **ASSUMPTIONS OF THE *PPF* :** The *PPF* provides a good example of the role played by simplifying assumptions in economic analysis. Clearly, no society in the world produces only two items. But by assuming that there are such "two-good" nations, we can gain invaluable insights into the real world. For instance, once a nation is producing on its production possibility frontier, no matter how many goods it produces, to increase the production of one good necessarily has an opportunity cost in terms of some other good or goods that must be foregone. In addition, the model allows us to explain several phenomena that we observe in the world, such as specialization and exchange. And the *PPF* also shows that countries that devote a larger proportion of their resources to capital accumulation will have more rapid growth.

    Like all economic models and theories, the *PPF* is based on assumptions that vastly simplify the complex reality in which we live. But, like all economic models and theories, the *PPF* is useful because these simplifications allow us to see more clearly the underlying issues and truths.

2. **INEFFICIENT PRODUCTION POINTS WITHIN THE *PPF* :** The production possibility frontier shows the *maximum* combinations of goods that can be produced. To produce fewer than the maximum is always possible — that is, to produce inside the *PPF* curve. This condition occurs whenever some inefficiency or misallocation emerges within the economy. Excessive unemployment of any resource or an inefficient use of resources cause a nation to produce at a point within the boundary illustrated by the *PPF*. However, a reduction in the resources available to the society does not cause it to produce within its *PPF*. Technology and the nation's resource base set the limits to production, that is, determine where the *PPF* boundary is located. So if, for some reason, resources shrink, the *PPF* shifts inward, but the nation does not necessarily produce at a point within the new *PPF* curve.

3. **CALCULATING OPPORTUNITY COST :** A helpful formula for opportunity cost, which works well in solving problems, results from the fact that opportunity cost is a ratio. In particular, opportunity cost

FIGURE **3.3**
A *PPF* Between Corn and Cloth

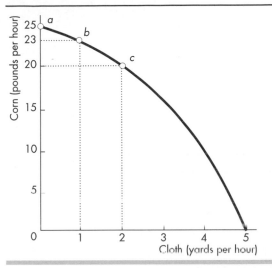

equals the quantity of goods you must give up divided by the quantity of goods you will get.

For instance, suppose Courtney can grow corn or produce cloth. Consider her *PPF* in Figure 3.3. If we move along the *PPF* from *a* to *b,* what is the opportunity cost of an additional yard of cloth? Courtney must give up 2 pounds of corn (25 – 23) to get 1 yard of cloth (1 – 0). Hence the opportunity cost of the first yard of cloth is 2 pounds of corn per yard of cloth. Next, if we move from *b* to *c,* the opportunity cost of the second yard of cloth is calculated the same way and is 3 pounds of corn. The opportunity cost is increasing as more cloth is produced, which accounts for the bowed-out shape of the *PPF*.

4. **OPPORTUNITY COST AND THE SLOPE OF THE *PPF* :** Opportunity cost can be related to the slope of the *PPF*. As we move down between any two points on the *PPF*, we gain more of the good on the horizontal axis. The opportunity cost of an additional unit of this good on the horizontal axis is equal to:

    $$|\text{Slope of the } PPF|$$

    The slope of the *PPF* is negative, but economists describe opportunity cost in terms of a positive quantity of foregone goods, so we use the absolute value of the slope to calculate the desired positive number. The fact that the slope equals the opportunity cost can be verified by looking at the slope between points *a* and *b* in Figure 3.3. The formula for the slope between *a* and *b* is:

$$\frac{\text{Change in vertical distance between } a \text{ and } b}{\text{Change in horizontal distance between } a \text{ and } b}$$

Comparing this formula with the calculations used to compute the opportunity cost of moving from point *a* to point *b* in the previous hint shows that they are identical.

Similarly, as we move *up* between any two points on the *PPF*, the opportunity cost of an additional unit of the good on the vertical axis is:

$$\left| \frac{1}{\text{Slope of } PPF} \right|$$

These formulas show us the inverse relation between the opportunity costs of moving from *b* to *c* and moving from *c* to *b* discussed in Chapter 3 of the textbook.

Questions

■ True/False/Uncertain and Explain

Resources and Wants

1. Wants are unlimited; resources are limited.

2. Scarcity affects only people who live in poverty.

Resources, Production Possibilities, and Opportunity Cost

3. In Figure 3.4 point *a* is <u>NOT</u> attainable.

4. In Figure 3.4 the opportunity cost of moving from point *b* to point *c* is 10 computers.

5. From a point on the *PPF*, rearranging production and producing more of *all* goods is possible.

6. From a point within the *PPF*, rearranging production and producing more of *all* goods is possible.

7. Production efficiency requires producing at a point on the *PPF*.

8. Along a bowed-out *PPF*, as more of a good is produced, the opportunity cost of producing the good diminishes.

FIGURE **3.4**

True/False/Uncertain Questions 3 and 4

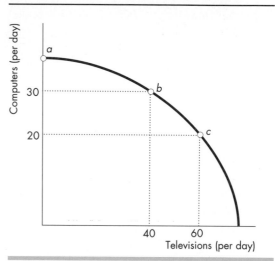

Using Resources Efficiently

9. The marginal cost of the 20th ton of cement equals the cost of producing all 20 tons of cement.

10. As people have more of a product, the product's marginal benefit decreases.

11. Efficiency is achieved by producing the amount of a good such that the marginal benefit of the last unit produced exceeds its marginal cost by as much as possible.

Economic Growth

12. Economic growth causes the *PPF* to shift outward.

13. Increasing a nation's economic growth rate has an opportunity cost.

Gains from Trade

14. Daphne has a comparative advantage in producing sweaters if she can produce more than Lisa.

15. If two individuals have different opportunity costs of producing goods, both can gain from specialization and trade.

16. If the United States has an absolute advantage in growing corn and making computers, it must have a comparative advantage in growing corn.

17. Learning-by-doing can lead to dynamic comparative advantage.

The Market Economy

18. Property rights refer only to the social rights given to owners of land.

19. Buyers and sellers must meet face-to-face in a market.

20. Price adjustments coordinate decisions in goods markets, but not in resource markets.

■ Multiple Choice

Resources and Wants

1. Which of the following accounts for scarcity?
   a. Nations always produce within their production possibility frontier.
   b. Resources are unlimited, but too many are wasted.
   c. Wants, though limited, exceed resources.
   d. Resources are limited and wants are unlimited.

2. Of the following, which is <u>NOT</u> a resource used to produce goods and services?
   a. Labor
   b. A company's money in the bank
   c. Capital equipment
   d. Entrepreneurship

Resources, Production Possibilities, and Opportunity Cost

3. Production points on the *PPF* itself are
   a. efficient but not attainable.
   b. efficient and attainable
   c. inefficient but not attainable.
   d. inefficient and attainable.

4. If the United States can increase its production of automobiles without decreasing its production of any other good, the
   a. United States must have been producing at a point within its *PPF*.
   b. United States must have been producing at a point on its *PPF*.
   c. problem of scarcity has been solved in the United States.
   d. None of the above are correct because increasing the production of one good without decreasing the production of another good is impossible.

FIGURE **3.5**
Multiple Choice Questions 5 and 6

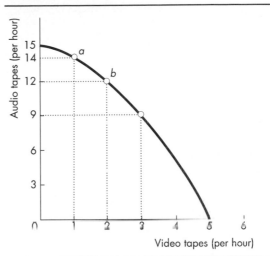

5. In Figure 3.5, at point *a* what is the opportunity cost of producing one more video tape?
   a. 14 audio tapes
   b. 3 audio tapes
   c. 2 audio tapes
   d. There is no opportunity cost.

6. In Figure 3.5, at point *b* what is the opportunity cost of producing one more video tape?
   a. 12 audio tapes
   b. 3 audio tapes
   c. 2 audio tapes
   d. There is no opportunity cost.

7. The scarcity of resources means that the *PPF* is
   a. bowed outward.
   b. linear.
   c. negatively sloped.
   d. positively sloped

8. Production efficiency means that
   a. scarcity is no longer a problem.
   b. producing more of one good without producing less of some other good is not possible.
   c. as few resources as possible are being used in production.
   d. producing another unit of the good has no opportunity cost.

9. The bowed-outward shape of a *PPF*
   a. is due to capital accumulation.
   b. reflects the unequal application of technology in production.
   c. illustrates the fact that no opportunity cost is incurred for increasing the production of the good measured on the horizontal axis but it is incurred to increase production of the good measured along the vertical axis.
   d. is due to the existence of increasing opportunity cost.

A nation produces only two goods — yak butter and rutabagas. Three alternative combinations of production that are on its *PPF* are given in Table 3.1. Use this information to answer the next three questions.

TABLE **3.1**

Production Possibilities

Possibility	Pounds of yak butter	Number of rutabagas
a	600	0
b	400	100
c	0	200

10. In moving from combination *a* to *b*, the opportunity cost of producing more rutabagas is
    a. 6 pounds of yak butter per rutabaga.
    b. 4 pounds of yak butter per rutabaga.
    c. 2 pounds of yak butter per rutabaga.
    d. 0 pounds of yak butter per rutabaga.

11. In moving from combination *b* to *a*, the opportunity cost of producing more pounds of yak butter is
    a. 0.10 rutabaga per pound of yak butter.
    b. 0.50 rutabaga per pound of yak butter.
    c. 1.00 rutabaga per pound of yak butter.
    d. 2.00 rutabagas per pound of yak butter.

12. Producing 400 pounds of yak butter and 50 rutabagas is
    a. not possible for this nation.
    b. possible and is an efficient production point.
    c. possible, but is an inefficient production point.
    d. an abhorrent thought.

Using Resources Efficiently

13. Moving along a bowed-out *PPF* between milk and cotton, as more milk is produced the marginal cost of an additional gallon of milk
    a. rises.
    b. does not change.
    c. falls.
    d. probably changes, but in an ambiguous direction.

14. The most anyone is willing to pay for another purse is $30. Currently the price of a purse is $40, and the cost of producing another purse is $50. Hence the marginal benefit of a purse is
    a. $50.
    b. $40.
    c. $30.
    d. An amount not given in the answers above.

15. If the marginal benefit from another computer exceeds the marginal cost of the computer, then to use resources efficiently,
    a. more resources should be used to produce computers.
    b. fewer resources should be used to produce computers.
    c. if the marginal benefit exceeds the marginal cost by as much as possible, the efficient amount of resources are being used to produce computers.
    d. none of the above is correct because marginal benefit and marginal cost have nothing to do with using resources efficiently.

Economic Growth

16. Economic growth
    a. creates unemployment.
    b. has no opportunity cost.
    c. shifts the *PPF* outward.
    d. makes it more difficult for a nation to produce on its *PPF*.

17. The *PPF* shifts if
    a. the unemployment rate falls.
    b. people decide they want more of one good and less of another.
    c. the prices of the goods and services produced rise.
    d. the resources available to the nation change.

18. An increase in the nation's capital stock or in its labor force will
    a. shift the *PPF* outward.
    b. cause a movement along the *PPF* upward and leftward.
    c. cause a movement along the *PPF* downward and rightward.
    d. move the nation from producing within the *PPF* to producing at a point closer to the *PPF*.

19. One of the opportunity costs of economic growth is
    a. capital accumulation.
    b. technological change.
    c. reduced current consumption.
    d. the gain in future consumption.

20. In general, the more resources that are devoted to technological research, the
    a. greater is current consumption.
    b. higher is the unemployment rate.
    c. faster the *PPF* shifts outward.
    d. more the *PPF* will bow outward.

Gains from Trade

21. In order to achieve the maximum gains from trade, people should specialize according to
    a. property rights.
    b. *PPF*.
    c. absolute advantage.
    d. comparative advantage.

In one day Brandon can either plow 40 acres of land or plant 20 acres. In one day Christopher can either plow 28 acres of land or plant 7 acres. Use this information to answer the next four questions.

22. Which of the following statements about absolute advantage is correct?
    a. Brandon has an absolute advantage in both plowing and planting.
    b. Brandon has an absolute advantage only in plowing.
    c. Brandon has an absolute advantage only in planting.
    d. Christopher has an absolute advantage both in plowing and planting.

23. Brandon has
    a. a comparative advantage both in plowing and planting.
    b. a comparative advantage only in plowing.
    c. a comparative advantage only in planting.
    d. a comparative advantage in neither in plowing and planting.

24. Christopher has
    a. an absolute advantage only in planting.
    b. an absolute advantage only in plowing.
    c. a comparative advantage only in planting.
    d. a comparative advantage only in plowing.

25. Brandon and Christopher can
    a. both gain from exchange if Brandon specializes in planting and Christopher in plowing.
    b. both gain from exchange if Brandon specializes in plowing and Christopher in planting.
    c. exchange, but only Brandon will gain from the exchange.
    d. exchange, but only Christopher will gain from the exchange.

26. A nation can *produce* at a point outside its *PPF*
    a. when it trades with other nations.
    b. when it is producing products as efficiently as possible.
    c. when there is no unemployment.
    d. at no time ever.

27. A nation can *consume* at a point outside its *PPF*
    a. when it trades with other nations.
    b. when it is producing products as efficiently as possible.
    c. when there is no unemployment.
    d. at no time ever.

The Market Economy

28. Which of the following does <u>NOT</u> help organize trade?
    a. Property rights
    b. Markets
    c. The production possibility frontier
    d. None of the above because all these answers given help organize trade.

29. In markets, people's decisions are coordinated by
    a. specialization according to absolute advantage.
    b. changes in property rights.
    c. learning-by-doing.
    d. adjustments in prices.

■ Short Answer Problems

1. What does the negative slope of the *PPF* mean? Why is a *PPF* bowed out?

2. How does the production possibility frontier illustrate the idea of scarcity?

3. In Figure 3.6 indicate which points are production efficient and which are inefficient. Also show which points are attainable and which are not attainable.

FIGURE 3.6
Short Answer Problem 3

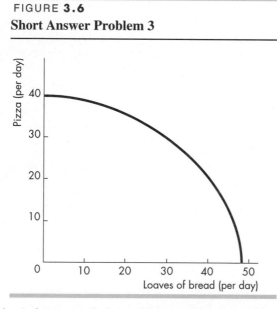

4. Sydna is stranded on a desert island and can either fish or harvest dates. Six points on her production possibility frontier are given in Table 3.2.
    a. In Figure 3.7 plot these possibilities, label the points, and draw the *PPF*.
    b. If Sydna moves from possibility *c* to possibility *d*, what is the opportunity cost per fish?
    c. If Sydna moves from possibility *d* to possibility *e*, what is the opportunity cost per fish?
    d. In general, what happens to the opportunity cost of a fish as more fish are caught?
    e. In general, what happens to the opportunity cost of dates as more dates are harvested?

TABLE 3.2
Sydna's Production Possibilities

Possibility	Dates gathered (per day)	Fish caught (per day)
a	54	0
b	50	1
c	42	2
d	32	3
e	20	4
f	0	5

FIGURE 3.7
Short Answer Problem 4

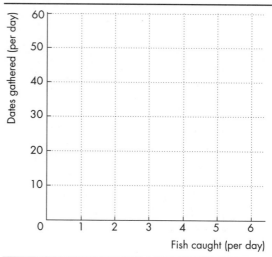

f. Based on the original *PPF* you plotted, is a combination of 40 dates and 1 fish attainable? Is this combination an efficient one? Explain.

5. If the following events occurred (each is a separate event, unaccompanied by any other event), what would happen to the *PPF* in Problem 4?
    a. A new fishing pond is discovered.
    b. The output of dates is increased.
    c. Sydna finds a ladder that enables her to gather slightly more dates.
    d. A second person, with the same set of fishing and date-gathering skills as Sydna, is stranded on the island.

TABLE **3.3**
Marginal Benefit and Marginal Cost of Pizza

Slice of pizza	Marginal benefit of slice	Marginal cost of slice	Marginal benefit minus marginal cost
1	6.0	1.5	____
2	5.0	2.0	____
3	4.0	2.5	____
4	3.0	3.0	____
5	2.0	3.5	____
6	1.0	4.0	____

6. A nation produces only pizza and tacos. Table 3.3 shows the marginal benefit and marginal cost schedules for slices of pizza in terms of tacos per slice of pizza.

   a. Complete Table 3.3

   b. For the first slice of pizza, after paying the marginal cost, how much marginal benefit — if any — is left?

   c. For the second slice, after paying the marginal cost, how much marginal benefit — if any — is left? How does your answer to this question compare to your answer to part (b)?

   d. Should the first slice of pizza be produced? Should the second one be produced? Explain you answers, especially your answer about the second slice.

   e. In a diagram, draw the marginal benefit and marginal benefit curves. Indicate the quantity of pizza slices that uses resources efficiently.

7. Bearing in mind the point that resources are limited and wants are not, explain why is it important for a nation to use its resources efficiently. What happens to the number of wants that can be satisfied if resources are used inefficiently?

8. Suppose that both the United States and France produce computers and wine. Table 3.4 shows what each country can produce in an hour.

   a. On graph paper, draw the *PPF* for the United States for one hour.

   b. On graph paper, draw the *PPF* for France for one hour.

   c. Complete Table 3.5

   d. In what good(s) does the United States have a comparative advantage? France?

TABLE **3.4**
Production in France and the United States

	Computers produced in an hour	Bottles of wine produced in an hour
United States	10,000	20,000
France	12,000	8,000

TABLE **3.5**
Short Answer Problem 8 (c)

	Opportunity cost of one computer	Opportunity cost of one bottle of wine
United States	____	____
France	____	____

   e. Initially the United States uses half its resources to produce wine and half to produce computers. How much wine and how many computers are produced in an hour in the United States? France also devotes half her resources to computers and half to wine. How many computers and bottles of wine does France produce in an hour? What is the total amount of wine produced by France and the United States in an hour? The total number of computers?

   f. Suppose that the United States specializes in wine and France in computers. What is the total amount of wine produced by France and the United States now? The total number of computers?

   g. What do your answers to parts (e) and (f) show?

9. How do property rights affect people's incentives to innovate?

■ You're the Teacher

1. "The idea of the production possibility frontier is stupid. I mean, after all, who ever heard of a nation that produces only two goods. Come on, every nation produces millions, probably billions of goods. Why do I have to bother to learn about the production possibility frontier when it is so unrealistic?" One reason for this student to learn about the production possibility frontier is that it will probably be on the exams. But there are other reasons,

too. Explain some of them to help motivate this student.

2. Your friend, who is not in your economics class, says: "I always thought that economic growth was good, and the more rapid the growth the better. At least, this is what I hear politicians saying. Now you tell me that economic growth inevitably has some costs. I don't understand this at all; can you explain it to me again?"

Answers

■ True/False Answers

Resources and Wants

1. **T** Because resources are limited, not all wants can be met, which means that people face scarcity.

2. **F** Scarcity means that not all wants can be satisfied, a condition true for everyone.

Resources, Production Possibilities, and Opportunity Cost

3. **F** *Any* point on the production possibility frontier is attainable, even points where the *PPF* intersects the axes.

4. **T** The opportunity cost equals the number of computers foregone, in this case the fall from 30 computers at point *b* to 20 at point *c*.

5. **F** Points on the frontier are production efficient, so increasing the production of one good necessarily requires producing fewer of some other good.

6. **T** Points within the frontier are inefficient, which means that rearranging production and boosting the output of all goods and services is possible. This condition is illustrated in Figure 3.8, where from (the inefficient) point *a*, it is possible to rearrange production and move to points such as *b* or *c* where more of both books and magazines are produced.

7. **T** Production efficiency implies that the production of one good can be increased *only if* the production of another good is decreased, which is true only on the *PPF* itself.

8. **F** As more of a good is produced, the opportunity cost of additional units increases.

Using Resources Efficiently

9. **F** The marginal cost is the cost of the 20th ton itself, not the cost of producing all 20 tons.

10. **T** As people have more of a product, they are willing to pay less for additional units, which means that the marginal benefit of the product will decrease.

11. **F** In order for resources to be allocated efficiently, it is necessary for the marginal benefit of the last unit produced to equal its marginal cost.

FIGURE **3.8**
True/False/Uncertain Question 6

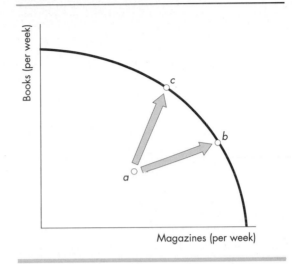

Economic Growth

12. **T** As the *PPF* shifts outward, the nation is able to produce more of all goods.

13. **T** The opportunity cost is the loss of current consumption.

Gains from Trade

14. **U** Based on the information in the problem, Daphne has an absolute advantage, but without more information we cannot tell whether she has a comparative advantage.

15. **T** A key observation is that *both* individuals gain.

16. **F** Comparative advantage requires *comparing* the opportunity cost of producing corn in the United States with the opportunity cost of producing it elsewhere.

17. **T** Learning-by-doing means that the cost of producing a good falls as more is produced, so the nation (or person) ultimately acquires a comparative advantage in making the good.

The Market Economy

18. **F** Property rights specify the ownership rights of *all* resources, goods, and services.

19. **F** Buyers and sellers communicate with each other in markets, but in most markets they do not meet face-to-face.

20. **F** Price adjustments coordinate decisions in all markets.

■ Multiple Choice Answers

Resources and Wants

1. **d** Because resources are limited, it is not possible to satisfy everyone's wants.

2. **b** The four general categories of resources are labor, land, capital, and entrepreneurship.

Resources, Production Possibilities, and Opportunity Cost

3. **b** *Only* points on the frontier are both attainable and efficient.

4. **a** Only from points within the frontier can the production of a good increase without decreasing the production of another good.

5. **c** By producing 1 more video tape, audio tape production falls by 2 (from 14 to 12), so the opportunity cost of the video tape is the ratio of 2 audio tapes to the 1 video tape, that is, 2 audio tapes per video tape.

6. **b** As more video tapes are produced, the opportunity cost of an additional video tape gets larger.

7. **c** Once production is on the *PPF*, if more of one good is produced, then because resources are limited, some other good must be foregone, which means that the *PPF* has a negative slope.

8. **b** This answer is the definition of production efficiency.

9. **d** Increasing opportunity costs means that, as more of a good is produced, its opportunity cost increases, which causes the *PPF* to bow out.

10. **c** Moving from *a* to *b* gains 100 rutabagas and loses 200 pounds of yak butter, so the opportunity cost is (200 pounds of yak butter)/(100 rutabagas), or 2 pounds of yak butter per rutabaga.

11. **b** 100 rutabagas are foregone, so the opportunity cost is (100 rutabagas)/(200 pounds of yak butter), or 0.50 rutabagas per pound of yak butter. Note how the opportunity cost of a rutabaga is the inverse of the opportunity cost of a pound of yak butter, as calculated in the answer to the previous question.

12. **c** When 400 pounds of yak butter are produced, a maximum of 100 rutabagas can be produced; if only 50 rutabagas are produced, the combination is inefficient.

Using Resources Efficiently

13. **a** Along a bowed-out *PPF*, as more of a good is produced, its marginal cost — the opportunity cost of producing another unit — rises.

14. **c** The marginal benefit from a good is the maximum that a person is willing to pay for the good.

15. **a** The benefit from the computer exceeds the cost of producing the computer, so society will gain if resources are allocated so that the computer is produced.

Economic Growth

16. **c** Economic growth makes attainable previously unattainable production levels.

17. **d** An increase in resources shifts the *PPF* outward; a decrease shifts it leftward. (A decrease in the unemployment rate moves the nation from a point in the interior of the *PPF* to a point closer to the frontier.)

18. **a** Increases in a nation's resources create economic growth and shift the nation's *PPF* outward.

19. **c** If a nation devotes more resources to capital accumulation or technological development, which are the main sources of growth, fewer resources can be used to produce goods for current consumption.

20. **c** The more resources used for technological research, the more rapid is economic growth.

Gains from Trade

21. **d** Specializing according to comparative advantage reduces the opportunity cost of producing goods and services.

22. **a** Brandon can produce more of both goods than Christopher, so Brandon has an absolute advantage in both goods.

23. **c** Brandon's opportunity cost of planting an acre of land is plowing 2 acres, whereas Christopher's opportunity cost of planting an acre is plowing 4 acres.

24. **d** Christopher's opportunity cost of plowing an acre is planting 1/4 an acre, while Brandon's opportunity cost is planting 1/2 an acre.

25. **a** By specializing according to their comparative advantages, both can gain from exchange.

26. **d** The *PPF* shows the maximum amounts that can be produced.

27. **a** When a nation specializes according to its comparative advantage and trades with another specialist nation, both can consume at levels beyond their *PPFs*.

The Market Economy

28. **c** The production possibility frontier shows the limits to production and does not help organize trade.

29. **d** Changes in prices create incentives for people to change their actions.

■ **Answers to Short Answer Problems**

1. The negative slope of the *PPF* indicates that increasing the production of one good causes the production of some other good to decline.

   A *PPF* is bowed out because the existence of nonidentical resources creates an increasing opportunity cost as the production of a good is increased. In other words, because resources are not identical, some are better suited for producing one good than another. So when resources are switched from producing items for which they are well suited to producing goods for which they are ill suited, the opportunity cost of increasing the output of these goods rises.

2. The very existence of the production possibility frontier indicates that unlimited production of all things (or anything) is impossible. The limits to production are the result of scarcity of resources, so the frontier illustrates the existence of scarcity.

   Additionally, the fact that the frontier has a negative slope shows that increasing the production of one good must be accompanied by producing less of some other good. The fundamental reason that the production of another good must be reduced is scarcity: not enough resources are available to produce more of one item without decreasing the production of some other good.

3. Figure 3.9 shows the efficient/inefficient points and attainable/not attainable points. The attainable but inefficient points are shaded; the attainable and efficient points lie on the *PPF* itself; and the unattainable points are located beyond the *PPF*.

4. a. Figure 3.10 shows the *PPF*.

   b. Moving from *c* to *d* means that the number of fish caught increases by 1 while the number of

FIGURE **3.9**
Short Answer Problem 3

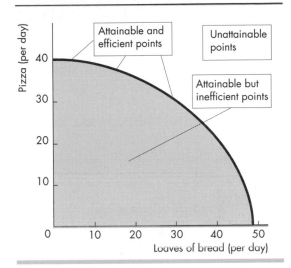

FIGURE **3.10**
Short Answer Problem 4

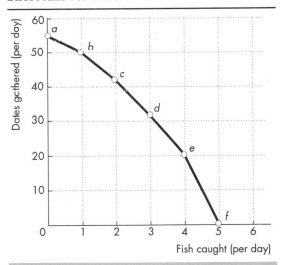

dates gathered falls from 42 to 32. Hence catching 1 fish costs 10 dates, so the opportunity cost of the fish is 10 dates. In terms of a formula, the opportunity cost of this fish is:

$$\frac{42 \ \text{dates} - 32 \ \text{dates}}{3 \ \text{fish} - 2 \ \text{fish}} = 10 \ \text{dates per fish}.$$

c. Moving from *d* to *e* indicates that the opportunity cost of the fish is 12 dates: The number of dates gathered falls from 32 to 20 while the number of fish caught increases by 1.

d. As more fish are caught, the opportunity cost of an additional fish rises. In particular, the first fish has an opportunity cost of only 4 dates; the second, 8 dates; the third, 10 dates; the fourth, 12 dates; and the fifth, 20 dates.

e. As more dates are gathered, the opportunity cost of a date rises. Moving from *f* to *e* shows that the first 20 dates cost only 1 fish so that the opportunity cost of a date here is 1/20 of a fish. Going from *e* to *d*, however, makes the opportunity cost of a date 1/12 of a fish. This pattern continues so that as more dates are gathered, their opportunity cost increases. Finally, moving from *b* to *a* has the largest opportunity cost for a date, 1/4 of a fish.

As parts (d) and (e) demonstrate, there is increasing opportunity cost moving along the *PPF*. That is, as more fish are caught, their opportunity cost — in terms of foregone dates — increases and as more dates are gathered, their opportunity cost — in terms of foregone fish — also increases. It is these increasing opportunity costs that account for the bowed-outward shape of the *PPF*.

f. This combination is within the *PPF* and is attainable. It is inefficient because Sydna could produce more of either or both goods. Therefore she is not organizing her activities as efficiently as possible.

5. a. A new fishing pond increases the number of fish Sydna can catch, but it does not affect the maximum number of dates she can gather. Her *PPF* shifts generally as shown in Figure 3.11.

b. Increasing her output of dates does not affect the *PPF*. Sydna might increase her gathering of dates either by moving from a point within the *PPF* curve to a point on (or closer to) the frontier or by moving along the frontier itself. However, neither of these actions changes the *PPF*, that is, the *PPF* does not shift.

c. The ladder increases the number of dates that Sydna can gather, but has no effect on the fish that she can catch. As a result, the maximum number of dates increases, but the maximum number of fish does not change. The *PPF* shifts in the same general pattern as shown in Figure 3.12.

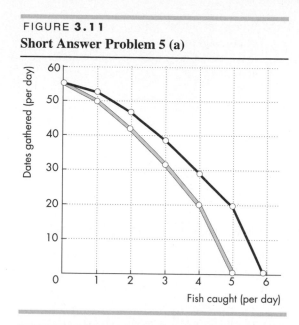

FIGURE **3.11**
Short Answer Problem 5 (a)

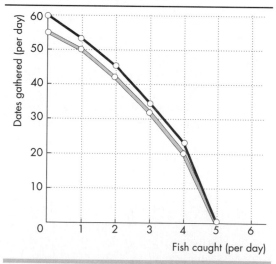

FIGURE **3.12**
Short Answer Problem 5 (c)

d. Having a second worker on the island boosts both the number of dates that can be gathered *and* the number of fish that can be caught. If the second person has the same set of skills as Sydna, the *PPF* shifts out in a "parallel" manner, as illustrated in Figure 3.13 (on the next page). Be sure to note that the scales on the axes in Figure 3.13 are different from those on the axes in Figures 3.10–3.12.

FIGURE **3.13**
Short Answer Problem 5 (d)

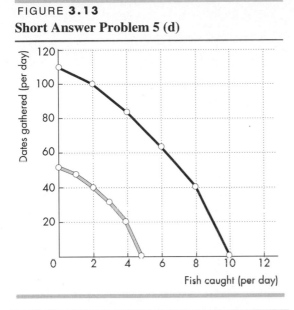

TABLE **3.6**
Marginal Benefit and Marginal Cost of Pizza

Slice of pizza	Marginal benefit of slice	Marginal cost of slice	Marginal benefit minus marginal cost
1	6.0	1.5	4.5
2	5.0	2.0	3.0
3	4.0	2.5	1.5
4	3.0	3.0	0.0
5	2.0	3.5	−1.5
6	1.0	4.0	−3.0

6. a. Table 3.6 shows the answers.

  b. For the first slice of pizza, after paying the marginal cost, there is 4.5 of marginal benefit left.

  c. For the second slice of pizza, after paying the marginal cost, there is 3.0 of marginal benefit left. After paying the marginal cost, there is less marginal benefit left for the second slice of pizza than for the first. There is less surplus because the marginal benefit of the second slice is less than that of the first slice and the marginal cost the second slice is more than that of the first one.

  d. Yes, the first slice should be produced because the marginal benefit from the first slice exceeds its marginal cost. The second slice also should be produced for the same reason. As long as the

marginal benefit from a slice of pizza exceeds its marginal cost, society benefits if the slice is produced. Notice that the "net benefit" from the first slice is more than that of the second slice, but as long as there is a positive net benefit, society benefits.

  e. Figure 3.14 shows the marginal cost and marginal benefit curves. Four slices of pizza are the quantity that uses resources efficiently because the marginal benefit from the fourth slice equals its marginal cost. The marginal benefit for any greater quantity of pizza slices is less than the marginal cost of the slice, so producing these units would result in a net loss for society.

FIGURE **3.14**
Short Answer Problem 6 (e)

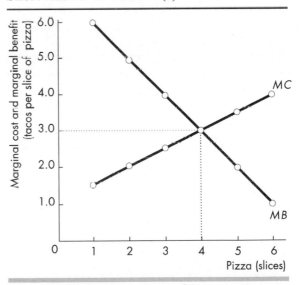

7. A nation should use its resources efficiently because it has only a limited quantity of them. If resources are used inefficiently, there is waste and fewer of people's wants can be satisfied. By producing efficiently, society ensures that as many of the most important wants — measured by the marginal benefit from the goods that satisfy those wants — are satisfied.

8. a. Figure 3.15 (on the next page) shows the *PPF* for the United States. The maximum amount of wine that can be produced is 20,000 bottles, when everyone specializes in producing only wine. The maximum number of computers that can be produced is 10,000, attainable when everyone produces only computers.

FIGURE **3.15**
Short Answer Problem 8 (a)

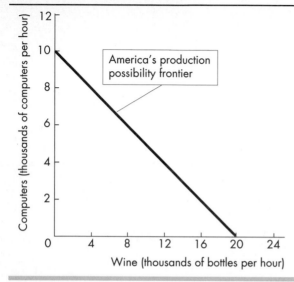

FIGURE **3.16**
Short Answer Problem 8 (b)

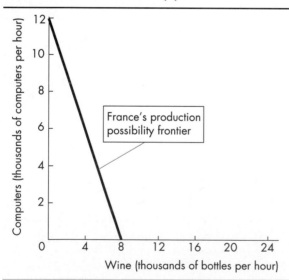

TABLE **3.7**
Short Answer Problem 8 (c)

	Opportunity cost of one computer	Opportunity cost of one bottle of wine
United States	2 bottles of wine	½ computer
France	⅔ bottles of wine	1½ computer

additional computer, resources must be switched from the wine industry to the computer industry for 1/10,000 of an hour. During this time, if left in the wine industry, the resources could otherwise have produced (1/10,000) (20,000 bottles of wine) or 2 bottles of wine. Hence to produce one additional computer in the United States, 2 bottles of wine are foregone. Two bottles of wine, then, are the opportunity cost of the computer. The rest of the opportunity costs are calculated similarly.

d. The United States has a comparative advantage in wine because the opportunity cost of a bottle of wine in the United States — ½ computer — is less than the opportunity cost of a bottle of wine in France —1½ computer. France has a comparative advantage in the production of computers, because its opportunity cost — 2/3 bottle of wine — is less than that in the United States — 2 bottles of wine.

e. In the United States, 5,000 computers and 10,000 bottles of wine are produced in an hour. In France, 6,000 computers and 4,000 bottles of wine are produced in an hour. Overall, 11,000 computers and 14,000 bottles of wine are produced in an hour.

f. With the United States specializing in wine, 20,000 bottles of wine are produced in an hour. Because France specializes in computers, 12,000 computers are produced in an hour.

g. With specialization, world computer production rises by 1,000 computers per hour and world production of wine rises by 6,000 bottles per hour. The fact that world production of wine and computers *both* increase demonstrates that specialization, according to comparative advantage, can boost world output of all goods.

b. Figure 3.16 shows the French *PPF*.

c. Table 3.7 shows the opportunity costs for the goods. To illustrate how this table was obtained, we can use the opportunity cost of a computer in the United States as an example. To produce one computer in the United States requires that resources work for 1/10,000 of an hour at manufacturing computers. Thus to produce an

9. Property rights play a key role in shaping incentives to innovate. Innovation — whether a new product

or a new, better way to manufacture an old good — benefits society. But innovation is costly: resources, time, and effort must be devoted to this process. By securing the property right to an innovation, the person who thought of the idea stands to benefit greatly from the resources expended. But if the innovator cannot obtain a property right, anyone can copy the new innovation. In that case the innovator's return will be dissipated when a lot of people copy the innovation and someone else may reap the rewards. Hence property rights, by promising that the innovator will personally benefit from the effort involved, motivate significantly more new development than would occur in the absence of property rights.

Incidentally, this fact may have played a role in the collapse of the former Soviet Union. Under the previous communist system, no property rights were offered to innovators. Interestingly, the Soviet Union was falling increasingly behind the Western world in developing new and improved products and methods of production.

■ You're the Teacher

1. "*All* economic models vastly simplify an incredibly complex reality. But that is no reason to throw them away. The lessons that can be learned from the simple two-good *PPF* carry over to the real world. For instance, the two-good *PPF* shows that there are limits to production. These limits are represented by the *PPF* curve, which divides attainable from unattainable production points. Now, just as you say, in the real world billions of goods are produced. But there are still limits. Regardless of the number of goods produced, every nation faces a limit of how much it can produce, just as in the simple two-good *PPF* case.

"Moreover, the simple *PPF* model demonstrates that production can be efficient or inefficient. This result is also true in the real world.

"Finally, the two-good *PPF* shows that once production is efficient — a point on the *PPF* — increasing the output of one good has an opportunity cost because the production of the other good must be reduced. The same is true in our real world. Once our nation is producing efficiently, if we want to produce more of one good, we have to give up other goods. So, based on the assumption that there are only two goods, the *PPF* teaches us stuff that we can apply everywhere, not just on the next test."

2. "The idea that economic growth has some costs is perhaps not surprising. But most of the time the costs we hear about have to do with pollution or stuff like that. Let's not worry about pollution; we haven't studied it yet in class. But even if we don't have any more pollution or such things, economic growth is costly. And that, perhaps, *is* surprising!

"Here's the idea: Suppose that we increase growth by building more factories and by developing better technology to manufacture faster computer chips. The essential point is that resources such as people and equipment, are required to build more factories or develop new technology. Because these people and resources are building factories and developing technology, they cannot be used to produce other stuff, like more clothes for us to wear or new video games for us to play. So the whole deal is that a higher economic growth rate costs us new clothes and new video games. While the increased growth may be good because we'll be able to get a lot of new clothes or video games after the growth, the growth sure hasn't been free."

Chapter Quiz

1. Consider a constant slope *PPF* with a vertical intercept of 80 guns and a horizontal intercept of 120 tons of butter. The opportunity cost of increasing butter output from 30 to 31 tons is
   a. 1/2 gun.
   b. 2/3 gun.
   c. 1 gun.
   d. 1 1/2 guns.

2. A nation produces at a point outside its *PPF*
   a   when it trades with other nations.
   b. when it produces inefficiently.
   c. when it produces efficiently.
   d. never.

3. Which of the following statements is true?
   a. All resources are made by people.
   b. Human resources are called labor.
   c. Capital is made only by labor.
   d. Human capital is a contradiction in terms.

4. A situation in which some resources are used inefficiently is represented in a *PPF* diagram by
   a. any point on either the vertical or horizontal axis.
   b. the midpoint of the *PPF*.
   c. a point outside the *PPF*.
   d. a point inside the *PPF*.

5. Robert has decided to write the essay that is due in his economics class rather than watch a movie. The movie he will miss is Robert's _____ of writing the essay.
   a. opportunity cost
   b. explicit cost
   c. implicit cost
   d. discretionary cost

6. The cost of textbooks _____ and the earnings foregone because of attending college _____ part of the opportunity cost of attending college.
   a. is; are
   b. is; are not
   c. is not; are
   d. is not; are not

7. The best alternative foregone from an action is called the action's
   a. "loss".
   b. "money cost".
   c. "direct cost".
   d. "opportunity cost".

8. The marginal benefit of a product is the
   a. benefit that the product gives to someone other than the buyer.
   b. maximum someone is willing to pay for that unit of the product.
   c. benefit of the product that exceeds the marginal cost of the product.
   d. benefit of the product divided by the total number of units purchased.

9. A marginal benefit curve has a _____ slope; a marginal cost curve has a _____ slope.
   a. positive; positive
   b. positive; negative
   c. negative; positive
   d. negative; negative

10. The production possibility frontier will shift inward as a result of
    a. an increase in the production of consumption goods.
    b. an increase in R&D expenditure.
    c. an increase in population.
    d. destruction of part of the nation's capital stock.

The answers for this Chapter Quiz are on page 327

Part Review **1** UNDERSTANDING THE SCOPE OF ECONOMICS

Reading Between the Lines

WITH FREE PCs, YOU GET WHAT YOU PAY FOR

With personal computers already selling for as little as $300, a growing number of companies are pushing prices to the limit: zero. But consumers would be well advised to read the fine print before signing up.

Most of these PCs aren't really free when you look closely. In exchange for the hardware, customers must typically sign up for a particular Internet service, sometimes for a monthly premium ranging from $6 to $30 or a two- to three-year contract. Some may be asked to divulge sensitive data about themselves for marketing purposes and may end up viewing advertising on their PC screens. "Free" PC customers also usually have to pay a delivery charge, may have to cough up a deposit and could be liable for hefty fees if they cancel early.

On the plus side, most of the companies simplify the process of getting on the Internet for many customers who never thought they could afford a PC. What's more, many companies promise to replace their machines with new models after two or three years, although sometimes for a fee, helping allay consumer fears that the PC will quickly become obsolete.

So far, there's no shortage of people willing to take a flier. Free-PC, a start-up in Pasadena, Calif., says it has received 1.2 million applications for the first 10,000 PCs it intends to distribute starting in May. Gobi Chief Executive Officer Ganesh Ramakrishnan says his service signs up two or three new customers every minute.

Competition between the vendors is already heating up. At the end of March, InterSquid.com started shipping free PCs with a $39.99 monthly fee for Internet access. A few days later, DirectWeb and Gobi announced similar services at lower prices. Just last week, InterSquid.com cut its monthly fee to $29.99.

"It's just the competition-it became fierce very quickly," says InterSquid.com Founder and CEO Joseph Calamari, whose name inspired the company's. "We just felt we should at least be competitive." One company, Free-PC itself, levies no monthly fees and allows customers to cancel the service and return their PC at any time. The catch is that Free-PC will constantly display advertising on its customers' PC screens and requires its users to log on to Free-PC's Internet service for at least 10 hours a month.

■ Analyze It

After years of falling in price, a new, lower price for PCs has been established: "Free!" Does this price disprove the saying that "There is no free lunch"? Or, are these PCs really free to the consumers? Or to society?

1. Are all these PCs truly free to the consumers or is there a cost? What is the cost of a computer from "Free-PC"? (Hint: Think in terms of "opportunity cost".)

2. Is there a cost to society of providing consumers with these free PCs? Be sure to use a production possibility frontier figure in your answer and to discuss the idea of opportunity cost.

3. The founder of one of the companies discussed the role that competition played in determining the deal the company offered consumers. Does competition help the consumers or the companies?

Web Resources

For more information about economics, browse the Parkin Web site to explore related links.

For career-related information in economics, try "Reference Shelf, try "Jobs," or "Economists". Alternatively, depending on your interests, look under "Law and Economics," "Business Economics," or "Economics and Teaching".

If you want a broader view of economics, choose "Economic History," "Methodology and History of Economic Thought," or "Microeconomics" and see where these links and your interests take you!

Mid-Term Examination

■ **Chapter 1**

1. Willy makes $25 an hour as a carpenter. He must take two hours off from work (unpaid) to go to the dentist to have a tooth pulled. The dentist charges $60. In terms of dollars, the opportunity cost of Willy's visit to the dentist is
   a. $25.
   b. $50.
   c. $60
   d. $110.

2. A company produces 100 units of a good at a cost of $400 or produces 101 units of the same good at a cost of $415 dollars. The $15 difference is
   a. the marginal benefit of producing 101 units.
   b. the marginal cost of producing the 101st unit.
   c. the marginal cost of producing the first unit.
   d. less than the average cost.

3. Positive statements are statements about
   a. prices.
   b. quantities.
   c. what is.
   d. what ought to be.

4. The branch of economics that studies individual markets within the economy is called
   a. macroeconomics.
   b. microeconomics.
   c. individual economics.
   d. market economy.

■ **Chapter 2**

5. A time-series graph displays the price of copper. The slope of the line is positive for periods when the
   a. price of copper is rising.
   b. price of copper is falling.
   c. quantity of copper is rising.
   d. quantity of copper is falling.

6. On the *x*-axis, smaller values usually will be
   a. directly above larger values.
   b. directly below larger values.
   c. farther to the right than larger values.
   d. farther to the left than larger values.

7. A positive relationship between two variables is shown by
    a. an upward-sloping line.
    b. a horizontal or vertical line.
    c. a downward-sloping line.
    d. a steeply sloping line.

8. Along a curved line, the slope at the minimum
    a. is greater than zero.
    b. is less than zero.
    c. is zero.
    d. may be greater than, less than, or equal to zero.

■ **Chapter 3**

9. Output combinations beyond the production possibility frontier
    a. result in more rapid growth.
    b. are associated with unused resources.
    c. are attainable only with the full utilization of all resources.
    d. are unattainable.

10. The *PPF* shifts inward as a result of
    a. a decrease in the production of consumption goods.
    b. an increase in R&D expenditure.
    c. an increase in population.
    d. the destruction of a portion of the capital stock.

11. Whenever a person can produce less of all goods than anyone else, that person
    a. should specialize in nothing.
    b. has a comparative advantage in something.
    c. should be self-sufficient.
    d. has a comparative advantage in nothing.

12. To obtain all the gains available from comparative advantage, individuals or countries must do more than trade, they must also
    a. specialize.
    b. save.
    c. invest.
    d. engage in research and development.

Answers

■ Reading Between the Lines

These PCs are not free to the consumers. For some of them, the price is obvious: A $29.99 per month fee to be connected to the Internet. This fee is significantly above the fees charged by companies that do not offer "free" personal computers, so it seems clear that the extra amount is actually a "hidden" price for the personal computer. The price for the personal computer provided by Free-PC is slightly more subtle. Indeed, it is similar to the cost of "free TV", namely the point that the personal computer owner must view the ads provided by Free-PC. Watching the ads has an opportunity cost, be it the time spent viewing them or in the space they occupy on the customer's monitor. However, apparently for many consumers the price of these personal computers is sufficiently low that they are rushing to take advantage of the deals.

From the perspective of society, these personal computers are not free regardless of the price charged the consumer: They have an opportunity cost in terms of the goods and services that are foregone to produce the computers. Figure 1 makes this point explicit. Suppose that the economy produces only personal computer, and televisions. Without the free PC offers, the economy would produce at point *a*, manufacturing T_0 televisions and PC_0 computers. With the increased marketing of "free PCs" and the large number of people taking advantage of these deals, the economy's production point moves from *a* to *b*. At *b*, more personal computer are produced — PC_1 rather than PC_0 — *and* fewer televisions are produced — T_1 instead of T_0. To the nation, the opportunity cost of producing the

FIGURE **1**

The Opportunity Cost of "Free PCs"

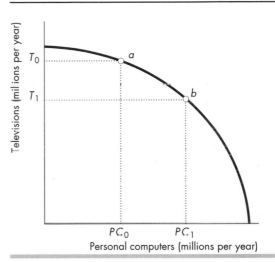

additional personal computers is the televisions that must be foregone. The opportunity cost of producing more computers arises because the nation has a limited amount of resources. To produce more computers, workers (and other resources) must stop producing other products, such as televisions.

Competition has benefited consumers. As the article tells, one of the companies initially charged $39.99 per month to be connected to the Internet. But, with increased competition, the company "felt it should at least be competitive" and so it was forced to lower its price to $29.99 a month. This point illustrates the result that competitive markets generally protect consumers by making it difficult for a firm to keep its price too high.

■ Mid-Term Exam Answers

1. d;   2. b;   3. c;   4. b;   5. a;   6. d;   7. a;   8. c;   9. d;   10. d;   11. b;   12. a

Chapter 4   DEMAND AND SUPPLY

Key Concepts

■ Price and Opportunity Cost

The ratio of the money price of one good to the money price of another good is the **relative price**. The relative price of a product is the product's opportunity cost. The demand for and supply of a product depend, in part, on its relative price.

■ Demand

The **quantity demanded** of a good is the amount that consumers plan to buy during a time period at a particular price. The **law of demand** states that "other things remaining the same, the higher the price of a good, the smaller is the quantity demanded." Higher prices decrease the quantity demanded for two reasons:

♦ **Substitution effect** — a higher relative price raises the opportunity cost of buying a good and so people buy less of it.

♦ **Income effect** — a higher relative price reduces the amount of goods people can buy. Usually this effect decreases the amount people buy of the product that rose in price.

Demand is the entire relationship between the price of a good and the quantity demanded. A **demand curve** shows the inverse relationship between the quantity demanded and price, everything else remaining the same. For each quantity, a demand curve shows the highest price someone is willing to pay for that unit. This highest price is the *marginal benefit* a consumer receives for that unit of output.

FIGURE **4.1**
Demand Curves

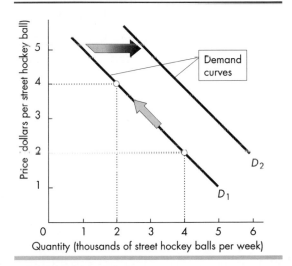

♦ Demand curves are negatively sloped, as illustrated in Figure 4.1.

♦ A change in the price of the product causes a **movement along the demand curve**, also called a **change in the quantity demanded**. The higher the price of a good, the lower is the quantity demanded. This relationship is shown in Figure 4.1 with the movement along D_1 from 4,000 to 2,000 street hockey balls demanded per week in response to a rise in price from $2 to $4 for a street hockey ball.

A shift in the demand curve is called a **change in demand**. An increase in demand means that the demand curve shifts rightward, such as the shift from D_1 to D_2 in Figure 4.1; a decrease in demand refers to a shift leftward. The demand curve shifts from changes in the following:

♦ *prices of related goods* — a rise in the price of a **substitute** increases demand and shifts the demand curve rightward; but a rise in the price of a **complement** decreases demand and shifts the demand curve leftward.

♦ *expected future prices* — if a product's price is expected to rise in the future, the current demand for it increases and the demand curve shifts rightward.

♦ *income* — for a **normal good**, an increase in income increases demand and shifts the demand curve rightward; but for an **inferior good** an increase in income decreases demand and shifts the demand curve leftward.

♦ *population* — an increase in population increases demand and shifts the demand curve rightward.

♦ *preferences* — if people decide they like a good more, its demand increases so the demand curve shifts rightward.

■ Supply

The **quantity supplied** is the amount of a good that producers plan to sell at a particular price during a given time period. **Supply** is the entire relationship between the price of a good and the quantity supplied.

The **law of supply** states that "other things remaining the same, the higher the price of a good, the greater is the quantity supplied." Supply curves show the positive relationship between the price and the quantity supplied. For each quantity, the supply curve shows the minimum price a supplier must receive in order to produce that unit of output.

♦ Supply curves are positively sloped, as shown in Figure 4.2.

♦ A change in the price of the product causes a **movement along the supply curve**, also called a **change in the quantity supplied**. It is illustrated in Figure 4.2 as the movement along S_1 from 2,000 street hockey balls supplied per week to 4,000 balls when the price rises from $2 for a ball to $4.

A **change in supply** is a shift in the supply curve. An increase in supply is equivalent to a shift rightward in the supply curve, shown in Figure 4.2 as the shift from S_1 to S_2; a decrease is a leftward shift in the

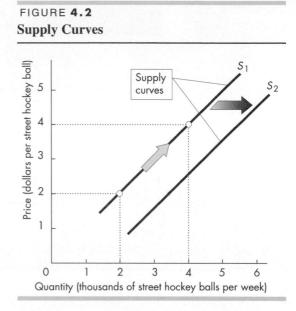

FIGURE **4.2**
Supply Curves

supply curve. The supply curve shifts in response to changes in the following:

♦ *prices of productive resources* — a rise in the price (cost) of an input decreases supply and shifts the supply curve leftward.

♦ *prices of related goods produced* — a rise in the price of a *substitute in production* decreases supply and shifts the supply curve leftward; a rise in the price of a *complement in production* increases supply and shifts the supply curve rightward.

♦ *expected future prices* — if the price is expected to rise in the future, the current supply decreases and the supply curve shifts leftward.

♦ *number of suppliers* — an increase in the number of suppliers increases the supply and shifts the supply curve rightward.

♦ *technology* — an advance in technology increases supply and thus shifts the supply curve rightward.

■ Market Equilibrium

The **equilibrium price** is determined by the intersection of the demand and supply curves. It is the price at which the quantity demanded equals the quantity supplied. The **equilibrium quantity** is the quantity bought and sold at the equilibrium price. Figure 4.3 shows the equilibrium price, $3, and the equilibrium quantity, 3,000 street hockey balls per week. Below the equilib-

FIGURE **4.3**
The Equilibrium Price and Quantity

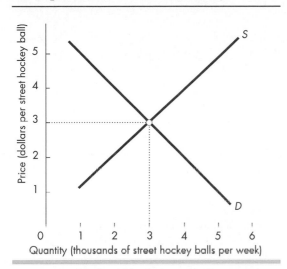

rium price, a shortage exists and the price will rise. Above the equilibrium price, a surplus exists and the price will fall. Only at the equilibrium price does the price not change.

■ Predicting Changes in Price and Quantity

When one of the demand or supply curves shifts, the effect on both the price (P) and quantity (Q) can be determined:

♦ An increase in demand (a shift rightward in the demand curve) raises P and increases Q.

♦ A decrease in demand (a shift leftward in the demand curve) lowers P and decreases Q.

♦ An increase in supply (a shift rightward in the supply curve) lowers P and increases Q.

♦ A decrease in supply (a shift leftward in the supply curve) raises P and decreases Q.

When both the demand and supply curves shift, the effect on the price *or* the quantity can be determined, but without information about the relative sizes of the shifts, the effect on the other variable is ambiguous.

♦ If both demand and supply increases (both curves shift rightward), the quantity increases but the price may rise, fall, or remain the same.

♦ If demand decreases (the demand curve shifts leftward) and supply increases (the supply curve shifts rightward), the price falls but the quantity may increase, decrease, or not change.

1. **DEVELOPING INTUITION ABOUT DEMAND :** When you are first learning about demand and supply, think in terms of concrete examples. Have some favorite examples in the back of your mind. For instance, when you hear "complementary goods" (goods used together), think about hot dogs and hot dog buns because few people eat hot dogs without using a hot dog bun. For "substitute goods" (things that take each other's place) think about hot dogs and hamburgers because they are obvious substitutes.

2. **DEVELOPING INTUITION ABOUT SUPPLY :** An easy and concrete way to identify with suppliers is to think of "profit": Anything that increases the profit from producing a product (except for the price of the good itself) increases the supply and shifts the supply curve rightward, whereas anything that decreases profit decreases the supply and shifts the supply curve leftward. Thus when studying the effect from a rise in the price of a productive resource, you could think about a rise in the wage rate paid to workers. That lowers the firm's profit, thereby shifting the supply curve leftward.

3. **SHIFT IN A CURVE VERSUS A MOVEMENT ALONG A CURVE :** Failing to distinguish correctly between a shift in a curve and a movement along a curve can lead to error and lost points on examinations. This distinction applies both to demand and supply curves. Many questions in this lesson are designed to reinforce your understanding of the distinction, and you can be sure that your instructor will test you heavily on it. The difference between "shift in" versus "movement along" a curve is crucial for thinking about the factors influencing demand and supply and for understanding the determination of the equilibrium price and quantity.

One important point to remember is *that a change in the price of a good does not shift its demand curve;* it causes a movement along the demand curve. If one of the other factors affecting demand changes, the demand curve itself shifts. The shift of the demand curve is referred to as a change in demand.

Similarly, the supply curve shifts if some relevant factor that affects the supply — *other than the price of the good* — changes. A change in the price of the good causes a movement along the supply curve.

4. **RULES FOR USING A SUPPLY/DEMAND DIAGRAM :** The safest way to solve any demand and supply problem is always to draw a graph. Do not make the common mistake of thinking that a problem is so easy that you can do it in your head, without drawing a graph.

A few mechanical rules can make using supply and demand graphs easy. First, when you draw the graph, be sure to label the axes. As the course progresses, you will encounter many graphs with different variables on the axes. You can easily become confused if you do not develop the habit of labeling the axes. Second, draw the supply and demand curves as straight lines. If you draw them with graceful and stylish curves, you might misread the answer from your figure and lose credit for a problem. Third, be sure to indicate and label the initial equilibrium price and quantity. Now come the two hard parts — which, with practice, actually are not difficult. Suppose that you are dealing with a situation in which one influence changes. First, determine whether the influence shifts the demand or the supply curve. Aside from the effect of the price expected in the future, most factors generally shift only one curve and you must decide which one. Second, determine whether the curve that is affected shifts rightward (increases) or shifts leftward (decreases). From here on, it's easy: Take the figure you have already drawn, shift the appropriate curve, and read off the answer.

5. **CHANGES IN DEMAND DO NOT CAUSE CHANGES IN SUPPLY ; CHANGES IN SUPPLY DO NOT CAUSE CHANGES IN DEMAND :** Do not make the common error of believing that an increase in demand, that is, a rightward shift in the demand curve, causes an increase in supply, a rightward shift in the supply curve. Use Figure 4.4, which illustrates the market for television sets, as an example. Television sets are a normal good, so an increase in income shifts the demand curve rightward, as shown. This shift in the demand curve causes the equilibrium price of a television to rise (from $300 for a set to $400) and also causes the equilibrium quantity to increase (from 3,000 sets per day to 4,000). But the shift in the demand curve does not cause the supply curve to *shift*. Instead, there is a movement *along* the unchanging supply curve.

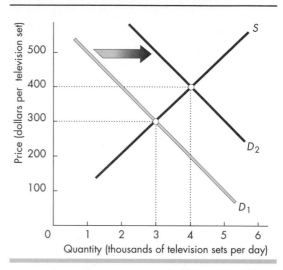

FIGURE **4.4**
The Effect of an Increase in Demand

Remember: Shifts in demand and supply curves cause the price to change. Changes in the price do NOT cause demand and supply curves to shift. Hence a shift in the demand curve does *not* cause the supply curve to shift and, similarly, a shift in the supply curve does *not* cause the demand curve to shift. Further, the price does *not* change unless one — or both — of the supply and demand curves shifts.

Questions

■ True/False/Uncertain and Explain

Price and Opportunity Cost

1. A good with a high relative price must have a low opportunity cost.

2. A product's relative price may fall even though its money price rises.

Demand

3. The law of demand states that, if nothing else changes, as the price of a good rises, the quantity demanded decreases.

4. A decrease in income decreases the demand for all products.

5. "An increase in demand" means a movement down and rightward along a demand curve.

6. New technology for manufacturing computer chips is developed. That shifts the demand curve for computer chips rightward.

Supply

7. A supply curve shows the maximum price required in order to have the last unit of output produced.

8. A rise in the price of chicken feed decreases the supply of chickens.

9. A rise in the price of orange juice shifts the supply curve of orange juice rightward.

Market Equilibrium

10. Once a market is at its equilibrium price, unless something changes, the price will not change.

11. If there is a surplus of a good, its price falls.

Predicting Changes in Price and Quantity

12. If the expected future price of a good rises, its current price rises.

13. The fact that a rise in the price of a product decreases the quantity demanded means that there can never be a situation with both the product's equilibrium price rising and equilibrium quantity increasing.

14. If both the demand and supply curves shift rightward, the equilibrium quantity increases.

15. If both the demand and supply curves shift rightward, the equilibrium price rises.

■ Multiple Choice

Price and Opportunity Cost

1. The opportunity cost of a product is the same as its
    a. money price.
    b. relative price.
    c. price index.
    d. None of the above.

2. The money price of a pizza is $12 per pizza and the money price of a taco is $2 per taco. The relative price of a pizza is
    a. $12 per pizza.
    b. $24 per pizza.
    c. 6 tacos per pizza.
    d. 1/6 pizza.

Demand

3. A rise in the price of a round of golf shifts the
    a. demand curve for golf balls leftward.
    b. demand curve for golf balls rightward.
    c. supply curve for golf balls leftward.
    d. supply curve of golf balls rightward.

4. If a rise in the price of gasoline decreases the demand for large cars,
    a. gasoline and large cars are substitutes in consumption.
    b. gasoline and large cars are complements in consumption.
    c. gasoline is an inferior good.
    d. large cars are an inferior good.

5. A normal good is one
    a. with a downward sloping demand curve.
    b. for which demand increases when the price of a substitute rises.
    c. for which demand increases when income increases.
    d. None of the above

6. Some sales managers are talking shop. Which of the following quotations refers to a movement along the demand curve?
    a. "Since our competitors raised their prices our sales have doubled."
    b. "It has been an unusually mild winter; our sales of wool scarves are down from last year."
    c. "We decided to cut our prices, and the increase in our sales has been remarkable."
    d. None of the above

FIGURE **4.5**
Multiple Choice Question 7

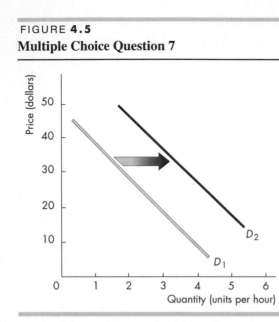

7. Which of the following could cause the shift in the demand curve illustrated in Figure 4.5?
   a. An increase in supply
   b. A rise in the price of a substitute good
   c. A rise in the price of a complement
   d. A fall in the price of the product

Supply

8. A decline in the price of a good causes producers to decrease the quantity of the good supplied. This result illustrates
   a. the law of supply.
   b. the law of demand.
   c. a change in supply.
   d. the nature of an inferior good.

9. Which of the following influences does <u>NOT</u> shift the supply curve?
   a. A rise in the wages paid workers
   b. Development of new technology
   c. People deciding that they want to buy more of the product
   d. A decrease in the number of suppliers

10. The price of jet fuel rises, causing the
    a. demand for airplane trips to increase.
    b. demand for airplane trips to decrease.
    c. supply of airplane trips to increase.
    d. supply of airplane trips to decrease.

11. In addition to showing the quantity that will be supplied at different prices, a supply curve may be viewed as the
    a. willingness-and-ability-to-pay curve.
    b. marginal benefit curve.
    c. minimum-supply price curve.
    d. maximum-supply price curve.

12. An increase in the number of producers of gruel _____ the supply of gruel and shifts the supply curve of gruel _____.
    a. increases; rightward
    b. increases; leftward
    c. decreases; rightward
    d. decreases; leftward

13. An increase in the cost of producing video tape shifts the supply curve of video tape _____ and shifts the demand curve for video tape _____.
    a. rightward; leftward
    b. leftward; leftward
    c. leftward; not at all
    d. not at all; leftward

14. To say that "supply increases" for any reason, means there is a
    a. movement rightward along a supply curve.
    b. movement leftward along a supply curve.
    c. shift rightward in the supply curve.
    d. shift leftward in the supply curve.

Market Equilibrium

15. If the market for Twinkies is in equilibrium, then
    a. Twinkies must be a normal good.
    b. producers would like to sell more at the current price.
    c. consumers would like to buy more at the current price.
    d. the quantity supplied equals the quantity demanded.

16. If there is a shortage of a good, the quantity demanded _____ the quantity supplied and the price will _____.
    a. is less than; rise
    b. is less than; fall
    c. is greater than; rise
    d. is greater than; fall

FIGURE **4.6**
Multiple Choice Question 17

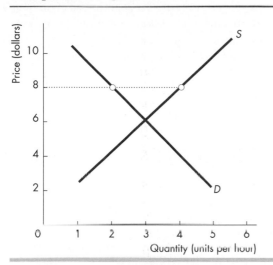

17. In Figure 4.6 at the price of $8 there is a
    a. shortage and the price will rise.
    b. shortage and the price will fall.
    c. surplus and the price will rise.
    d. surplus and the price will fall

18. In a market, at the equilibrium price,
    a. neither buyers nor sellers can do business at a better price.
    b. buyers are willing to pay a higher price, but sellers do not ask for a higher price.
    c. buyers are paying the minimum price they are willing to pay for any amount of output and sellers are charging the maximum price they are willing to charge for any amount of production.
    d. None of the above is true.

Predicting Changes in Price and Quantity

19. For consumers, pizza and hamburgers are substitutes. A rise in the price of a pizza causes _____ in the price of a hamburger and _____ in the quantity of hamburgers.
    a. a rise; an increase
    b. a rise; a decrease
    c. a fall; an increase
    d. a fall; a decrease

20. How does an unusually cold winter affect the equilibrium price and quantity of anti-freeze?
    a. It raises the price and increases the quantity.
    b. It raises the price and decreases the quantity.
    c. It lowers the price and increases the quantity.
    d. It lowers the price and decreases the quantity.

21. You notice that the price of wheat rises and the quantity of wheat increases. This set of observations can be the result of the
    a. demand for wheat curve shifting rightward.
    b. demand for wheat curve shifting leftward.
    c. supply of wheat curve shifting rightward.
    d. supply of wheat curve shifting leftward.

22. A technological improvement lowers the cost of producing coffee. As a result, the price of a pound of coffee _____ and the quantity of coffee _____.
    a. rises; increases
    b. rises; decreases
    c. falls; increases
    d. falls; decreases

23. The number of firms producing computer memory chips decreases. As a result, the price of a memory chip _____ and the quantity of memory chips _____.
    a. rises; increases
    b. rises; decreases
    c. falls; increases
    d. falls; decreases

For the next five questions, suppose that the price of paper used in books rises and simultaneously (and independently) more people decide they want to read books.

24. The rise in the price of paper shifts the
    a. demand curve rightward.
    b. demand curve leftward.
    c. supply curve rightward.
    d. supply curve leftward.

25. The fact that more people want to read books shifts the
    a. demand curve rightward.
    b. demand curve leftward.
    c. supply curve rightward.
    d. supply curve leftward.

26. The equilibrium quantity of books
    a. definitely increases.
    b. definitely does not change.
    c. definitely decreases.
    d. might increase, not change, or decrease.

27. The equilibrium price of a book
    a. definitely rises.
    b. definitely does not change.
    c. definitely falls.
    d. might rise, not change, or fall.

28. Suppose that the effect from people deciding they want to read more books is larger than the effect from the increase in the price of paper. In this case, the equilibrium quantity of books
    a. definitely increases.
    b. definitely does not change.
    c. definitely decreases.
    d. might increase, not change, or decrease.

29. Which of the following definitely causes a product's equilibrium price to rise?
    a. An increase in both demand and supply.
    b. A decrease in both demand and supply.
    c. An increase in demand combined with a decrease in supply.
    d. A decrease in demand combined with an increase in supply

■ **Short Answer Problems**

1. a. This year the price of a hamburger is $2 and the price of a compact disc is $12. In terms of hamburgers, what is the relative price of a compact disc? In terms of hamburgers, what is the opportunity cost of buying a compact disc? How are the two answers related?
   b. Next year the (money) price of a compact disc doubles to $24 and the (money) price of a hamburger remains at $2. Now what is the relative price of a compact disc?
   c. The following year the (money) price of a compact disc stays at $24 and the (money) price of a hamburger doubles to $4. What is the relative price of a compact disc?
   d. In the next year, the (money) price of a compact disc doubles to $48 and the money price of a

hamburger triples to $12. What is the relative price of a compact disc?
   e. Can a product's relative price fall even though its money price has risen? Why or why not?

2. a. When drawing a demand curve, what five influences are assumed not to change?
   b. If any of these influences change, what happens to the demand curve?
   c. When drawing a supply curve, what five influences are assumed not to change?
   d. If any of these influences change, what happens to the supply curve?

TABLE **4.1**

Demand and Supply Schedules

Price (per comic book)	Quantity demanded (per month)	Quantity supplied (per month)
$2.50	14,000,000	8,000,000
3.00	13,000,000	10,000,000
3.50	12,000,000	12,000,000
4.00	11,000,000	13,000,000
4.50	10,000,000	14,000,000

3. a. Table 4.1 presents the demand and supply schedules for comic books. Graph these demand and supply schedules in Figure 4.7. What is the equilibrium price? The equilibrium quantity?

FIGURE **4.7**

Short Answer Problem 3

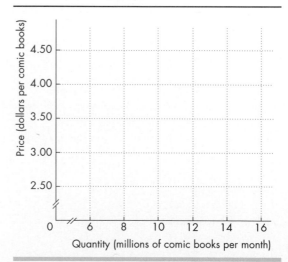

b. What is the marginal benefit received by the consumer of the 12,000,000th comic book? What is the minimum price for which a producer is willing to produce the 12,000,000th comic book?

c. Suppose that the price of a movie, a substitute for comic books, rises so that at every price of a comic book consumers now want to buy 2,000,000 more comic books than before. That is, at the price of $2.50, consumers now will buy 16,000,000 comics; at the price of $3.00, consumers now will buy 15,000,000 comic books; and so on. Plot this new demand curve in Figure 4.7. What is the new equilibrium price? The new equilibrium quantity?

4. New cars are a normal good. Suppose that the economy enters a period of strong economic expansion so that people's incomes increase substantially. Use a supply and demand diagram to determine what happens to the equilibrium price and quantity of new cars.

5. Used records and used compact discs are substitutes. Use a supply and demand diagram to determine what happens to the equilibrium price and quantity of used records when the price of a used compact disc falls because of an increase in the supply of used discs.

6. Suppose we observe that the consumption of peanut butter increases at the same time its price rises. What must have happened in the market for peanut butter? Is the observation that the price rose and the quantity increased consistent with the law of demand? Why or why not?

7. Suppose that the wages paid oil workers fall. Use a supply and demand diagram to determine the effect this action has on the equilibrium price and quantity of gasoline.

8. Chemical companies discover a new, more efficient technology for producing benzene. Use a supply and demand model to determine the impact that this new method has on the equilibrium price and quantity of benzene.

9. The price of a personal computer has continued to fall in the face of increasing demand. Explain.

10. a. The market for chickens initially is in equilibrium. Suppose that eating buffalo wings (which, contrary to the name, are made from chicken wings) becomes so stylish that people eat them for breakfast, lunch, and dinner. Use a supply and demand diagram to determine how the equilibrium price and quantity of chicken change.

b. Return to the initial equilibrium, before eating buffalo wings became stylish. Now suppose that a heat wave occurred and caused tens of thousands of chickens to die or commit suicide. Keeping in mind that dead chickens cannot be marketed, use a supply and demand diagram to determine what happens to the equilibrium price and quantity of chicken.

c. Now assume that both the heat wave and fad strike at the same time. Use a supply and demand diagram to show what happens to the equilibrium price and quantity of chicken. (Hint: Can you tell for sure what happens to the price? The quantity?)

■ You're the Teacher

1. When you and a friend are studying Chapter 4, the friend says to you, "I really don't understand the difference between a 'shift in a curve' and a 'movement along' a curve. Can you help me? It's probably important to understand this, so what's the difference?" Explain the difference to your friend.

2. "This supply and demand model is nonsense. It says that if demand for some product decreases, the price of that good falls. But, come on — except for computers, how many times have you actually seen a price fall? Prices *always* rise, so don't try telling me that that they fall." The supply and demand model is sound; it is this statement that is nonsense. Show the speaker the error in that analysis.

■ Answers

■ True/False Answers

Price and Opportunity Cost

1. **F** A product's relative price is its opportunity cost.

2. **T** As illustrated in the text, the money price of wheat has tended to rise while its relative price has tended to fall.

Demand

3. **T** The law of demand points out the negative relationship between a product's price and the quantity demanded.

4. **F** Demand decreases for normal goods but increases for inferior goods.

5. **F** The term "increase in demand" refers to a rightward shift in the demand curve.

6. **F** Technology is a factor that shifts the supply curve; new technology shifts the supply curve rightward.

Supply

7. **F** The supply curve shows the *minimum* price that suppliers must receive in order to produce the last unit supplied.

8. **T** Chicken feed is a resource used to produce chickens, so a rise in its price shifts the supply curve of chickens leftward.

9. **F** The rise in the price of orange juice creates a movement along the supply curve to a larger quantity supplied (that is, upward and rightward), but it does not shift the supply curve.

Market Equilibrium

10. **T** Once at the equilibrium price, because the opposing forces of supply and demand are in balance, the situation can persist indefinitely until something changes.

11. **T** A surplus of a product causes its price to fall until it reaches the equilibrium price.

Predicting Changes in Price and Quantity

12. **T** The rise in the future price shifts the demand curve rightward and the supply curve leftward, unambiguously raising the current price.

13. **F** The inverse relationship between the price and quantity demanded holds along a fixed demand curve. But if the demand curve shifts rightward, the equilibrium price rises and the equilibrium quantity increases.

14. **T** The equilibrium quantity definitely increases when both the demand and supply increase.

15. **U** The price rises if the shift in the demand curve is larger than that in the supply curve; but if the shifts are the same size, the price does not change and if the supply shift is larger, the price falls.

■ Multiple Choice Answers

Price and Opportunity Cost

1. **b** A product's relative price tells how much of another good must be foregone to have another unit of the product, which is the opportunity cost of the product.

2. **c** The relative price of the pizza is its money price relative to the money price of a taco, which equals ($12 per pizza)/($2 per taco) or 6 tacos per pizza.

Demand

3. **a** Golf balls and playing a round of golf are complements; hence a rise in the price of playing a round of golf causes the demand curve for golf balls to shift leftward.

4. **b** The definition of complementary goods is that a rise in the price of one decreases the demand for the other.

5. **c** This is the definition of a "normal good."

6. **c** A reduction in the price of the product causes a movement along its demand curve.

7. **b** A rise in the price of a substitute shifts the demand curve rightward.

Supply

8. **a** The law of supply points out the positive relationship between the price of a product and the quantity supplied.

9. **c** A change in preferences shifts the demand curve, not the supply curve.

10. **d** Jet fuel is a resource used to produce airplane trips, so a rise in the price (cost) of this resource decreases the supply of airplane trips.

11. **c** For any unit of output, the supply curve shows the minimum price for which a producer is willing to produce and sell that unit of output.

12. **a** An increase in supply is reflected in a rightward shift of the supply curve.

13. **c** A change in the cost to produce a product shifts the supply curve but does not shift the demand curve.

14. **c** An "increase in supply" means that the supply curve shifts rightward; a "decrease in supply" means the supply curve shifts leftward.

Market Equilibrium

15. **d** At equilibrium, consumers and suppliers are simultaneously satisfied insofar as the quantity consumers are willing to buy matches the quantity producers are willing to sell.

16. **c** A shortage occurs when the price is below the equilibrium price. The quantity demanded exceeds the quantity supplied and the resulting shortage causes the price to rise to its equilibrium level.

FIGURE **4.8**
Multiple Choice Question 17

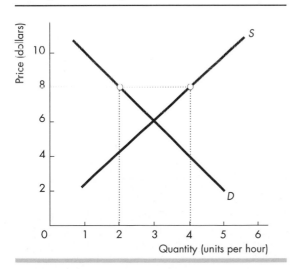

17. **d** There is surplus because, as illustrated in Figure 4.8, the quantity supplied at the price of $8 is 4. This quantity exceeds 2, the quantity demanded.

18. **a** Buyers cannot find anyone willing to sell to at a lower price and sellers cannot find anyone willing to buy at a higher price.

Predicting Changes in Price and Quantity

19. **a** The rise in the price of a pizza increases the demand for hamburgers, which results in a rise in

the price of a hamburger and an increase in the quantity of hamburgers.

20. **a** The cold winter shifts the demand curve rightward, as consumers increase their demand for antifreeze; the supply curve does not shift. As a result, the equilibrium price rises and the quantity increases.

FIGURE **4.9**
Multiple Choice Question 21

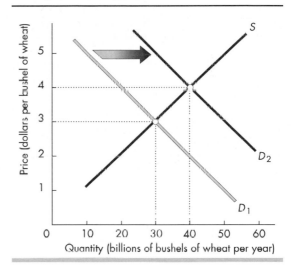

21. **a** Figure 4.9 shows that an increase in the demand for wheat, so that the demand curve shifts from D_1 to D_2, raises the price of wheat from $3 a bushel to $4 and increases its quantity from 30 billion bushels of wheat a year to 40 billion.

22. **c** The technological improvement increases the supply, that is, the supply curve shifts rightward. As a result, the quantity increases and the price falls.

23. **b** The decrease in the number of firms producing memory chips decreases the supply of memory chips, which raises the price and decreases the quantity of chips.

24. **d** Paper is a resource used in the manufacture of books, so a rise in the price of paper shifts the supply curve of books leftward.

25. **a** When people's preferences change so that they want to read more books, the demand curve for books shifts rightward.

26. **d** The equilibrium quantity increases if the increase in demand is larger than the decrease in

supply, decreases if the change in supply is larger, and does not change if the changes are the same size.

27. **a** Both the increase in demand and decrease in supply cause the price to rise, so the equilibrium price unambiguously rises.

FIGURE **4.10**
Multiple Choice Question 28

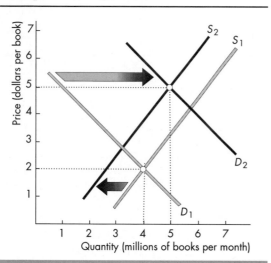

28. **a** If the shift in the demand curve exceeds the shift in the supply curve, the equilibrium quantity increases. This result is illustrated in Figure 4.10, where the quantity increases from 4 to 5 million.

29. **c** Both the increase in demand and decrease in supply serve to raise the price, so the two of them occurring together definitely must raise the price.

■ **Answers to Short Answer Problems**

1. a. The money price of a compact disc is $12 per compact disc; the money price of a hamburger is $2 per hamburger. The relative price of a compact disc is the ratio of the money prices, $12 per compact disc/$2 per hamburger, or 6 hamburgers per compact disc. For the opportunity cost, buying 1 compact disc means using the funds that otherwise could purchase 6 hamburgers. Hence the opportunity cost of buying 1 compact disc is 6 hamburgers. The relative price and the opportunity cost are identical.

b. The relative price of a compact disc is $24 per compact disc/$2 per hamburger or 12 hamburgers per compact disc.

c. The relative price of a compact disc is $24 per compact disc/$4 per hamburger, or 6 hamburgers per compact disc.

d. The relative price of a compact disc is $48 per compact disc/$12 per hamburger, or 4 hamburgers per compact disc.

e. Yes, a product's relative price can fall even though its money price rises. Part (d) gives an example of how that can occur: If a good's money price rises by a smaller percentage than the money price of other goods, then the product's relative price falls. Keep this result in mind when you use the supply and demand model because when the model predicts that the equilibrium price will fall, it means that the *relative* price, and not necessarily the money price, falls.

2. a. The five influences that do not change along a demand curve are prices of related goods, income, the expected future price, population, and preferences.

b. If any of these factors change, the demand curve shifts.

c. The five influences that are held constant when you draw a supply curve are prices of productive resources, technology, number of suppliers, prices of related goods produced, and the expected future price.

d. If any of these influences change, the supply curve shifts. It is very important to remember what influences shift a supply curve and what shift a demand curve.

3. a. Figure 4.11 (on the next page) shows the graph of the supply and demand schedules as S and D_1. The equilibrium price is $3.50 a comic book, and the equilibrium quantity is 12,000,000 comic books.

b. The person who buys the 12,000,000th comic book pays $3.50 for the comic book, and so $3.50 is the benefit this person receives from this comic book. The firm that produces the 12,000,000th comic book receives $3.50 for the book, and the supply curve shows that $3.50 is the minimum price for which this firm is willing to produce and sell the comic book.

FIGURE **4.11**
Short Answer Problem 3

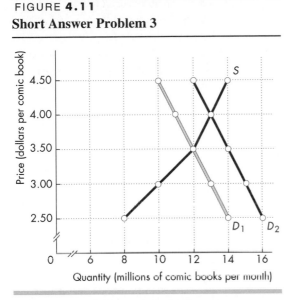

Quantity (millions of comic books per month)

c. The new demand curve is plotted in Figure 4.11 as D_2. The new equilibrium price is $4, and the new equilibrium quantity is 13 million.

FIGURE **4.12**
Short Answer Problem 4

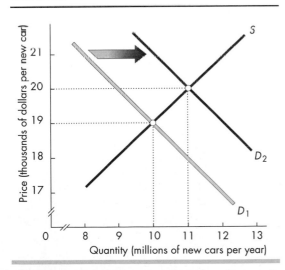

Quantity (millions of new cars per year)

4. Because new cars are a normal good, an increase in income increases the demand for them. Hence the demand curve shifts rightward, as shown in Figure 4.12. As a result, the equilibrium price rises (from $19,000 to $20,000 in the figure) and the equilibrium quantity also increases (from 10 million a year to 11 million in the figure).

FIGURE **4.13**
Short Answer Problem 5

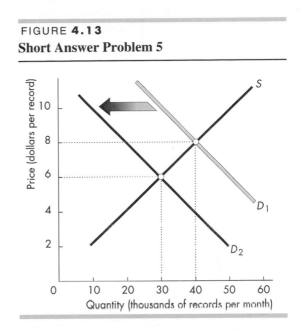

Quantity (thousands of records per month)

5. The fall in the price of a used compact disc, a substitute for used records, decreases the demand for used records. This change causes the demand curve for used records to shift leftward, as shown in Figure 4.13. As a result, the price of a used record falls, (from $8 a record to $6 in the figure) and the quantity decreases (from 40,000 per month to 30,000 in the figure). Note that it is the shift in the demand curve that changed the price and that the shift in the demand curve did *not* shift the supply curve.

6. In order for both the equilibrium price and quantity of peanut butter to increase, the demand for peanut butter must have increased. The increase in demand leads to a rise in the price and an increase in the quantity of peanut butter.

The observation that both the price rose and the quantity increased is not at all inconsistent with the law of demand. The law of demand states that "other things remaining the same, the higher the price of a good, the smaller is the quantity demanded." A key part of this law is the "other things remaining the same" clause. When the demand curve for peanut butter shifts rightward, something else that increased the demand for peanut butter changed. Hence "other things" have not remained the same and by changing have resulted in a higher price and increased quantity of peanut butter.

FIGURE **4.14**
FIGURE **4.14**
Short Answer Problem 7

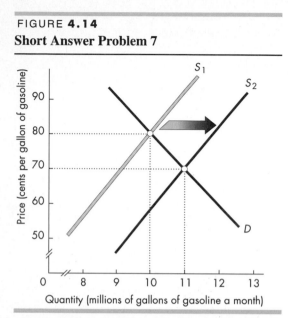

7. Lower wages reduce the price of a resource (labor) used to produce gasoline. As a result, the supply of gasoline increases. This change is illustrated in Figure 4.14, where the supply curve shifts rightward from S_1 to S_2. The increase in supply lowers the price of gasoline (from 80 cents a gallon to 70 cents in the figure) and increases the quantity (from 10 million gallons a month to 11 million).

FIGURE **4.15**
Short Answer Problem 8

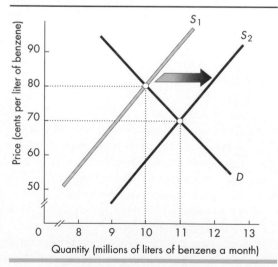

8. New technology increases the supply, so the supply curve shifts rightward. Then, as Figure 4.15 shows, the price falls (from 80 cents a liter to 70 cents in

the figure) and the equilibrium quantity increases from (10 million liters of benzene a month to 11 million).

This answer and the figure are virtually the same as those in problem 7. Even though a fall in wages and the development of new technology appear dissimilar, the demand and supply model reveals that both have the same effect on the price and quantity of the product. This model can easily accommodate these quite different changes. For this reason the demand and supply model is a very important economic tool.

FIGURE **4.16**
Short Answer Problem 9

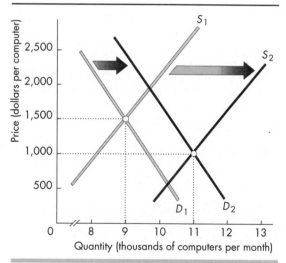

9. Personal computers have fallen in price although the demand for them has increased because the supply has increased even more rapidly. Figure 4.16 illustrates this situation. From one year to the next the demand curve shifted from D_1 to D_2. But over the year the supply curve shifted from S_1 to S_2. Because the supply has increased more than the demand, the price of a personal computer fell (in the figure, from $1,500 for a personal computer to $1,000). The quantity increased (from 9,000 personal computers a month to 11,000 in the figure).

10. a. With the change in people's preferences — so that they want more chicken wings and hence more chickens — the demand for chickens increases. The increase in the demand for chickens means that the demand curve for chickens shifts rightward. Figure 4.17 (on the next page) shows this change. As it demonstrates, the equilibrium

FIGURE **4.17**
Short Answer Problem 10 (a)

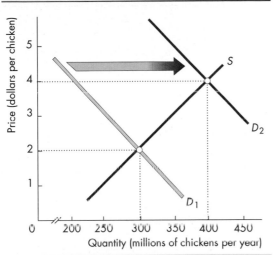

price rises (from $2 to $4 per chicken) and the equilibrium quantity of chickens increase (from 300 million to 400 million). Note that the change in people's preferences does not affect the supply of chicken, so the supply curve does *not* shift.

FIGURE **4.18**
Short Answer Problem 10 (b)

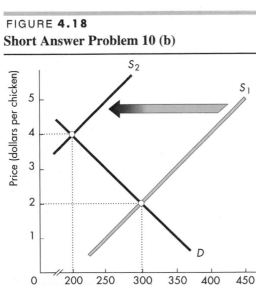

b. The heat wave decreases the number of chickens that can be supplied. This change shifts the supply curve for chickens leftward, as Figure 4.18 shows. Hence the heat wave raises the price

FIGURE **4.19**
Short Answer Problem 10 (c)

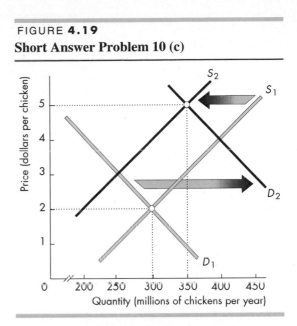

FIGURE **4.20**
Short Answer Problem 10 (c)

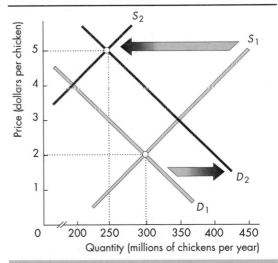

of a chicken (from $2 to $4) and decreases the quantity (from 300 million to 200 million).

c. If the demand increases *and* the supply decreases, the equilibrium price of a chicken rises. But the effect on the quantity is ambiguous. Figures 4.19 and 4.20 reveal the nature of this ambiguity. In Figure 4.19, the demand shift is larger than the supply shift, and the equilibrium quantity increases to 350 million chickens. But in Figure 4.20, the magnitude of the shifts is reversed, and the supply shift exceeds the demand shift. Because the supply shift is larger, the equilibrium quantity decreases to 250 million chickens. Thus unless you know which shift is larger, you cannot determine whether the quantity increases (when the demand shift is larger); decreases (when the supply shift is larger); or stays the same (when both shifts are the same size). However, regardless of the relative sizes, Figures 4.19 and 4.20 show that the price will unambiguously rise, coincidentally to $5 in both figures.

■ You're the Teacher

1. "The distinction between a 'shift in a curve' and a 'movement along a curve' is really crucial. Let's think about the demand curve; once you understand the difference for the demand curve, understanding it for the supply curve is easier. Take movies, OK? A lot of things affect how many movies we see in a month: the ticket price, our income, and so on. Start with the price. Obviously, if the price of a movie ticket rises, we'll buy fewer. The slope of a demand curve shows this effect. For the demand curve in Figure 4.21, when the price rises from $5 to $6 for a movie, the movement is from point *a* on the demand curve to point *b*. Our quantity demanded decreases from 5 movies a month to 4. Thus the rise in the price of the product has caused a movement along the demand curve. The negative slope of the demand curve shows the negative effect that higher prices have on the quantity demanded.

"Now, let's suppose that our incomes fall and that as a result we're going to go to fewer movies. The demand curve's slope can't show us this effect because the slope indicates the relationship between the price and the quantity demanded. Instead, the whole demand curve is going to shift. That is, at any price we'll buy fewer tickets. Look at Figure 4.22 for instance. If the price stays at $6 a movie, the quantity we demand decreases from 4 movies a month to 2.

"But the same is true if the price is $5: If the price stays at $5 the quantity we demand decreases from 5 movies a month to only 3. Now, I don't mean to say that the price has to stay at $6 or at $5. All I'm saying is that at any possible price, the number of movies we'll see has decreased and I'm just using $6 and $5 as examples. Thus we're going to decrease the quantity demanded at $6 and at $5, *and* at every

FIGURE **4.21**
You're the Teacher Question 1

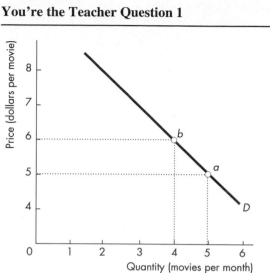

FIGURE **4.22**
You're the Teacher Question 1

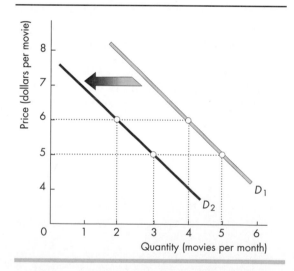

other possible price. That means that we can draw a new demand curve (D_2) to show how much we demand at every price after our incomes fall. So, the drop in income has shifted the demand curve from D_1 to D_2. And, that's all there is to the difference between a 'movement along the demand curve' and a 'shift in the demand curve.'"

2. "You're missing a key point about the demand and supply model. This model predicts what happens to *relative* prices, not *money* prices. You're certainly right when you say that we don't often see a money

price fall. We live in inflationary times and most money prices usually rise. But when the demand and supply model says that the price falls, it means that the *relative* price falls. A good's relative price can fall even though its money price rises. For instance, if the money price of some product rises by 2 percent when the money prices of all other goods are rising by 4 percent, the first product's relative price has fallen. That is, its money price relative to every other money price is lower. If you think about it, relative prices change all the time, and at least half the time relative prices fall. Drops in relative prices aren't rare; they're common. So, don't be too hasty to throw away the demand and supply model. Not only are we going to see it on tests in this class, but it also works well to help us understand what happens to a product's (relative) price and quantity whenever there's a change in a relevant factor."

Chapter Quiz

1. When demand increases
   a. price falls and quantity decreases.
   b. price falls and quantity increases.
   c. price rises and quantity decreases.
   d. price rises and quantity increases.

2. Wants differ from demands insofar as
   a. wants are limited by income but demands are unlimited.
   b. wants require a plan to acquire a good, while demands require no such plan.
   c. wants imply a decision about which demands to satisfy, while demands require no such specific plans.
   d. wants are unlimited and involve no specific plan to acquire the good, while demands reflect a decision about which wants to satisfy and a plan to buy the good(s).

3. A complement is a good
   a. that can be used in place of another good.
   b. that is used with another good.
   c. of lower quality than another.
   d. of higher quality than another.

4. Suppose that people buy less of good 1 when the price of good 2 falls. These goods are
   a. complements.
   b. substitutes.
   c. normal.
   d. inferior.

5. A change in the price of a good _____ its supply curve and _____ a movement along its supply curve.
   a. shifts; causes
   b. shifts; does not cause
   c. does not shift; causes
   d. does not shift; does not cause

6. Which of the following will shift the supply curve for good X leftward?
   a. A situation in which the quantity demanded of good X exceeds the quantity supplied.
   b. An increase in the price of machinery used to produce X.
   c. A technological improvement in the production of X.
   d. A decrease in the wages of workers employed to produce X.

7. A surplus causes the
   a. demand curve to shift rightward.
   b. supply curve to shift rightward.
   c. price to fall.
   d. price to rise.

8. If a product is a normal good and people's incomes rise, then the new equilibrium quantity is _____ the initial equilibrium quantity.
   a. greater than
   b. equal to
   c. less than
   d. perhaps greater than, less than, or equal to depending on how suppliers react to the change in demand.

9. In the market for oil, the development of a new deep sea drilling technology _____ the demand curve for oil and _____ the supply curve of oil.
   a. shifts rightward; shifts rightward
   b. does not shift; shifts rightward
   c. shifts leftward; shifts leftward
   d. does not shift; shifts leftward

10. Taken by itself, an increase in supply causes
    a. the price to rise.
    b. the price to fall.
    c. the demand curve to shift rightward.
    d. the demand curve to shift leftward.

The answers for this Chapter Quiz are on page 327

2 UNDERSTANDING HOW MARKETS WORK

Part Review

Reading Between the Lines

OIL PRICES SURGE AS OPEC WEIGHS CUTS

Oil prices surged on news that key members of the Organization of Petroleum Exporting Countries (OPEC) were discussing a sharp reduction in the world's oil supply.

Meeting in Shaybah, a new Saudi oil development deep in the desert known as the Empty Quarter, Gulf oil ministers were reported to be considering an agreement that would take as much as two million barrels a day off of world markets.

The cuts under discussion could amount to as much as a 3% reduction in world supply ... .

The (price) for the benchmark West Texas Intermediate crude gained 82 cents on the news to close at $14.68 in trading yesterday on the New York Mercantile Exchange.

What remains unclear is how OPEC would achieve its cut. The organization, responsible for about 40% of the world's output, has still not delivered fully on cuts agreed to by its members last June. In January, for example, it produced about 800,000 barrels more daily than called for in the agreement.

But analysts said that low prices have caused such financial pain in Saudi Arabia, as well as in neighboring allied states such as Iran, that the (Saudi) kingdom may now have decided to reverse policy and overlook noncompliance..

A new round of cuts would also require the cooperation of a reluctant Venezuela, the third-largest OPEC producer. The country only this month came near to fulfilling cutback promises made in June, and its leaders offer contradictory statements almost daily about their appetite for further reductions

... some analysts believe that a sustained upturn in oil prices can only be sustained by a rebound in demand, not output cuts.

Steve Liesman and Bhushan Bahree, "Oil Price Surge as OPEC Weighs Cuts," March 11, 1999, p. A2. Reprinted by permission of The Wall Street Journal, ©1999 Dow Jones & Co., Inc. All Rights Reserved Worldwide.

■ Analyze It

The price of oil had fallen to near historic lows in early 1999 when the meeting of the Organization of Petroleum Exporting Countries (OPEC) leaders discussed in the article took place. The governments of the OPEC countries obtain most of their revenue from selling oil, so when the revenue they collect from oil decreases, they suffer. Thus OPEC nations are rather single minded about trying to increase the revenue from oil sales.

1. In a supply and demand diagram, illustrate the effect of the proposed OPEC policy.
2. What impact would a decrease in the quantity of oil have on the U.S. production possibility frontier (*PPF*)?

Web Resources

For more information, browse the Parkin Web site to explore related links.

On the Top 10 list, visit the "National Bureau of Economic Research." The National Bureau of Economic Research (NBER) is the nation's premier group of research oriented economists. This link is certainly not to be missed!

Mid-Term Examination

■ **Chapter 4**

1. The law of demand states that, other things remaining the same, the higher the price of a good, the
   a. smaller will be the demand for the good.
   b. larger will be the demand for the good.
   c. smaller will be the quantity of the good demanded.
   d. larger will be the quantity of the good demanded.

2. Which of the following shifts the supply curve?
   a. An increase in income but only if the good is a normal good.
   b. An increase in income regardless of whether the good is normal or inferior.
   c. A rise in the price of the good.
   d. An increase in the cost of producing the product.

3. A surplus causes the
   a. demand curve to shift to the left.
   b. supply curve to shift to the right.
   c. price to fall.
   d. price to rise.

4. When supply increases, the equilibrium quantity
   a. increases and the price rises.
   b. decreases and the price falls.
   c. increases and the price falls.
   d. decreases and the price rises.

Answers

■ Reading Between the Lines

If OPEC is successful in decreasing the supply of oil, OPEC's action shifts the supply curve of oil leftward. Such a shift is illustrated in Figure 1, which shows the shift from the initial supply curve, S_1, to the new supply curve, S_2. The demand curve does not shift; it stays at D. As a result of the decrease in supply, the price of a barrel of oil rises, in the article and in the figure from $13.86 per barrel to $14.68 per barrel. The equilibrium quantity decreases, as indicated in the figure by the decrease from Q_1 to Q_2.

The effect of this action on the production possibility frontier for the United States is illustrated in Figure 2. OPEC is decreasing the quantity of oil that it supplies. As a result, the resources available to the U.S. economy decrease. When the quantity of resources decreases, the nation's *PPF* curve shifts inward, as illustrated in Figure 2. (Though the inward shift that may occur as a result of OPEC's action would be significantly smaller than what is illustrated in the figure!) Essentially, because the United States has fewer resources available to it, the maximum quantities of the goods and services produced in the United States decrease.

The article raises doubts about OPEC's ability to make the reduction stick. If OPEC is unable to force all its member nations to cooperate with the scheduled decreases, more oil will be available and thus the decrease in supply will be less than otherwise. As a result, the rise in price will be less and the inward shift in the U.S. *PPF* will be smaller. As it happens, in the two months following OPEC's meeting, the member nations did decrease their supply of oil, but by less than what was called for by the plan. Analysts continued to wonder if, as additional time passed, more OPEC members would increase production beyond the limits established by the plan. By the time you read this analysis, you may in a position to determine if the March 1999 OPEC plan succeeded or failed!

FIGURE **1**

The Oil Market

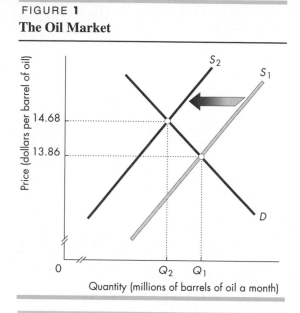

FIGURE **2**

The Production Possibility Frontier

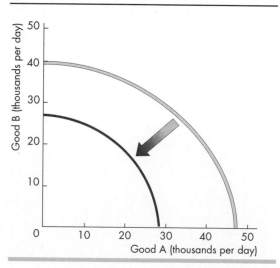

■ Mid-Term Exam Answers
1. c;   2. d;   3. c;   4. c

5 A FIRST LOOK AT MACROECONOMICS*

Key Concepts

■ Origins and Issues of Macroeconomics

Modern macroeconomics began during the **Great Depression**, 1929–1939. At that time, massive unemployment was the major economic problem, so macroeconomic's focus was initially on short-term problems, such as high unemployment. Recently the focus has changed so that long-term problems, such as economic growth, are also considered vital.

■ Economic Growth

Economic growth is the expansion in the economy's ability to produce goods and services. It is measured by the increase in **real gross domestic product**, also called **real GDP**. Real GDP is the value of a nation's aggregate (total) production of goods and services linked back to prices from one year.

Potential GDP is the quantity of real GDP that is produced when all resources are fully employed.

♦ The **productivity growth slowdown** caused potential GDP to grow more slowly in the 1970s and afterwards than it had in the 1950s and 1960s.

Real GDP fluctuates irregularly around potential GDP, leading to the **business cycle**. It has four phases:

♦ *Trough* — the lower turning point, when a recession ends and an expansion begins.

♦ **Expansion** — when real GDP increases.

♦ *Peak* — the upper turning point, when an expansion ends and a recession begins.

♦ **Recession** — when real GDP decreases for at least two consecutive quarters.

The 1990–1991 recession was mild compared to earlier recessions.

♦ Before the 1990s, business cycles in the U.S., Germany, and Japan occurred at about the same time. During the 1990s, business cycles have diverged.

♦ Similar 1970s productivity growth slowdowns occurred in the U.S., Germany, and Japan.

♦ From 1960 to 1990, on average growth in real GDP per person was been fastest in Japan. But, in the 1990s growth has been slowest in Japan.

Economic growth expands future consumption possibilities. However, economic growth allows less current consumption as resources must be devoted to capital accumulation; might lead to more rapid depletion of resources and more pollution; and can cause more frequent changes in jobs and consumption patterns.

■ Jobs and Unemployment

On the average, the U.S. economy creates 1.8 million new jobs per year, with more created during expansions and fewer during recessions.

A person is unemployed if he or she does not have a job but is looking for work. The **unemployment rate** is the number of unemployed workers as a percentage of the total number of employed plus unemployed workers.

♦ Unemployment increases during a recession and decreases during an expansion.

♦ The average unemployment rate in the United States is higher than in Japan, but lower than in Canada and Europe.

Unemployment is a serious problem because unemployed workers lose income and can find their future job prospects limited.

---

* This is Chapter 22 in *Economics*.

■ Inflation

The **price level** is the average level of prices. **Inflation** occurs when prices rise. The inflation rate is the percentage change in the price level. **Deflation** occurs when the inflation rate is negative so that the price level falls. In recent years, deflation has been rare in the United States.

Inflation was high in the 1970s and early 1980s, but has been lower since then. The U.S. experience with inflation has been similar to that of other industrialized nations.

Inflation reduces the value of money, and thus unpredictable inflation makes transactions spread over time more difficult to carry out. Moreover, people use resources to predict inflation rather than to produce goods and services. A *hyperinflation* is a period when the inflation rate exceeds 50 percent per month. At such rates, inflation causes economic chaos.

■ Surpluses and Deficits

A **government budget surplus** occurs when the government collects more in taxes than it spends; a **government budget deficit** occurs when the government spends more than it collects in taxes. The U.S. federal government had a surplus in 1998. From 1970 to 1997 it had a deficit every year.

The **current account balance** equals exports plus interest income minus the sum of imports plus interest expense. Payments greater than (less than) receipts create a current account deficit (surplus). The United States has run a current account deficit since 1982.

Deficits used to finance investment are not necessarily harmful; deficits used to finance consumption may be troublesome because such deficits do not create the income necessary to repay the debt incurred.

■ Macroeconomic Policy Challenges and Tools

Five widely agreed upon challenges for macroeconomic policy are:

♦ To boost long-term growth

♦ To stabilize the business cycle

♦ To lower unemployment

♦ To keep inflation low

♦ To reduce the government and international deficits

Achieving these challenges will help the economy.

The two general macroeconomic policy tools the government has at hand to help attain the five goals are:

♦ **Fiscal policy** — setting and changing taxes and the amount of government spending. The federal government may use fiscal policy in efforts to accomplish some of the policy challenges.

♦ **Monetary policy** — changes in the interest rate and money supply. Monetary policy is under the control of the Federal Reserve, or Fed. The Federal Reserve may use monetary policy in order to meet some of the policy challenges.

Helpful Hints

1. **THE MACROECONOMIC CHALLENGES :** The chapter discusses five widely agreed upon macroeconomic challenges. As you study the forthcoming chapters, keep these challenges in mind because ultimately we return to see what policies, if any, the government might adopt to help meet these goals. While these challenges are widely agreed upon, there is dispute among economists about ranking their importance as well as dispute about the proper polices necessary to attain some of them. The first disagreement matters because at times the goals collide, so that achieving one causes setbacks in others. In this case, the decision whether attaining the first goal is worth the cost of falling behind in others will differ from person to person. The second area of contention can arise even with agreement on the ranking of the goals. You will see in future chapters that there is disagreement amongst macroeconomists about how to meet the macroeconomic challenges and that this can lead to different policy advice.

Questions

■ True/False/Uncertain and Explain

Origins and Issues of Macroeconomics

1. Modern macroeconomics was developed during the decade of the Great Depression.

2. All macroeconomic goals are long-term goals.

Economic Growth

3. Real GDP is the amount of goods and services that are produced in a year when resources are fully employed.

4. Real GDP per person grew slowly in the 1960s and quite rapidly in the 1970s.

5. The trough is the lower turning point of the business cycle.

6. For the last four decades, on average the growth rate of real GDP per person has been lower in the United States than in Japan.

Jobs and Unemployment

7. Unemployment rates in recent years have been lower than those during the Great Depression.

8. In the recession phase of a business cycle, the unemployment rate rises.

Inflation

9. The inflation rate can never be negative.

10. Inflation in the U.S. has been similar to that in other industrialized nations.

Surpluses and Deficits

11. Ignoring interest income and expense, if U.S. exports exceed U.S. imports, the U.S. has a current account deficit.

12. A current account deficit harms the nation.

Macroeconomic Policy Challenges and Tools

13. The government can use fiscal policy and monetary policy to pursue its macroeconomic goals.

14. Fiscal policy includes government engineered changes in the interest rate.

■ Multiple Choice Questions

Origins and Issues of Macroeconomics

1. During the Great Depression,
   a. the major focus of macroeconomics switched to preventing inflation.
   b. the productivity growth slowdown occurred.
   c. economists switched their focus so that macroeconomics began to emphasize business cycles.
   d. long-term economic growth was the major problem facing capitalist nations.

Economic Growth

2. Real GDP
   a. measures only the output of real goods, such as machines and food, not "unreal" things such as services.
   b. includes all the goods and services produced in the economy, including those produced in the home.
   c. is measured by linking prices to a single year in order to eliminate the effects of inflation.
   d. is the amount of goods and services that the nation is able to produce when its resources are fully employed.

3. Which is the proper order for the business cycle?
   a. Peak, recession, trough, expansion
   b. Peak, trough, expansion, recession
   c. Peak, expansion, trough, recession
   d. Peak, recession, expansion, trough

4. Real GDP rose in all four quarters of 1998; thus 1998 was definitely a year
   a. of expansion.
   b. with a business cycle peak.
   c. of recession.
   d. with a business cycle trough.

5. Which of the following statements about the productivity growth slowdown is correct?
   a. The productivity growth slowdown was confined to the United States.
   b. The productivity growth slowdown occurred in the 1960s.
   c. The growth of potential GDP slowed during the productivity growth slowdown.
   d. Extremely low oil prices were a major cause of the productivity growth slowdown.

6. Comparing the United States, Germany, and Japan reveals that
   a. the United States and Germany have similar business cycles but that Japan has no business cycle.
   b. the business cycle is the most severe in the United States.
   c. business cycles last longer in Germany than in the United States or Japan.
   d. Japan's economic growth was the slowest of the three in the 1990s.

7. Comparing the United States, Germany, and Japan shows that
   a. the United States and Germany both experienced the slowdown in productivity growth but Japan did not.
   b. the slowdown in productivity growth was most severe in the United States.
   c. the slowdown in productivity growth lasted longer in Germany than in the United States and Japan.
   d. all three nations had a slowdown in productivity growth.

8. Which of the following is NOT a cost of more rapid economic growth?
   a. Current consumption must be foregone in order to develop new technology or new capital.
   b. Environmental damage may increase because of economic growth.
   c. Consumption possibilities expand in the future because of economic growth.
   d. Jobs and consumption patterns change more rapidly.

Jobs and Unemployment

9. On average, each year the total number of jobs in the United States increases by
   a. 18,000.
   b. 180,000.
   c. 1,800,000.
   d. 180,000,000.

10. The unemployment rate generally rises during _____ in the business cycle.
   a. a peak
   b. a recession
   c. a trough
   d. an expansion

11. Comparing the United States, Western Europe, and Japan, in recent years the unemployment rate has been highest in
   a. the United States.
   b. Western Europe.
   c. Japan.
   d. the United States and Japan.

Inflation

12. In the United States, the average inflation rate was highest over the decade of the
   a. 1960s.
   b. 1970s.
   c. 1980s.
   d. 1990s.

13. Which of the following is a cost of unpredictable inflation?
   a. People use resources to predict inflation rather than to produce output.
   b. It becomes too easy to obtain loans.
   c. Deflation becomes an increasing problem.
   d. All of the above are costs of unpredictable inflation.

Surpluses and Deficits

14. Which of the following statements about the government budget is correct?
   a. Whenever tax revenues exceed government spending, the government has a budget deficit,
   b. As a fraction of GDP (income), the budget deficit has increased steadily since 1980.
   c. The government has had a budget deficit every year since 1970.
   d. None of the above are correct.

15. Since 1982, the U.S. current account has had
   a. a deficit.
   b. a surplus that has been consistently large.
   c. a deficit that has gotten consistently larger.
   d. alternating small surpluses and deficits.

Macroeconomic Policy Challenges and Tools

16. Which of the following is NOT a policy challenge?
   a. Boosting long-term growth.
   b. Lowering unemployment.
   c. Stabilizing the business cycle.
   d. Raising the government budget deficit.

17. Which of the following is an example of monetary policy?
   a. Changing the interest rate.
   b. Changing government spending.
   c. Changing tax rates.
   d. Changing the government's deficit.

■ Short Answer Problems

1. What was the productivity growth slowdown? Why is it important?

2. Suppose that real GDP per person in the United States in 1999 is $30,000.

   a. If the U.S. real GDP per person grows at 2 percent per year, what is real GDP per person in 2000? In 2001? In 2004? In 2009?

   b. If the U.S. real GDP per person grows at 3 percent per year, what is real GDP per person in 2000? In 2001? In 2004? In 2009?

   c. In 2009 what is the difference in real GDP per person if the growth rate is 3 percent per year versus 2 percent? What does this result illustrate?

3. How has the growth rate of real GDP per person in the United States compared to that in Germany and Japan? What about business cycles; how have they compared?

4. Complete Table 5.1.

TABLE **5.1**

Employment and Unemployment

Employed workers (millions)	Unemployed workers (millions)	Unemployment rate (percent)
90	10	___
114	6	___
120	5	___

5. What happens to real GDP and the unemployment rate during each of the four phases of the business cycle?

6. What are the costs of unemployment?

7. How has inflation in the United States compared to inflation in other countries?

■ You're the Teacher

1. After class, your friend asks you: "You know, I wonder what's more important: stabilizing the business cycle or boosting long-term economic growth. Both seem important, and it would be cool if we could achieve both of these goals, but do you think one is more important than the other? You know, what I mean is that if we can actually achieve only one of these goals, which one do you think it ought to be?" Your friend has posed a very thoughtful question; what is your equally thoughtful response?

Answers

■ True/False Answers

Origins and Issues of Macroeconomics

1. **T** The initial focus of modern macroeconomics was on overcoming the very high unemployment that existed in the Great Depression.

2. **F** Short-term goals, such as avoiding a depression, as well as long term goals, such as the rate of economic growth, are both important parts of macroeconomics.

Economic Growth

3. **F** Potential real GDP is the amount of goods and services produced when all resources are fully employed.

4. **F** Real GDP per person started growing more slowly in the 1970s. Indeed, that was the "productivity growth slowdown."

5. **T** After the trough, the economy enters the expansion phase of the business cycle.

6. **T** Over the last forty years, on average Japanese economic growth has exceeded U.S. economic growth. But, for the last decade, the U.S. has grown more rapidly than Japan.

Jobs and Unemployment

7. **T** In the Great Depression, unemployment rates approximated 25 percent; during the past 50 years, at its monthly peak, the unemployment rate was approximately 12 percent.

8. **T** As real GDP falls during a recession, the unemployment rate rises.

Inflation

9. **F** The inflation rate can be negative (called deflation), though in recent years inflation has rarely been negative.

10. **T** In industrial nations worldwide, the inflation rate was very high in the 1970s and lower in recent years.

Surpluses and Deficits

11. **F** If exports exceed imports, the United States has a current account *surplus*.

12. **U** If the current account deficit occurs because the nation is buying capital equipment and other investments from abroad, the deficit may help the nation; if the nation is buying consumption goods and services, it may prove harmful to the nation.

Macroeconomic Policy Challenges and Tools

13. **T** In chapters to come, we explore fiscal and monetary policy in detail.

14. **F** Interest rate changes are part of monetary policy.

■ Multiple Choice Answers

Origins and Issues of Macroeconomics

1. **c** During the Great Depression, the extraordinarily high unemployment rates caused economists to stress short-term goals, such as reducing the severity of recessions or depressions.

Economic Growth

2. **c** By linking prices to a single year, real GDP eliminates the effects of inflation.

3. **a** Keep in mind that the business cycle is not a "smooth" cycle; some expansions last longer than others, some troughs are deeper than others, and so on.

4. **a** By definition, an expansion is a period of time during which real GDP increases.

5. **c** The slowdown in productivity growth is reflected in the slower growth rate of potential GDP.

6. **d** Japanese economic growth slowed dramatically during the 1990s.

7. **d** The productivity growth slowdown occurred in all nations but slowed Japanese economic growth the most, although until the last decade, Japanese growth rate remained higher than U.S. growth.

8. **c** The expansion of future consumption possibilities is a benefit of economic growth.

Jobs and Unemployment

9. **c** In recessions, fewer jobs are created; in expansions, more jobs are created.

10. **b** As real GDP falls in a recession, the unemployment rate rises.

11. **b** Relatively high unemployment rates in Western Europe have emerged as a major economic problem in those countries.

Inflation

12. **b** The inflation rate was markedly highest during the 1970s.

13. **a** By becoming "amateur inflation predictors," people take time and effort away from their occupations and so the nation produces fewer goods and services.

Surpluses and Deficits

14. **d** Until 1998, when it had a budget surplus, the government had had a budget deficit every year since 1970.

15. **a** The United States has had a deficit that initially became quite large, then diminished in size, and recently started to increase once again.

Macroeconomic Policy Challenges and Tools

16. **d** *Lowering* any government budget deficit is the macroeconomic policy challenge.

17. **a** Monetary policy includes changing the interest rate and/or the nation's money supply. The other answers are examples of fiscal policy.

■ Answers to Short Answer Problems

1. The productivity growth slowdown refers to period that started in the 1970s when growth in real GDP fell. During the 1970s, growth in real GDP slowed and has remained lower since than. Growth in real GDP is important because economic growth increases people's consumption possibilities; the larger real GDP, then the more goods and services people can consume. Basically, because of the productivity growth slowdown, today we all have smaller incomes than we would have had if productivity growth had not slowed.

2. a. In 2000 real GDP per person equals $30,600; in 2001 it equals $31,212; in 2004 it equals $33,122.42; and in 2009 it equals $36,569.83.

   b. In 2000 real GDP per person equals $30,900; in 2001 it equals $31,827; in 2004 it equals 34,778.22; and in 2009 it equals $40,317.49.

   c. The difference is $3,747.66, or almost $4,000 per person. This result illustrates the point that a relatively small difference in the growth rate of real GDP per person can eventually make a large difference in the total amount of real GDP per person.

3. Real GDP per person has grown in Japan, Germany, and the United States. Over the last several decades, on average, it has grown more rapidly in Japan than in the United States. The growth rate of GDP per person in Germany has been between that of Japan and the United States.

   All three countries have experienced the productivity growth slowdown, so that the growth rate of real GDP per person in the 1970s and 1980s was less than in the two earlier decades, though Japan's growth rate remained the highest. However, in the 1990s Japan's growth virtually ceased. In this decade, U.S. economic growth has been much higher than Japan's growth.

   Business cycles in the three nations generally were similar until the last decade. Until then, there were small differences in timing, so that, say, an expansion started slightly earlier in the United States than in Japan, are minor. In the 1990s, however, business cycles in these nations have had quite different timing.

TABLE 5.2

Employment and Unemployment

Employed workers (millions)	Unemployed workers (millions)	Unemployment rate (percent)
90	10	10.0
114	6	5.0
120	5	4.0

4. Table 5.2 completes Table 5.1. The unemployment rate equals the number of unemployed workers divided by the sum of employed plus unemployed workers times 100 or, for the first row in the table,
$$\frac{10 \text{ million}}{100 \text{ million}} \times 100 = 10.0 \text{ percent}.$$

5. During the recession phase of the business cycle, real GDP falls. During this phase of the cycle, the unemployment rate rises, although the rise in unemployment starts somewhat after the time that real GDP starts falling. At the trough, real GDP reaches its lowest point below trend, and soon thereafter the unemployment rate is at its highest point over the business cycle. The trough is the turning point between the recession phase and the expansion phase. During the expansion, real GDP grows and the unemployment rate generally falls. At the end of an

expansion, the economy reaches the peak of the business cycle. The peak is characterized by real GDP at its highest point above its trend and the rate of unemployment is either then or soon thereafter at its lowest point over the business cycle.

6. There are two important costs of unemployment: one "paid" immediately and the other incurred over a longer time horizon. First, and immediately, unemployed workers suffer a loss of income and the nation loses production. Second, and perhaps equally significant, when workers are unemployed for long periods of time, their skills and abilities deteriorate, which hurts their future job prospects.

7. Inflation in the United States has been similar to that in other industrialized countries. In particular, inflation rates rose in the 1970s and early 1980s and have fallen substantially since then.

■ You're the Teacher

1. "That's an excellent question. I asked our teacher about it, and our teacher said that economists don't agree about which of these macroeconomic challenges is more important.

   "Some economists think that boosting long-term growth is most important. They point out that if we are able to increase the growth rate of potential real GDP by 1 percentage point, after one generation, or two decades, real GDP per person would be over 22 percent higher than otherwise. That means that our consumption possibilities would expand by 22 percent so that, on the average, we could buy 22 percent more goods and services than otherwise. These economists also point out that this 22 percent increase in consumption possibilities dwarfs the fall of real GDP per person in a recession. So they argue that increasing the growth rate of potential GDP is more important than eliminating business cycles.

   "Other economists disagree. Although they agree that boosting the growth rate of potential real GDP is important, they point out that sustaining even a 1 percent increase in real GDP over 20 years is extremely difficult. Instead, they argue that taming the business cycle should be considered the major goal of macroeconomic policy. They contend that this task is easier than increasing the growth rate of potential real GDP. Indeed, some of these economists suggest that we have tamed the business cycle a bit because there hasn't been a recession nearly as severe as the Great Depression since 1940.

   "But our teacher says that *neither* of these objectives is easy to meet because if either were easy, we'd already be doing it. But, both challenges really are important. You know, I learned that our instructor became an economist exactly because these are crucial challenges and that by becoming a professional economist, our instructor hoped to help resolve these issues."

Chapter Quiz

1. The unemployment rate was approximately 25 percent
   a. during the Great Depression.
   b. during the most recent recession.
   c. during the 1974-1975 recession.
   d. in most years during the 1990s.

2. Which of the following are examples of short-term economic policy issues?
   a. Reducing inflation and increasing economic growth.
   b. Increasing economic growth and smoothing business cycles.
   c. Smoothing business cycles and reducing unemployment.
   d. All of the above.

3. Economic growth allows people to buy more goods and services. Economic growth is the expansion in the economy's real GDP.
   a. Both sentences are true.
   b. The first sentence is true and the second is false.
   c. The first sentence is false and the second is true.
   d. Both sentences are false.

4. Which of the following is included in real GDP?
   a. Purchases of hair styling.
   b. Transactions in the underground economy.
   c. Purchase of a used car.
   d. Production in the home.

5. The productivity growth slowdown refers to the
   a. increase in output growth during the 1970s.
   b. decrease in output growth during the 1970s.
   c. increase in employment growth in the 1980s.
   d. recession that occurred in 1991.

6. You notice that over the last year the unemployment rate has gone from 8.2 percent to 6.2 percent and growth in real GDP has increased. Hence over this year the economy is likely
   a. in a recession.
   b. at the trough of a business cycle.
   c. in an expansion.
   d. at the peak of a business cycle.

7. If real GDP increases by 1 percent and population increases by 3 percent, then
   a. real GDP per person increases.
   b. real GDP per person remains constant.
   c. real GDP per person decreases.
   d. real GDP per person probably changes, but without more information it is not possible to determine if it increases, decreases, or remains constant.

8. One of the costs of increasing growth in GDP is
   a. it does not increase the wealth available for all.
   b. it makes too many goods available for consumption in the future.
   c. people must give up current consumption.
   d. inflation must rise.

9. In recent decades, unemployment in the United States has been
   a. higher than in Western Europe.
   b. lower than in Japan.
   c. lower than in Canada.
   d. None of the above answers are correct.

10. The government collects $500 billion in taxes and spends $550 billion. The government has
    a. a budget surplus of $500 billion.
    b. a budget surplus of $50 billion.
    c. a budget deficit of $550 billion.
    d. a budget deficit of $50 billion.

The answers for this Chapter Quiz are on page 327

Chapter 6 MEASURING GDP, ECONOMIC GROWTH, AND INFLATION*

Key Concepts

■ Gross Domestic Product

Gross domestic product, **GDP**, is the value of the aggregate production in a country during a given time period.

A **flow** is an amount over a unit of time. A **stock** is a quantity that exists at a moment in time. **Capital**, the amount of plant, equipment, and inventories used to produce other goods, is a stock. Investment (the purchase of new capital) and **depreciation** (the decrease in the capital stock because of wear or obsolescence) are flows.

♦ **Gross investment** is the total amount of investment.

♦ **Net investment** is gross investment minus depreciation. Net investment is the amount by which the capital stock changes.

Wealth, or what people own, is a stock; **income**, or what people earn, is a flow.

The circular flow of income and expenditure shows real and monetary flows in the economy. The circular flow involves:

♦ Four economic sectors — households, firms, governments, and the rest of the world.

♦ Three major markets — resource markets, goods markets, and financial markets.

In these markets people make their economic decisions by choosing the amounts of key economic variables:

♦ **Consumption expenditures** (C) — total household spending on consumption goods and services.

♦ **Saving** — the amount of income left after spending on consumption. Saving is a flow that adds to wealth.

♦ Investment (I) — the purchase of plants, equipment, buildings, and additions to inventories by firms.

♦ **Net taxes** (T) — taxes paid to the government minus transfer payments from the government to firms and households.

♦ **Government purchases** (G) — government spending on goods and services.

♦ **Net exports** (NX) — exports (X, sales of U.S. goods abroad) minus imports (M, purchases of foreign goods by U.S. firms).

Aggregate expenditure, $C + I + G + NX$, equals aggregate production, GDP, and also equals aggregate income, Y. This equality is the basis for measuring GDP.

♦ **National saving** equals household saving plus government saving: $S + (T - G)$.

♦ Borrowing from the rest of the world equals $M - X$.

Investment is financed by national saving plus borrowing from the rest of world.

---

* This is Chapter 23 in *Economics*.

■ Measuring U.S. GDP

♦ The *expenditure approach* measures GDP by adding final expenditures, $C + I + G + NX$. Intermediate goods and services, used goods, and financial securities are not included because they are not final expenditures on newly produced goods and services.

♦ The *incomes approach* adds the compensation of employees, net interest, rental income, corporate profits and proprietors' income to give *net domestic income at factor cost*. Then indirect taxes and depreciation are added and subsidies subtracted to obtain GDP.

♦ A firm's **value added** equals the value of its output minus the value of the intermediate goods it bought from other firms.

■ The Price Level and Real GDP

The price level (the average level of prices) is measured by a price index.

♦ **Consumer Price Index (CPI)**, the average level of prices of goods and services purchased by a typical urban family. The CPI equals the current cost of a base-period basket of consumer goods and services relative to base-period cost.

Nominal GDP is GDP valued in current year prices; it is the dollar value of GDP. **Real GDP** equals GDP in a base year (currently 1992), scaled up by the growth in real GDP that has occurred each year since the base year. The growth rate of real GDP is calculated using a **chain-weighted output index**.

♦ The chain-weighted index first calculates the value of GDP for this year and last year, using prices from last year and then calculates a quantity index by dividing this year's GDP by last year's GDP.

♦ Next the chain-weighted index calculates the value of GDP for this year and last year, using prices from this year and calculates a second quantity index for GDP between the two years.

♦ The two quantity indices are averaged using their geometric mean. This average is used to scale up last year's real GDP by multiplying last year's GDP by the average and dividing by 100.

GDP deflator measures the average price level of the goods and services in GDP. The GDP deflator equals

$$\frac{\text{Nominal GDP}}{\text{Real GDP}} \times 100.$$

■ Measuring Economic Growth

The **economic growth rate** is the percentage change in real GDP from one year to the next.

Real GDP is used for economic welfare comparisons, for making international comparisons of output, and for business cycle forecasting.

Economic welfare is a general measure of economic well being. Real GDP is an imperfect measure of economic welfare because real GDP omits:

♦ Quality improvements — many quality improvements that lead to higher prices are counted as only price hikes.

♦ Household production — all household production is omitted.

♦ The underground economy — the underground economy (transactions hidden from the government) is not included.

♦ Health and life expectancy — neither people's health nor life expectancy are indicated by real GDP.

♦ Leisure time — the value of leisure time is not included.

♦ The environment — the consequences of adverse and beneficial environmental changes are omitted.

♦ Political freedom and social justice — the extent of political freedom or social justice within a nation is not measured.

Making international comparisons of real GDP can be tricky because the real GDP of one country must be converted into the other nation's currency. Using exchange rates for such conversions may understate the real GDP in less developed nations. However, use of purchasing power parity prices may give a more accurate comparison.

Though real GDP probably overstates the size of fluctuations in total production and economic welfare, it is a reasonably good indicator of the phase of the business cycle, e.g., expansion, peak, and so on.

■ Measuring Inflation

The **inflation rate** is the percentage change in the price level from one year to the next. In terms of a formula, the inflation rate is:

$$\frac{(\text{CPI this year}) - (\text{CPI last year})}{(\text{CPI last year})} \times 100.$$

The CPI overstates the actual inflation rate:

♦ New goods bias — when new, higher priced goods replace older goods.

♦ Quality change bias — failing to take account of quality improvements that raise prices.

♦ Commodity substitution bias — when consumers shift their purchases away from goods whose relative prices rise toward lower priced goods.

♦ Outlet substitution bias — with higher prices, people switch to low-cost outlets such as discount stores.

The CPI is estimated to overstate inflation by 1.1 percentage points per year. This CPI bias distorts private contracts, increases government spending, and reduces estimates of real earnings.

Helpful Hints

1. **GDP, AGGREGATE EXPENDITURE, AND AGGREGATE INCOME :** Some of the most important results in this chapter show the equality between GDP, aggregate expenditure, and aggregate income. A key point about these equalities is that GDP, aggregate expenditure, and aggregate income are linked. For instance, the production of output (GDP) creates income (aggregate income) as firms pay their workers and also creates expenditure (aggregate expenditure) as households use their incomes to buy goods and services.

2. **THE DIFFERENCE BETWEEN GOVERNMENT PURCHASES AND GOVERNMENT TRANSFER PAYMENTS :** Government spending on goods and services (G) and government transfer payments are fundamentally different. Both involve payments by the government, but transfer payments are not payments for goods and services. Instead, they are simply a flow of money, just like taxes. We "give" the government taxes and do not directly receive a good or service in exchange. Think of transfer payments as negative taxes. (Indeed, we define net taxes *[T]* as taxes minus transfer payments.) Transfer payments are like gifts; they do not buy a good or service for the government in exchange. Transfer payments are not payment for a good or service, so they are not part of the G component of aggregate expenditure, $C + I + G + NX$, because aggregate expenditure measures purchases of goods and services.

3. **THE DIFFERENCE BETWEEN THE PRICE LEVEL AND THE INFLATION RATE :** Whether you are using the CPI or the GDP deflator, always keep in mind the difference between the *price level* and the *inflation rate*. The price level tells the average level of prices in a given year. In contrast, the inflation rate is the growth rate of the price level. Thus the inflation rate tells you by how much the price level has grown over a period of time, usually a year. For example, at the end of 1999 the price level might equal 140. If, at the end of 2000, the price level equals 154, it has grown by 10 percent, so that the inflation rate over 2000 has been 10 percent. If you keep this discussion in mind, you should not confuse the price level and the inflation rate.

Questions

■ True/False/Uncertain and Explain

Gross Domestic Product

1. Capital is a stock; investment is a flow.

2. The payment of wages to households for their labor services is part of aggregate income.

3. Transfer payments are included in the government purchases component of aggregate expenditure.

4. Aggregate income equals aggregate expenditure.

Measuring U.S. GDP

5. GDP can be measured only one way.

6. The expenditure approach to measuring GDP adds firms' expenditures on wages, rent, interest, and profit.

7. The purchase and sale of used goods is excluded from real GDP.

The Price Level and Real GDP

8. The market basket used in calculating the CPI changes each year.

9. The GDP deflator is calculated as real GDP divided by nominal GDP, multiplied by 100.

Measuring Economic Growth

10. If two economies have the same GDP, economic welfare is the same in each one.

11. Real GDP is a good measure of economic welfare in less developed nations, but is a bad measure in developed nations.

12. Real GDP is a good measure of the phase of the business cycle.

Measuring Inflation

13. Inflation measured using the GDP deflator is much different than inflation measured using the consumer price index.

14. Consumers shift their purchases away from goods whose relative prices increase and thereby cause the CPI to overstate the actual inflation rate.

15. The CPI is estimated to overstate inflation by about 1.1 percentage points a year.

■ Multiple Choice

Gross Domestic Product

1. Which of the following is a flow?
   a. GDP
   b. Wealth
   c. The amount of money in a savings account
   d. None of the above because all the answers above are stocks.

2. Which of the following is a stock?
   a. Income
   b. Depreciation
   c. Investment
   d. Capital

3. GDP equals
   a. aggregate expenditure.
   b. aggregate income.
   c. the value of the aggregate production in a country during a given time period.
   d. all of the above.

4. A nation's investment must be financed by
   a. national saving only.
   b. the government's budget deficit.
   c. borrowing from the rest of the world only.
   d. national saving plus borrowing from the rest of the world.

Measuring U.S. GDP

5. Which of the following is <u>NOT</u> an example of investment in the expenditure approach to measuring GDP? General Motors
   a. buys a new auto stamping machine
   b. adds 500 new cars to inventories
   c. buys government bonds
   d. replaces some worn-out stamping machines

6. Which of the following is <u>NOT</u> a component of the factor incomes approach to GDP?
   a. Net exports
   b. Wages and salaries
   c. Corporate profits
   d. Proprietors' income

7. Net interest plus compensation of employees are components of which approach to measuring GDP?
   a. Factor incomes approach
   b. Expenditure approach
   c. Linking approach
   d. Output approach

Use Table 6.1 for the next eight questions. Assume there are no indirect taxes, subsidies, or depreciation.

TABLE **6.1**

Multiple Choice Questions 9–16

Consumption expenditure	$200 billion
Government purchases	60 billion
Net taxes	50 billion
Investment	50 billion
Corporate profits	30 billion
Imports	20 billion
Exports	10 billion

8. How much is aggregate expenditure?
   a. $440 billion
   b. $330 billion
   c. $300 billion
   d. $270 billion

9. How much is GDP?
   a. $440 billion
   b. $330 billion
   c. $300 billion
   d. $270 billion

10. How much is aggregate income?
    a. $440 billion
    b. $330 billion
    c. $300 billion
    d. $270 billion

11. How much are net exports?
    a. $20 billion
    b. $10 billion
    c. $0
    d. −$10 billion

12. How much is household saving?
    a. $300 billion
    b. $200 billion
    c. $100 billion
    d. $50 billion

13. How much is government saving?
    a. $60 billion
    b. $50 billion
    c. $0
    d. −$10 billion

14. How much is national saving?
    a. $200 billion
    b. $50 billion
    c. $40 billion
    d. −$10 billion

15. How much is borrowing from the rest of the world?
    a. $20 billion
    b. $10 billion
    c. $0
    d. −$10 billion

16. A firm pays its workers $1 million in wages, buys $3 million of intermediate goods and services, and sells what it produces for $7 million. The firm's value added equals
    a. $7 million.
    b. $4 million.
    c. $3 million.
    d. $1 million.

The Price Level and Real GDP

Use Table 6.2 for the next three questions.

TABLE **6.2**

Multiple Choice Questions 17, 18, and 19

Year	Nominal GDP (billions of dollars)	Real GDP (billions of 1992 dollars)	GDP deflator
1999	$4,500	____	150
2000	____	$3,100	156

17. What is the real GDP in 1999?
    a. $675,000 billion
    b. $4,500 billion
    c. $3,100 billion
    d. $3,000 billion

18. What is the nominal GDP in 2000?
    a. $4,836 billion
    b. $3,100 billion
    c. $3,000 billion
    d. $1,987 billion

19. What is the inflation rate between 1999 and 2000?
    a. 156 percent
    b. 150 percent
    c. 6 percent
    d. 4 percent

20. In years with inflation, nominal GDP increases ____ real GDP.
    a. more rapidly than
    b. at the same rate as
    c. less rapidly than
    d. sometimes more rapidly, sometimes less rapidly, and sometimes at the same speed as

Measuring Economic Growth

21. Pollution is a by-product of some production processes, so real GDP as measured
    a. is adjusted downward to take into account the pollution.
    b. is adjusted upward to take into account the expenditures that will be made in the future to clean up the pollution.
    c. tends to overstate economic welfare.
    d. tends to understate economic welfare.

22. Which of the following is <u>NOT</u> a reason that real GDP is a poor measure of a nation's economic welfare?
    a. Real GDP omits measures of political freedom.
    b. Real GDP does not take into account the value of people's leisure time.
    c. Real GDP does not include the underground economy.
    d. Real GDP overvalues household production.

23. Which of the following statements about the comparison between GDP in China and in the U.S. is correct?
    a. Using the exchange rate to value China's GDP in dollars shows that China's GDP per person exceeds the GDP per person in the United States.
    b. Using purchasing power parity prices to value China's GDP in dollars shows that China's GDP per person exceeds the GDP per person in the United States.
    c. China's GDP per person is higher using purchasing power parity prices rather than the exchange rate when valuing China's GDP in dollars.
    d. None of the above answers are correct because they are all false statements.

Measuring Inflation

24. At the end of last year, the CPI equaled 120. At the end of this year, the CPI equals 132. What is the inflation rate over this year?
    a. 6 percent.
    b. 10 percent.
    c. 12 percent.
    d. None of the above answers are correct because more information is needed to calculate the inflation rate.

25. The technique used to calculate the consumer price index is based on the assumption that consumers buy
    a. more goods whose relative prices rise.
    b. fewer goods whose relative prices rise.
    c. the same quantities of goods as in the base period.
    d. goods and services whose quality improves at the rate of growth of real income.

26. The commodity substitution bias is that
    a. consumers substitute high-quality goods for low-quality goods.
    b. government spending is a good substitute for investment expenditures.
    c. national saving and foreign borrowing are interchangeable.
    d. consumers decrease the quantity they buy of goods whose relative prices rise and increase the quantity of goods whose relative price falls.

■ Short Answer Problems

1. Betty receives a Social Security check for $1,500 from the government. Is her check part of the government purchases component of GDP? Explain your answer.

2. How is a nation's investment financed? Define national saving and borrowing from the rest of world in your answer.

3. How can we measure gross domestic product, GDP, with either the expenditure or the incomes approach, when neither of these approaches actually measures production?

4. Robert buys 100 shares of stock in Microsoft and pays a total of $10,000. Is his expenditure of $10,000 part of the investment component of GDP? Explain your answer.

TABLE **6.3**

Data From Mallville

Consumption expenditure	$400 billion
Government purchases	120 billion
Net taxes	100 billion
Investment	80 billion
Corporate profits	50 billion
Imports	50 billion
Exports	60 billion

5. Table 6.3 shows data for the nation of Mallville. Depreciation in Mallville is zero. Using these data, what is the value of Mallville's
    a. GDP?
    b. aggregate expenditure?
    c. net exports?
    d. aggregate income?
    e. household saving?

f. government saving?

g. national saving?

h. borrowing from the rest of world?

6. Use the data and your answers from problem 6 to show how Mallville's investment of $80 billion is financed.

7. A small economy has only 10 firms. It has no government and no foreign trade. Its top economist calculates its GDP by adding up the sales of all 10 firms. Do you agree with this procedure? Explain.

8. What is a firm's value added?

TABLE 6.4
A Loaf of Bread

Transaction	Price	Value Added
Farmer sells wheat to miller	20¢	_____
Miller sells flour to baker	35¢	_____
Baker sells bread to grocery store	60¢	_____
Grocery store sells bread to consumer	75¢	_____

9. Table 6.4 describes the (simplified) process by which wheat is grown and eventually transformed into a loaf of bread that is sold to a consumer as a final good. In the first stage of the production process, the farmer raises the wheat and sells enough for one loaf of bread to the miller for 20¢. The miller grinds the wheat into flour and sells the flour to the baker for 35¢. The baker uses the wheat to bake a loaf of bread which is sold to a grocer for 60¢. Finally, the grocer sells the bread to a consumer for 75¢.

a. Complete the last column of Table 6.4 by computing the value added at each of the four stages of the production process.

b. What is the total value added at all stages of production for this loaf of bread? How does that sum compare with the price of the loaf of bread as a final good?

TABLE 6.5
Consumption in Snowville

	1999		2000	
	Price	Quantity	Price	Quantity
Rutabaga	$0.50	200	$0.70	110
Parka	$50.00	2	$75.00	1
Book	$40.00	5	$30.00	10

10. In 1999, consumers in Snowville consumed only rutabagas, parkas, and books. The prices and quantities for 1999 and 2000 are listed in Table 6.5. The base year for Snowville's CPI is 1999.

a. What is the CPI for Snowville in 1999?

b. What is the CPI for Snowville in 2000?

c. What is the inflation rate between 1999 and 2000?

d. What is the percentage change in the price of a rutabaga? A parka? A book?

e. Comparing your answers to parts (c) and (d), does the inflation rate equal the rate of increase in the prices of all three goods and services? Did any commodity substitution take place? Explain your answer.

11. Igor has been hired to calculate the chain-weighted growth rate for Transylvania's GDP between 1998 and 1999. Igor likes chains, so he thought he would be good at his new job, but he needs help. Igor calculates that GDP using 1998 prices is $1,000 in 1998 and $1,100 in 1999. He also calculates that GDP using 1999 prices is $1,200 and $1,440 in 1999. Help Igor avoid chains himself by calculating the chain-weighted growth rate of real GDP between 1998 and 1999.

■ You're the Teacher

1. "Even though I studied this chapter a lot, just like our teacher told us to, I don't understand why I had to study it so much. What's the big deal? Do you know why?" Your friend probably didn't study this chapter quite enough. Because you did, you can help your friend by explaining why this chapter is worthy of study.

Answers

■ True/False Answers

Gross Domestic Product

1. **T** Investment is the flow that adds to the stock of capital.

2. **T** Indeed, compensation of employees (wages) is the single largest component of aggregate income.

3. **F** The government purchases component of aggregate expenditure is the goods and services the government buys. Transfer payments buy no good or service — they are essentially "gifts" to the recipients — and so are not part of government purchases.

4. **T** Aggregate income equals aggregate expenditure and both equal GDP.

Measuring U.S. GDP

5. **F** Because of the equality between aggregate expenditure, aggregate income, and GDP, GDP can be measured using the expenditure approach or using the income approach.

6. **F** The expenditure approach to measuring GDP adds consumption expenditure, investment, government purchases, and net exports.

7. **T** Real GDP measures *current* period production (usually the current year's production), so the purchase or sale of used goods is excluded from real GDP.

The Price Level and Real GDP

8. **F** The market basket stays the same, that is, the quantities used in the basket do not change. However, the prices used change.

9. **F** The GDP price deflator is defined as
$$\frac{\text{Nominal GDP}}{\text{Real GDP}} \times 100.$$

Measuring Economic Growth

10. **U** Economic welfare depends on more than just real GDP, so even if the nations' real GDPs are equal, their economic welfare may be different.

11. **F** In developed nations real GDP is not a perfect measure of economic welfare and is an even poorer measure in less developed nations.

12. **T** Real GDP generally is a reliable indicator of business cycle phases.

Measuring Inflation

13. **F** Both measures yield similar inflation rates.

14. **T** The CPI is based on a fixed market basket and thereby assumes that people continue to buy the same quantities of goods and services whose relative prices have increased.

15. **T** Because of this bias, if the reported inflation rate is, say, 3.4 percent, the "true" inflation rate is 2.3 percent.

■ Multiple Choice Answers

Gross Domestic Product

1. **a** GDP is the flow of production during a year.

2. **d** Capital is the total amount of plant, equipment, and inventories that exists at a moment in time.

3. **d** The equality of these three measures of GDP is a key result developed in this chapter.

4. **d** A nation's investment can be financed through borrowing from foreigners and/or saving by domestic citizens.

Measuring U.S. GDP

5. **c** The investment component of aggregate expenditure includes purchases of capital goods, not purchases of financial assets.

6. **a** Net exports is a component of the expenditure approach to measuring GDP.

7. **a** The factor incomes approach adds the incomes paid to all the resources in order to estimate the GDP.

8. **c** Aggregate expenditure equals the sum of consumption expenditure ($200 billion) plus gross investment ($50 billion) plus government purchases ($60 billion) plus net exports (–$10 billion, exports minus imports).

9. **c** GDP equals aggregate expenditure.

10. **c** Aggregate income equals GDP.

11. **d** Net exports equals exports ($10 billion) minus imports ($20 billion).

12. **d** Household saving equals aggregate income ($300 billion) minus consumption expenditure ($200 billion) and net taxes ($50 billion), so household saving is $50 billion.

13. **d** Government saving equals net taxes ($50 billion) minus government purchases ($60 billion) so government saving is –$10 billion.

14. **c** National saving equals the sum of household saving plus government saving. From question 13, household saving is $50 billion. From question 14, government saving is –$10 billion. Thus national saving is $40 billion.

15. **b** Borrowing from the rest of the world equals the negative of net exports.

16. **b** Value added equals the value of the firm's sales ($7 million) minus its purchases of intermediate goods ($3 million).

The Price Level and Real GDP

17. **d** Real GDP equals nominal GDP deflated by (divided by) the GDP deflator, then multiplied by 100.

18. **a** Nominal GDP equals real GDP multiplied by the GDP deflator, then divided by 100.

19. **d** The inflation rate equals $\frac{156-150}{150} \times 100$, or 4 percent.

20. **a** Real GDP increases only because production increases; nominal GDP increases because production increases and also because prices rise.

Measuring Economic Growth

21. **c** Because pollution is not subtracted from real GDP, real GDP overstates economic welfare.

22. **d** Real GDP omits household production.

23. **c** When the exchange rate is used to value China's GDP, GDP per person in the United States is 69 times larger than China's GDP per person. If purchasing power parity prices are used to value China's GDP, U.S. GDP per person is only 12 times that in China.

Measuring Inflation

24. **b** The inflation rate is the percentage change in the price index, $\frac{132-120}{120} \times 100$, or 10 percent.

25. **c** Each month, the quantities used in the CPI are the same as the quantities from the base period.

26. **d** In part because of the commodity substitution bias, the CPI tends to overstate the true increase in the cost of living.

■ Answers to Short Answer Problems

1. No, Betty's $1,500 Social Security check is not part of the government purchases (G) component of GDP. That measures the government's purchases of goods and services. The government is not buying a good or service when it gives Betty her Social Security check. Instead, the check is a transfer payment, that is, a transfer of income from the people who paid Social Security taxes to Betty. Transfer payments are not part of the government purchases component of GDP.

2. Investment can be financed by national saving and/or borrowing from the rest of the world. National saving equals the sum of household saving, S, plus government saving, $T - G$. Hence national saving equals $S + (T - G)$. Borrowing from the rest of world is $M - X$. Thus investment must equal what is saved in the nation plus what is borrowed from abroad, which in terms of a formula is equal to $S + (T - G) + M - X$.

3. The analysis of the circular flow showed that firms produce goods and services (what we want to measure, GDP); sell them (what the expenditure approach measures); and then use the proceeds to pay for factor incomes, such as rents, profits, and the like (what the incomes approach measures). Therefore aggregate expenditure = aggregate income = production = GDP.

4. No, Robert's purchase of Microsoft stock is not part of the investment (I) component of GDP. The investment part of GDP includes the actual purchase of capital goods. Thus investment would include, say, Microsoft's purchase of a new telephone system because this is the purchase of a piece of capital. Robert's purchase of Microsoft stock is a purely financial transaction; that is, no good or service changed hands. Hence it is excluded from the expenditure components of GDP because the expenditures in GDP represent the purchase of goods or services.

5. a. GDP in Mallville equals the sum of consumption expenditure (C, $400 billion) plus investment (I, $80 billion) plus government purchases (G, $120 billion) plus net exports (NX), which equals exports (X, $60 billion) minus imports (M, $50 billion). Thus GDP in Mallville is $610 billion.

b. Aggregate expenditure equals GDP, so aggregate expenditure is $610 billion.

c. Net exports, NX, equal exports ($60 billion) minus imports ($50 billion), or $10 billion.

d. Aggregate income, Y, equals GDP, or $610 billion.

e. Household saving equals aggregate income ($610 billion) minus net taxes ($100 billion) minus consumption expenditure ($400 billion), or $110 billion.

f. Government saving is net taxes minus government purchases, or $T - G$. Thus government saving equals $100 billion − $120 billion, or −$20 billion.

g. National saving equals household saving plus government saving. From parts (e) and (f), national saving in Mallville is $90 billion.

h. Borrowing from the rest of the world equals imports minus exports, $M - X$. Thus Mallville's borrowing from the rest of the world is $50 billion − $60 billion = −$10 billion, that is, Mallville's residents *loan* $10 billion to the rest of the world.

6. Investment is financed by national saving and borrowing from the rest of the world. In Mallville's case, gross investment is $80 billion. That equals the sum of national saving, $90 billion plus borrowing from the rest of world, −$10 billion. Basically, Mallville has national saving of $90 billion, but only $80 billion of investment. Hence the difference, $10 billion, is loaned to the rest of the world.

7. Adding all the sales gives an incorrect answer because it counts both intermediate and final products, resulting in "double counting." For example, counting the value of the steel sold to General Motors (one of the 10 firms!) to build a car and then counting it again when the car is sold as a final good overstates the value of goods and services because the steel is counted twice.

8. Value added for a firm equals the value of the firm's output minus the cost of the intermediate goods and services it purchased. Basically, value added measures the extent to which a firm increases the value of the product it produces.

9. a. Table 6.6 shows the answer. The value added equals the price of the product (its "value") minus the cost of any intermediate goods. The

TABLE 6.6
A Loaf of Bread

Transaction	Price	Value Added
Farmer sells wheat to miller	20¢	20¢
Miller sells flour to baker	35¢	15¢
Baker sells bread to grocery store	60¢	25¢
Grocery store sells bread to consumer	75¢	15¢

farmer buys no intermediate goods, so the value added of the farmer is the price received for the wheat, or 20¢. The miller's value added is the price of the flour, 35¢, minus the cost of the intermediate good wheat, 20¢. Hence the miller's value added is 15¢. The remainder of the values added are calculated similarly.

b. The total value added is the sum of the value added at each step, or 20¢ + 15¢ + 25¢ + 15¢ = 75¢. This sum, or value, equals the price of the loaf of bread as a final good. Thus the loaf of bread adds 75¢ of value to the GDP.

TABLE 6.7
Consumption in Snowville

	1999		2000	
	Price	Quantity	Price	Quantity
Rutabaga	$0.50	200	$0.70	110
Parka	$50.00	2	$75.00	1
Book	$40.00	5	$30.00	10

10. a. The CPI in 1999 is 100. This answer may be calculated in two ways. First, the CPI in *any* base year equals 100. Alternatively, the CPI may be calculated directly. From Table 6.7, in 1999, the market basket cost ($0.50 per rutabaga) × (200 rutabagas) + ($50.00 per parka) × (2 parkas) + ($40.00 per book) × (5 books) or $400. The CPI is defined as 100 times the ratio of the cost of the basket in the current year divided by the cost of the basket in the base year. Thus the CPI equals

$$\frac{(\$400)}{(\$400)} \times 100, \text{ or } 100.$$

b. As the first step in calculating the CPI for 2000, calculate the cost using 2000 prices of the 1999 market basket: ($0.70 per rutabaga) × (200 rutabagas) + ($75.00 per parka) × (2 parkas) + ($30 per book) × (5 books) or $440. The CPI equals 100 times the ratio of the cost of the basket in the current year divided by the cost of the basket in the base year, or $\frac{(\$440)}{(\$400)} \times 100 = 110$.

c. The inflation rate between 1999 and 2000 equals $(110 - 100)/(100)$, or 10 percent.

d. The percentage change in price of a rutabaga is $(\$0.70 - \$0.50)/(\$0.50) = 40$ percent. The percentage change in the price of a parka is $(\$75.00 - \$50.00)/(\$50.00) = 50$ percent. Finally, the percentage change in the price of a book is $(\$30.00 - \$40.00)/(\$40.00) = -25$ percent.

e. The inflation rate does not equal the amount by which all prices change. In part (c) the inflation rate is 10 percent, but in part (d) none of the prices of rutabagas, parkas, and books rose by 10 percent. Instead, two goods, rutabagas and parkas, rose by more than 10 percent and one good, books, actually fell in price. Essentially, the inflation rate is a weighted average of price changes. Hence the inflation rate of 10 percent means that between 1999 and 2000 the average good purchased by consumers in Snowville rose in price by 10 percent, not that the price of every good purchased increased by exactly 10 percent.

Commodity substitution took place. As Table 6.7 shows, the relative prices of a rutabaga, parka, and book have changed: Rutabagas and parkas have increased in price relative to books and books have fallen in price relative to them. Changes in relative prices cause consumers to make substitutions away from goods whose relative prices have risen to goods whose relative prices have fallen: consumers have purchased fewer rutabagas and parkas and have increased their consumption of books. These changes in consumption reduce the effect of inflation on the cost of living. Indeed, Table 6.7 reveals that, in 2000, Snowville consumers spent $417 on their 2000 market basket, an increase of about 4 percent, not 10 percent, over the amount spent in 1999.

11. Using 1998 prices, Transylvania's GDP grew from $1,000 in 1998 to $1,100 in 1999. Hence using 1998 prices, the quantity index between these years

equals $\frac{\$1100}{\$1000}$ or 1.100. Then, when using 1999 prices, GDP increased from $1,200 in 1998 to $1,440 in 1999. Hence using 1999 prices, the quantity index between the years is $\frac{\$1440}{\$1200}$, which equals 1.200. (Thus when using 1998 prices, Transylvania's GDP grew at a rate of 10.0 percent and when using 1999 prices, Transylvania's GDP grew at 20.0 percent.) The last step to compute the chain-weighted growth rate takes the geometric average of the two indices: $\sqrt{1.100 \times 1.200} = 1.149$. Thus the chain-weighted growth rate between 1998 and 1999 is 14.9 percent.

■ You're the Teacher

1. "Yes, I have an idea why this chapter is important. Basically, it is a lot of the foundation for the next 10 or so chapters!

"That statement sure got your attention! Now, listen: We're trying to learn what factors affect the aggregate economy in order to discover what makes our economy grow more or less rapidly and what causes business cycles. Look, these are important issues! I don't know about you, but I sure hope the economy's not in a recession when we graduate and have to look for jobs. At least I sure hope there's no recession going on when *I* have to look for a job! And once we get jobs, I sure hope that the economy grows rapidly so that our incomes grow rapidly along with it.

"Anyway, we have to know what GDP is in order to understand growth and business cycles. After all, how would we measure these things if we didn't know what the GDP is? So, we're going to be studying what makes GDP grow faster and what makes it fluctuate. And, when we do, a lot of the stuff we learned in this chapter will be important, like the idea that aggregate expenditure equals aggregate income and both equal GDP.

"Finally, the other stuff in this chapter, like price indices and inflation, will be important in the next 10 chapters too. So, I'm glad you studied this stuff, because if you'd blown it off, I'd be alone, without any friends, in the last half of the class."

Chapter Quiz

1. Which of the following is an example of a flow variable?
   a. Capital.
   b. GDP.
   c. Inventories.
   d. The money in your wallet.

2. Two factors that both directly change the amount of capital are
   a. consumption and government expenditure.
   b. exports and net exports.
   c. depreciation and investment.
   d. investment and government expenditure.

3. In the national income accounts, government purchases of goods and services exclude
   a. transfer payments.
   b. state and local government spending.
   c. spending on national defense.
   d. local government spending, though it does include state government spending.

4. A government budget surplus equals
   a. net taxes minus government spending on goods and services.
   b. government spending on goods and services minus investment.
   c. consumption expenditure minus net taxes.
   d. None of the above.

5. When calculating real GDP between this year and last year, prices from last year and this year _____ used and the quantities produced last year and this year _____ used.
   a. are; are
   b. are; are not
   c. are not; are
   d. are not; are not

6. Which component of GDP has been negative in recent years?
   a. Consumption expenditure.
   b. Investment.
   c. Government purchases of goods and services.
   d. Net exports.

7. Income minus saving equals
   a. investment.
   b. consumption.
   c. GDP.
   d. net spending on government goods.

8. Inflation as measured by the CPI apparently
   a. exceeds the actual inflation rate by about 11 percentage points a year.
   b. exceeds the actual inflation rate by about 1.1 percentage points a year.
   c. is less than the actual inflation rate by about 11 percentage points a year.
   d. is less than the actual inflation rate by about 1.1 percentage points a year.

9. Substitution bias in the CPI refers to the fact that the CPI
   a. takes into account the substitution of goods by consumers when relative prices change.
   b. takes no account of the substitution of goods by consumers when relative prices change.
   c. substitutes new goods every year into the computation of the index.
   d. substitutes relative prices for money prices of goods.

10. GDP equals
   a. $C + I - S - T$.
   b. $C + S - NX$.
   c. $C + I + G + NX$.
   d. $C + S + G$.

The answers for this Chapter Quiz are on page 327

Chapter 7 MEASURING EMPLOYMENT AND UNEMPLOYMENT*

■ **Employment and Wages**

The U.S. Census divides the **working-age population** (those people 16 years old and older who are not in jail, hospital, or other institution) into categories:

♦ Employed — people working at a full-time or part-time job.

♦ Unemployed — people who are (1) without a job but have made efforts to find a job within the past four weeks; or, (2) waiting to be called back to work from a layoff; or, (3) waiting to start a new job within 30 days.

♦ Not in the labor force — people who are not employed and not looking for work, that is, are not unemployed.

The **labor force** equals the sum of employed plus unemployed workers. **Discouraged workers** are unemployed people who have stopped looking for work. Discouraged workers are not in the labor force.

♦ **Unemployment rate** — percentage of the labor force that is unemployed. The unemployment rate is

$$\frac{\text{Number of people unemployed}}{\text{Labor force}} \times 100$$

From 1960 to 1998, the average unemployment rate has been about 6 percent. It rises during recessions.

♦ **Labor force participation rate** — percentage of the working-age population that is in the labor force. This rate is

$$\frac{\text{Labor fore}}{\text{Working-age population}} \times 100$$

Since 1960, the labor force participation rate has increased to almost 67 percent. It falls during recessions because of discouraged workers, who may temporarily leave the labor force during the recession and then rejoin it during expansions.

♦ **Employment-to-population ratio** — the percentage of working age people who have jobs. This ratio has increased since 1960 and in 1998 is 64 percent. The employment-to-population ratio falls during recessions.

Both the labor force participation rate and the employment-to-population ratio have increased because significantly more women are working at market jobs.

Aggregate hours, the total number of hours worked, is a measure of labor input. Aggregate hours have maintained an upward trend, but have increased less rapidly than the number of people employed because the average work week has become shorter. Aggregate hours fall during recessions.

The **real wage rate** is the number of goods and services an hour's work can buy. It equals the money wage rate divided by the price level. Real wage growth slowed during the slowdown in productivity growth during the 1970s and 1980s.

■ **Unemployment and Full Employment**

Unemployed workers include:

♦ **Job losers** (workers who were laid off or fired).

♦ **Job leavers** (workers who quit).

♦ Labor force **entrants** or **reentrants** (people who are entering the labor force for the first time or are returning to it after leaving).

Job losers are the largest source of unemployment; job leavers are the smallest. Unemployment ends when a person is hired, recalled, or leaves the labor

* This is Chapter 24 in *Economics*.

force. The duration of unemployment increases during recessions.

Unemployment rates are highest for young workers and black workers.

Unemployment can be classified as:

♦ **Frictional unemployment** — caused by normal labor market turnover, such as people entering the labor force and businesses expanding or contracting. Frictionally unemployed workers are searching for good job matches, and the length of their searches can be influenced by the level of unemployment compensation payments.

♦ **Structural unemployment** — caused by industries or regions declining because of technological change or international competition.

♦ **Cyclical unemployment** — caused by the business cycle. Cyclical unemployment increases during recessions and decreases during expansions.

Full employment occurs when there is no cyclical unemployment.

The **natural rate of unemployment** is the unemployment rate when there is full employment. It equals the sum of the frictional and structural unemployment rates.

During recessions, the unemployment rate is higher than the natural rate. At a business cycle peak, the unemployment rate is lower than the natural rate, at which time cyclical unemployment is negative.

Structural unemployment is different from frictional unemployment because structurally unemployed workers are not going to get a new job without retraining or relocation. Thus the cost to the worker is much greater — for example, structurally unemployed workers typically are unemployed for long time periods. They bear the brunt of the cost of restructuring industries in our economy. So, although society benefits because goods and services in higher demand are produced, structural unemployment can impose a significant cost on the worker.

2. **FULL EMPLOYMENT :** Full employment does not mean that everyone has a job. Rather, it means that the only unemployment is frictional and structural in nature so that there is no cyclical unemployment. When there is no cyclical unemployment, the unemployment rate is called the natural rate of unemployment.

The actual rate of unemployment may be less than the natural rate of unemployment, so that the level of employment can exceed full employment. In these situations, people are spending too little time searching for jobs, and therefore less productive job matches are being made. Conversely, the actual rate of unemployment may exceed the natural rate. In this case, too many workers are searching for jobs and so the economy is able to produce fewer goods and services.

Helpful Hints

1. **BENEFITS FROM UNEMPLOYMENT :** In a dynamic economy, not all unemployment is bad. In fact, frictional unemployment benefits both the individual and society. For instance, younger workers typically experience periods of frictional unemployment as they search for jobs that match their skills and interests. The benefit to them of the resulting frictional unemployment is a more satisfying and productive work life. Society benefits because the frictional unemployment that accompanies such searches allows workers to find jobs in which they are most productive. As a result, the total production of goods and services in the economy rises.

Questions

■ True/False/Uncertain and Explain

Employment and Wages

1. Full-time students not looking for work are counted as unemployed.

2. The unemployment rate equals the total number of unemployed workers divided by the total working-age population.

3. Lesline lost her job and looked for a new job for eight months. She stopped looking for work because she believes she cannot find a job. Lesline is counted as unemployed.

4. The labor force participation rate has been rising over the past several decades because more women are working in the marketplace.

5. The aggregate hours worked in the United States have not grown as quickly as the number of people employed.

6. The real wage rate is the wage rate including all fringes, that is, the wage rate that workers "really" receive.

7. The growth rate of real wages accelerated during the 1970s and 1980s.

Unemployment and Full Employment

8. More unemployed workers have quit their previous jobs than were fired or laid off.

9. In a recession, the duration of unemployment generally increases.

10. Bill has just graduated from high school and is looking for his first job. Bill is frictionally unemployed.

11. Jill worked in a steel mill in Pittsburgh, but when the industry contracted because of foreign competition, she lost her job. Jill is structurally unemployed.

12. The natural rate of unemployment equals the sum of frictional and structural unemployment.

13. At full employment, there is no unemployment.

■ Multiple Choice

Employment and Wages

1. In a country with a working-age population of 200 million, 130 million workers are employed and 10 million are unemployed. The size of the labor force is
   a. 200 million.
   b. 140 million.
   c. 130 million.
   d. 10 million.

2. In a country with a working-age population of 200 million, 130 million workers are employed and 10 million are unemployed. The unemployment rate is
   a. 5.0 percent.
   b. 7.1 percent.
   c. 7.7 percent.
   d. 65.0 percent.

3. In a country with a working-age population of 200 million, 130 million workers are employed and 10 million are unemployed. The labor force participation rate is
   a. 100 percent.
   b. 70 percent.
   c. 65 percent.
   d. 5 percent.

4. Which of the following statements about the labor force participation rates of men and women is correct?
   a. Over the past 30 years, the labor force participation rates for both men and women alike have increased.
   b. Over the past 30 years, the labor force participation rate for men has increased and for women has decreased.
   c. Over the past 30 years, the labor force participation rate for men has decreased and for women has increased.
   d. Over the past 30 years, the labor force participation rates for men and for women have both decreased.

5. Suppose that the money wage rate is $5 per hour, and that the price level is 100. If the money wage rate rises to $10 per hour and the price level does not change, what happens to the real wage rate?
   a. The real wage rate doubles.
   b. The real wage rate rises, but does not double.
   c. The real wage rate does not change.
   d. The real wage rate falls.

6. Suppose that the money wage rate is $5 per hour and that the price level is 100. If the money wage rate rises to $10 per hour and simultaneously the price level rises to 200, what happens to the real wage rate?

    a. The real wage rate doubles.
    b. The real wage rate rises but does not double.
    c. The real wage rate does not change.
    d. The real wage rate falls.

7. Which of the following statements about the last 35 years is correct?

    a. The average hours of work per week has declined.
    b. The unemployment rate generally has increased.
    c. Aggregate hours of work have declined.
    d. The real wage increased most rapidly in the 1970s and early 1980s.

Unemployment and Full Employment

8. Which of the following accounts for largest amount of unemployment?

    a. Job leavers
    b. Job losers
    c. New entrants to the labor force
    d. Reentrants to the labor force

9. For which of the following groups is the unemployment rate the lowest?

    a. Black teenagers
    b. White teenagers
    c. Blacks, 20 years old and older
    d. Whites, 20 years old and older

10. Unemployment resulting from a recession is called

    a. cyclical unemployment.
    b. frictional unemployment.
    c. structural unemployment.
    d. cycle unemployment.

11. Who of the following is a discouraged worker?

    a. Cara, who lost her job because of foreign competition and is unemployed until retrained.
    b. Omar, a fishery worker who is searching for a better job closer to home.
    c. Eugene, a steelworker who was laid off but has stopped looking for a new job because the economy is in a recession and he thinks he won't be able to find a job.
    d. Amanda, an office worker who lost her job because of a slowdown in economic activity.

12. Who of the following is frictionally unemployed?

    a. Cara, who lost her job because of foreign competition and is unemployed until retrained.
    b. Omar, a fishery worker who is searching for a better job closer to home.
    c. Eugene, a steelworker who was laid off but has stopped looking for a new job because the economy is in a recession and he thinks he won't be able to find a job.
    d. Amanda, an office worker who lost her job because of a slowdown in economic activity.

13. Who of the following is structurally unemployed?

    a. Cara, who lost her job because of foreign competition and is unemployed until retrained.
    b. Omar, a fishery worker who is searching for a better job closer to home.
    c. Eugene, a steelworker who was laid off but has stopped looking for a new job because the economy is in a recession and he thinks he won't be able to find a job.
    d. Amanda, an office worker who lost her job because of a slowdown in economic activity.

14. Who of the following is cyclically unemployed?

    a. Cara, who lost her job because of foreign competition and is unemployed until retrained.
    b. Omar, a fishery worker who is searching for a better job closer to home.
    c. Eugene, a steelworker who was laid off but has stopped looking for a new job because the economy is in a recession and he thinks he won't be able to find a job.
    d. Amanda, an office worker who lost her job because of a slowdown in economic activity.

15. At the natural rate of unemployment, there is no
    a. frictional unemployment.
    b. structural unemployment.
    c. cyclical unemployment.
    d. unemployment.

16. If the economy is at full employment, the
    a. entire population is employed.
    b. entire labor force is employed.
    c. only unemployment is frictional unemployment plus discouraged workers.
    d. only unemployment is frictional and structural unemployment.

■ **Short Answer Problems**

TABLE **7.1**

Short Answer Question 1

Employed workers	Unemployed workers	Labor force	Unemployment rate
100	10	——	——
80	——	100	——
——	——	200	5.0%
130	8	——	——

1. Complete Table 7.1.
2. Can the unemployment rate increase while the total amount of employment also increases? Be sure to take account of the behavior of discouraged workers in your answer.
3. Describe the trends in the labor force participation rate and employment-to-population ratio since 1960. Is there any difference in these trends for men and women?
4. Describe the trends in aggregate hours and total employment since 1960. How do they behave during recessions?
5. For the following time periods, describe Igor's labor market status. When Igor is unemployed, tell whether it is frictional, structural, or cyclical unemployment.
    a. From January 1 through June 30, 1999, Igor was a full-time student pursuing his bachelor's degree.

    b. On July 1, Igor graduated with his degree in body building. He spent three months looking for work before Dr. Frankenstein hired him on October 1.
    c. From October 1 to January 1, 2000, Igor worked full-time on the night shift.
    d. On January 1, because of generally worsening economic conditions, Igor was put on part-time on the night-shift even though he wanted to work full time.
    e. On February 28, as economic conditions worsened, Dr. Frankenstein fired Igor. Igor looked for work until May 1.
    f. On May 1, Igor became convinced that he couldn't find a job, so until October 31 Igor tended house and dug in his garden but did not look for work.
    g. On October 31, Count Dracula dropped by for a bite and offered Igor a job, which Igor accepted.

■ **You're the Teacher**

1. "I really don't understand why we bother with the ideas of 'frictional,' 'structural,' and 'cyclical' unemployment. I mean, unemployment is unemployment, so who really cares about these types?" Your friend is being unnecessarily negative; explain why understanding these different types of unemployment is useful.
2. "Okay, now I see that the book is right — we should divide unemployment into frictional, structural, and cyclical. But, I still can't see why we should have any unemployment. I think that the government should reduce the unemployment rate to zero because that has to be best for the nation!" Your friend sees some of the lessons from the book, but your friend's vision is far from 20/20. Help this student by explaining why a goal of zero unemployment is neither realistic nor desirable.

Answers

■ True/False Answers

Employment and Wages

1. **F** These students are not in the labor force.

2. **F** The unemployment rate equals the total number of unemployed workers divided by the labor force, not the total working-age population.

3. **F** Lesline is a discouraged worker because she stopped looking for a job and discouraged workers are not counted as unemployed.

4. **T** The labor force participation rate for men has been falling, but it has been rising for women. The increase in the female labor force participation rate has been enough to cause the overall participation rate to increase.

5. **T** The average work week has gotten shorter, so the growth in total employment has been greater than the growth in aggregate hours of work.

6. **F** The real wage is the purchasing power of the wage, so the real wage rate shows the quantity of goods and services that can be purchased with an hour's work.

7. **F** The growth rate of real wages fell in the 1970s and 1980s, reflecting the slowdown in productivity growth.

Unemployment and Full Employment

8. **F** The greatest number of unemployed workers were fired or laid off.

9. **T** The duration of unemployment refers to length of time workers are unemployed, and the duration increases during a recession.

10. **T** Bill is part of the normal turnover in the labor market and thus is frictionally unemployed.

11. **T** Structural unemployment occurs when a job is lost because of structural changes in the economy, such as an industry contracting because of foreign competition.

12. **T** The natural rate of unemployment is *defined* as the sum of frictional and structural unemployment.

13. **F** At full employment, the unemployment rate equals the natural rate, comprising frictional and structural unemployment.

■ Multiple Choice Answers

Employment and Wages

1. **b** The labor force equals the sum of employed workers (130 million) and unemployed workers (10 million), or 140 million.

2. **b** The unemployment rate equals the number of unemployed workers divided by the labor force, multiplied by 100.

3. **b** The labor force participation rate equals the percentage of the working-age population in the labor force, that is, the total labor force (140 million) divided by the total working-age population (200 million), times 100.

4. **c** The increase for women has been larger than the decrease for men, so the overall labor force participation rate has increased.

5. **a** The real wage rate equals the money wage rate divided by the price level, so when the money wage rate doubles and the price level does not change, the real wage rate doubles.

6. **c** As in question 5, the real wage rate equals the money wage rate divided by the price level. Thus when both the money wage rate and price level double, the real wage rate does not change.

7. **a** The average work week has declined in length primarily because the number of part-time jobs has increased.

Unemployment and Full Employment

8. **b** Job losers include workers who have been fired or laid off, and these workers account for the majority of unemployment.

9. **d** The unemployment rate for whites, 20 years old or older is the lowest and for teenage blacks is the highest.

10. **a** Cyclical unemployment is positive when the economy is in a recession and negative when it is an expansion.

11. **c** Eugene has stopped looking for work, so he is no longer considered an unemployed worker.

12. **b** Omar is part of the normal turnover in the labor force, so he is frictionally unemployed.

13. **a** Cara lost her job because of structural change (more foreign competition) in the economy, so she is structurally unemployed.

14. **d** Amanda's job was lost because of a recession, so Amanda is cyclically unemployed.

15. **c** The natural rate consists of only frictional and structural unemployment.

16. **d** At full employment, the unemployment rate is the natural rate, which equals the sum of frictional and structural unemployment.

■ Answers to Short Answer Problems

TABLE 7.2

Short Answer Question 1

Employed workers	Unemployed workers	Labor force	Unemployment rate
100	10	110	9.1%
80	20	100	20.0%
190	10	200	5.0%
130	8	138	5.8%

1. The answers are in Table 7.2. To calculate them, recall that the labor force equals the sum of employed and unemployed workers. Hence in the first line the total labor force equals 100 + 10 or 110. In the second line, the number of unemployed workers equals the labor force, 100, minus the total number of employed workers, 80. Thus unemployed workers number 20. The unemployment rate equals the total number of unemployed workers divided by the labor force, multiplied by 100. So in the first row the unemployment rate equals (10)/(110) × 100 = 9.1 percent. In the third row, rearranging the definition of the unemployment rate shows that the total number of unemployed workers equals the unemployment rate multiplied by the labor force. Hence in the third row the total number of unemployed workers is (5.0%) × (200) so that unemployment is 10. The number of employed workers in that row therefore is 190.

2. Although uncommon, both the number of employed workers and the unemployment rate can increase at the same time. This situation occurs most often just after the trough of the business cycle when the economy moves into an expansion. In these months, the economy is growing, and real GDP is expanding, so the total amount of employment rises. In addition, previously discouraged workers begin to perceive that they may now be able to find a job. A large number of discouraged workers may rejoin the labor force, start searching for jobs, and add significantly to the number of unemployed workers. (Recall that as discouraged workers, they were not counted as unemployed; rather they were not in the labor force.) Hence the unemployment rate may increase even though the total number of employed workers increases.

3. Both the labor force participation rate and the employment-to-population ratio have increased since 1960. The primary reason is more women in the labor force. The female labor force participation rate and the female employment-to-population ratio each have increased substantially since 1960. In contrast, the male labor force participation rate and the male employment-to-population ratio both have decreased slightly.

4. Both aggregate hours and total employment have increased since 1960. However, the changes have not been steady; during recessions, they have increased at a slower rate or have even decreased, but in total both have increased significantly over the past three decades. The growth in employment has exceeded the growth in total hours because the average work week has shortened.

6. a. As a full-time student, Igor was not in the labor force.

    b. While Igor searched for his first job, he was frictionally unemployed.

    c. When working full-time for Dr. Frankenstein, Igor was an employed worker.

    d. Even though Igor wanted full-time work, he nonetheless was still counted as (fully) employed when he was on the part-time night shift.

    e. From February 28 to May 1, Igor was cyclically unemployed because his unemployment was the result of a downturn in the economy.

    f. From May 1 to October 31, Igor was not in the labor force because he was not looking for work. Igor was a discouraged worker.

    g. Igor is employed after October 31.

■ You're the Teacher

1. "You're right, it probably doesn't make any difference to the unemployed worker whether he or she is frictionally, structurally, or cyclically unemployed. And determining which classification a particular unemployed worker falls into is difficult — perhaps impossible. But, this division can be *very* useful for us, as students, because it makes clear some of the causes of unemployment. And, once we know the causes, we can get insight into what we can do.

"Take the idea of structural unemployment, for instance. Helping workers who are structurally unemployed has to take a different tack than helping those who are cyclically unemployed. A worker who is cyclically unemployed doesn't necessarily need a lot of retraining. But one who is structurally unemployed may well benefit from this type of training. So, by recognizing that structural reasons are one cause of unemployment, we can see that offering retraining may be a good idea if we want to reduce the unemployment rate.

"Now, if we hadn't divided unemployment into different types, we may very well have thought that all unemployment was cyclical in nature. And in this case, we would probably have completely overlooked retraining. So dividing unemployment into three categories is helpful because it helps us think more deeply about unemployment."

2. "Look, here's another case where the division of unemployment into frictional, structural, and cyclical unemployment can help you avoid these outlandish statements. Think about frictional unemployment: What would it take to reduce this type of unemployment to zero? I mean, the laws and regulations would be awful! For instance, you'd need a law that says you couldn't graduate from college until you already had a job lined up because if you had to look for a job after graduation, you'd be frictionally unemployed. And once you had a job, you couldn't leave it until you had another job lined up. I don't know about you, but even though I like college, I don't want to spend the rest of my life as a student and, if I get stuck in a job I hate, I want to be able to quit to look for a better one.

"You can see that reducing frictional unemployment to zero would be way too costly. The laws it would take are too strict and would really hurt our economy! It would probably be equally impossible to reduce structural unemployment to zero. But cyclical unemployment is a different issue. The more we can tame the business cycle, the more we can reduce cyclical unemployment. So, possibly what we want to aim for is to reduce cyclical unemployment to zero. In other words, forget the idea of eliminating *all* unemployment; let's concentrate instead on eliminating cyclical unemployment."

Chapter Quiz

1. The unemployment rate
   a. rises during an expansion and falls during a recession.
   b. measures the percentage of the working-age population who can't find a job.
   c. includes workers who have quit looking for work because they think they cannot find a job, that is, the unemployment rate includes discouraged workers.
   d. equals the percentage of the labor force that is without a job.

2. Over the last three decades, the labor force participation rate _____ and the employment-to-population ratio _____.
   a. increased; increased
   b. increased; decreased
   c. decreased; increased
   d. decreased; decreased

3. In a country with a working-age population of 200 million, 90 million workers are employed and 10 million are unemployed. What is the unemployment rate?
   a. 45.0 percent
   b. 11.1 percent
   c. 10.0 percent
   d. 5.0 percent

4. If money wages rise by a greater percentage than the price level, real wages
   a. increase.
   b. do not change.
   c. decrease.
   d. probably change, but without knowledge of the labor demand and labor supply, it is impossible to tell the direction.

5. Most unemployed people are
   a. job leavers.
   b. job losers.
   c. discouraged workers.
   d. new entrants into the labor force.

6. Unemployment that is associated with changing jobs in a normally changing economy is best characterized as
   a. cyclical unemployment.
   b. structural unemployment.
   c. frictional unemployment.
   d. long-term unemployment.

7. When thirty workers are laid off because the economy has entered a recession, _____ unemployment has increased.
   a. cyclical
   b. structural
   c. frictional
   d. discouraged worker

8. When thirty workers enter the labor force after graduation from school, _____ unemployment has increased.
   a. cyclical
   b. structural
   c. frictional
   d. discouraged worker

9. When thirty workers are laid off and cannot find new jobs because they lack the necessary skills, _____ unemployment has increased.
   a. cyclical
   b. structural
   c. frictional
   d. discouraged worker

10. Which of the following is correct?
    a. Aggregate hours have increased more rapidly than employment so the average work week has lengthened.
    b. Aggregate hours have increased more rapidly than employment so the average work week has shortened.
    c. Aggregate hours have increased less rapidly than employment so the average work week has lengthened.
    d. Aggregate hours have increased less rapidly than employment so the average work week has shortened.

The answers for this Chapter Quiz are on page 327

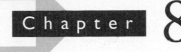

Chapter 8

AGGREGATE SUPPLY AND AGGREGATE DEMAND*

■ Aggregate Supply

The **aggregate production function** shows that the quantity of real GDP (Y) supplied depends on the quantity of labor (N), the quantity of capital (K), and the state of technology.

♦ When the wage rate makes the quantity of labor supplied equal the quantity of labor demanded, there is **full employment**. At full employment, the unemployment rate is the **natural rate of unemployment**, and the amount of GDP produced is **potential GDP**.

Aggregate supply is the relationship between the quantity of real GDP supplied and the price level. Aggregate supply depends on the time frame.

The **macroeconomic long run** is the period of time necessary for all changes to have occurred so that real GDP equals potential GDP.

♦ The **long-run aggregate supply curve**, *LAS*, is the relationship between the price level and real GDP when real GDP equals potential GDP. The *LAS* curve is vertical, as illustrated in Figure 8.1.

♦ Along the *LAS* curve, both the prices of goods and services *and* the prices of productive resources change.

In contrast, the **macroeconomic short run** is the period of time during which real GDP is above or below potential GDP.

FIGURE **8.1**
Long-Run and Short-Run Aggregate Supply

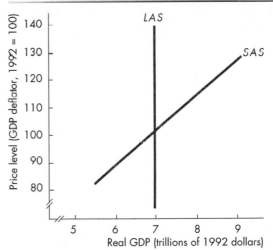

♦ The **short-run aggregate supply curve**, *SAS*, is the relationship between the price level and the quantity of real GDP supplied in the short run when the money wage and other resource prices are constant. The *SAS* curve slopes upward, as illustrated in Figure 8.1.

♦ Along the *SAS* curve, only the price level changes; money wages and other resource prices are constant.

♦ The *SAS* curve shifts leftward when money wages (or other costs) rise.

When the *LAS* curve shifts, so does the *SAS* curve. Three factors shift the *LAS* curve:

♦ Changes in the full-employment quantity of labor.

---

* This is Chapter 25 in *Economics*.

♦ Changes in the quantity of capital, including human capital.

♦ Advances in technology.

The short-run aggregate supply decreases when the cost of resources rises.

♦ A rise in the money wage rate shifts the *SAS* curve leftward, but does not shift the *LAS* curve.

■ Aggregate Demand

The quantity of real GDP demanded equals the sum of consumption expenditure (C), investment (I), government purchases (G), and exports (X) minus imports (M).

Aggregate demand shows the relationship between the quantity of real GDP demanded and the price level.

As illustrated in Figure 8.2 the **aggregate demand curve**, *AD*, slopes downward. It does so for two reasons:

♦ Wealth effect — A higher price level decreases the amount of *real* wealth (that is, the purchasing power of wealth), which decreases the quantity of real GDP demanded.

♦ Substitution effects — An increase in the price level raises the interest rate, which reduces the quantity of real GDP demanded. In addition, an increase in the U.S. price level raises the price of U.S. goods relative to foreign goods.

When aggregate demand increases, the *AD* curve shifts rightward. Three key factors shift the *AD* curve:

♦ Expectations — higher expected future incomes, higher expected inflation, or higher expected profits increase current aggregate demand.

♦ **Fiscal policy** and **monetary policy** — Fiscal policy is government attempts to influence economic activity by changing taxes or government spending. An increase in government spending increases aggregate demand. Reduced taxes and increased transfer payments raise **disposable income**, and thereby increase consumption expenditures and hence aggregate demand. **Monetary policy** is changes the money supply and interest rates. Increasing the quantity of money or lowering interest rates increases aggregate demand.

♦ International factors — a decline in the foreign exchange rate or an increase in foreign incomes increase net exports and hence aggregate demand.

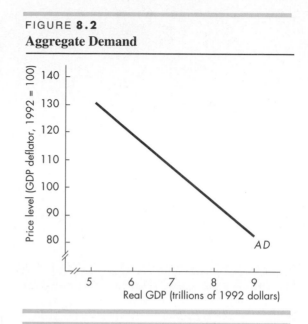

FIGURE **8.2**
Aggregate Demand

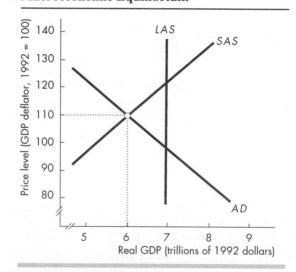

FIGURE **8.3**
Macroeconomic Equilibrium

■ Macroeconomic Equilibrium

Short-run macroeconomic equilibrium occurs where the *AD* and *SAS* curves intersect. In Figure 8.3 the equilibrium level of real GDP is $6 trillion and the price level is 110. The price level adjusts to achieve equilibrium. Short-run equilibrium does not necessarily take place at full employment.

Long-run macroeconomic equilibrium occurs when real GDP equals potential GDP so that the economy is on the *LAS* curve.

Economic growth takes place when potential GDP increases. Inflation occurs when aggregate demand increases more than long-run aggregate supply. Business cycles because aggregate demand and short-run aggregate supply do not grow at the same rate.

♦ Figure 8.3 shows a **below full-employment equilibrium** because potential GDP exceeds real GDP. The **recessionary gap** is the amount by which potential GDP exceeds real GDP, or $1 trillion in the figure.

♦ An **above full-employment equilibrium** occurs when real GDP exceeds potential GDP. The **inflationary gap** is the difference between real GDP and potential GDP.

The *AD/AS* framework illustrates how the economy responds to an increase in aggregate demand:

♦ In the short run, in response to the rightward shift in the *AD* curve, the equilibrium moves along the initial *SAS* curve, so real GDP increases and the price level rises.

♦ Money wages rise to reflect the higher prices, and the *SAS* curve shifts leftward, thereby decreasing real GDP and further raising the price level.

♦ In the long run, the *SAS* curve shifts leftward enough so that real GDP returns to potential GDP. Further adjustments cease. Real GDP is at potential GDP, and the price level is permanently higher than before the increase in aggregate demand.

The *AD/AS* model also explains how the economy responds to a decrease in aggregate supply:

♦ The *SAS* curve shifts leftward, real GDP decreases and the price level rises. A period of time with combined recession and inflation is known as *stagflation*.

■ U.S. Economic Growth, Inflation, and Cycles

GDP and the price level have changed dramatically over time in the U.S. economy. Both real GDP and the price level have grown over time.

♦ Growth in GDP results from growth in potential GDP, owing to increases in the labor force, capital stock, and advances in technology.

♦ Persistent inflation occurs when aggregate demand grows faster than long-run aggregate supply.

♦ Growth in real GDP is not steady but goes in cycles because aggregate demand and short-run aggregate supply do not increase at the same rate.

Helpful Hints

1. **SHORT-RUN AND LONG-RUN AGGREGATE SUPPLY :** The distinction between suppliers' short-run and long-run behavior is crucial. The short run and long run are not defined as particular, fixed lengths of time but in terms of whether resource prices change. In the short run, the prices of productive resources do not change in response to change in prices; in the long run, resource prices do change.

Consider what happens when the price level rises. In the short run, resource prices do not change. Firms find that the prices of their outputs rise while the costs of their inputs do not change. Firms react by hiring more resources and supplying more real GDP, so the short-run aggregate supply curve slopes upward: As the price level rises, the quantity of real GDP supplied increases.

In the long run, resource prices adjust by the same amount as the price level, which means that firms find their costs have risen by the same percentage as their revenue. These two effects offset each other, so firms do not change their supply as the price level rises. Hence the long-run aggregate supply curve is vertical.

2. **SHIFTS AND MOVEMENTS ALONG THE *AD* AND *AS* CURVES :** Be sure to distinguish between a shift of a curve and a movement along a curve. This distinction is crucial in understanding the factors that influence *AD* and *AS*, and you can be sure that your instructor will test you on it! The slope of the *AD* curve reflects the impact of a change in the price level on aggregate demand. A change in the price level produces a movement along the *AD* curve. A change in any of the factors affecting the *AD* curve *other* than the price level is reflected by a shift of the entire *AD* curve.

Similarly, a change in the price level produces a movement along the *SAS* curve or the *LAS* curve, but does not shift these curves. Instead, these curves shift when any relevant factor *other* than the price level changes.

These rules are similar to those you learned about the supply and demand curves for specific products. For those curves, changes in the price of the product created movements along the curves and changes in other relevant factors shifted the curves.

Questions

■ True/False/Uncertain and Explain

Aggregate Supply

1. At full employment, there is no unemployment.

2. Along the *LAS* curve, a rise in the price level and all resource prices increase the aggregate quantity of goods and services supplied.

3. Along the *SAS* curve, a rise in the price level increases the aggregate quantity of goods and services supplied.

4. Both the long-run and short-run aggregate supply curves shift rightward when the quantity of capital increases.

5. Any factor that shifts the short-run aggregate supply curve also shifts the long-run aggregate supply curve.

Aggregate Demand

6. Aggregate demand equals consumption expenditure plus investment plus government purchases plus exports minus imports.

7. According to the wealth effect, the lower the quantity of real wealth, the larger will be the quantity of real GDP demanded.

8. The term "monetary policy" refers to the government's spending more money to purchase more goods and services.

Macroeconomic Equilibrium

9. Long-run macroeconomic equilibrium occurs when real GDP equals potential GDP.

10. In the short run, an increase in expected future profits raises the price level and increases real GDP.

11. If the economy is in equilibrium at below full employment, there is a recessionary gap.

12. A rise in money wages increases short-run aggregate supply, that is, shifts the short-run aggregate supply curve rightward.

13. If aggregate demand increases so the economy is producing more output than potential real GDP, then, with the passage of time, money wages will rise in response to the higher price level.

U.S. Economic Growth, Inflation, and Cycles

14. If the aggregate demand curve and the short-run aggregate supply curve both shift rightward at the same time, the price level rises.

15. If the aggregate demand curve and the short-run aggregate supply curve both shift rightward at the same time, real GDP increases.

16. The main forces generating persistent growth in real GDP are those that cause increases in long-run aggregate supply.

17. The *AD/AS* model shows that growth in potential GDP causes inflation.

■ Multiple Choice

Aggregate Supply

1. Long-run aggregate supply is the level of real GDP at which
   a. aggregate demand always equals short-run aggregate supply.
   b. full employment occurs.
   c. more than full employment occurs.
   d. prices are sure to rise

2. Along which curve do money wages and the price level change in the same proportion?
   a. The *AD* curve.
   b. The *SAS* curve.
   c. The *LAS* curve.
   d. None of the above because there is no curve along which both money wages and the price level change in the same proportion.

3. Long-run aggregate supply will increase for all the following reasons EXCEPT
   a. reduced money wages.
   b. increased human capital.
   c. introduction of new technology.
   d. increased capital.

4. A technological improvement shifts
   a. both the *SAS* and *LAS* curves rightward.
   b. both the *SAS* and *LAS* curves leftward.
   c. the *SAS* curve rightward, but it leaves the *LAS* unchanged.
   d. the *LAS* curve rightward, but it leaves the *SAS* curve unchanged.

5. An increase in money wages shifts
   a. both the *SAS* and *LAS* curves rightward.
   b. both the *SAS* and *LAS* curves leftward.
   c. the *SAS* curve leftward, but leaves the *LAS* curve unchanged.
   d. the *LAS* curve rightward, but leaves the *SAS* curve unchanged.

Aggregate Demand

6. The aggregate demand curve (*AD*) illustrates that, as the price level falls,
   a. the quantity of real GDP demanded increases.
   b. the quantity of real GDP demanded decreases.
   c. the *AD* curve shifts rightward.
   d. the *AD* curve shifts leftward.

7. As the price level rises, the quantity of real wealth _____ and the aggregate quantity demanded _____.
   a. increases; increases
   b. increases; decreases
   c. decreases; increases
   d. decreases; decreases

8. Which of the following is classified as monetary policy?
   a. The government changing the amount of its purchases.
   b. The government changing its level of taxation.
   c. The government changing interest rates.
   d. The government financing a change in money wages.

9. Which of the following will cause the aggregate demand curve to shift rightward?
   a. An increase in expected inflation.
   b. An increase in taxes.
   c. A fall in the price level.
   d. A rise in the price level.

Macroeconomic Equilibrium

10. Short-run macroeconomic equilibrium occurs at the level of GDP where the
    a. economy is at full employment.
    b. *AD* curve intersects the *SAS* curve.
    c. *SAS* curve intersects the *LAS* curve.
    d. *AD* curve intersects the *LAS* curve.

Use Table 8.1 for the next four questions.

TABLE **8.1**

Multiple Choice Questions 11, 12, 13, 14

Price level	Aggregate demand (billions of dollars)	Short-run aggregate supply (billions of dollars)	Long-run aggregate supply (billions of dollars)
100	$800	$600	$600
110	700	700	600
120	600	800	600
130	500	900	600

11. In the short-run macroeconomic equilibrium, the price level is _____ and the level of real GDP is _____ billion.
    a. 100; $600
    b. 110; $700
    c. 120; $600
    d. 130; $600

12. In the short run, the economy is in a(n)
    a. full-employment equilibrium and resource prices will not change.
    b. above full-employment equilibrium and resource prices will rise.
    c. above full-employment equilibrium and resource prices will fall.
    d. below full-employment equilibrium and resource prices will fall.

13. In the short-run equilibrium, there is
    a. an inflationary gap of $100 billion.
    b. an inflationary gap of $50 billion.
    c. a recessionary gap of $50 billion.
    d. a recessionary gap of $100 billion.

14. Assuming no changes in aggregate demand or long-run aggregate supply, in the long-run macroeconomic equilibrium, the price level is _____ and the level of real GDP is _____ billion.
    a. 100; $600
    b. 110; $700
    c. 120; $600
    d. 130; $600

15. If real GDP is greater than potential real GDP, then the economy is
    a. not in macroeconomic equilibrium.
    b. in a full-employment equilibrium.
    c. in an above full-employment equilibrium.
    d. in a below full-employment equilibrium.

16. A below full-employment equilibrium can be caused by
    a. the *AD* curve shifting rightward.
    b. the *SAS* curve shifting rightward.
    c. the *LAS* curve shifting leftward.
    d. the *AD* curve shifting leftward.

Use Figure 8.4 for the next four questions.

FIGURE **8.4**
Multiple Choice Questions 17, 18, 19, 20

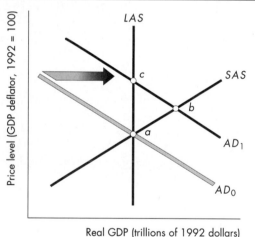

Real GDP (trillions of 1992 dollars)

17. Which of the following factors might have shifted the aggregate demand curve rightward?
    a. Reduced taxes
    b. Less investment
    c. A decrease in government purchases
    d. Higher money wages

18. After the aggregate demand curve has shifted permanently to AD_1, the new short-run macroeconomic equilibrium is at point
    a. point *a*.
    b. point *b*.
    c. point *c*.
    d. No point identified with a letter in the figure.

19. When the economy in Figure 8.4 is moving to its long-run equilibrium, which curve shifts?
    a. The *LAS* curve shifts rightward.
    b. The *LAS* curve shifts leftward.
    c. The *SAS* curve shifts rightward.
    d. The *SAS* curve shifts leftward.

20. After the aggregate demand curve has shifted permanently to AD_1, the new long-run macroeconomic equilibrium will be at
    a. point *a*.
    b. point *b*.
    c. point *c*.
    d. No point identified with a letter in the figure.

21. The price level rises and real GDP falls. Which of the following is a possible explanation?
    a. Higher profits are expected in the future.
    b. The price of raw materials has increased.
    c. The stock of capital has increased.
    d. The money supply has increased.

U.S. Economic Growth, Inflation, and Cycles

22. The fact that the short-run aggregate supply and aggregate demand curves do not shift at a fixed, steady pace explains
    a. persistent inflation.
    b. business cycles.
    c. trend growth in real GDP.
    d. large government budget deficits.

23. Persistent inflation is caused by
    a. persistent rightward shifts in the *AD* curve.
    b. persistent rightward shifts in the *SAS* curve.
    c. the tendency for long-run aggregate supply to increase faster than aggregate demand.
    d. persistent leftward shifts in the *SAS* and *AD* curves.

24. Which of the following statements about economic growth in the United States is most accurate?
    a. Inflation was high in the 1960s, low in the 1970s, and moderate in the 1980s and 1990s.
    b. Economic growth was rapid in the 1960s, slow in the 1970s, and rose in the 1980s and 1990s.
    c. Economic growth and inflation were both high in the 1970s, but lower in the 1980s and 1990s.
    d. Economic growth and inflation were both low in the 1970s, but higher in the 1980s and 1990s.

■ **Short Answer Problems**

1. Why is the *LAS* curve vertical?
2. Why does the *SAS* curve have a positive slope?
3. The international substitution effect implies that an increase in the price level will lead to a decrease in the aggregate quantity of goods and services demanded. Explain why.

FIGURE **8.5**
Short Answer Problem 4

4. In Figure 8.5 illustrate an economy in long-run equilibrium, producing at the full-employment level of production. Indicate the equilibrium price level and level of real GDP. Also indicate the potential level of real GDP.

5. In Figure 8.6 illustrate an economy in short-run equilibrium producing at a below full-employment level of production. Indicate the equilibrium price level and level of real GDP and show the amount of the recessionary gap.

6. In Figure 8.7 illustrate an economy in short-run equilibrium producing at an above full-employment level of production. Indicate the equilibrium price level and level of real GDP and show the amount of the inflationary gap.

FIGURE **8.6**
Short Answer Problem 5

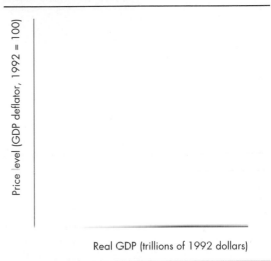

FIGURE **8.7**
Short Answer Problem 6

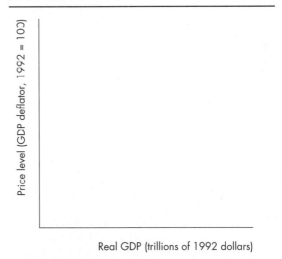

FIGURE **8.8**
Problem 7

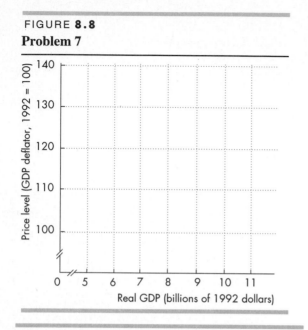

TABLE **8.2**
Short Answer Problem 7

Price level	Aggregate demand (billions of 1992 dollars)	Short-run aggregate supply (billions of 1992 dollars)	Long-run aggregate supply (billions of 1992 dollars)
100	$9	$ 7	$8
110	8	8	8
120	7	9	8
130	6	10	8
140	5	11	8

7. Table 8.2 shows the initial aggregate demand, short-run, and long-run aggregate supply schedules for the nation of Macro.

 a. Draw the *AD*, *SAS*, and *LAS* curves for Macro in Figure 8.8. Label the equilibrium point *a*. What is the equilibrium level of real GDP and price level?

 b. Suppose that government purchases increase so that aggregate demand increases by $2 billion at every price level. In Figure 8.8 draw the new aggregate demand curve. Label the new short run equilibrium point *b*. What is the equilibrium level of real GDP and price level in the short run?

 c. Why is point *b* not a long-run equilibrium? In your answer, mention the level of potential real GDP, and describe whether point *b* represents

an above full-employment, a full-employment, or a below full-employment equilibrium. If either an inflationary or recessionary gap exists, calculate what it equals.

 d. As time passes, what happens to move the economy back to its long-run equilibrium? Illustrate this process in Figure 8.8 by drawing any other curves you need. Label the long-run equilibrium point *c*. What is the equilibrium level of GDP and price level in the long run?

8. Suppose that the *AD* curve shifts rightward. In the long run, how does this shift affect the *SAS* curve? Why does the *SAS* change only in the long run?

FIGURE **8.9**
Short Answer Problem 9

9. Suppose that new, productivity enhancing technologies are discovered. In Figure 8.9 show how these technological advances affect the equilibrium level of real GDP and the price level.

10. Why are increases in the quantity of money the likely cause of the persistent inflation that the United States has experienced for the last several decades?

■ You're the Teacher

1. "I've really tried, but I just don't see why a change in the price level doesn't shift the short-run aggregate supply curve. After all, it seems like when the price level falls, firms should decrease the amount they produce and that this should shift the *SAS* curve. Plus, I'm a little shaky on how to use the

AD/AS model. I sure hope the *AD/AS* model isn't too important so that I don't get hurt badly by not knowing this." In truth, your friend may be mortally wounded by not understanding the difference between a shift of a curve and a movement along a curve. Use an example in which the *AD* curve shifts leftward to help explain to your friend how to use the *AD/AS* model for the short run and also why a drop in the price level does not shift the *SAS* curve.

2. After you have helped overcome the previous problems, your friend offers an observation: "I think I'm catching on to this stuff now. And the diagram you just drew was really helpful. But, is that diagram the end of the story? Or does something else happen as more time passes?" Basically, your friend is asking you to complete the explanation you started by showing what happens in the long run. Doing so would help reinforce your friend's grasp of the *AD/AS* model. So, using another diagram, show what happens in the long run after an initial decrease in aggregate demand has occurred.

Answers

■ True/False Answers

Aggregate Supply

1. **F** Even at full employment, there is some unemployment, which is called the natural rate of unemployment.

2. **F** The *LAS* curve is vertical at the level of potential GDP. This fact indicates that the amount of potential GDP does not change when the price level and all resource prices rise.

3. **T** The *SAS* curve slopes upward, which means that an increase in the price level increases the quantity of real GDP supplied.

4. **T** An increase in the capital stock increases the nation's potential real GDP, thereby shifting both the *LAS* and *SAS* curves rightward.

5. **F** A change in money wages shifts the *SAS* curve, but does not shift the *LAS* curve. The *LAS* curve shifts *only* when potential GDP changes.

Aggregate Demand

6. **T** Any factor that changes consumption expenditure, investment, government purchases, exports, or imports will have an affect on aggregate demand.

7. **F** The lower the quantity of real wealth, the smaller is the quantity of real GDP demanded, which is a reason for the negative slope of the aggregate demand curve.

8. **F** Monetary policy refers to changes in the quantity of money or interest rates.

Macroeconomic Equilibrium

9. **T** At the long-run macroeconomic equilibrium, the economy is on its long-run aggregate supply curve.

10. **T** The increase in expected future profits shifts the *AD* curve rightward, thereby raising the price level and increasing real GDP.

11. **T** The recessionary gap is the amount by which actual GDP falls short of potential GDP.

12. **F** An increase in money wages causes short-run aggregate supply to decrease (not increase), which means the short-run aggregate supply curve shifts leftward (not rightward).

13. **T** If the economy is producing more than potential GDP, the amount of employment exceeds full employment. The tight labor market then puts upward pressure on money wages and money wages rise.

U.S. Economic Growth, Inflation, and Cycles

14. **U** If the shift of the *AD* curve exceeds that of the *SAS* curve, the price level rises. But if the shift of the *SAS* curve exceeds that of the *AD* curve, the price level falls.

15. **T** Both shifts increase real GDP.

16. **T** As the nation's potential real GDP grows, the long-run aggregate supply curve shifts rightward.

17. **F** If the *AD* curve does not shift rightward, growth in potential real GDP, which shifts the *LAS* curve rightward, lowers the price level.

■ Multiple Choice Answers

Aggregate Supply

1. **b** Long-run aggregate supply is at potential GDP, which occurs when the economy is at full employment.

2. **c** Moving along the *LAS* curve, *both* money wages and the price level change in the same proportion. (Moving along the *SAS* curve, *only* the price level changes.)

3. **a** Along the *LAS* curve, both the price level and money wage rate change, so a change in the money wage rate does not shift the *LAS* curve.

4. **a** Any factor that shifts the *LAS* curve, such as technological advances, also shifts the *SAS* curve.

5. **c** The change in money wages shifts the *SAS* curve but not the *LAS* curve.

Aggregate Demand

6. **a** As the price level falls, a movement occurs along a stationary *AD* curve to a larger quantity of real GDP demanded.

7. **d** Real wealth equals the amount of wealth divided by the price level, so an increase in the price level decreases real wealth. In turn, this reduction decreases the quantity of real GDP demanded.

8. **c** Monetary policy includes changes in the money supply and interest rates.

9. **a** An increase in expected inflation causes people to increase their demand now in order to beat

the higher prices expected in the future. Note that answers (c) and (d) are wrong because changes in the price level do not shift the aggregate demand curve but instead cause movements along it.

Macroeconomic Equilibrium

10. **b** The intersection of the *AD* and *SAS* curves always determines the equilibrium level of real GDP and price level. (In the long run, where the *AD* and *SAS* curves cross, the both also cross the *LAS* curve.)

11. **b** The equilibrium price level is 110 because that is the price level at which the quantity of real GDP demanded equals the (short-run) quantity supplied, $700 billion.

12. **b** Potential GDP is only $600 billion, so, with actual GDP greater than potential GDP, the economy is at an above full-employment equilibrium.

13. **a** The inflationary gap equals the difference between actual GDP ($700 billion) and potential real GDP ($600 billion).

14. **c** In long-run equilibrium, the price level is such that the aggregate quantity demanded equals potential real GDP. (In the long run, the *SAS* curve shifts so that it goes through the point where the *AD* and *LAS* curves cross.)

15. **c** Whenever real GDP exceeds potential GDP, the economy is in an above full-employment equilibrium.

16. **d** A leftward shift of the *AD* curve decreases real GDP and causes a below full-employment equilibrium.

17. **a** Lower taxes increase consumption expenditure, thereby shifting the aggregate demand curve rightward.

18. **b** The short-run equilibrium is where the *SAS* curve intersects the *AD* curve.

19. **d** At point *b*, real GDP exceeds potential GDP, so point *b* is an above full-employment equilibrium. Hence money wages rise and the *SAS* curve shifts leftward, moving the economy to its (new) long-run equilibrium.

20. **c** The long-run equilibrium occurs where the *LAS* curve crosses the *AD* curve. In the long run, the *SAS* curve will have shifted so that it, too, goes through point *c*.

21. **b** A leftward shift in the *SAS* curve causes the price level to rise and real GDP to decrease. One reason the *SAS* curve may shift leftward is an increase in the price of raw materials (such as oil).

U.S. Economic Growth, Inflation, and Cycles

22. **b** If the short-run aggregate supply and aggregate demand curves shifted rightward steadily, economic growth would be steady.

23. **a** As the *AD* curve shifts rightward, the price level rises, so persistent rightward shifts of the *AD* curve cause persistent increases in the price level; that is, cause inflation.

24. **b** The fluctuations in economic growth reflect the uneven growth in long-run aggregate supply.

■ Answers to Short Answer Problems

1. Long-run aggregate supply is the level of real GDP supplied at full employment. Because this level of real GDP, potential GDP, is independent of the price level, the long-run aggregate supply curve is vertical. Potential real GDP is attained when prices of resources, such as the money wage rate, have had enough time to adjust so as to restore full employment in all resource markets.

2. The short-run aggregate supply curve has a positive slope because it holds prices of productive resources constant. Thus when the price level rises, firms see the prices of their output (revenues) rising, but the prices of their inputs (costs) remain unchanged. Each firm is then induced to increase output because by so doing it can increase its profits. Hence, as firms increase their output, aggregate output (real GDP) increases.

3. International substitution means substituting domestically produced goods for foreign-produced ones or vice versa. If the price of domestic goods rises and foreign prices remain constant, domestic goods become relatively more expensive, and households buy fewer domestic and more foreign goods. This substitution decreases the demand for real (domestic) GDP. Thus a rise in the price level (the prices of domestic goods) leads to a decrease in the aggregate quantity of (domestic) goods and services demanded via the international price effect. Conversely, a fall in the price level leads to an increase in the aggregate quantity of domestic goods and services demanded.

FIGURE **8.10**
Short Answer Problem 4

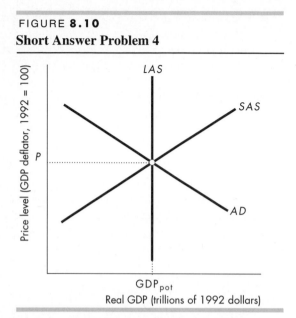

4. Figure 8.10 shows the economy in a long-run, full
employment equilibrium. The equilibrium price
level is P, and the equilibrium level of real GDP is
GDP_{pot}. Potential real GDP also equals GDP_{pot}.

FIGURE **8.11**
Short Answer Problem 5

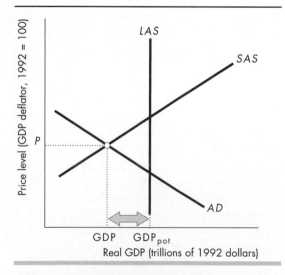

5. Figure 8.11 shows the economy when it is in a below full-employment equilibrium. The price level is
P, and the level of real GDP is GDP. The recessionary gap is the difference between potential real
GDP, GDP_{pot}, and the actual GDP, so it equals
the length of the arrow in Figure 8.11.

FIGURE **8.12**
Short Answer Problem 6

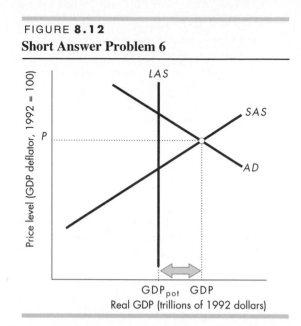

6. Figure 8.12 shows the economy in a short-run,
above full-employment equilibrium. The equilibrium price level is P, and the level of real GDP is
GDP. The inflationary gap is the difference between
actual GDP and potential real GDP, GDP_{pot}. The
inflationary gap equals the length of the double-
headed arrow in the figure.

FIGURE **8.13**
Problem 7 (a) and (b)

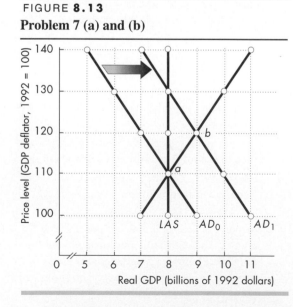

7. a. Figure 8.13 shows the initial aggregate demand
curve (AD_0), the initial short-run aggregate
supply curve (SAS_0), and the long-run aggregate supply curve (LAS). Point a is the equilib-

rium point, where the aggregate demand curve crosses the short-run aggregate supply curve. This point also is a long-run equilibrium because it is on the *LAS* curve. The price level is 110 because this price level sets the aggregate quantity demanded equal to the aggregate quantity supplied. The level of real GDP is $8 billion.

b. As illustrated in Figure 8.13, the increase in government purchases shifts the aggregate demand curve from AD_0 to AD_1. The new, short-run equilibrium point is labeled *b*. The price level rises to 120 and the level of real GDP increases to $9 billion.

c. Point *b* cannot be the long-run equilibrium because the economy is producing more than the potential level of real GDP. The long-run *AS* curve shows the potential level of real GDP to be $8 billion. Hence the situation illustrated by point *b* in Figure 8.13 is an above full-employment equilibrium. The inflationary gap in Figure 8.13 equals $1 billion, the difference between real GDP and potential real GDP.

short-run aggregate supply curve shifts leftward. Figure 8.14 illustrates this process, whereby the short-run aggregate supply curve has shifted from SAS_0 to SAS_1. When the short-run aggregate supply curve is SAS_1, the economy has reached its new long-run equilibrium at point *c*. At point *c*, the price level is 130 and the level of real GDP has returned to potential real GDP, $8 billion.

8. A rightward shift of the *AD* curve raises the price level. In the short run, money wages do not change, but in the long run money wages will rise to reflect the higher price level. Hence, in the long run, the increase in money wages shifts the *SAS* curve leftward. The curve does not shift in the short run because money wages do not respond immediately to higher prices. Initially, prices rise but money wages are constant. But then, over time, workers demand higher money wages to make up for the fact that they must pay higher prices for the goods and services they purchase. Thus in the long run, money wages rise along with prices.

FIGURE **8.14**
Problem 7 (d)

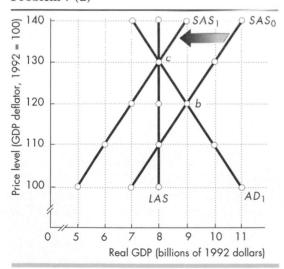

FIGURE **8.15**
Short Answer Problem 9

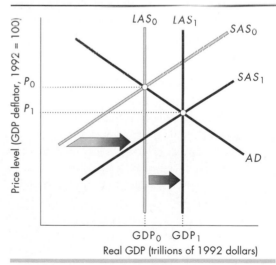

d. As the answer in part (c) just described, the short-run equilibrium at point *b* is an above full-employment equilibrium. Unemployment is below its natural rate. As a result of the tight conditions in the labor market (and other resource markets), money wages (and other resource prices) rise. As money wages rise, the

9. As Figure 8.15 shows, technological advances shift both the *LAS* and *SAS* curves rightward. However, the *AD* curve does not shift. As a result, the equilibrium price level falls from P_0 to P_1, and the level of real GDP increases, from GDP_0 to GDP_1.

10. The price level can rise as the result of either an increase in aggregate demand or a decrease in aggregate supply. However, the steady and persistent in-

creases in the price level have been caused by aggregate demand increasing faster than aggregate supply. (In terms of the *AD/AS* diagram, the *LAS* curve generally shifts rightward and thus, for prices to rise, the *AD* must be moving rightward even faster.) The most important reason for this behavior of aggregate demand is persistent increases in the quantity of money. Hence the persistent inflation in the United States during the past several decades is the result of persistent increases in the quantity of money.

■ You're the Teacher

1. "Look, using the *AD/AS* model has to be important because a whole chapter's devoted to it and, when I flipped through the next chapters in the book, I saw *lots* of *AD/AS* figures. So, you've got to get this straight, or I won't be seeing you in class after a while.

   "Here's the deal: A change in the price level does not shift the *AD* or the *AS* curves. Instead, the price level changes in response to a shift of the *AD* or *AS* curve.

   "Let me give you an example to hammer this point home. I need to draw a figure — let's call it Figure 8.16. Now in Figure 8.16, the initial equilibrium is at point *a* because that's where the initial aggregate demand curve, AD_0, and short-run aggregate supply curve, SAS_0, cross.

   "Let's figure out what happens in our model when firms lose confidence in future profits. I think this is what happened in the recession in 1991, so I think this example is a good one. Anyway, the drop in expected future profit from new investment leads to a decrease in aggregate demand, which means that the aggregate demand curve shifts leftward from AD_0 to AD_1.

   "You can best understand what happens next by imagining that the curve AD_0 can be peeled off the page so that it no longer exists. I mean, this is reasonable because, after all, the factors that created it no longer exist! Now before any adjustments take place, this leaves us with the curves SAS_0 and AD_1, and with the price level of 100. At this price level, there is a surplus of goods and services: SAS_0 shows that the quantity of real GDP supplied is equal to $7 trillion, but the AD_1 curve shows that the quantity of real GDP demanded is only $5 trillion. Firms find their inventories piling

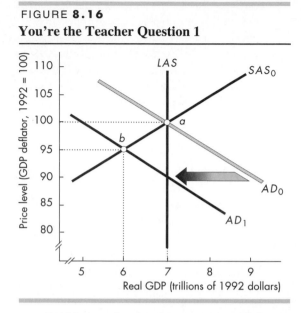

FIGURE **8.16**
You're the Teacher Question 1

up. In this case, they cut prices to try to sell the output, and the price level falls. Once the price level reaches 95, there is no longer a surplus of output and firms stop cutting their prices. This, then, is the new equilibrium, with a price level of 95 and a real GDP of $6 trillion.

"The key here is that the price level falls *because* the *AD* curve shifted. The fall in the price level did *not* shift the *AD* curve. In addition, the fall in the price level does not shift the *SAS* curve. If you want, you can think that we have moved along the SAS_0 curve from point *a* to point *b* (that is, from the old equilibrium point to the new equilibrium point), but the key thing is that the *SAS* curve has not shifted! After all, SAS_0 tells us that when the price level is 100, then $7 trillion of goods and services are supplied and when the price level is 95, then $6 trillion of goods and services are supplied. The slope of the *SAS* curve — and not a shift of the *SAS* curve — shows us that, when the price level falls, so, too, does the quantity of goods and services supplied."

2. "I'm really glad that you're starting to catch on because I like having a friend in class. Now that you understand what happens at the start, it won't be hard to see the rest of the story.

   "You're right that what we called point *b* in Figure 8.16 can't be the end of the story. So far the only thing that has happened is that the price level has fallen and we've moved along SAS_0 to a lower level of real GDP. From the firms' standpoint, the prices of the things they sell have fallen, but their costs haven't changed. As a result, their profits are being squeezed. This is why they cut production. But, as they were cutting back on output, they were firing and laying off workers. Point b is a below full-employment equilibrium, with more unemployment than the natural rate. So workers start to accept lower wages and, in general, the prices of resources start to fall.

"Whenever we get to a below full-employment equilibrium, these sorts of adjustments occur. And as the prices of resources such as the money wage rate fall, firms find their profits starting to bounce back. As a result, they are willing to increase their supply of goods and services even if the price level doesn't change. For instance, even if the price level stays at 95, because their costs are falling, firms are willing to produce more than $6 trillion of goods and services. To reflect this change, the SAS curve *shifts* rightward. As long as the money wage rate continues to fall, the SAS curve continues to shift rightward.

"Suppose that eventually the SAS curve has shifted from SAS_0 to SAS_1 in Figure 8.17. In this case, just like in Figure 8.16, where we pretended to erase the AD_0 curve once it was no longer relevant, in Figure 8.17 we can now pretend to erase the SAS_0 curve because the fall in money wages makes SAS_1 the relevant curve. So Figure 8.17 shows us that the new equilibrium will occur at point c, where SAS_1 crosses AD_1. The price level is 90 and real GDP is $7 trillion.

FIGURE **8.17**
You're the Teacher Question 2

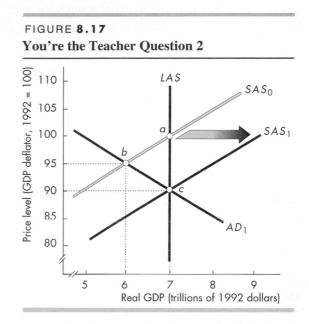

"The new level of real GDP is on the LAS curve; that is, the new equilibrium level of GDP is equal to potential real GDP. This situation is a full-employment equilibrium so unemployment is back at its natural rate, eliminating downward pressure on money wages. So money wages stop falling, which means that the SAS curve stops shifting rightward. As a result, point c is the new long-run equilibrium point. Compared to the initial point a, at point c, once all the adjustments are completed, we see that the price level is lower (90 versus 100), but that real GDP is the same (both are $7 trillion)."

Chapter Quiz

1. Which curve is vertical?
   a. The *AD* curve.
   b. The *SAS* curve.
   c. The *LAS* curve.
   d. None of the above.

2. The short-run aggregate supply curve shifts right-ward when
   a. the price level rises.
   b. the price level falls.
   c. money wages rise.
   d. the level of potential GDP increases.

3. A change in money wages
   a. shifts the *AD* curve.
   b. shifts the *SAS* curve.
   c. shifts the *LAS* curve.
   d. causes a movement along the *SAS* curve.

4. Short-run equilibrium is always at the point where the
   a *AD* curve crosses the *LAS* curve.
   b. *LAS* curve crosses the *SAS* curve.
   c. *AD* curve crosses the *SAS* curve.
   d. None of the above because the short-run equilibrium point is always moving.

5. Aggregate demand increases when
   a. investment spending increases.
   b. government spending increases.
   c. net exports increase.
   d. All of the above increase aggregate demand.

6. The amount of capital increases. Hence the price level _____ and real GDP _____.
   a. rises; increases
   b. rises; decreases
   c. falls; increases
   d. falls; decreases

7. An inflationary gap occurs when
   a. GDP is below full-employment GDP.
   b. GDP equals full-employment GDP.
   c. GDP is above full-employment GDP.
   d. The *AD* curve shifts leftward.

8. Which of the following is <u>NOT</u> a reason why the aggregate demand curve slopes downward?
   a. Wealth effect.
   b. Intertemporal substitution effect.
   c. International substitution effect.
   d. Real wage effect.

9. In the short run, a temporary increase in oil prices causes the price level to _____ and level of real GDP to _____.
   a. rise; increase
   b. rise; decrease
   c. fall; increase
   d. fall; decrease

10. Which of the following does <u>NOT</u> shift the aggregate demand curve?
    a. A decrease in the money supply.
    b. An increase in consumption expenditure.
    c. An increase in taxes.
    d. A rise in the price level.

The answers for this Chapter Quiz are on page 327

3 UNDERSTANDING
THE THEMES OF
MACROECONOMICS

Reading Between the Lines

GDP SHOOTS UP AT A 4.5% ANNUAL RATE

Consumers were buying up everything in sight in the first quarter, keeping the U.S. economy roaring ahead ...

The Commerce Department said the gross domestic product, or the value of all goods and services produced in the U.S., shot up at a 4.5% annual rate in the first quarter, following a stunning fourth-quarter surge of 6%. Over the four quarters of 1998, the U.S. economy expanded by 4.3%.

Friday's report had few signs of the slowdown that had been projected by many economists last year.

"This is a stunning report," said Martin A. Regalia, chief economist for the U.S. Chamber of Commerce. "Consumption is driving this strong economy virtually single-handedly."

Consumer spending surged at a 6.7% rate in the first quarter, the largest rise in 11 years. The combination of low interest rates, insatiable consumer demand for big ticket items like cars, homes and computers and the astronomical rise in the Dow Jones Industrial Average has created a consumer-friendly environment.

Consumers continue to be inspired by the lowest levels of inflation in a generation. The most meaningful inflation gauge, known as the chain-weighted gauge, rose at a 1.4% annual rate.

Analysts said some of the consumer spending boom reflected warmer-than-usual winter weather, which brought consumers out of their homes for spring shopping earlier than usual.

Spending by businesses also was robust in the first quarter, jumping at a 10% rate, as corporations shelled out money to address year-2000 computer problems.

"This quarter has shown smooth growth that is very much in line with what we've grown accustomed to over the last year," said Patrick Dimick, an economist at Warburg Dillon Read. "I'm starting to wonder why are we continuing to allow ourselves to be surprised by the 4% year-over-year GDP growth."

Alejandro Bodipo-Memba, "GDP Shoots Up at a 4.5% Annual Rate," May 3, 1999, p. A2. Reprinted by permission of The Wall Street Journal, ©1999 Dow Jones & Co., Inc. All Rights Reserved Worldwide.

■ Analyze It

In 1998 and 1999 the U.S. economy grew very strongly. In the first quarter of 1999, U.S. real GDP grew at an annual rate of 4.5 percent. Simultaneously, the inflation rate remained low. During the first quarter the annual inflation rate was only 1.4 percent. (The phrase "chain-weighted gauge" used in the article is a technical term for the GDP deflator.) Some observers credited the rapid growth in

GDP to growth in consumption expenditure. Other analysts suggested that rapid growth in GDP should no longer be a surprise but perhaps ought to be expected.

1. Using a diagram with long-run aggregate supply and aggregate demand curves, show how the U.S. economy would grow over the year if it continued at the pace reported for the quarter of the year reported in the article. Assume that the initial price level was 100 and that the initial level of real GDP was $8 trillion.

2. From the news article, what factors influenced consumption expenditure?

3. Some analysts had predicted a slowdown in economic growth. In fact, some of these analysts had "hoped" for a slowdown because they fear that excessively rapid growth will create inflation. Illustrate these concerns using an aggregate demand/aggregate supply diagram showing the type of equilibrium these forecasters fear.

Web Resources

For more information, browse the Parkin Web site to explore related links.

One place to start is by looking under "Economic Data". Also, on the Top 10 list, visit the "Economic Report of the President - Macroeconomic Policy and Performance". There you can see the latest on U.S. economic performance and policy proposals.

Mid-Term Examination

■ **Chapter 5**

1. All of the following are included in GDP <u>EXCEPT</u>
   a. purchases of the services of attorneys.
   b. purchases of short-lived goods such as cotton candy.
   c. steel production.
   d. production in the underground economy.

2. Which is the proper order for the business cycle?
   a. Peak, expansion, recession, trough
   b. Peak, trough, expansion, recession
   c. Peak, expansion, trough, recession
   d. Peak, recession, trough, expansion

3. The value of money increases during time periods when
   a. inflation is rapid.
   b. inflation is slow.
   c. the price level falls.
   d. none of the above because the value of money never increases.

4. Over the last twenty five years, the U.S. has
   a. had a current account surplus every year.
   b. had a current account surplus more than half the years.
   c. had a current account deficit more than half the years.
   d. had a current account deficit every year.

■ **Chapter 6**

5. At the beginning of the year, your wealth is $5,000. During the year, you have
   an income of $20,000 and you spend $21,000. Your wealth at the end of the
   year is
   a. $11,000.
   b. $10,000.
   c. $6,000.
   d. $4,000.

6. Investment
   a. is a flow that adds to capital.
   b. plus consumption equals national income.
   c. minus saving equals consumption.
   d. includes the flow of money from firms to households.

7. Let C equal consumption expenditure, S saving, I investment, G government
   purchases, and NX net exports. Then GDP equals
   a. $C + S + G + NX$
   b. $C + S + G - S$
   c. $C + I + G + NX$
   d. $C + I + G - NX$.

8. If the CPI in 1999 is 100 and the CPI in 2000 is 105, then the rate of inflation is
   a. 1.5 percent.
   b. 5 percent.
   c. 100 percent.
   d. 105 percent.

■ **Chapter 7**

9. The working age population is 150 million, there are 120 million employed workers and 10 million unemployed workers. The unemployment rate equals
   a. 80.0 percent.
   b. 25.0 percent.
   c. 8.3 percent.
   d. 7.7 percent.

10. Since 1960, in the United States the unemployment rate has averaged
    a. 15 percent.
    b. 9 percent.
    c. 6 percent.
    d. 3 percent.

11. The natural rate of unemployment includes
    a. only frictional unemployment.
    b. only structural unemployment.
    c. only frictional and structural unemployment.
    d. frictional, structural, and cyclical unemployment.

12. In an expansion, which unemployment rate can be negative?
    a. The cyclical unemployment rate.
    b. The frictional unemployment rate.
    c. The structural unemployment rate.
    d. None of the above because no unemployment rate can be negative.

■ **Chapter 8**

13. When the economy is operating at above full-employment,
    a. there is a recessionary gap.
    b. the economy is at its long-run equilibrium.
    c. there is an inflationary gap.
    d. the short-run aggregate supply curve has shifted rightward.

14. The long-run aggregate supply curve is
    a. vertical.
    b. positively sloped.
    c. negatively sloped.
    d. horizontal.

15. A decrease in government purchases directly shifts
    a. the long-run, but not the short-run, aggregate supply curve leftward.
    b. the short-run, but not the long-run, aggregate supply curve leftward
    c. both the long-run and the short-run aggregate supply curves leftward.
    d. the aggregate demand curve leftward.

16. An economy characterized by very high unemployment and low inflation is likely to be in a(n)
    a. strong expansionary phase of the business cycle.
    b. full employment equilibrium.
    c. inflationary gap.
    d. recessionary gap.

Answers

■ Reading Between the Lines

Figure 1 shows the growth in the U.S. economy. Over the year in question, long-run aggregate supply increased, in the figure from LAS_0 to LAS_1. Over the same year, aggregate demand also increased, in Figure 1 from AD_0 to AD_1. The increase in aggregate demand, that is, the size of the rightward shift in the aggregate demand curve, was just slightly larger than the increase in long-run aggregate supply, the rightward shift in the long-run aggregate supply curve. Because the increase in aggregate demand exceeded that in long-run aggregate supply, the price level rose, by 1.4 percent. The 1.4 percent rise in the price level corresponds to the 1.4 percent inflation rate described in the article and analysis. The figure shows a substantial increase in real GDP, from $8 trillion to $8.36 trillion, which corresponds to the 4.5 percent growth rate in real GDP.

Several factors were mentioned in the article as leading to an increase in consumption expenditure: low interest rates (which presumably created the "insatiable consumer demand for big items such as cars, homes, and computers"), the rise in the Dow Jones Industrial Average (which created an increase in the purchasing power of net assets), low inflation, and warm weather. Of this list, low inflation is probably incorrect: Consumption expenditure increases when the inflation rate is expected to increase, not when the current rate is low. And, warm weather likely had, at best, a small impact on consumption expenditure: If consumers shopped early, the implication is that they won't shop late!

Figure 2 illustrates some analysts' concern. They worry that rapid growth in GDP is caused by a large increase in aggregate demand accompanied by a little increase in aggregate supply. This situation is illustrated in Figure 2, in which the aggregate demand curve has shifted rightward from AD_0 to AD_1 and with no increase in aggregate supply. In this case, the economy (temporarily) might be at a point such as *a*. This point is one with an inflationary gap because the economy is producing more than its potential output. As time passes, money wages will rise and short-run aggregate supply

FIGURE 1
The U.S. Economy

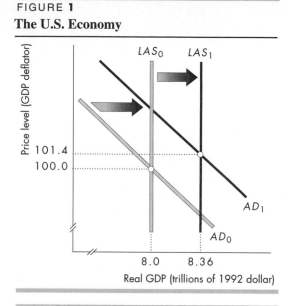

FIGURE 2
The Concern: An Inflationary Gap

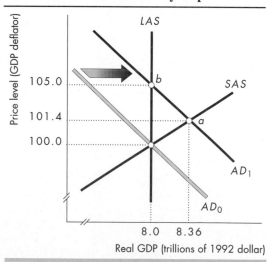

will decrease, so that eventually the economy moves to point *b*, a long-run equilibrium point. At point *b* the price level will have increased to 105, a 5 percent inflation from the initial price level of 100.

■ Mid-Term Exam Answers

1. d; 2. d; 3. c; 4. d; 5. d; 6. a; 7. c; 8. b; 9. d; 10. c; 11. c; 12. a;
13. c; 14. a; 15. d; 16. d.

Chapter 9 THE ECONOMY AT FULL EMPLOYMENT*

Key Concepts

■ Real GDP and Employment

A production possibility frontier between real GDP and leisure shows that GDP can be increased if time spent at leisure is decreased, that is, if employment increases.

The **production function** shows the relationship between real GDP and employment. A production function is illustrated in Figure 9.1.

♦ When employment increases, there is a movement along the production function, as illustrated by the movement from point *a* to point *b* along PF_0.

An increase in **labor productivity**, real GDP per hour of work, shifts the production function upward, as illustrated by the shift from PF_0 to PF_1. Labor productivity increases with:

♦ an increase in physical capital;

♦ an increase in **human capital**, people's skill and training;

♦ an increase in technology.

In the United States, capital accumulation and technological change have shifted the production function upward.

■ The Labor Market and Aggregate Supply

The demand for labor and the supply of labor depend on the **real wage rate**, the quantity of goods and services an hour of labor earns. The **money wage rate** is the number of dollars an hour of labor earns.

♦ The real wage rate equals the money wage rate divided by the price level.

FIGURE 9.1
Production Function

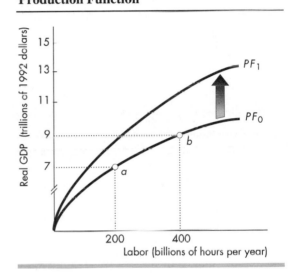

The **demand for labor** is the relationship between the real wage rate and the quantity of labor firms demand. As the real wage rate increases, the quantity of labor demanded decreases.

♦ The **marginal product of labor** is the additional real GDP produced by an additional hour of labor. As more hours of labor are employed, the marginal product diminishes.

♦ Because the marginal product of labor diminishes as employment increases, firms will hire additional workers only if the real wage rate falls. Thus the labor demand curve, *LD*, slopes downward, as illustrated in Figure 9.2 (on the next page).

♦ The demand for labor increases when the marginal product of labor increases.

---

* This is Chapter 26 in *Economics*.

FIGURE 9.2
The Labor Market

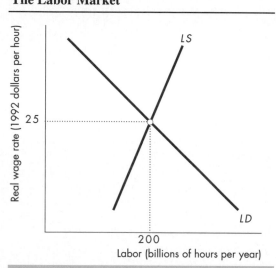

Labor (billions of hours per year)

The **supply of labor** is the relationship between the real wage rate and the quantity of labor households supply.

♦ The **labor supply curve**, *LS*, slopes upward, as illustrated in Figure 9.2, because higher real wages increase the amount of goods and services that can be purchased for an hour's work.

In Figure 9.2 the equilibrium real wage rate is $25 per hour and the equilibrium quantity of employment is 200 billion hours.

♦ The equilibrium quantity of employment from the labor market and the production function determine potential GDP. The *LAS* curve is vertical at this level of real GDP.

In the short run, the labor market may depart from equilibrium.

♦ If the price level rises and the money wage does not change, the real wage falls. Firms hire more workers so that real GDP increases and the economy moves along the *SAS* curve. A shortage of labor results so that the money wage rises. Eventually the real wage returns to its equilibrium and GDP again equals potential GDP.

♦ If the price level falls and the money wage does not change, the real wage rises. Firms hire fewer workers so that real GDP decreases and the economy moves along the *SAS* curve. A surplus of labor results so that the money wage falls. Eventually the real wage returns to its equilibrium and GDP again equals potential GDP.

■ Changes in Potential GDP

Real GDP increases if the economy recovers from a recession or it potential GDP increases. Potential GDP increases if the population increases or if labor productivity increases.

♦ An increase in population increases the supply of labor so that the labor supply curve shifts rightward. The production function does not shift. Employment increases and the economy moves along its (unchanged) production function to a higher level of potential GDP.

♦ An increase in productivity (because of an increase in physical capital, human capital, or technology) shifts the production function upward and increases the demand for labor. Employment increases because of the increase in demand for labor. Potential GDP increases because employment increases *and* because the production function has shifted upward.

In the United States, over the last fifteen years, the population increased, thereby increasing the supply of labor. The demand for labor increased because the capital stock increased and because technology advanced. Both these last two factors increased productivity and thus shifted the production function upward. Hence potential GDP has increased because equilibrium employment has increased and because the production function has shifted upward.

■ Unemployment at Full Employment

Two factors help explain why unemployment is always present even at full employment (when the unemployment rate equals the **natural rate of unemployment**):

♦ **Job search** — the activity of looking for an acceptable job. The length of time spent searching, and hence the natural rate of unemployment, increases when more young people enter the labor market; when unemployment compensation payments become more generous; and when structural change in the economy increases.

♦ **Job rationing** — paying workers an above-equilibrium wage rate, so that there is an excess supply of labor and a shortage of jobs. Jobs may be rationed because of **efficiency wages** (paying a higher wage to increase productivity) or because of the minimum wage (which prevents some workers from finding jobs).

Helpful Hints

1. **FROM THE LABOR MARKET TO POTENTIAL GDP :** The production function stands between the labor market and the aggregate output market. The equilibrium level of employment is determined in the labor market and then the production function indicates how much output results from that level of employment.

   The labor market functions like the "typical" supply and demand markets you studied in Chapter 4. Everything you learned there about how to use the supply and demand model applies to the labor market in this chapter. In particular, the key difference between shifts in a curve versus movements along a curve continues to apply: Changes in the real wage rate create movements along the labor demand and labor supply curves while other relevant factors shift these curves.

2. **PRODUCTION FUNCTION :** The production function graphically illustrates the relationship between the amount of labor employment and the level of real GDP.

   In the next chapters you will meet a similar concept, the "productivity function". The productivity function relates output per hour of work to capital per hour of work. Graphically, the productivity function appears similar to the production function. The productivity function is related to the production function but it is not the same. Thoroughly study the production function now so that you are not confused between the two when you study the productivity function.

Questions

■ True/False/Uncertain and Explain

Real GDP and Employment

1. If the production possibility frontier does not shift, real GDP can be increased only if leisure is increased.

2. An increase in employment causes a movement along the production function.

3. Labor productivity increases when the amount of the nation's human capital increases.

4. Learning-by-doing increases the nation's physical capital.

5. In the United States, there have been movements along the U.S. production function but no shifts in the function.

The Labor Market and Aggregate Supply

6. The demand for labor curve is downward sloping.

7. As more workers are employed, the marginal product of labor increases.

8. A rise in the real wage rate increases the quantity of labor supplied.

9. When employment equals the equilibrium quantity, the economy is on its *LAS* curve.

Changes in Potential GDP

10. An increase in the demand for labor raises the real wage rate.

11. An increase in the demand for labor increases potential GDP.

12. An increase in the nation's physical capital stock decreases the demand for labor.

13. An increase in labor productivity shifts the production function downward and decreases the quantity of employment.

14. Since 1984 in the United States, the supply of labor has increased more than the demand for labor.

Unemployment at Full Employment

15. When the unemployment rate equals the natural rate, there is no job search.

16. An increase in unemployment compensation will decrease job search.

17. Efficiency wages can be a cause of unemployment.

■ Multiple Choice

Real GDP and Employment

1. The production possibility frontier between real GDP and leisure
   a. shifts inward when the capital stock increases because unemployment rises.
   b. shows that increasing leisure will decrease real GDP.
   c. shifts if employment increases.
   d. All of the above answers are correct.

2. Which of the following shifts the nation's production function upward?

   a. An increase in employment.
   b. A decrease in employment.
   c. An increase in human capital.
   d. A decrease in human capital.

3. A movement along the production function with no shift in the production function is created by

   a. changes in the amount of physical capital.
   b. changes in the amount of human capital.
   c. advances in technology.
   d. changes in employment.

4. Between 1980 and 1998, the U.S. production function shifted _____ and the quantity of labor hours _____.

   a. upward; increased
   b. upward; decreased
   c. downward; increased
   d. downward; decreased

The Labor Market and Aggregate Supply

5. The money wage rate is $10 per hour and the price level is 100. If the price level rises to 200 and the money wage rate does not change, what happens to the real wage rate?

   a. The real wage rate doubles.
   b. The real wage rate rises, but does not double.
   c. The real wage rate does not change.
   d. The real wage rate falls.

6. Five workers produce output of $200; six workers produce output of $222. The marginal product of the sixth worker equals

   a. $40.
   b. $37.
   c. $22.
   d. None of the above answers is correct.

7. The demand curve for labor is downward sloping because

   a. the marginal product of labor diminishes as more workers are employed.
   b. the supply curve of labor is upward sloping.
   c. the demand curve shifts when capital increases.
   d. None of the above answers are correct because the demand curve for labor is upward sloping.

8. As the real wage rate increases, the quantity of labor supplied increases

   a. only because people already working increase the quantity of labor they supply.
   b. only because the higher wage rate increases labor force participation.
   c. because people already working increase the quantity of labor they supply *and* because the higher wage rate increases labor force participation.
   d. None of the above answers is correct because an increase in the real wage rate decreases the quantity of labor supplied.

9. A rise in the real wage rate

   a. shifts the labor demand curve rightward.
   b. shifts the labor demand curve leftward.
   c. shifts the labor supply curve leftward.
   d. does not shift the labor demand or labor supply curve.

10. If the economy is at full employment, the

    a. entire population is employed.
    b. entire labor force is employed.
    c. long-run aggregate supply curve is upward sloping.
    d. the quantity of labor supplied equals the quantity of labor demanded.

11. At potential GDP,

    a. the labor market is in equilibrium, with the quantity of labor demanded equal to the quantity supplied.
    b. there is no necessary relationship between the quantity of labor demanded and the quantity supplied.
    c. the real wage has adjusted so that it equals the money wage.
    d. the real wage rate must be rising because otherwise people will not work.

Changes in Potential GDP

12. An increase in population

    a. shifts the labor demand curve rightward.
    b. shifts the labor demand curve leftward.
    c. shifts the labor supply curve rightward.
    d. shifts the labor supply curve leftward.

13. An increase in productivity from new technology shifts the production function _____ and shifts the demand for labor curve _____.
   a. upward; rightward
   b. upward; leftward
   c. downward; rightward
   d. downward; leftward

14. An increase in the demand for labor causes the real wage rate to _____ and the quantity of employment to _____.
   a. rise; increase
   b. rise; decrease
   c. fall; increase
   d. fall; decrease

15. Which of the following will NOT increase labor productivity?
   a. An increase in physical capital.
   b. An increase in human capital.
   c. An increase in employment.
   d. An advance in technology.

16. In the United States, from 1984 to 1998, the demand for labor has
   a. increased more than the supply of labor has increased.
   b. increased less than the supply of labor increased.
   c. increased while the supply of labor has decreased.
   d. decreased while the supply of labor increased

17. The demand for labor and the supply of labor are both increasing over time, but the demand for labor is increasing at a faster rate. Over time, therefore, you would expect to see the real wage rate _____ and employment _____.
   a. rise; increase
   b. rise; decrease
   c. fall; increase
   d. fall; decrease

Unemployment at Full Employment

18. An increase in unemployment compensation payments will
   a. decrease the extent of search unemployment.
   b. lead to more job rationing.
   c. decrease the extent of demographic change.
   d. increase the length of time a worker searches for a job.

19. Which of the following is a reason that jobs might be rationed?
   a. Efficiency wages
   b. Equilibrium real wage rate.
   c. The vertical *LAS* curve.
   d. An increase in the demand for labor

20. An efficiency wage refers to
   a. workers being paid wages below the equilibrium wage rate in order to increase the economy's efficiency.
   b. wages being set to generate the efficient level of unemployment.
   c. workers being paid wages above the equilibrium wage rate in order to increase their productivity.
   d. None of the above.

21. Suppose that real wages are above the equilibrium real wage rate. Then the quantity demanded of labor ____ the quantity supplied of labor and there _____ unemployment.
   a. is more than; is
   b. is more than; is not
   c. is less than; is not
   d. is less than; is

■ **Short Answer Problems**

1. What is the connection between the production possibility frontier showing the relationship between leisure and real GDP and the production function showing the relationship between employment and real GDP?

2. a. What does diminishing marginal product of labor mean?
   b. Moving along a production function, why does the marginal product of labor diminish as employment increases?

3. Why is the marginal product of labor curve the same as the labor demand curve? What does this equality imply for the slope of the labor demand curve?

4. a. What is the real wage rate? How does it differ from the money rate? How is the real wage rate constructed?
   b. Why does the supply of labor depend on the real wage rate rather than the money wage rate?

FIGURE **9.3**

Short Answer Problem 5

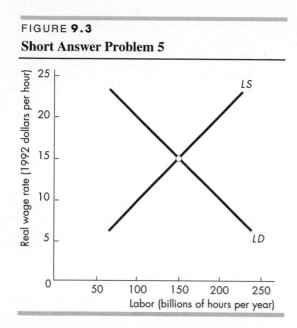

FIGURE **9.4**

Short Answer Problem 7

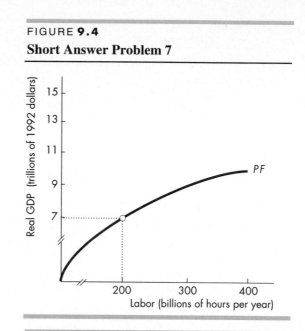

FIGURE **9.5**

Short Answer Problem 7

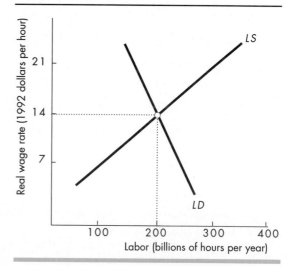

5. In Figure 9.3 what is the equilibrium real wage rate? Illustrate a real wage rate at which jobs are rationed. Indicate the amount of unemployment.

6. What can account for job rationing?

7. Suppose that new technology shifts the production function upward and increases labor productivity. Using Figures 9.4 and 9.5, show what happens in both. Does the equilibrium quantity of employment rise or fall? Does real GDP increase or decrease?

■ **You're the Teacher**

1. "Look, I really studied this chapter, but why bother? I mean, I thought we were going to be learning about stuff like money, and recessions, and stuff like that. I know that unemployment is important, but why do we bother to study unemployment at full employment?" It is undoubtedly good that your friend has been studying this chapter, but it undoubtedly would be better if your friend understood why this chapter is important. Can you help your friend grasp this key point?

Answers

■ True/False Answers

Real GDP and Employment

1. **F** Increasing leisure decreases employment and hence *decreases* real GDP.

2. **T** An increase in employment causes a movement along the production function to a higher level of real GDP.

3. **T** When productivity increases, the nation's production function shifts upward.

4. **F** Learning-by-doing increases human capital, not physical capital.

5. **F** The U.S. production function has shifted upward because of increases in capital and advances in technology.

The Labor Market and Aggregate Supply

6. **T** The demand for labor curve is downward sloping because the marginal product of labor diminishes as more workers are employed.

7. **F** As more workers are employed, the marginal product diminishes.

8. **T** If the real wage rate rises, more workers enter the labor force and workers already in the labor force supply more hours of work.

9. **T** Equilibrium employment is full employment, which means the economy is at potential GDP on its *LAS* curve.

Changes in Potential GDP

10. **T** An increase in the demand for labor raises both the real wage rate and employment.

11. **T** Because an increase in the demand for labor increases employment, it also increases potential GDP.

12. **F** An increase in capital raises the marginal product of labor, which increases the demand for labor.

13. **F** An increase in productivity shifts the production function upward and increases the quantity of employment.

14. **F** The demand for labor has increased by more than the supply of labor and, as a result, the real wage has risen.

Unemployment at Full Employment

15. **F** Job search *always* exists.

16. **F** An increase in unemployment compensation creates more job search and hence increases unemployment.

17. **T** When wages are set above the equilibrium level, unemployment results.

■ Multiple Choice Answers

Real GDP and Employment

1. **b** If leisure increases, people are spending less time at work. As a result, real GDP decreases.

2. **c** Changes in employment, answers (a) and (b), create movements along the production function. An increase in human capital shifts the production function upward.

3. **d** As the previous answer pointed out, changes in employment create a movement along the production function. Changes in other relevant factors shift the production function.

4. **a** The production function shifted upward because of increases in productivity.

The Labor Market and Aggregate Supply

5. **d** The real wage rate equals the money wage rate divided by the price level so when the price level rises and the money wage does not change, the real wage rate falls

6. **c** The marginal product of labor equals the change in output divided by the change in employment, or, in this case, ($222 − $200)/(6 − 5) = $22.

7. **a** The demand for labor curve is the same as the marginal product of labor curve.

8. **c** For both reasons given in the answer, the supply of labor curve is upward sloping, indicating that an increase in the real wage rate increases the quantity of labor supplied.

9. **d** A change in the real wage rate creates a movement along the labor demand and labor supply curves but does not shift either curve.

10. **d** When the labor market is in equilibrium, the economy is at full employment.

11. **a** When the labor market is in equilibrium — the quantity of labor supplied equals the quantity of labor demanded — the economy is producing its potential GDP.

Changes in Potential GDP

12. **c** With more people, the supply of labor increases.

13. **a** The increase in productivity increases the marginal product of labor, which shifts the demand for labor curve rightward.

14. **a** As Figure 9.6 illustrates, the increase in the demand for labor is reflected in the rightward shift in the demand curve from LD_0 to LD_1. The wage rate rises from $10 an hour to $15 and the level of employment increases from 100 billion hours to 150 billion. This answer demonstrates how an increase in productivity and the resulting increase in the demand for labor (the last question) results in a higher real wage rate.

FIGURE **9.6**
Multiple Choice Question 14

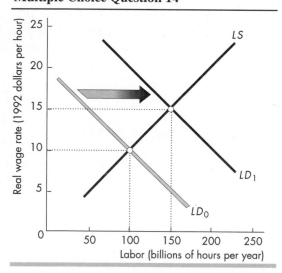

15. **c** By itself, an increase in employment will cause a movement along the production function to a lower level of productivity.

16. **a** Because the demand for labor has increased more than the supply of labor, the real wage rate has risen.

17. **a** The situation outlined in the question is what occurred in the United States, so in the United States employment and the real wage rate have increased.

Unemployment at Full Employment

18. **d** Unemployment compensation payments reduce the cost of being unemployed, so an increase in these payments makes unemployed workers more willing to search for longer periods of time to find better jobs.

19. **a** Efficiency wages and the minimum wage both may cause job rationing.

20. **c** Answer (c) is the definition of an efficiency wage.

21. **d** With the real wage rate above the equilibrium wage rate, there are workers who cannot find jobs and these workers are unemployed.

■ Answers to Short Answer Problems

1. The production possibility frontier and the production function are basically opposite sides of the same coin.

   The production possibility frontier shows that if leisure is decreased — so that employment is increased — then real GDP increases. Because of increasing opportunity cost, the production possibility frontier also shows that as more additional time is spent in employment, the additional GDP that results diminishes.

   The production function shows similar results. The production function demonstrates that if employment increases, real GDP increases. Because of diminishing marginal product, the production function also shows that as employment increases, the additional GDP that results diminishes.

2. a. Diminishing marginal product of labor means that as the quantity of labor increases, the additional GDP that results diminishes. In other words, the 1,000,001st hour of labor by itself creates less additional GDP than does the 1,000,000th hour of labor.

   b. Moving along a production function, the marginal product of labor diminishes because along the production function the amount of the capital stock and technology are constant. Thus additional labor must work with the same number of factories, assembly lines, and so forth. In this situation, an added worker may not create much additional output because the assembly lines, machine tools, and so forth are already efficiently stocked with enough workers.

3. The marginal product of labor is the same as the labor demand curve because firms want to earn the maximum possible profit. When a firm is considering hiring another worker, the firm looks at two

factors: How much it costs to hire the worker and how much the worker adds to the firm's output. If the worker adds more to the firm's output than it costs to hire the worker, the firm will employ the worker. (Conversely, if it costs more to hire the worker than the worker adds to output, the firm will not hire the worker.)

The cost of hiring another worker is the real wage rate. And, the amount of output that the worker produces is the marginal product of labor. If the marginal product exceeds the real wage rate, the firm hires the worker because it is profitable. As the firm hires more and more workers, the marginal product of labor diminishes. But, as long as the marginal product exceeds the real wage rate, the firm hires the workers because by so doing the firm raises its profit. Eventually the firm hires enough workers so that the marginal product of an additional worker just equals the real wage. The firm will hire this worker but will hire no more workers because for all additional workers the marginal product of labor would be less than the real wage rate. Thus the quantity of workers that the firm hires is determined by the marginal product of labor curve, so that the quantity hired is given by the marginal product of labor curve. But the quantity of workers the firm hires is the same as the quantity it demands, so therefore the marginal product of labor curve is the same as the labor demand curve.

4. a. The real wage rate shows the quantity of goods and services that can be purchased with an hour's labor. The money wage rate is the quantity of money received for an hour's labor. The real wage rate is defined as the money wage rate divided by the price level.

    b. The supply of labor depends on the real wage rate because workers are interested in what they can buy in exchange for their work. The money wage rate just shows the number of dollar bills that the worker will receive for an hour's labor. But the worker is concerned with what can be purchased with these dollar bills, which is what the real wage rate indicates.

5. In Figure 9.7 the equilibrium wage rate is $15 an hour. Any wage rate higher than the equilibrium wage rate creates some job rationing. For instance, at the wage rate of $20 an hour, the demand for labor is only 100 billion hours of labor, yet at this wage rate 200 billion hours of labor are supplied. At

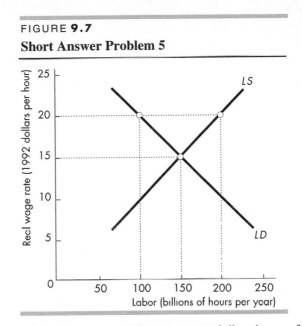

FIGURE **9.7**

Short Answer Problem 5

this wage rate unemployment is 100 billion hours of labor.

More generally, at any wage rate, the extent of unemployment equals the difference between the quantity of labor supplied and the quantity demanded.

6. Two factors can account for job rationing: efficiency wages and the minimum wage.

    Efficiency wages occur when firms pay above-equilibrium wage rates to increase their workers' productivity. Firms might pay a wage rate that exceeds the equilibrium wage rate knowing that, although the higher wage rate increases their costs, this effect is more than offset by the higher productivity of the workers receiving the higher wage rate.

    Finally, the minimum wage may be at a level that is above the equilibrium wage rate. In this case the quantity of labor demanded is less than that supplied, and jobs are rationed because not everyone who wants to work at the going (minimum) wage rate can find employment.

7. Start with the production function, illustrated in Figure 9.8 (on the next page). The upward shift and increase in productivity are illustrated. (Your diagram does not need to look exactly like what is illustrated, but the production function must shift upward and become steeper.)

    The key feature of this change is that labor productivity increased, so the change increases the demand for labor. Hence in Figure 9.9, the demand for

FIGURE **9.8**
Short Answer Problem 7

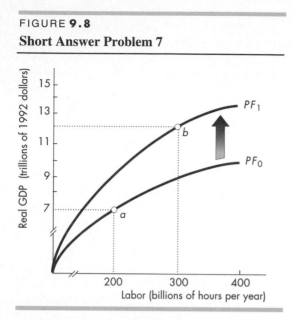

FIGURE **9.9**
Short Answer Problem 7

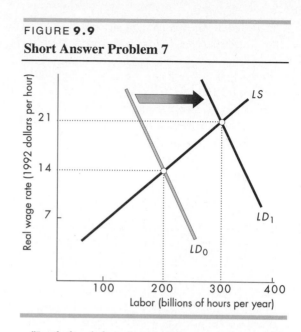

labor curve has shifted rightward, from LD_0 to LD_1. (Your figure does not need to look exactly like Figure 9.9, as long as the labor demand curve has shifted rightward.) As a result, the equilibrium quantity of employment increases, to 300 billion hours, and the equilibrium real wage rate rises, to $21 per hour in the figure.

GDP changes for two reasons: First, the production function has shifted upward, so even if employment did not change, GDP would increase. But, employment *does* increase. Thus as Figure 9.8 demonstrates, GDP increases from $7 trillion to $12 trillion as the economy moves from point *a* on production function PF_0 to point *b* on production function PF_1.

■ You're the Teacher

1. "Well the things you mentioned, money, recessions, and so on *are* important and when I flip through the book I see that we'll get to them a little later in the class. But they are not the only really important macroeconomic topics. I mean, one of the really important topics is economic growth, how rapidly our economy grows. And it's this topic that this chapter is concerned about.

"Look, here's how I see it. We want to know how fast our economy can grow and what we can do to make sure that it grows at the best speed possible, right? Well, economic growth basically depends on two things: the resources our nation has and the technology we can use. Well, one of the most important resources is labor and this chapter is focusing on that. This chapter helped me understand what factors change the equilibrium amount of labor, like the productivity growth. I mean, productivity *has* to be important because it not only increases the demand for labor and so increases the amount of labor that will be employed, but it also increases our real wages.

"And look, I've been talking with our teacher again and our teacher said that this chapter and the next two concentrate on economic growth. This chapter talks about one resource, labor. The next covers another resource, capital. And the one after that puts all this together with a discussion of technology. So, this chapter is part of an important group.

"So look, don't get upset because we aren't talking about money or recessions or other stuff yet. Be patient; we'll get there. But in the meantime let's settle back and learn all about economic growth!"

Chapter Quiz

1. A nation's production function shifts upward if
   a. employment increases.
   b. employment decreases.
   c. human capital increases.
   d. physical capital decreases.

2. Diminishing marginal product of labor means that
   a. the supply of labor curve is upward sloping so that a higher real wage increases the quantity of labor supplied.
   b. as more labor is employed, GDP decreases.
   c. the demand for labor curve is upward sloping.
   d. as more labor is employed, the additional amount of GDP produced diminishes.

3. If money wages rise by a greater percentage than the price level, real wages
   a. increase.
   b. do not change.
   c. decrease.
   d. probably change, but without knowledge of the labor demand and labor supply, it is impossible to tell the direction.

4. When the economy producing more than potential GDP,
   a. the labor market is in equilibrium.
   b. the real wage rate is below the equilibrium real wage rate.
   c. the real wage is above the equilibrium real wage rate.
   d. None of the above answers are correct.

5. If the demand for labor increases, the equilibrium quantity of employment ___ and potential GDP ____.
   a. increases; increases
   b. increases; decreases
   c. decreases; increases
   d. decreases; decreases

6. In the United States, from 1984 to 1998, which of the following accurately describes what occurred?
   a. Employment increased because population growth increased the labor supply and technological change increased the demand for labor.
   b. Employment decreased because population growth lead to increased amounts of unemployment and technological change decreased the demand for labor.
   c. Employment grew because population growth increased the supply of labor but the real wage fell because technological change decreased the demand for labor.
   d. None of the above answers are correct.

7. The demand for labor is ____ sloped; the supply of labor curve is ____ sloped.
   a. positively; positively
   b. positively; negatively
   c. negatively; positively
   d. negatively; negatively

8. If the supply of labor increases more than the demand for labor, then the real wage rate ____ and the level of employment ____.
   a. rises; increases
   b. rises; decreases
   c. falls; increases
   d. falls; decreases

9. Job search occurs
   a. only when the supply of labor increases.
   b. only when the quantity of labor demanded exceeds the quantity of labor supplied.
   c. only when the quantity of labor supplied exceeds the quantity of labor demanded.
   d. at all times.

10. Job search increases if
    a. the minimum wage falls.
    b. efficiency wages are lowered.
    c. unemployment compensation payments increase.
    d. the demand for labor increases.

The answers for this Chapter Quiz are on page 327

10 CAPITAL, INVESTMENT, AND SAVING*

Key Concepts

■ Capital and Interest

The **capital stock** is the total quantity of plant, equipment, buildings, and inventories. **Gross investment** is the purchase of new capital. **Depreciation** is the decrease in capital because of its use. **Net investment** is gross investment minus depreciation.

♦ The capital stock has grown every year; net investment has fluctuated relatively widely.

♦ Investment in the United States has ranged between 15 and 19 percent of GDP.

♦ Investment in developing nations has generally been higher than in developed countries.

The return on capital is the **real interest rate**, the nominal interest rate minus the inflation rate. The real interest rate was low in the 1970s, high in the early 1980s, and steady between 4 and 6 percent in the decade of the 1990s.

■ Investment Decisions

Investment depends on two factors:

♦ *Expected profit rate* — the profit rate from an investment. The expected profit rate rises during expansions and falls during recessions. New technology may at first cause only a small increase in the expected profit rate followed by a larger increase as firms learn how to use the technology.

♦ *Real interest rate* — the opportunity cost of the funds used to make an investment.

***

* This is Chapter 27 in *Economics*.

FIGURE **10.1**

Investment Demand Curve

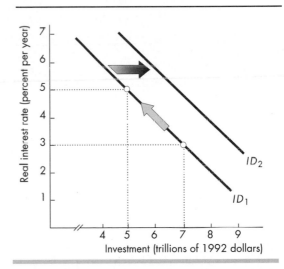

Investment demand is the relationship between the real interest rate and the amount of investment. Figure 10.1 shows an investment demand curve.

♦ The relationship between the real interest rate and the quantity of investment demanded is negative. In Figure 10.1, an increase in the real interest rate from 3 to 5 percent causes a movement along investment demand curve ID_1 from \$7 trillion of investment to \$5 trillion.

♦ If the expected profit rate rises, the investment demand curve shifts rightward, from ID_1 to ID_2.

Investment in the United States fluctuates because of changes in the real interest rate and expected profit rate. Changes in the expected profit rate have increased investment demand in most years and decreased it in others.

■ Saving Decisions

National saving is the sum of private saving plus government saving.

Households divide disposable income between consumption expenditure and saving. Saving depends on:

♦ *Real interest rate* — the lower the real interest rate, the smaller is the quantity of saving.

♦ *Disposable income* — the higher a household's disposable income, the more it saves.

♦ *Purchasing power of net assets* — the higher the purchasing power of a household's net assets, the lower is its saving.

♦ *Expected future income* — the lower a household's expected future income, the greater is its (current) saving.

Saving supply is the (positive) relationship between the real interest rate and the quantity of saving. Figure 10.2 shows a saving supply curve.

A change in disposable income, the purchasing power of net assets, or expected future income change saving supply and shift the saving supply curve.

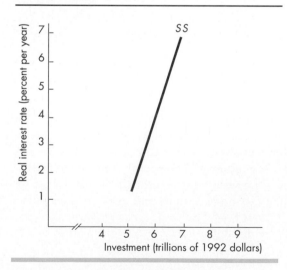

FIGURE **10.2**
Saving Supply Curve

■ Equilibrium in the World Economy

The equilibrium real interest rate is determined in the *world* market because capital is free to move to the nation that promises the highest return. Hence it is world investment demand and saving supply that determine

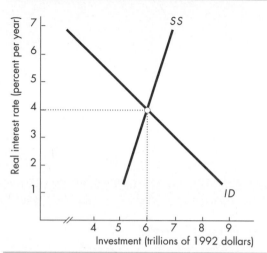

FIGURE **10.3**
Equilibrium in the World Capital Market

the real interest rate. In Figure 10.3, the equilibrium real interest rate is 4 percent, the real interest rate that sets the quantity of investment demanded equal to the quantity supplied, and the equilibrium quantity of investment is $6 trillion.

Changes in saving supply or investment demand change the real interest rate.

♦ In 1975 the investment demand curve shifted leftward and the saving supply curve rightward so that the real interest rate was low.

♦ By 1984 both the investment demand and saving supply curves had shifted rightward, but the shift in the investment demand curve exceeded that in the saving supply curve, so the real interest rate rose.

♦ During the late 1980s and the 1990s, investment demand increased less than saving supply, so the real interest rate fell from its high level in 1984.

■ The Role of Government

Total government saving in the world as a whole is close to 10 percent of total saving, but government saving is *negative*.

Combining the two equalities, GDP = $C + I + G$ and GDP = $C + S + T$, shows how investment is financed,

$$I = S + T - G,$$

where I is investment, S is private saving, T is net taxes, and G is government expenditure, so that $T - G$ is government saving. Thus total saving is the sum of private saving plus government saving. If government purchases exceed net taxes ($G > T$), then the government has a budget deficit and government saving is negative. Government saving has two effects on total saving and hence on the real interest rate and the equilibrium quantity of investment:

♦ Direct effect — a decrease in government saving (increase in the budget deficit) decreases total saving, thereby raising the real interest rate and decreasing investment. The **crowding-out effect** refers to a decrease in investment caused by an increase in the government budget deficit.

♦ Indirect effect — The Barro-Ricardo effect says that private saving increases by the amount of a government budget deficit, so that total saving is unaffected by a decrease in government saving. In this case, a government budget deficit has no effect on the real interest rate or investment.

Probably a government deficit does increase private saving, but by less than the Barro-Ricardo effect indicates.

As a fraction of GDP, the deficits of most industrial nations peaked in 1993. Since then these deficits as a fraction of GDP have decreased and the U.S. budget deficit has turned to a budget surplus.

■ Saving and Investment in the National Economy

♦ The world real interest rate determines the quantity of each nation's saving and investment.

♦ If the quantity of national saving exceeds the quantity of investment, that nation lends to the rest of the world and runs an export surplus.

♦ If the quantity of investment exceeds the quantity of national saving, that nation borrows from the rest of the world and runs an export deficit.

♦ An increase in the government budget deficit can decrease national saving and thereby cause an export deficit.

Helpful Hints

1. **KEY THEMES :** This chapter is a building block to understanding economic growth. Economic growth results from growth in productive resources and from growth in technology. The two most impor-

tant resources are labor, which we discussed in the last chapter, and capital, which we examine in this chapter. The next chapter integrates these topics with some new material (the role of technology and incentives that help foster economic growth) to permit a thorough analysis of economic growth. This chapter also is helpful to understanding business cycles, that is, the recurring fluctuations in economic activity. Investment, and particularly fluctuations in investment, play a crucial role in business cycles. Thus the discussion of the demand for investment is significant in terms of key issues concerning causes of business cycles.

2. **SAVING AND INVESTMENT AS A SUPPLY AND DEMAND MODEL :** The saving supply curve is just another supply curve, and the investment demand curve is simply another demand curve. Thus all the lessons and rules that you have learned about "ordinary" supply and demand curves directly apply to these two curves. For instance, the equilibrium point is where the two curves cross. And, the difference between a movement along a curve and a shift in a curve is exactly the same as before: A change in the variable on the vertical axis (the real interest rate in this case) causes a movement along the (saving) supply curve and (investment) demand curve. A change in any other relevant variable (such as disposable income) shifts the curve(s).

Questions

■ True/False/Uncertain and Explain

Capital and Interest

1. Over the past three decades in the United States, the capital stock has grown each year.

2. The amount of net investment is smaller during recessions and larger during expansions.

3. On average, as a percentage of GDP, investment in developing nations has been higher than that in developed countries.

4. The real interest rate equals the nominal interest rate plus the inflation rate.

Investment Decisions

5. The real interest rate is the opportunity cost of investment.

6. In the United States, over the past two decades the expected profit rate has only increased so the investment demand curve has only shifted rightward.

Savings Decisions

7. An increase in the real interest rate increases the quantity of people's saving.

8. An increase in the purchasing power of a household's net assets decreases its saving.

9. An increase in the expected profit rate shifts the saving supply curve rightward.

Equilibrium in the World Economy

10. Equilibrium in the world capital market is such that in nations with the same amount of risk, the real interest rate is higher in the country with less savings.

11. If the world saving supply curve shifts rightward more rapidly than the investment demand curve, the real interest rate falls.

The Role of the Government

12. Government saving equals government purchases minus net taxes.

13. The crowding-out effect refers to the situation in which an increase in investment decreases ("crowds out") government purchases.

14. The Barro-Ricardo effect concludes that a government budget deficit has no effect on the real interest rate.

Saving and Investment in the National Economy

15. The total amount of a nation's investment can never exceed the total amount of the nation's saving.

16. An export deficit can be caused by an increase in the government's budget deficit that decreases national saving.

■ Multiple Choice

Capital and Interest

1. Which of the following is largest?
   a. Gross investment
   b. Net investment
   c. Depreciation
   d. The capital stock

2. As a fraction of GDP, investment in developing nations is _____ that in developed nations.
   a. generally more than
   b. generally the same as
   c. generally less than
   d. generally less in recent years but in past years was generally more than

3. If the nominal interest rate is 8 percent and the inflation rate is 2 percent, the real interest rate is
   a. 16 percent.
   b. 10 percent.
   c. 6 percent.
   d. 4 percent.

Investment Decisions

4. The expected profit rate rises
   a. when the real interest rate falls.
   b. during business cycle recessions.
   c. when sales fall so that the company has time to make investments.
   d. during business cycle expansions.

5. What does an increase in the real interest rate do?
   a. It causes a movement along the investment demand curve.
   b. It shifts the investment demand curve rightward.
   c. It shifts the investment demand curve leftward.
   d. Two of the above answers are correct.

6. What does an increase in the expected profit rate do?
   a. It causes a movement along the investment demand curve.
   b. It shifts the investment demand curve rightward.
   c. It shifts the investment demand curve leftward.
   d. Two of the above answers are correct.

7. Which of the following statements about investment and the investment demand curve is true for the United States?
   a. The investment demand curve has a positive slope.
   b. Fluctuations in the expected profit rate have created changes in both investment and in the real interest rate.
   c. An increase in the real interest rate has no effect on the amount of firms' investment.
   d. The U.S. investment demand curve never shifts.

Savings Decisions

8. Which of the following increases saving, that is, shifts the saving supply curve rightward?
   a. An increase in disposable income.
   b. An increase in the purchasing power of net assets.
   c. An increase in expected future income.
   d. A decrease in the expected profit rate.

9. An increase in disposable income shifts the _____.
   a. investment demand curve rightward.
   b. investment demand curve leftward.
   c. saving supply curve leftward.
   d. saving supply curve rightward.

10. Which of the following causes a movement along the saving supply curve?
    a. A change in disposable income.
    b. A change in the purchasing power of net assets.
    c. A change in expected future income.
    d. A change in the real interest rate.

11. After 1980 the saving supply curve in the United States has
    a. rotated so that in the 1990s it has a negative slope.
    b. shifted leftward in the early 1980s because the real interest rate fell, shifted rightward until the late 1980s because the real interest rate rose, and then shifted leftward after that because the real interest rate has fallen again.
    c. generally shifted rightward during most years.
    d. shifted rightward until it reached its maximum position in 1984 and since then has shifted leftward.

Equilibrium in the World Economy

12. Why is the real interest rate determined in the world economy?
    a. Because no nation has enough saving to finance all its investment.
    b. Because every nation has some excess saving that it must lend to foreigners.
    c. Because international trade means that each nation must borrow from its trading partners.
    d. Because capital moves from one country to another, seeking the highest possible return.

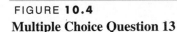

FIGURE **10.4**

Multiple Choice Question 13

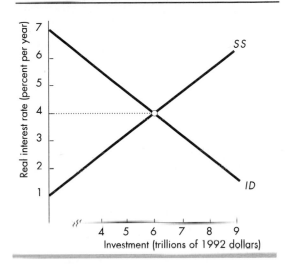

13. In Figure 10.4, the equilibrium real interest rate is
    a. 7 percent.
    b. between 7 percent and 4 percent.
    c. 4 percent.
    d. less than 4 percent

14. If the real interest rate in the world investment demand and saving supply market is less than the equilibrium real interest rate, the quantity of
    a. savings exceeds the quantity of investment and the real interest rate rises.
    b. savings exceeds the quantity of investment and the real interest rate falls.
    c. investment exceeds the quantity of savings and the real interest rate falls.
    d. investment exceeds the quantity of savings and the real interest rate rises.

15. Which of the following raises the equilibrium real interest rate and increases the equilibrium quantity of investment?
    a. A rightward shift of the saving supply curve combined with a leftward shift of the investment demand curve.
    b. A leftward shift of the saving supply curve.
    c. A leftward shift of the investment demand curve.
    d. A rightward shift of the investment demand curve.

16. An increase in the expected profit rate shifts the
    _____ curve rightward and _____ the real interest rate.
    a. saving supply; lowers
    b. investment demand; raises
    c. saving supply; raises
    d. investment demand; lowers

17. People come to expect their future incomes will be
    lower than they had previously thought. As a result,
    the
    a. investment demand curve shifts rightward and
       the real interest rate rises.
    b. investment demand curve shifts leftward and the
       real interest rate falls.
    c. saving supply curve shifts rightward and the real
       interest rate falls.
    d. saving supply curve shifts leftward and the real
       interest rate rises.

18. The real interest rate was unusually low in the _____
    and unusually high in the _____.
    a. 1990s; 1970s
    b. 1970s; 1980s
    c. 1980s; 1990s
    d. 1980s; 1970s

The Role of Government

19. Government saving equals
    a. $S + T - G.$
    b. $S + T.$
    c. $G - T.$
    d. $T - G.$

20. A government budget deficit
    a. occurs when the government has positive saving.
    b. is negative saving.
    c. helps finance the nation's private investment.
    d. equals $T - S.$

21. The idea that an increase in the budget deficit de-
    creases the quantity of investment is called the
    a. Barro-Ricardo effect.
    b. indirect effect of government saving.
    c. adverse effect.
    d. crowding-out effect.

22. Which of the following statements is true?
    a. Taken as a percentage of GDP, budget deficits in
       developing countries have risen over the last
       decade.
    b. Taken as a percentages of GDP, the U.S. budget
       deficit has risen over the last decade.
    c. Taken as percentages of GDP, over the last dec-
       ade the U.S. budget deficit — as well as the
       budget deficits in other industrial nations —
       peaked in the early 1990s and have fallen since
       then.
    d. Taken as percentages of GDP, the U.S. budget
       deficit has fallen over the last decade while the
       budget deficits of other industrial countries have
       risen.

Saving and Investment in the National Economy

23. If the quantity of a nation's investment exceeds the
    quantity of its national saving, the country _____ the
    rest of the world and has _____ net exports.
    a. borrows from; negative
    b. borrows from; positive
    c. lends to; positive
    d. lends to; negative

24. If a nation has negative net exports, a decrease in its
    national saving will
    a. cause the nation's net exports to become more
       negative.
    b. increase the government budget deficit.
    c. decrease the amount of the nation's investment.
    d. cause the nation's net exports to become positive.

■ **Short Answer Problems**

1. The nominal interest rate in 1974 was 12 percent;
   twenty-five years afterwards, in 1999, the compara-
   ble nominal interest rate was 8 percent. Based on
   this information alone, can you determine in which
   year the real interest rate was the highest? Explain
   your answer.

2. The Rush household receives the very good news
   that it will get a big pay raise next year. What happens to the Rush household's saving supply curve
   this year — that is, the year the news is received but
   before their income actually increases?

FIGURE **10.5**
Short Answer Problem 3

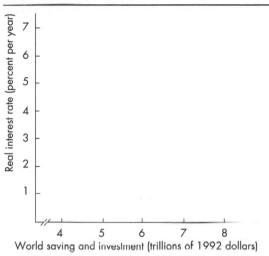

TABLE **10.1**
Investment and Private Saving in Nirvana

Real interest rate (percent)	Private saving (S) (billions of dollars)	Investment (I) (billions of dollars)
3%	$19	$24
4	21	21
5	23	18
6	25	15
7	27	12

3. In Figure 10.5, draw a world investment demand and saving supply curve. Show the equilibrium real interest rate and the amount of saving and investment. Use the figure to illustrate what happens when the expected profit rate increases.

5. Table 10.1 gives the saving supply and the investment demand for the nation of Nirvana. The government of Nirvana buys $10 billion of goods and levies net taxes equal to $10 billion. There is no international trade.

   a. What is the equilibrium real interest rate? The equilibrium quantity of investment?

   b. Government spending rises to $15 billion, while net taxes do not change. Private saving stays as shown in Table 10.1. What is the government budget deficit? What is the equilibrium real interest rate? The equilibrium quantity of investment?

   c. Government spending stays at $15 billion and net taxes stay at $10 billion. Now, however, private savers increase their savings by the amount of the deficit. What is the equilibrium real interest rate? The equilibrium quantity of investment?

FIGURE **10.6**
Short Answer Problem 4

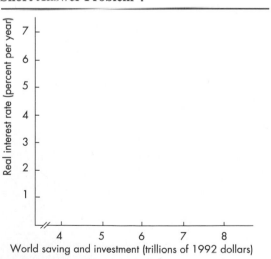

4. In Figure 10.6 draw a world investment demand and saving supply curve. Show the equilibrium real interest rate and the amount of saving and investment. Use the figure to illustrate what happens when saving increases.

6. What is the relationship between the crowding-out effect and the Barro-Ricardo effect?

7. What is the connection between the quantity of a nation's investment and savings and its net export surplus or deficit? Explain the relationship.

8. Initially, the small country of Primus has net exports equal zero so it has neither a net export deficit nor surplus. Then the expected profit rate in Primus increases. Because Primus is a small part of the world economy, the world real interest rate does not change. How does this change affect Primus's

   a. investment demand curve?

   b. equilibrium quantity of investment?

   c. equilibrium quantity of net exports?

9. In question 8, how does Primus finance the change in its investment?

■ **You're the Teacher**

1. "I really don't understand one thing about this
    chapter: Why does investment decrease when the
    real interest rate rises? I just don't get this! After all,
    if I could get more interest, I'd sure invest more in
    my savings account at my bank!" Your friend is
    making a fundamental error. Correct it and perhaps
    you can earn your friend's undying gratitude ... or
    your friend's help in another course you're both
    taking!

Answers

■ True/False Answers

Capital and Interest

1. **T** The average growth rate for the capital stock has been 2 percent per year.

2. **T** Net investment fluctuates with the business cycle; it is higher during expansions and lower during recessions.

3. **T** Although not true for all developing countries, on the average, as a percentage of GDP investment in developing nations exceeds that in developed countries.

4. **F** The real interest rate equals the nominal interest rate *minus* the inflation rate.

Investment Decisions

5. **T** Because the real interest rate is the opportunity cost of investment, an increase in the real interest rate decreases the quantity of investment demanded.

6. **F** Though the investment demand curve has generally shifted rightward, during recessions the expected profit rate fell, thereby (temporarily) shifting the investment demand curve leftward.

Savings Decisions

7. **T** As the real interest rate rises, the "reward" from saving increases, so people increase the quantity they save.

8. **T** As the purchasing power of net assets increase, the saving supply curve shifts leftward.

9. **F** An increase in the expected profit rate shifts the investment demand curve rightward; it does not shift the saving supply curve.

Equilibrium in the World Economy

10. **F** The real interest rates in similar nations are equal because international borrowing and lending drive them to equality.

11. **T** The rightward shift in the saving supply curve lowers the equilibrium real interest rate.

The Role of Government

12. **F** Government savings equal net taxes (the equivalent of government "income") minus government purchases.

13. **F** Crowding out refers to the situation in which an increase in the government budget deficit raises the real interest rate, thereby decreasing or crowding out investment.

14. **T** The Barro-Ricardo effect says that government budget deficits have no effect on total savings because private savings change to "cancel" the budget deficit.

Saving and Investment in the National Economy

15. **F** A nation can borrow from or lend to the rest of the world, so the amount of its investment does not need to equal the amount of its saving.

16. **T** The United States has had an export deficit (negative net exports) probably in part because government budget deficits have helped lower national saving.

■ Multiple Choice Answers

Capital and Interest

1. **d** The capital stock in the United States is about $22 trillion.

2. **a** On the average, the investment rate in developing nations exceeds that in developed nations, so, on average, the capital stock in developing nations is growing more rapidly than in developed countries.

3. **c** The real interest rate equals the nominal interest rate, 8 percent, minus the inflation rate, 2 percent.

Investment Decisions

4. **d** As the expected profit rate rises, the demand curve for investment shifts rightward.

5. **a** An increase in the real interest rate decreases the quantity of investment, which translates into a movement along an investment demand curve.

6. **b** An increase in the expected profit rate increases investment, thereby shifting the investment demand curve rightward.

7. **b** Changes in the expected profit rate have shifted the investment demand curve and resulted in changes in the real interest rate and investment.

Savings Decisions

8. **a** An increase in disposable income boosts a household's savings.

9. **d** An increase in disposable income increases saving, so the saving supply curve shifts rightward.

10. **d** The other answers given *shift* the saving supply curve.

11. **c** In some years it shifted rightward more than in others, but the general trend has been rightward.

Equilibrium in the World Economy

12. **d** If the return from investing in one nation exceeds that from investing in another, many savers will send their funds to the country that offers the highest return. By so doing, they will increase that nation's saving and drive down the real interest rate in that nation.

13. **c** The equilibrium real interest rate is the real interest rate that sets the quantity of world saving equal to the quantity of investment, 4 percent in the figure.

14. **d** The excess of the quantity of investment demanded over the quantity of saving supplied creates upward pressure on the real interest rate that moves the real interest rate toward its equilibrium.

15. **d** The rightward shift in the investment demand curve raises both the equilibrium real interest rate and equilibrium quantity of investment.

FIGURE **10.7**
Multiple Choice Question 16

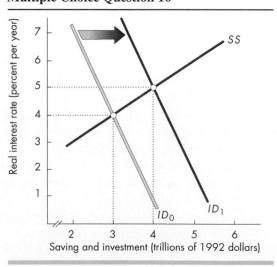

16. **b** As Figure 10.7 shows, the rightward shift in the investment demand curve raises the equilibrium real interest rate from 4 to 5 percent.

17. **c** As people's expectations about their future income fall, they increase their savings so that the saving supply curve shifts rightward and the real interest rate falls.

18. **b** The real interest rate was negative for some years in the 1970s and then quite high for some years in the 1980s.

The Role of Government

19. **d** Answer d is the definition of government saving.

20. **b** Whenever the government runs a budget deficit, it subtracts from private saving.

21. **d** The crowding-out effect occurs when an increase in the government budget deficit raises the real interest rate, thereby decreasing the amount of investment.

22. **c** The U.S. government budget deficit peaked in 1992; the deficits in other industrialized nations peaked in 1993.

Saving and Investment in the National Economy

23. **a** The nation borrows from the rest of the world to finance its investment. To do so, the country's net exports are negative.

24. **a** As national saving decreases, the country borrows more from other nations, thus increasing its export deficit.

■ **Answers to Short Answer Problems**

1. From what is given, determining when the real interest rate is the highest is impossible. The real interest rate equals the nominal interest rate minus the inflation rate. If the inflation rates in the two years were the same, the real interest rate in 1974 was higher. But if the inflation rate was enough higher in 1974 than in 1999, the real interest rate in 1974 was lower than in 1999. For instance, suppose that the inflation rate in 1974 was 11 percent and in 1999 was 3 percent. Then the real interest rate in 1974 is 1 percent and in 1999 is 5 percent. Indeed, in the United States, nominal interest rates in 1974 generally were higher than in 1999, but the inflation rate in 1974 was much higher than in 1997, so real interest rates in 1974 were lower than in 1999.

2. The Rush family will "cash in" on its higher future income by decreasing its current saving supply and using the funds to buy more current consumption. Thus the Rush's saving supply curve shifts leftward.

FIGURE **10.8**
Short Answer Problem 3

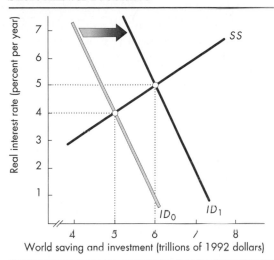

3. Figure 10.8 shows an investment demand ID_0 and a saving supply curve SS. Your curves do not need to be identical to those shown; however, the investment demand curve must slope downward, and the saving supply curve must slope upward. The equilibrium real interest rate is the interest rate at which the two curves cross — 4 percent in the figure. The equilibrium quantity of saving and investment in the figure is $5 trillion.

An increase in the expected profit rate shifts the investment demand curve rightward, to ID_1 in the figure. As a result, the equilibrium real interest rate rises to 5 percent in the figure, and the equilibrium quantity of saving and investment also increases (to $6 trillion in the figure).

4. Figure 10.9 shows an investment demand ID and a saving supply curve SS_0. As in problem 3, your curves do not need to be identical to those shown, but they need the same slopes. The equilibrium real interest rate is the interest rate at which the quantity of investment equals the quantity of saving — 4 percent in the figure. The equilibrium quantity of investment and saving is $5 trillion in the figure.

An increase in saving shifts the saving supply curve rightward, to SS_1 in the figure. Your figure does not need to be identical, but the saving supply curve must shift rightward. As a result of the increase in saving, the real interest rate falls (to 3 percent in the figure), and the quantity of investment and saving increase (to $6 trillion in the figure).

FIGURE **10.9**
Short Answer Problem 4

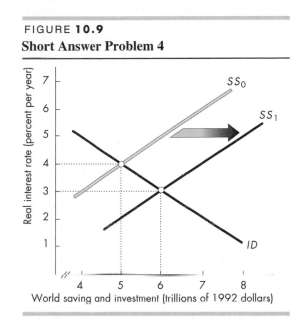

TABLE **10.2**
Short Answer Problem 5 (b)

Real interest rate (percent)	Private saving (billions of dollars)	Government saving (billions of dollars)	Total saving (billions of dollars)
3%	$19	–$5	$14
4	21	–5	16
5	23	–5	18
6	25	–5	20
7	27	–5	22

5. a. The equilibrium real interest rate is 4 percent because that is the real interest rate at which the quantity of investment demanded equals the quantity of saving supplied. The equilibrium amount of investment is $21 billion.

b. The government budget deficit equals government purchases minus net taxes, so the government budget deficit is $5 billion. Hence the government has negative savings of –$5 billion. To determine the equilibrium real interest rate, it is necessary to determine total savings, which equals the sum of private plus government savings. Table 10.2 presents Nirvana's total savings. Because government saving is negative, total saving equals private saving minus $5 billion. The equilibrium real interest rate is 5 percent because at that interest rate the quantity of total savings equals the quantity of investment. Hence the equilibrium amount of investment is $18 billion, $3 billion less than in part (a), without the deficit. The $5 billion government budget deficit crowded out $3 billion of investment.

c. The equilibrium real interest rate in part (a) is identical to the real interest rate in this part. Part (c) describes the Barro-Ricardo effect, in which private savers offset the government budget deficit so that total saving remains unchanged. Hence, the equilibrium real interest rate is 4 percent and the quantity of investment is $21 billion. Thanks to the Barro-Ricardo effect, the government budget deficit did not crowd out any investment.

6. The crowding-out effect refers to a direct effect from government saving. In particular, say the government has negative saving, that is, it is running a budget deficit. Total saving is the sum of personal saving plus government saving, so negative saving from the government decreases total saving. If the budget deficit increases — so that the magnitude of the government's negative saving increases — total saving decreases. As a result the real interest rate rises and hence the equilibrium quantity of investment decreases because it has been crowded out by government borrowing.

The Barro-Ricardo effect refers to an indirect effect from government saving. It suggests that households increase their private saving in response to negative government saving. When the government runs a budget deficit, so that its saving is negative, households increase their saving by an amount equal to the budget deficit. In this case, total saving, the sum of private and government saving, does not change. As a result, the real interest rate does not change and neither does the quantity of investment.

Basically these two effects run opposite to each other. Crowding out suggests budget deficits decrease the amount of investment, while the Barro-Ricardo effect says that budget deficits have no effect on the quantity of investment.

7. The tie between the quantity of a nation's investment and saving and its export surplus or deficit is direct. A nation can finance its investment either through national saving, through international borrowing, or through some combination of the two. If the amount of the nation's investment exceeds the amount of its national saving, the country borrows

from the rest of the world. And, when it does, the country runs a net export deficit, that is, its net exports are negative.

Conversely, if the quantity of a country's investment is less than the quantity of its saving, the nation lends the "excess" saving to the rest of the world. When a nation lends abroad, it runs a net export surplus, that is, its net exports are positive.

8. a. The increase in the expected profit rate increases investment demand, shifting the investment demand curve rightward.

b. The increase in the expected profit rate combined with no change in the real interest rate means that the quantity of investment increases.

c. The country borrows from the rest of the world, so it runs a net export deficit. Net exports become negative.

9. Investment can be financed by national saving and borrowing from the rest of the world. In the case of Primus, national saving does not change because the real interest rate is constant. Thus the increase in investment is financed by borrowing from the rest the world. When it borrows, Primus uses the funds to run a net export deficit, that is, Primus uses the funds to buy more from foreign countries than it sells to foreign nations.

■ **You're the Teacher**

1. "No, you're making a fundamental error. Once you get the point here, I bet the rest of the chapter will be a *lot* easier! Anyway, the deal is that you're confusing investment and saving. 'Investment' means the purchase of new capital goods; that is, investment refers to buying the actual capital good. When you think about your funds in a savings account, you're thinking about 'saving.' And, yeah, I agree with you that if the real interest rate you get on your savings increases, you'll save more. In fact, that's exactly what our book says! But when you think about investment, you have to realize that the real interest rate is a cost of investment. It's the same way with you and me: If the real interest rate goes up, I know that I am less likely to borrow to buy a car or anything else. Companies behave the same way: If the real interest rate goes up, companies will borrow less, cutting back on their investments. So, you can see, that when the real interest rate rises, the quantity of investment demanded decreases."

Chapter Quiz

1. Which of the following directly decreases the capital stock?
   a. Gross investment
   b. Net investment
   c. Depreciation
   d. Consumption expenditure

2. The capital stock has more than doubled since 1970. The capital stock's growth rate is steady and does not change in a recession.
   a. Both sentences are true.
   b. The first sentence is true and the second is false.
   c. The first sentence is false and the second is true.
   d. Both sentences are false.

3. The real interest rate is the return on capital. The real interest rate has trended higher since 1980.
   a. Both sentences are true.
   b. The first sentence is true and the second is false.
   c. The first sentence is false and the second is true.
   d. Both sentences are false.

4. If the nominal interest rate is 8 percent and the inflation rate is 2 percent, the real interest rate is approximately
   a. 16 percent.
   b. 10 percent.
   c. 6 percent.
   d. 4 percent.

5. During a recession, the expected profit rate _____ and the investment demand curve shifts _____.
   a. rises; rightward
   b. rises; leftward
   c. falls; rightward
   d. falls; leftward

6. National saving equals
   a. private saving plus government saving.
   b. private saving plus foreign saving.
   c. private saving plus foreign lending.
   d. government saving plus foreign lending.

7. If saving supply increases by the same amount as investment demand, the real interest rate _____ and the quantity of investment _____.
   a. rises; increases
   b. does not change; increases
   c. falls; increases
   d. rises; does not change

8. The saving supply curve has a negative slope. The investment demand curve has a positive slope.
   a. Both sentences are true.
   b. The first sentence is true and the second is false.
   c. The first sentence is false and the second is true.
   d. Both sentences are false.

9. During the year, there is both technological progress and an increase in incomes throughout the world. As a result, the equilibrium real interest rate _____ and the quantity of investment _____.
   a rises; increases
   b. probably changes, but in an ambiguous direction; increases
   c. falls; probably changes, but in an ambiguous direction
   d. None of the above

10. Because saving equals investment in the world economy,
    a saving must equal investment in each nation.
    b. saving may exceed investment in some nations.
    c. saving may be less than investment in some nations.
    d. Both b and c are correct.

The answers for this Chapter Quiz are on page 327

11 ECONOMIC GROWTH*

■ Long-Term Growth Trends

♦ Over the past 100 years, growth in real GDP per person in the United States has averaged 2 percent per year. The growth rate varies from one period to the next and it has slowed to 1.5 percent after 1973.

♦ Some rich nations are catching up to the U.S. level of real GDP per person.

♦ Many poor nations are not catching up, but Hong Kong, Korea, Singapore, and Taiwan are generally growing more rapidly than the U.S. and so they are catching up.

■ The Causes of Economic Growth: A First Look

Three institutions are the basic precondition for economic growth:

♦ Markets — enable buyers and sellers to conduct transactions. They also convey information (in the form of prices) that create incentives for people to change their quantities demanded and supplied.

♦ Property rights — social arrangements that govern the ownership, use, and disposal of productive resources and goods and services.

♦ Monetary exchange — facilitates buying and selling of goods and services.

Markets, property rights, and monetary exchange create incentives to specialize. For growth to continue, incentives are needed to pursue three crucial activities:

♦ Saving and investment in new capital — the accumulation of capital adds to the nation's productivity and level of output.

♦ Investment in human capital — human capital, the skills and talents people possess, is a key ingredient for economic growth. Much human capital is acquired through education; some is obtained through doing the same task over and over.

♦ Discovery of new technologies — technological advancement is crucial to economic growth.

■ Growth Accounting

Growth accounting calculates how much of real GDP growth is the result of growth in labor and capital and how much is the result of technological change.

The **aggregate production function** shows that the quantity of real GDP supplied is determined by employment, capital, and technology.

Labor productivity is real GDP per hour of work; it equals real GDP divided by aggregate labor hours. Productivity growth slowed after 1973. It speeded up after 1983, but did not return to the levels reached in the 1960s.

Growth accounting divides growth in productivity into two components:

♦ Growth in capital per hours of labor, and

♦ Technological change.

---

* This is Chapter 28 in *Economics*.

FIGURE **11.1**
Productivity Function

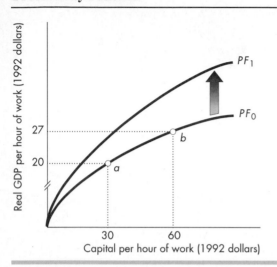

The **productivity function** is a relationship that shows how real GDP per hour of labor varies as the amount of capital per hour of labor changes with no change in technology. Figure 11.1 shows two productivity functions.

◆ An increase in the amount of capital per hour causes a movement along a productivity function curve, as shown in Figure 11.1 by the movement from point *a* to point *b* on PF_0.

◆ An increase in technology shifts the productivity function upward, as shown in this figure by the shift from PF_0 to PF_1.

The **law of diminishing returns** is that, as the quantity of one input increases without changing the quantities of the other inputs, output increases but by increasingly smaller amounts. The **one-third rule** states that a 1 percent increase in capital per hour of work yields a one third of 1 percent increase in output per hour of work. The one-third rule divides growth in productivity into growth resulting from increases in capital per hour of work and growth resulting from advances in technology.

The one-third rule and productivity function show that the slowdown in productivity growth after 1973 occurred because technological change was offsetting negative shocks to productivity.

◆ From 1973 to 1983, technological change contributed very little to productivity growth.

◆ After 1983, technological change's contribution to growth in productivity resumed, but at a slower pace than in the 1960s.

Two factors accounted for the slowdown between 1973 and 1983:

◆ Energy price shocks — the price of oil skyrocketed in the 1970s, so research and development was redirected toward technologies designed to conserve energy.

◆ Environmental protection laws — new capital was used to protect the environment. This protection is not counted as output, so although the quality of life improves, real GDP does not increase.

Policies for increasing the economic growth rate are:

◆ Stimulate saving — tax incentives could be directed at increasing saving.

◆ Stimulate research and development — inventions can be copied, so government subsidies can lead to more inventions that spread throughout the economy.

◆ Target high-technology industries — by encouraging such industries, a country temporarily can earn above-average profits.

◆ Encourage international trade — free international trade encourages economic growth because free trade extracts all the possible gains from specialization and exchange.

◆ Improve the quality of education — education creates benefits beyond the ones enjoyed by the students who receive education, so without government action, too little education is provided.

■ Growth Theories

Three theories of economic growth are *classical, neoclassical*, and *new growth*.

The **classical growth theory** holds that population growth is determined by the level of income per person.

◆ As productivity increases, income per person rises, which causes the population growth rate to increase.

◆ The increase in population increases labor supply, which drives the real wage rate back to the **subsistence real wage rate**, the minimum wage rate necessary to maintain life.

◆ Economic growth ceases until new technological change occurs.

Contrary to the classical theory assumption, the data show that the population growth rate is approximately independent of the economic growth rate.

The **neoclassical growth theory** stresses that real GDP per person grows because technological changes increase saving and investment. Population growth and technological change are determined by factors outside the model, such as luck.

♦ Investment demand is a negative function of the real interest rate; saving supply is a positive function of the real interest rate. In Figure 11.2, the initial investment demand curve is ID_0 and the initial saving supply curve is SS. The initial equilibrium real interest rate is 4 percent and the quantity of saving and investment is \$1 trillion.

♦ Technological change increases the productivity of capital, shifting the investment demand curve rightward to ID_1. The real interest rate rises (to 6 percent in the figure), and the quantity of investment increases (to \$1.5 trillion in the figure).

♦ The increase in investment adds to the nation's capital stock, so the capital supply curve shifts rightward. The increase in the capital stock causes economic growth.

♦ If the real interest rate exceeds the target level, saving is positive and the capital supply curve shifts rightward.

♦ As the capital stock increases, the interest rate falls until eventually it reaches the target rate. At that point, all new investment replaces the capital that wears out in use. There is no additional increase in the capital stock, so economic growth ceases.

One difficulty with the neoclassical model is that it predicts all nations will converge to the same level of per capita income.

The **new growth theory** is based on the idea that technological change results from the choices that people make in the pursuit of profit. Four facts about market economies are key:

♦ Discoveries result from people's choices, such as whether to look for something new and, if so, how intensively to look.

♦ A new discovery offers the innovator the chance at a temporary, above-average profit.

♦ Discoveries can be used by everyone without reducing their availability to others, so the benefits from a new discovery spread everywhere.

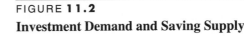

FIGURE 11.2

Investment Demand and Saving Supply

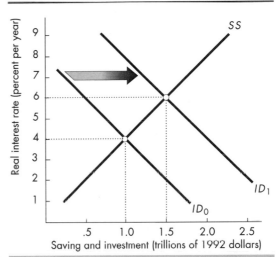

♦ Most production processes can be replicated so that the economy as a whole does not suffer diminishing returns.

Because there are no diminishing returns to capital, the capital demand curve is horizontal at the expected rate of profit on capital.

♦ If the return on capital exceeds the target real interest rate, people save in order to accumulate additional capital. As the amount of capital increases, the economy grows.

♦ Because the demand curve for capital is horizontal, even as the amount of capital increases, the return on additional capital does not fall. Hence the incentive to accumulate more capital does not diminish and, as a result, the economy grows perpetually.

Helpful Hints

1. **CLASSICAL VERSUS NEW GROWTH THEORY :** Economics is sometimes called the "dismal science." This nickname came about because of the classical growth theory. The main conclusion from the classical approach is that, in the long run, workers are bound to earn only a subsistence wage. This result is, indeed, dismal!

The fact that the classical model of growth was developed right at the beginning of the industrial revolution is ironic. The classical model focuses on population growth and does not allow for continuing technological change and capital growth, two features of the industrial revolution that were to become an increasingly important aspect of our world. It is these omissions that account for the dismal, subsistence-wage conclusion of the classical model.

New growth theory examines the factors that lead to technological change. In this theory, economic growth can persist indefinitely because the incentive to accumulate more capital persists indefinitely. Perhaps the nickname for economics should be changed, to the "happy science"!

2. **THE NEOCLASSICAL DEMAND FOR CAPITAL CURVE :** In the neoclassical model, an increase in technology sets off a spurt of economic growth. However, this growth does not continue forever; eventually, unless another technological change occurs, it dies out. The reason that growth eventually stops is the downward slope of the capital demand curve.

To understand the slope of this demand curve, we need to examine how the return (the additional output that additional capital creates) of capital changes as more capital is accumulated. One concrete example is industrial robots. The first such robot may be quite valuable. That's because it fits well into the factory's operations, a relatively large number of workers are available to service it, and it can produce a lot of output. Thus its return is quite high and, because the robot is producing a lot of additional output, economic growth is robust. Now consider, say, the 20th robot installed in the plant. With 20 robots, the factory is starting to get crowded. Workers servicing the robots are starting to be spread thin, with the result that the robots may spend a substantial period waiting to be repaired or reprogrammed. Thus the 20th robot likely will produce significantly less additional output than the first one.

Because the return from additional robots diminishes, the return from installing additional robots falls as more are obtained. As a result, more are installed only if the opportunity cost of buying them (the real interest rate) falls, which means that the demand curve for industrial robots — or, more generally, capital — slopes downward. Additional

capital is demanded only when the opportunity cost of acquiring it, the real interest rate, falls.

3. **THE NEW GROWTH THEORY DEMAND FOR CAPITAL CURVE :** In contrast to the neoclassical theory of growth, discussed in the second helpful hint, in the new growth theory, economic growth can persist forever. The crucial ingredient in the new growth theory is the assumption that the economy-wide demand for capital curve is horizontal. What accounts for the assumption?

The answer to this question lies in idea of replication: Factories and production techniques can be duplicated throughout the economy. Thus adding, say, a 20th industrial robot to a factory may not create much in the way of additional output, but adding an identical 20th factory to the economy will produce precisely as much as did the first factory.

As a result, unlike the neoclassical model, the new growth model asserts that the return from additional capital does not diminish. New capital will continue to be produced even if the opportunity cost of developing it (the real interest rate) does not fall. Hence the capital demand curve does not slope downward: it is horizontal. The fact that the capital demand curve is horizontal indicates that the real interest rate will not fall back to its target level. Thus more capital will be produced indefinitely and, as a result, economic growth will continue indefinitely.

Questions

■ True/False/Uncertain and Explain

Long-Term Growth Trends

1. Over the past 100 years, real GDP per person in the United States has grown at an average rate of 5 percent per year.

2. Because real GDP per person is highest in the United States, over the past 30 years economic growth has been most rapid in the United States.

The Causes of Economic Growth: A First Look

3. Once a nation has in place markets, property rights, and monetary exchange, economic growth is inevitable.

4. Discovery of new technologies help generate economic growth.

Growth Accounting

5. An increase in the amount of capital per hour of work shifts the productivity function upward.

6. The law of diminishing returns states that as more capital is used, total output produced diminishes.

7. Productivity growth slowed between 1973 and 1983 because capital per worker did not grow during this period.

8. Energy price hikes are one of the causes of the productivity growth slowdown.

9. Limiting the extent of international trade increases the rate of economic growth.

Growth Theories

10. An assumption of the classical growth theory is that an increase in real wages and incomes increase the population growth rate.

11. A subsistence real wage is the minimum real wage necessary to sustain life.

12. In the neoclassical theory of growth, a technological advance that increases the productivity of capital increases demand for investment.

13. The neoclassical growth theory stresses the role played by people's incentives for discovering new technology.

14. In the new growth theory, the demand curve for capital is vertical.

15. In the new theory of economic growth, economic growth can continue indefinitely.

■ Multiple Choice

Long-Term Growth Trends

1. For the last 100 years in the United States, growth in real GDP per person
   a. has averaged 2 percent per year.
   b. has accelerated in the last half century because of the technological revolution.
   c. was never negative for any year.
   d. has averaged about 8 percent per year.

2. Which of the following best describes the facts?
   a. Almost all rich and poor nations are catching up to the level of GDP per person in the U.S.
   b. Almost all rich nations are growing fast enough to catch up to the level of GDP per person in the U.S., but virtually no poor nation is growing fast enough to catch up.
   c. Some rich and some poor nations are catching up to the level of GDP per person in the U.S., but many poor nations are not catching up.
   d. No nation, rich or poor, is growing fast enough to catch up to the level of GDP per person in the U.S.

3. Which of the following is NOT a source of economic growth?
   a. Saving and investment in new capital
   b. The productivity function
   c. Investment in human capital
   d. Discovery of new technologies

Growth Accounting

4. Growth accounting divides changes in productivity into changes resulting from
   a. markets and property rights.
   b. saving and investment.
   c. capital per hour of labor and technology.
   d. human capital and other capital.

5. An increase in the amount of capital per hour of work causes
   a. the productivity function to shift upward.
   b. the productivity function to shift downward.
   c. a movement along the productivity function to a higher level of output per hour of work.
   d. a movement along the productivity function to a lower level of output per hour of work.

6. Technological advancement causes
   a. the productivity function to shift upward.
   b. the productivity function to shift downward.
   c. a movement along the productivity function to a higher level of output per hour of work.
   d. a movement along the productivity function to a lower level of output per hour of work.

7. The law of diminishing returns
   a. holds that additional workers produce less additional output.
   b. applies only to labor and not to any kind of capital.
   c. explains why the productivity function shifts upward when technology increases.
   d. does not apply to labor.

8. The one-third rule states that
   a. one third of all technology helps replace capital per hour of work.
   b. an increase in productivity can be traced to one third of the firms in the nation.
   c. a 1 percent increase in capital per hour of work creates a 3 percent increase in productivity.
   d. a 1 percent increase in capital per hour of work creates a 1/3 percent increase in productivity.

9. Suppose that capital per hour of work increases by 30 percent and that real GDP per hour of work increases by 18 percent. The increase in capital per hour of work increased real GDP per hour of work by ____.
   a. 30 percent
   b. 18 percent
   c. 10 percent
   d. 8 percent

10. Suppose that capital per hour of work increases by 30 percent while real GDP per hour of work increases by 18 percent. The change in technology increased real GDP per hour of work by ____.
    a. 30 percent
    b. 18 percent
    c. 10 percent
    d. 8 percent

11. When did productivity grow most rapidly?
    a. 1960 to 1973
    b. 1973 to 1983
    c. 1983 to 1997
    d. 1960 to 1983

12. All of the following are a cause of the slowdown in productivity growth EXCEPT
    a. a reduction in capital per hour of work.
    b. large increases in the price of oil.
    c. passing more environmental protection laws.
    d. an increase in the rate at which gas-guzzling capital was replaced.

13. Economic growth can be increased by
    a. taxing savings.
    b. limiting international trade.
    c. using government funds to help finance basic research.
    d. decreasing the length of time for which a patent is effective.

Growth Theories

14. A key assumption of the classical growth theory is that
    a. the population growth rate increases when real GDP per person increases.
    b. saving is more important than investment in determining economic growth.
    c. capital plays a major role in determining how rapidly the economy grows.
    d. human capital is the ultimate cause of economic growth.

15. A factor that turned out to be a weakness of the classical theory of growth is its
    a. emphasis on saving and investment.
    b. assumption that the growth rate of the population increases when income increases.
    c. reliance on constant growth in technology.
    d. neglect of the subsistence real wage.

16. In the neoclassical theory of growth, growth in ____ is the result of luck.
    a. saving
    b. income
    c. technology
    d. the real interest rate

17. The demand curve for capital in the neoclassical model
    a. is vertical.
    b. slopes downward.
    c. slopes upward.
    d. is horizontal.

18. If the real interest rate exceeds the target interest rate, the capital ____ shifts ____.
    a. demand curve; rightward
    b. demand curve; leftward
    c. supply curve; rightward
    d. supply curve; leftward

19. An assumption of the new growth theory is that
    a. in the long run, people earn only a subsistence real wage.
    b. all technological advances are the result of chance.
    c. the economy-wide return to capital diminishes as more capital is accumulated.
    d. production can be replicated in identical firms.

20. A key assumption of new growth theory is that
    a. all technological change is the result of luck.
    b. higher incomes lead to a higher birth rate.
    c. a successful innovator has the opportunity to earn a temporary, above-average profit.
    d. the target interest rate is greater than the real interest rate.

21. If the demand curve for capital slopes downward, an increase in the supply of capital _____ the equilibrium real interest rate and _____ the equilibrium quantity of capital.
    a. lowers; increases
    b. does not change; increases
    c. raises; increases
    d. lowers; does not change

22. If the demand curve for capital is horizontal, an increase in the supply of capital _____ the equilibrium real interest rate and _____ the equilibrium quantity of capital.
    a. lowers; increases
    b. does not change; increases
    c. raises; increases
    d. lowers; does not change

23. Which theory of economic growth concludes that in the long run people will be paid only a subsistence real wage?
    a. The classical theory
    b. The neoclassical theory
    c. The new theory
    d. All of the theories

24. Which theory of economic growth concludes that growth can continue indefinitely?
    a. The classical theory
    b. The neoclassical theory
    c. The new theory
    d. All of the theories

■ Short Answer Problems

1. What are the three basic preconditions for economic growth? Explain the role that each plays in promoting economic growth. Are these preconditions sufficient for economic growth to continue forever? Why or why not?

2. a. In 1999 real GDP per person in the nation of Slow is $2,000 and is growing at the rate of 1 percent per year. After 1 year, what is real GDP per person? After 2 years? After 10 years? After 30 years?

   b. In 1999 real GDP per person in Fast is half of that in Slow, $1,000, but is growing at the rate of 3 percent per year. After 1 year, what is real GDP per person? After 2 years? After 10 years? After 30 years?

   c. Initially the ratio of GDP per person in Fast to GDP per person in Slow is 0.50. What is the ratio after 1 year? After 30 years?

FIGURE **11.3**

Short Answer Problem 3

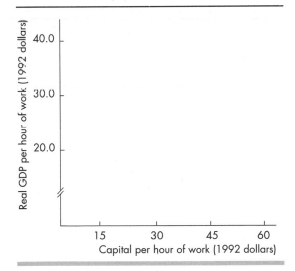

3. a. In Figure 11.3 illustrate a productivity function that shows this situation: When capital per hour of work is $30 then $20 of real GDP per hour of work will be produced. Label this point *a*.

   b. In Figure 11.3 show what happens to the amount of real GDP per hour of work when the amount of capital per hour of work increases from $30 to $60. After the increase in capital per hour of work, what is the new amount of real GDP per hour of work? (Use the one-third rule.)

c. In Figure 11.3 show what happens to the productivity function when new technology is developed.

4. Would the slowdown in productivity growth in the United States have been as large if real GDP included the value of improving the environment? Explain your answer.

5. Why can't a high level of GDP per person persist in classical growth theory? In particular, what mechanism drives the economy back to the situation in which workers receive only a subsistence wage?

6. What does "replication of activities" mean? What role does this replication play in the new theory of economic growth?

7. In Figure 11.4 draw the demand curve for capital assumed by the neoclassical approach. Label this curve KD_0. Also in Figure 11.4, draw the demand curve for capital assumed by the new growth theory and label it KD_1. If these curves are similar, explain why; if they are dissimilar, explain why.

8. Igor was recently named economic minister. His first assigned task is to predict his nation's long-term growth prospects. Igor expects that capital per hour of labor will grow at 1 percent per year. Moreover, he expects technological change of 1 percent per year. What productivity growth rate will Igor predict?

9. After Igor announces his prediction from question 8, the nation's president suggests to Igor that Igor's current position will be short-lived unless productivity growth picks up. Igor likes his current job because it involves no night work and very little digging. What government policies to speed up growth might Igor suggest and why?

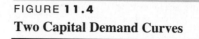

FIGURE 11.4
Two Capital Demand Curves

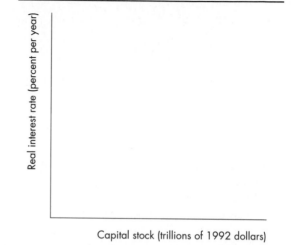

Capital stock (trillions of 1992 dollars)

■ **You're the Teacher**

1. "This is a really great chapter, but you know, there's one thing that puzzles me just a bit. I just don't get the relationship between the saving supply curve, which we talked about in the last chapter, and the capital supply curve, which we talked about in this chapter. I know these things have to be related, but I just can't see how and it's really bugging me!" Help debug your friend by explaining the relationship between the saving supply curve and capital supply curve.

2. After you explain the relationship between the two curves, your friend still has a couple of bugs left: "Okay, I've got you; I can sort of see how these things relate. But, what about the shifts? I really can't see why the capital supply curve shifts and, you know, this bugs me a little." You've managed to remove many but not all of your friend's bugs. Complete the job; free your friend from bugs by relating shifts in the capital supply curve to the saving supply curve.

Answers

■ True/False Answers

Long-Term Growth Trends

1. **F** Real GDP growth per person has averaged 2 percent per year, not 5 percent.

2. **F** Other nations have grown more rapidly and these nations are catching up to the level of GDP per person in the United States.

The Causes of Economic Growth: A First Look

3. **F** Markets, property rights, and monetary exchange are necessary for economic growth, but they do not guarantee that it will occur.

4. **T** The discovery of new technologies is a key method of creating growth in GDP per person.

Growth Accounting

5. **F** An increase in the quantity of capital per hour of work causes a movement along a productivity function, not a shift in the function.

6. **F** The law of diminishing returns states that as more capital is used the *additional* output produced diminishes.

7. **F** The main cause of the productivity growth slowdown was the failure of technological change to contribute to increasing productivity.

8. **T** As a result of massive hikes in the price of energy, technological development was devoted to reducing the amount of energy used in production rather than increasing overall productivity.

9. **F** Allowing unhindered international trade is good economic growth policy because nations that do so generally grow more rapidly than nations that restrict international trade.

Growth Theories

10. **T** The data, however, show that increases in real wages and incomes is associated with little change in the population growth rate.

11. **T** The question gives the definition of the subsistence real wage, the real wage rate that the classical growth theory predicted would occur.

12. **T** By increasing investment demand, the quantity of capital increases and so, too, does the nation's real GDP.

13. **F** The neoclassical growth theory stresses the role played by saving and investment; the new growth theory emphasizes people's incentives.

14. **F** The demand curve for capital is horizontal.

15. **T** Economic growth can persist forever because the return from new capital does not diminish.

■ Multiple Choice Answers

Long-Term Growth Trends

1. **a** The long-term average of 2 percent per year is above the recent average since the productivity growth slowdown that started in the 1970s.

2. **c** If a nation *grows* more rapidly than the United States, eventually that nation's *level* of GDP per person will catch up to that in the United States.

3. **b** The productivity function can illustrate economic growth, but it is not a source of growth.

Growth Accounting

4. **c** Growth accounting is used to divide changes in productivity into different factors so that the factors responsible for growth can be identified.

5. **c** An increase in capital per hour of work causes a movement along the productivity function.

6. **a** Technological advances shift the productivity function upward.

7. **a** Answer (a) is the law of diminishing returns applied to labor.

8. **d** Answer (d) is the definition of the one-third rule.

9. **c** The one-third rule states that the increase in real GDP per hour of work from the increase in capital per hour of work is (1/3)(30 percent), or 10 percent.

10. **d** Based on the answer to question 9, the increase in capital per hour of work raised productivity by 10 percent, leaving technology to account for the remaining 8 percent.

11. **a** Between 1960 and 1973, rapid technological progress shifted the productivity function upward and productivity growth was high.

12. **a** Between 1973 and 1983, the growth rate of capital per hour of work slowed a bit to 15 percent, so the total amount of capital per hour of work increased, albeit slowly.

13. **c** Private markets will allocate too few funds to basic research because an inventor's profit can be limited by copying the inventions.

Growth Theories

14. **a** This assumption is important because it leads to the (dismal!) conclusion that people are paid only a subsistence wage.

15. **b** The previous answer pointed out the importance of the assumption that population growth increases when income increases. However, this assumption is a weakness because the data show it to be false: Population growth does not change when income increases.

16. **c** Technological growth is the driving force behind economic growth in the neoclassical theory. However, because technological growth depends on chance and luck in this approach, the neoclassical model advanced no reasons for the occurrence or continuance of technological growth.

17. **b** The demand curve is downward sloping because in the neoclassical approach, capital is subject to diminishing returns.

18. **c** When the real interest rate exceeds the target interest rate, people save and the supply of capital increases.

19. **d** Because production can be replicated in different firms, the economy as a whole does not have a diminishing returns to capital .

20. **c** The opportunity to earn an above-average profit gives innovators the incentive to develop new technologies.

21. **a** In the neoclassical theory of growth, the demand curve for capital slopes downward.

22. **b** In contrast to the neoclassical theory of growth, the new theory of growth holds that the demand curve for capital is horizontal.

23. **a** This long-run conclusion of the classical theory was based on the (faulty!) assumption that the population growth rate rises when income increases.

24. **c** Only in the new theory can economic growth continue forever as the natural course of the economy. In both the neoclassical and classical theories, economic growth slows and eventually ceases.

■ Answers to Short Answer Problems

1. The three necessary preconditions for economic growth are markets, property rights, and monetary exchange. Markets enable people to buy and sell at low cost. In addition, markets create and convey important information in the form of prices. Monetary exchange also facilitates buying and selling. Thus markets and monetary exchange help promote specialization, which can vastly increase the amount of goods and services produced. Secure property rights are a key to specialization. Without secure property rights, people would be less willing to specialize because what they produce might be taken from them without their deriving any personal benefit from it. In this case, people likely would not specialize.

These preconditions are not sufficient for growth to continue forever. To have persistent growth, saving, investing in new capital (both physical and human), and developing new technologies must occur. Without the necessary three preconditions, saving, investing, and developing new technologies will not occur. But simply having the three preconditions in place is no guarantee that saving, investing, and developing new technologies will occur.

2. a. After 1 year, real GDP per person in Slow is ($2,000.00)(1.01) or $2,020.00. After 2 years, real GDP per person in is ($2,000.00)$(1.01)^2$ or $2,040.20. Similarly, after 10 years real GDP per person is $2,209.24 and after 30 years is $2,695.70.

   b. Real GDP per person in Fast after 1 year is $1,030.00; after 2 years is $1,060.90; after 10 years is $1,343.92; and after 30 years is $2,427.26.

   c. After 1 year the ratio of real GDP per person in Fast to real GDP per person in Slow is equal to $1,030.00/$2,020.00 = 0.51. After 30 years the ratio is $2,427.26/$2,695.70 = 0.90. By growing more rapidly than Slow, the nation of Fast has been able to close a large part of the gap in the GDP per person. In other words, by growing more rapidly than the (advanced) nation of Slow, the (poorer) nation of Fast is able to catch up to the (higher) level of GDP in Slow. In fact, the level of GDP in Fast will equal that in Slow in less than 6 more years!

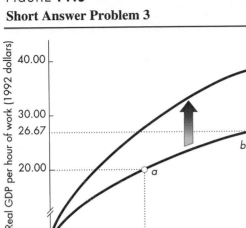

FIGURE **11.5**
Short Answer Problem 3

ple's real wage. Real GDP per person increases. But in response to the higher real wage, the classical theory holds that the population growth rate increases. As a result, the supply of labor increases, which depresses the real wage. As long as the real wage is above the subsistence real wage, population growth remains rapid and the real wage ultimately is driven back to its subsistence level. Thus a high level of real GDP per person is only temporary.

6. The replication of activities plays a crucial role in the new theory of economic growth. Replicating an activity means that the activity of, say, producing a good, can be duplicated. That is, another firm can use the same types and amounts of capital and labor to produce exactly the same amount of the good as the first firm. Consequently when new technology is developed, it can be used by any number of different firms and, because each new firm produces the same amount of output as the previous ones, the return from the capital that embodies the new technology does not fall.

3. a. Figure 11.5 shows the initial productivity function, PF_0, going through point a.

b. An increase in the amount of capital per hour from \$30 to \$60 causes a movement along productivity function PF_0 from point a (real GDP of \$20 per hour) to point b. The increase in capital per hour is 100 percent. Thus the one-third rule states that real GDP per hour of work will increase by one third of 100 percent, or 33 percent. The new level of real GDP per hour of work is \$26.67.

c. An increase in technology shifts the productivity function upward. This shift is from productivity function PF_0 to the new productivity function PF_1.

4. No, the slowdown in productivity growth would not have been as large. One of the reasons for the slowdown was that the value of an improved environment is not included in real GDP. During the 1970s, investment often was aimed at reducing pollution. If the benefit of the resulting cleaner environment had been included, real GDP would have been larger and, as a result, productivity, which equals real GDP divided by aggregate hours of work, also would have been larger.

5. High levels of real GDP per person do not persist in classical growth theory because an assumption of classical growth theory is that population growth is directly related to people's real wage or real income. In particular, an increase in productivity raises peo-

FIGURE **11.6**
Two Capital Demand Curves

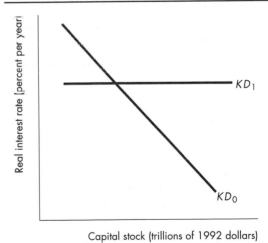

Capital stock (trillions of 1992 dollars)

7. Figure 11.6 illustrates the two demand curves. There is an important difference between the two: The neoclassical demand for capital curve slopes downward, whereas the new growth theory demand for capital curve is horizontal. The difference in the slopes reflects the difference in how the theories treat the return to capital when more capital is acquired. In the neoclassical model, as more capital is acquired the return from the capital falls. Thus the

quantity demanded of physical capital increases only if the opportunity cost of the new capital decreases, that is, only if the real interest rate falls. However, in the new growth theory, with its emphasis on technological change and the replication of activities, the return from capital does not diminish. So if new technology increases the return to capital, this return exceeds the real interest rate. Hence firms throughout the economy acquire additional capital even if the real interest rate does not fall farther.

8. Use the one-third rule to predict the productivity growth rate: Capital per hour of labor is growing at 1 percent and will contribute productivity growth of 1/3 percent. Technological change contributes another 1 percent, so Igor will predict that total productivity growth will be 1 1/3 percent.

9. Igor can suggest five policies. First, he can recommend that his nation stimulate saving by using tax incentives. By increasing saving, his country can increase its growth rate of capital per hour. Second, Igor can recommend that the government subsidize research and development. Research and development will spur technological advances. Third, Igor can propose a government policy of targeting high-tech industries with, say, favorable tax treatment. This policy also should translate into more rapid technological growth. Fourth, Igor can recommend encouraging international trade. Finally, Igor can suggest that his nation undertake policies to improve the quality and increase the quantity of education.

■ **You're the Teacher**

1. "You know, I had to think about this subject a bit myself, and then I finally figured out what's going on. The capital supply curve shows us the stock of capital, that is, the total amount of capital in the economy. The saving supply curve shows us the flow of saving, that is, the additional new capital. So the amount of saving — which we get from the saving supply curve — shows us the addition to the capital stock — which we measure from the capital supply curve."

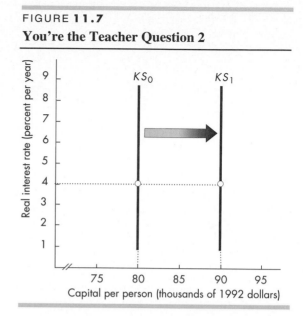

FIGURE 11.7

You're the Teacher Question 2

2. "Look, I can give you an example, but let's start by keeping this simple by ignoring depreciation. Now, I've got to draw a figure. Let's call it Figure 11.7. Suppose that at the beginning of this year the capital supply curve is KS_0. Also, let's say that the real interest rate is 4 percent so that the quantity of capital supplied is $80,000 per person. During the year, suppose that the real interest rate remains at 4 percent and that people save an additional $10,000 of capital per person. Consequently at the end of the year, the supply of capital will have increased by $10,000 per person. Hence the supply curve of capital will shift rightward to KS_1, which shows that, at a real interest rate of 4 percent, $90,000 of capital per worker now is supplied. In other words, the deal is that, when people save, more total capital is available. As a result, the supply curve of capital shifts rightward and it shifts rightward by the amount of the saving.

"Now, of course, depreciation decreases the supply of capital. Thus if people saved nothing during the year, the capital stock would decrease and so the capital supply curve would shift leftward. Thus the net effect on the capital stock — and hence on the capital supply curve — is the balance of these two effects: saving, which increases the supply of capital, and depreciation, which decreases it."

Chapter Quiz

1. Over the last 100 years, in the U.S. economic growth per person has averaged _____.
   a. 15
   b. 10
   c. 5
   d. 2

2. For the past three decades, the nation with the highest GDP per person has been _____ and the industrialized nation with the most rapid growth in GDP on average per person has been _____ .
   a. Japan; Japan
   b. the United States; the United States
   c. Germany; Japan
   d. the United States; Japan

3. Markets, property rights, and monetary exchange
   a. guarantee that economic growth will occur.
   b. are unrelated to economic growth.
   c. cause nations to trade with each other.
   d. are needed for economic growth to occur, but do not guarantee that growth takes place.

4. Continuing economic growth requires
   a. investment in human capital.
   b. saving and investment in new capital.
   c. technological progress.
   d. All of the above.

5. The purpose of growth accounting is to
   a. estimate the productivity function for the United States
   b. verify the one-third rule.
   c. measure how much technological progress, increased labor, and increased capital have contributed to economic growth.
   d. determine whether the United States is saving and investing enough in new capital.

6. A movement along a productivity function occurs when
   a. technological progress takes place.
   b. the amount of capital and labor grow by the same proportion.
   c. the amount of capital grows more rapidly than the amount of labor.
   d. the amount of output per hour of labor does not change.

7. The slope of the productivity function reflects the
   a. effects of capital accumulation.
   b. effects of technological progress.
   c. law of diminishing returns.
   d. effects of population growth.

8. Capital per hour of work rises by 6 percent and technology has increased output per hour of work by 9 percent. Hence the total increase in output per hour of work equals
   a. 15 percent.
   b. 11 percent.
   c. 9 percent.
   d. None of the above.

9. The new theory of economic growth assumes that
   a. the supply of labor increases whenever the wage rate exceeds the subsistence level.
   b. technological change is the result of luck.
   c. production processes can be replicated.
   d. people save as long as the real interest rate is less than the target interest rate.

10. Which theory of economic growth predicts that nations eventually converge to the same level of GDP per person?
    a. The classical theory.
    b. The neoclassical theory.
    c. The new theory of economic growth.
    d. None of the theories make this prediction.

The answers for this Chapter Quiz are on page 327

Part Review

4 UNDERSTANDING AGGREGATE SUPPLY AND ECONOMIC GROWTH

Reading Between the Lines

PRODUCTIVITY ROSE AT 4% RATE IN 1st PERIOD

The productivity of American workers outside of agriculture surged at a 4% annual pace in the first quarter, compared with the fourth quarter, adding more evidence to the case that productivity is perking up after a 25-year snooze.

Growth in productivity, or output per hour of work, is "just about the single most important measurement of economic prosperity and how the economy performs," said Frank Lichtenberg, a Columbia Business School economist.

A lasting rise in the trend would mean bigger wage increases, an economy that grows faster without inflation ... . The more workers produce for each hour on the job, the more employers can afford to pay them without raising prices.

Nonfarm businesses paid workers 4.1% more an hour in the first quarter than they did a year earlier. But the workers produced 2.8% more for each hour of work, the Bureau of Labor Statistics said yesterday. The bottom line: Employers' labor costs rose only 1.3%, the smallest increase in more than two years, despite remarkably tight labor markets.

After World War II, nonfarm business productivity grew 2.8% a year on average. The pace slowed around 1973, and for the next 20 years, productivity growth averaged only 1% a year. Since then, however, the pace has quickened.

Economists debate whether this is a blip or a trend, and whether the increase is a few tenths of a percentage point or much more. "It is increasingly difficult to deny that there has been an acceleration in underlying productivity growth, compared to the record of the past quarter-century, ..." said Mark Zandi of Regional Financial Associates in West Chester, Pa.

All sides agree that a lasting upturn in productivity growth would have huge economic consequences.

How big?

If productivity were to grow 1% a year, it would take 70 years to double American families' standard of living; at 2%, it would take only 35 years. Or, as Isabel Sawhill of the Brookings Institution, a Washington think tank, puts it: The typical American family earned $44,568 in 1997, nearly all from wages. At 1%-a-year growth in productivity, a similar family would have income of $56,029 in 2020, assuming nothing else in the economy changed. At 2% a year, the income would be $70,279 in 2020-$14,250 a year more without working longer hours.

Analysts who have been expecting computers, deregulation and globalization to produce the long-sought upturn in productivity see the latest data as proof. Skeptics, including Ms. Sawhill, are more open minded than they once were. She still wants to see "a few more years " of data before she is persuaded. But she admits to being impressed that productivity growth hasn't followed the usual pattern: a rapid increase early in an expansion and a slowdown later.

"What's surprising is that it hasn't tapered off," she said. "Maybe this is the fruits of the information revolution finally paying off. Plus the competition from abroad finally forcing American business to get its act together."

■ Analyze It

Recent data seem to indicate that productivity is on an up-turn, with an annualized increase of 4 percent during the first three months of 1999. Some observers, such as Frank Lichtenberg, look at productivity as "the single-most important measurement of economic prosperity". If productivity has increased, good news abounds: Wage increases will be greater, the economy will grow more rapidly, and people's incomes will increase more rapidly. However, there is still some question about whether the measured increase in productivity will be long lasting or if it is a blip so that productivity will soon return to its lower growth rate.

1. Use a labor demand/labor supply diagram to illustrate the impact on the wage rate of increases in productivity; in particular, how will an increase in productivity allow for greater wage hikes?.

2. What is the effect of an increase in productivity on potential GDP and the *LAS* curve? Suppose that aggregate demand grows at the same rate as does productivity; that is, the *AD* curve shifts at the same rate as does the *LAS* curve. Using an aggregate demand/aggregate supply framework with the long-run aggregate supply curve, what are the consequences of an increase in the growth rate of productivity for the growth rate of real GDP and the price level?

Web Resources

For more information, browse the Parkin Web site to explore related links.

On the Top 10 list, visit the "Bureau of Labor Statistics" to see how employment, wages, and so forth have been changing recently. For a site of immediate relevance to the topics you have just studied, under "Economic Development, Technological Change, and Growth," look at "Growth".

Mid-Term Examination

■ Chapter 9

1. Real wages fall if
   a. money wages rise and the price level is constant.
   b. money wages rise more rapidly than the price level.
   c. money wages are constant and the price level rises.
   d. money wages and the price level fall by the same proportion.

2. Suppose that real wage rates increase. Then
   a. the labor demand curve shifts rightward.
   b. the labor demand curve shifts leftward.
   c. the labor supply curve shifts leftward.
   d. there is a movement along the labor demand curve.

3. If unemployment compensation benefits are reduced in value, then the opportunity cost of search will be ____ for the economy as a whole and the natural rate of unemployment will ____.
   a. increased; increase
   b. increased; decrease
   c. decreased; decrease
   d. decreased; increase

4. Which of the following is an example of economic practices which causes unemployment?
   a. Efficiency wages.
   b. Real wages.
   c. The downward sloping demand curve for labor.
   d. People not being in the labor force.

■ Chapter 10

5. In a recession, gross investment ____ and net investment ____.
   a. increases; increases
   b. increases; decreases
   c. decreases; increases
   d. decreases; decreases

6. Greater pessimism about expected future profits from potential investment projects
   a. shifts the investment demand curve rightward.
   b. shifts the investment demand curve leftward.
   c. causes a movement up and to the left along the investment demand curve.
   d. causes a movement down and to the right along the investment demand curve.

7. Without a Barro-Ricardo effect, an increase in the government budget deficit
    a. raises the real interest rate and increases investment.
    b. raises the real interest rate and decreases investment.
    c. lowers the real interest rate and decreases investment.
    d. lowers the real interest rate and increases investment.

8. The quantity supplied of world saving exceeds the quantity of investment demanded if
    a. the real interest rate exceeds the equilibrium real interest rate.
    b. the real interest rate equals the equilibrium real interest rate.
    c. the real interest rate is less than the equilibrium real interest rate.
    d. the world-wide total of government budget deficits is positive.

■ **Chapter 11**
9. An example of capital is
    a. land owned by IBM.
    b. a factory owned by IBM.
    c. 100 shares of stock in IBM.
    d. a $1000 bond issued by IBM.

10. If capital per worker falls, then generally
    a. labor productivity declines.
    b. long-term economic growth increases.
    c. labor productivity is increased.
    d. potential GDP increases.

11. Productivity
    a. has been falling over the period 1960 to 1994.
    b. has been rising over the period 1960 to 1994.
    c. has been constant over the period 1960 to 1994.
    d. was high in the 1960s, slowed after 1973, and speeded up again after 1983.

12. In the new growth theory, the demand curve for capital
    a. has a positive slope
    b. has a negative slope.
    c. is vertical.
    d. is horizontal.

Answers

■ Reading Between the Lines

The increase in productivity increases the demand for labor. Hence the labor demand curve shifts rightward, as illustrated in Figure 1. As a result of the increase in the demand for labor, the (real) wage rate rises, in the figure from $10 an hour to $15. The increase in demand also boosts the level of employment, as illustrated in the figure.

A productivity increase boosts potential GDP and thus shifts the LAS curve rightward, from LAS_0 to LAS_1 in Figure 2. If aggregate demand grows at the same rate as potential GDP, the rightward shift in the aggregate demand curve equals that of the long-run aggregate supply curve. Figure 2 shows this change as the shift from AD_0 to AD_1. Thus the combined growth in potential GDP and aggregate demand mean that GDP increases (from $6 trillion to $7 in the figure) and the price level remains unchanged, at 120 in the figure. (Indeed, if aggregate demand had remained at AD_0, the price level would have *fallen* rather than remained constant.) Thus if productivity is now growing more rapidly than before, real GDP will grow more rapidly than before. And, with more rapid growth in GDP combined with higher wage rates, Isabel Sawhill of the Brookings Institution points out that the typical American family's income will rise substantially.

Has U.S. productivity growth increased? Has the information revolution finally paid off? Unfortunately, only time can tell! But, when you read this, more data will have accumulated and you can check out the Parkin web site to see the latest information.

FIGURE 1
FIGURE 1
Higher Productivity in the Labor Market

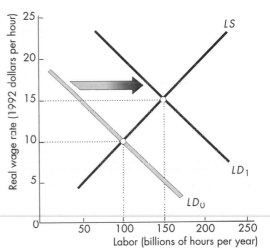

FIGURE 2
Productivity, GDP, and the Price Level

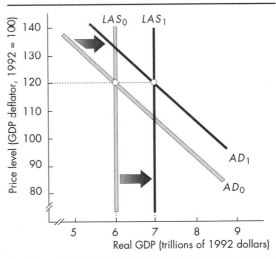

■ Mid-Term Exam Answers

1. c;   2. d;   3. b;   4. a;   5. d;   6. b;   7. b;   8. a;   9. b;   10. a;   11. d;   12. d

Chapter **12** EXPENDITURE MULTIPLIERS*

Key Concepts

■ Fixed Prices and Expenditure Plans

In the very short run, firms do not change their prices and they sell the amount that is demanded. As a result:

♦ The price level is fixed.

♦ GDP is determined by aggregate demand.

Aggregate planned expenditure is the sum of planned consumption expenditure, planned investment, planned government purchases, and planned exports minus planned imports.

GDP and aggregate planned expenditures have a two-way link: An increase in real GDP increases aggregate planned expenditures, and an increase in aggregate expenditures increases real GDP.

Consumption expenditure, C, and saving, S, depend on disposable income (**disposable income**, YD, is income minus taxes plus transfer payments), the real interest rate, the purchasing power of net assets, and expected future income.

The **consumption function** is the relationship between consumption expenditure and disposable income. Figure 12.1 illustrates a consumption function.

♦ The amount of consumption when disposable income is zero ($1 trillion in Figure 12.1) is called *autonomous consumption*. Consumption above this amount is called *induced consumption*.

♦ The **marginal propensity to consume, *MPC*,** is the fraction of a *change* in disposable income that is

FIGURE **12.1**
The Consumption Function

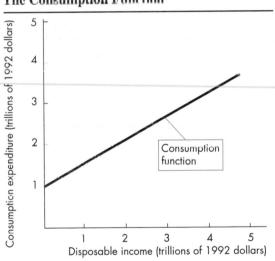

spent on consumption, or $MPC = \dfrac{\Delta C}{\Delta YD}$,

where Δ means "change in."

♦ The slope of the consumption function equals the *MPC*. The slope of the U.S. consumption function is about 0.75.

♦ Changes in the real interest rate, purchasing power of net assets, or expected future income shift the consumption function.

Consumption varies when real GDP changes because changes in real GDP change disposable income.

The **saving function** is the relationship between saving and disposable income. The **marginal propensity to**

---

* This is Chapter 29 in *Economics*.

save, *MPS*, is the fraction of a change in disposable income that is saved, or $MPS = \dfrac{\Delta S}{\Delta YD}$.

The sum of the *MPC* plus *MPS* equals 1.

Domestic imports are determined in the short run mainly by U.S. GDP. The **marginal propensity to import** is the fraction of an increase in real GDP spent on imports.

■ Real GDP with a Fixed Price Level

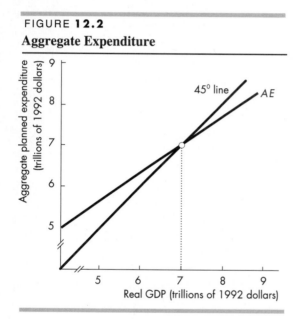

FIGURE **12.2**
Aggregate Expenditure

The aggregate planned expenditure schedule shows how aggregate expenditure depends on real GDP. The aggregate expenditure curve plots the aggregate planned expenditure schedule. Figure 12.2 illustrates an aggregate expenditure curve, $AE = C + I + G + NX$, where *NX* is exports minus imports.

♦ **Autonomous expenditure** is the part of aggregate expenditure that does not change when real GDP changes. In Figure 12.2 autonomous expenditure is $5 trillion.

♦ **Induced expenditure** is the sum of the components of aggregate expenditure that change with GDP.

Equilibrium expenditure is the level of aggregate expenditure at which aggregate planned expenditure equals real GDP. In Figure 12.2 the equilibrium expenditure is the point at which the 45° line crosses the *AE* line, or $7 trillion.

♦ If real GDP exceeds equilibrium expenditure, unplanned inventories accumulate; if real GDP is less than equilibrium expenditure, inventories are drawn down in an unplanned manner.

■ The Multiplier

A change in autonomous expenditure creates an additional change in induced expenditure. The **multiplier** is the amount by which a change in autonomous expenditure is multiplied to determine the change in equilibrium expenditure and real GDP. The multiplier is larger than 1.0 because a change in autonomous expenditure also changes induced expenditure.

♦ With no income taxes or imports, the multiplier equals $\dfrac{1}{(1-MPC)}$, or, equivalently, $\dfrac{1}{MPS}$.

♦ Income taxes and imports shrink the multiplier.

♦ Imports and income taxes reduce the slope of the *AE* curve. With them the multiplier equals

$$\dfrac{1}{(1-\text{slope of the } AE \text{ curve})}.$$

♦ A business cycle expansion occurs when autonomous expenditure increases and the multiplier effect increases equilibrium expenditure; a business cycle recession occurs when autonomous expenditure decreases.

■ The Multiplier and the Price Level

The *aggregate expenditure curve (AE)* shows the relationship between aggregate planned expenditure and disposable income; the *aggregate demand curve (AD)* shows the relationship between the aggregate quantity of goods demanded and the price level. The *AD* curve is derived from the *AE* curve.

♦ An increase in the price level shifts the *AE* curve downward and equilibrium expenditure decreases.

♦ Figure 12.3 (on the next page) illustrates this effect: When the price level rises from 130 to 170, the *AE* curve shifts from AE_0 to AE_1 and equilibrium expenditure decreases from $7 to $5 trillion.

♦ Figure 12.3 shows that, when the price level is 130, the aggregate quantity demanded is $7 trillion and, when the price level is 170, the aggregate quantity demanded is $5 trillion. These are two points on the *AD* curve in Figure 12.4.

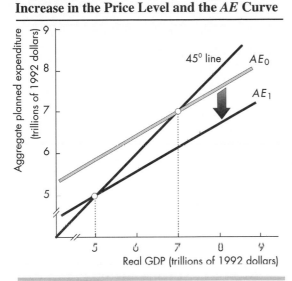

FIGURE 12.3

Increase in the Price Level and the *AE* Curve

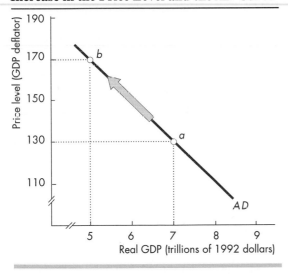

FIGURE 12.4

Increase in the Price Level and the *AD* Curve

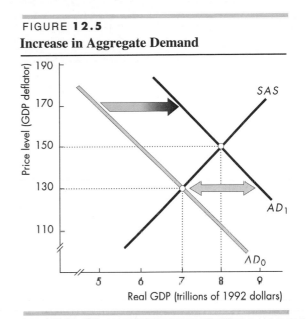

FIGURE 12.5

Increase in Aggregate Demand

♦ The size of the shift in the *AD* curve equals the multiplier times the change in autonomous expenditure. Figure 12.5 shows this result, where the *AD* curve shifts rightward and the multiplied change in equilibrium expenditure is equal to the length of the double-headed arrow, $2 trillion.

♦ The change in real GDP is less than the shift in the *AD* curve. In Figure 12.5 the shift in the *AD* curve is $2 trillion. The increase in the price level reduces the increase in GDP; in the short run, real GDP in the figure increases by only $1 trillion.

♦ In the long run, real GDP returns to potential real GDP and does not change as a result of a change in aggregate demand. In the long run, the multiplier is zero.

♦ An increase in the price level causes a movement along the aggregate demand curve. Figure 12.4 shows how an increase in the price level from 130 to 170 causes a movement along the *AD* curve from point *a* to point *b*. The *AD* curve does *not* shift in response to a change in the price level.

♦ The *AD* curve shifts when autonomous expenditure changes for any reason other than a change in the price level, such as a change in investment or government purchases.

Helpful Hints

1. **AUTONOMOUS AND INDUCED EXPENDITURE:** Autonomous expenditure is independent of changes in real GDP, whereas induced expenditure varies as real GDP changes. In general, a change in autonomous expenditure creates a change in real GDP, which in turn creates a change in induced expenditure. The induced changes are at the heart of the multiplier effect.

However, even though autonomous expenditure may be independent of changes in real GDP, it will not be independent of changes in other variables (e.g., the price level).

2. **THE INTUITION OF THE MULTIPLIER :** The concept of the multiplier is very important. It is a result of the interaction of the various components of aggregate expenditure. In particular, an initial increase in autonomous expenditure, such as invest-ment, increases real GDP directly, but that is not the end of the story. The initial increase in real GDP generates an increase in induced expenditure, which further increases real GDP and thus creates further increases in (induced) expenditure. When prices are fixed, the total effect on real GDP is larger than the initial increase in autonomous expenditure because of the induced expenditure.

Induced expenditure occurs because the increase in real GDP created by the increase in autonomous expenditure raises disposable income. For instance, an increase in investment purchases of personal computers raises the incomes of workers who are hired to manufacture the additional computers. Then, the increase in disposable income increases these workers' (induced!) consumption expenditures. You should become thoroughly familiar with the concept of the multiplier.

3. **THE MULTIPLIER AND THE AGGREGATE SUPPLY CURVE :** The multiplier shows the change in equilibrium expenditure. Thus if the multiplier is, say, 5.0 and investment (a component of autonomous expenditure) increases by $10 billion, the equilibrium expenditure increases by $50 billion.

However, an increase in the equilibrium expenditure of $50 billion does not necessarily mean that equilibrium real GDP also increases by $50 billion. The change in equilibrium real GDP depends on the interaction of aggregate demand and aggregate supply. The $50 billion increase in equilibrium expenditure implies that the *AD* curve shifts rightward by $50 billion, but this shift is one part of the picture. Depending on the aggregate supply curve, real GDP could increase by an amount close to $50 billion (if the *SAS* curve is relatively flat) or by an amount less than $50 billion (how much less depends on the steepness of the *SAS* curve).

Keep in mind that the multiplier gives the shift in the *AD* curve, that is, the change in equilibrium aggregate expenditure. However, the short-run change in equilibrium GDP depends on both the *AD* and *SAS* curves.

Questions

■ True/False/Uncertain and Explain

Fixed Prices and Expenditure Plans

1. A change in disposable income shifts the consumption function.

2. The marginal propensity to consume equals consumption divided by disposable income.

3. The sum of the marginal propensity to consume and the marginal propensity to save equals 1.

Real GDP with a Fixed Price Level

4. When real GDP increases, induced expenditure increases along the *AE* curve.

5. Planned aggregate expenditure can be different than the actual aggregate expenditure.

6. Equilibrium expenditure occurs when aggregate planned expenditure equals real GDP.

7. When aggregate planned expenditure exceeds real GDP, inventories rise more than planned.

The Multiplier

8. The multiplier is greater than 1 because an increase in autonomous expenditure leads to an induced increase in consumption expenditure.

9. The multiplier equals $\dfrac{1}{(1 - MPS)}$.

10. The larger the marginal propensity to consume, the smaller the multiplier.

11. If the marginal propensity to consume is 0.8 and there are no income taxes nor imports, the multiplier equals 5.0.

The Multiplier and the Price Level

12. When the *AE* curve shifts downward, the *AD* curve shifts leftward.

13. An increase in investment shifts the *AE* curve upward and the *AD* curve rightward.

14. In the short run, an increase in investment expenditure of $1 billion increases equilibrium GDP by more than $1 billion.

15. In the long run, an increase in investment expenditure of $1 billion increases equilibrium GDP by more than $1 billion.

■ Multiple Choice

Fixed Prices and Expenditure Plans

1. The fraction of a change in disposable income saved is called
   a. the marginal propensity to consume.
   b. the marginal propensity to save.
   c. the marginal tax rate.
   d. none of the above.

Use Figure 12.6 for the next question.

FIGURE **12.6**

Multiple Choice Question 2

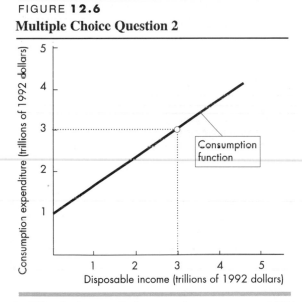

2. What is the marginal propensity to consume, *MPC*, in Figure 12.6?
   a. 1.00.
   b. 0.90.
   c. 0.67.
   d. $3 trillion.

3. The *MPC* plus *MPS* equals
   a. 1.
   b. 0.
   c. A number between 1 and 0.
   d. A number not between 0 and 1.

4. Consumption expenditure increases when ___ increases.
   a. the interest rate
   b. the price level
   c. real GDP
   d. saving

5. Which of the following causes a household to increase the amount it saves?
   a. A decrease in the household's current disposable income.
   b. An increase in the household's expected future income.
   c. An increase in the household's net taxes.
   d. A decrease in the household's expected future income.

6. Which of the following shifts the consumption function downward?
   a. An increase in current disposable income.
   b. An increase in future expected income.
   c. An increase in the purchasing power of net assets.
   d. A decrease in the purchasing power of net assets.

7. An increase in expected future income ___ consumption expenditure and ___ saving.
   a. increases; increases
   b. increases; decreases
   c. decreases; increases
   d. decreases; decreases

Real GDP with a Fixed Price Level

8. The aggregate expenditure, *AE*, curve shows the relationship between aggregate planned expenditure and
   a. government purchases.
   b. real GDP.
   c. the interest rate.
   d. the price level.

9. Autonomous expenditure is <u>NOT</u> influenced by
   a. the interest rate.
   b. taxes.
   c. real GDP.
   d. any variable.

10. If unplanned inventories rise, aggregate planned expenditure is
   a. greater than real GDP and firms will increase their output.
   b. greater than real GDP and firms will decrease their output.
   c. less than real GDP and firms will increase their output.
   d. less than real GDP and firms will decrease their output.

11. If aggregate planned expenditure exceeds real GDP, in the short run,
    a. aggregate planned expenditure will increase.
    b. real GDP will increase.
    c. the price level will fall to restore equilibrium.
    d. exports fall to restore equilibrium.

The Multiplier

12. If investment increases by $200 and, in response, equilibrium expenditure rises by $800,
    a. the multiplier is 0.25.
    b. the multiplier is 4.0.
    c. the slope of the AE curve is 0.25.
    d. None of the above.

13. The multiplier equals
    a. $1/(MPC)$.
    b. $(MPC)/(1 - MPC)$.
    c. $MPS/(MPC)$.
    d. $1/(1 - MPC)$.

14. When the marginal propensity to consume is 0.50 and there are no income taxes or imports, the multiplier equals
    a. 10.0.
    b. 5.0.
    c. 2.0.
    d. 0.5.

15. If the marginal propensity to consume is 0.75 and there are no income taxes nor imports, what is the multiplier?
    a. 1.33
    b. 1.50
    c. 2.00
    d. 4.00

16. An increase in autonomous expenditure shifts the AE curve
    a. upward and leaves its slope unchanged.
    b. upward and makes it steeper.
    c. upward and makes it flatter.
    d. downward and makes it steeper.

17. Income taxes ___ the magnitude of the multiplier.
    a. increase
    b. do not change
    c. decrease
    d. sometimes increase and sometimes decrease

18. A recession begins when
    a. the multiplier falls in value because the marginal propensity to consume has fallen in value.
    b. autonomous expenditure increases.
    c. autonomous expenditure decreases.
    d. the marginal propensity to consume rises in value, which boosts the magnitude of the multiplier.

The Multiplier and the Price Level

19. An increase in the price level shifts the AE curve ____ and ____ equilibrium expenditure.
    a. upward; increases
    b. upward; decreases
    c. downward; increases
    d. downward; decreases

20. A fall in the price level causes
    a. the aggregate expenditure curve to shift downward and produces a movement along the aggregate demand curve.
    b. the aggregate expenditure curve to shift upward and the aggregate demand curve to shift rightward.
    c. the aggregate expenditure curve to shift upward and produces a movement along the aggregate demand curve.
    d. a movement along both the aggregate expenditure curve and the aggregate demand curve.

21. The multiplier is 2.0 and, owing to an increase in expected future profit, investment increases by $10 billion. The increase in investment and the multiplier cause the AD curve
    a. to shift rightward by exactly $20 billion.
    b. to shift rightward by more than $20 billion.
    c. to shift rightward by less than $20 billion.
    d. not to shift and the SAS curve to shift rightward by $20 billion.

22. The multiplier is 2.0 and, owing to an increase in expected future profit, firms increase their investment by $10 billion. As long as the SAS curve is not horizontal, in the short run, equilibrium real GDP will
    a. increase by $20 billion.
    b. increase by more than $20 billion.
    c. increase by less than $20 billion.
    d. be unaffected.

23. The multiplier is 2.0 and, owing to an increase in expected future profit, investment increases by $10 billion. If potential real GDP is unaffected, in the long run, equilibrium real GDP will

a. increase by $20 billion.

b. increase by more than $20 billion.

c. increase by less than $20 billion.

d. be unaffected.

24. Investment increases by $10 billion. In the short run, which of the following increases the effect of this change on equilibrium real GDP?

a. A smaller value for the marginal propensity to consume.

b. The presence of income taxes.

c. A steeper short-run aggregate supply curve.

d. A flatter short-run aggregate supply curve.

■ Short Answer Problems

1. Explain why the *MPC* plus the *MPS* must total 1.

2. What is the difference between autonomous and induced expenditure?

3. Suppose that aggregate planned expenditure is greater than real GDP so that inventories are decreasing. If prices are sticky, explain the process by which equilibrium expenditure is achieved.

4. Table 12.1 shows the components of aggregate expenditure in the nation of Woodstock. All quantities are in billions of 1994 dollars. Woodstock has no foreign trade and no taxes.

a. Plot these components of aggregate expenditure in Figure 12.7. Label the consumption line *C*, the investment line *I*, and the government purchases line *G*.

b. Complete Table 12.2 to show aggregate expenditure in Woodstock.

c. Use Table 12.2 and plot the aggregate expenditure line in Figure 12.7. Label it *AE*.

d. Draw a 45° line in Figure 12.7. What is equilibrium expenditure in Woodstock?

e. Now use either Figure 12.7 or Table 12.1 to determine the equilibrium amount of consumption expenditure, investment, and government purchases.

TABLE **12.1**

Aggregate Expenditure Components

Real GDP	Consumption expenditure	Investment	Government purchases
0.5	0.2	0.3	0.2
1.0	0.6	0.3	0.2
1.5	1.0	0.3	0.2
2.0	1.4	0.3	0.2
2.5	1.8	0.3	0.2

TABLE **12.2**

Aggregate Expenditure

Real GDP (billions of 1994 dollars)	Aggregate expenditure (billions of 1994 dollars)
0.5	_____
1.0	_____
1.5	_____
2.0	_____
2.5	_____

FIGURE **12.7**

Short Answer Problem 4

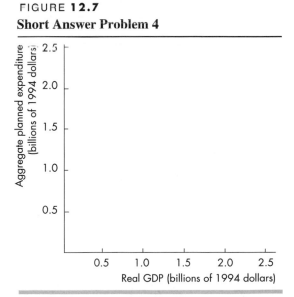

TABLE **12.3**

New Aggregate Expenditure Components

Real GDP	Consumption expenditure	Investment	Government purchases
0.5	0.2	0.4	0.2
1.0	0.6	0.4	0.2
1.5	1.0	0.4	0.2
2.0	1.4	0.4	0.2
2.5	1.8	0.4	0.2

TABLE **12.4**

New Aggregate Expenditure

Real GDP (billions of 1994 dollars)	Aggregate expenditure (billions of 1994 dollars)
0.5	____
1.0	____
1.5	____
2.0	____
2.5	____

5. Continuing with the Woodstock nation, investment increases by $0.1 billion to $0.4 billion, as shown in Table 12.3.

   a. Taking into account the increase in investment, complete Table 12.4 to show aggregate expenditure in Woodstock.

   b. What is the new equilibrium level of expenditure? What is the increase in equilibrium consumption expenditure? Equilibrium investment? Equilibrium government purchases?

   c. Compared to problem 4, what is the increase in consumption expenditure? In investment? In government purchases?

   d. What is Woodstock's multiplier? How does the fact that the multiplier exceeds 1.0 relate to your answers to part (c)?

6. Explain why the multiplier is larger if the marginal propensity to consume is larger.

7. a. Complete Table 12.5.

   b. Based on Table 12.5, how does a decrease in the size of the MPC affect the multiplier?

TABLE **12.5**

The *MPC*, *MPS*, and Multiplier

MPC	MPS	Multiplier
0.9	____	____
0.8	____	____
0.7	____	____
0.6	____	____
0.5	____	____

8. The island nation of Wet has no international trade and no income taxes. The marginal propensity to consume in Wet is 0.75.

   a. Investment increases by $20 billion. Before prices change, what is the change in equilibrium expenditure?

   b. By how much and in what direction does the aggregate demand curve shift?

   c. Suppose that instead of being 0.75, the marginal propensity to consume is 0.90. With this marginal propensity to consume, what is the change in equilibrium expenditure? The shift in the aggregate demand curve?

   d. In the short run, prices rise. Without giving a precise numeric answer, what is the effect of the higher price level on the change in equilibrium expenditure? The shift in the aggregate demand curve?

9. Briefly explain what the AE curve illustrates and how it is related to the AD curve.

10. Figure 12.8 (on the next page) shows the aggregate expenditure curve when the price level is 110. When the price level rises to 120, the AE curve shifts vertically downward from AE_0 by $1 trillion. When the price level falls to 100, the AE curve shifts vertically upward from AE_0 by $1 trillion.

    a. Draw two new AE curves in Figure 12.8 for the price levels of 100 and 120. What are the equilibrium levels of aggregate expenditure for these two price levels? Label as *b* the equilibrium point when the price level is 100 and as *c* the equilibrium when the price level is 120

FIGURE **12.8**
Short Answer Problem 10 (a)

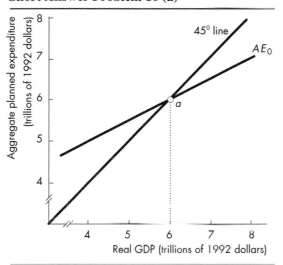

FIGURE **12.9**
Short Answer Problem 10 (b)

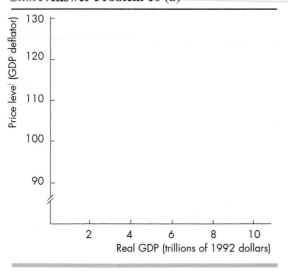

b. Use Figure 12.8 to obtain three points, *a*, *b*, and *c*, on the aggregate demand curve. Plot these three points in Figure 12.9. Assume that the aggregate demand curve is linear and draw the *AD* curve in Figure 12.9.

■ **You're the Teacher**

1. "I've got something of an idea about how the multiplier, *AD*, *SAS*, and *LAS* curves all fit together, but I know I'm still a little confused. Remember when I helped you in our other class? C'mon, don't you still owe me for that? Can you help me with this stuff?" Well, you actually might owe your friend some help. And, after all, your friend *is* asking you about a lot of material that is really important. So pay back your debt by explaining to your friend how these topics all fit together by using the example of an increase in investment. Explain how the shift in the *AD* curve is determined, what the short-run effects are on the price level and real GDP, and what the long-run effects are on the price level and real GDP.

Answers

■ True/False Answers

Fixed Prices and Expenditure Plans

1. **F** A change in disposable income creates a movement along the consumption function, not a shift in it.

2. **F** The marginal propensity to consume equals the *change* in consumption divided by the *change* in disposable income.

3. **T** Because $MPC + MPS = 1$, the two formulas for the multiplier, $\dfrac{1}{(1-MPC)}$ and $\dfrac{1}{MPS}$, are equivalent.

Real GDP with a Fixed Price Level

4. **T** The increase in GDP induces increases in aggregate expenditure. Indeed, that is why the *AE* curve has a positive slope.

5. **T** If the economy is not in equilibrium, actual aggregate expenditure is different from planned aggregate expenditure.

6. **T** The question gives the definition of equilibrium expenditure.

7. **F** When aggregate planned expenditure exceeds real GDP, inventories fall because more goods and services are being purchased than are being produced.

The Multiplier

8. **T** The question presents the essential reason why a multiplier exists.

9. **F** With the *MPC*, the multiplier is $\dfrac{1}{(1-MPC)}$; with the *MPS*, the multiplier is $\dfrac{1}{MPS}$.

10. **F** The larger the marginal propensity to consume, the larger is the change in consumption resulting from any change in disposable income, which causes the multiplier to be larger.

11. **T** The multiplier is $\dfrac{1}{(1-MPC)}$, so when the *MPC* is 0.8, the formula equals $1/(1-0.8)$, and the multiplier is 5.0.

The Multiplier and the Price Level

12. **U** The effect on the *AD* curve depends on the reason for the shift in the *AE* curve. If the *AE* curve shifts downward because the price level has risen, the *AD* curve does not shift; there is a movement along the *AD* curve. If the *AE* curve shifts downward for any other reason, the *AD* curve does, indeed, shift leftward.

13. **T** Any increase in autonomous expenditure *not* caused by a change in the price level shifts the *AE* curve upward and the *AD* curve rightward.

14. **T** An increase in investment creates a larger increase in GDP because of the multiplier.

15. **F** In the long run, the economy returns to potential GDP, so the long-run change in GDP is zero.

■ Multiple Choice Answers

Fixed Prices and Expenditure Plans

1. **b** The question presents the definition of the marginal propensity to save.

2. **c** The *MPC* is $(\Delta C)/(\Delta YD)$, which here is ($2 trillion)/($3 trillion) = 0.67.

3. **a** The fact that $MPC + MPS = 1.0$ means that knowing a value for one (say, the *MPC*) allows us to calculate the value of the other.

4. **c** A rise in real GDP induces increases in consumption expenditure.

5. **d** When people expect less income in the future than they did before, they respond by increasing their savings in order to (partially) make up for the newly recognized shortfall in future income.

6. **d** A decline in the purchasing power of net assets makes people poorer, so they decrease their consumption expenditure.

7. **b** As people perceive that their income will be higher in the future, they increase current spending and decrease current saving.

Real GDP with a Fixed Price Level

8. **b** The aggregate expenditure curve shows that, as real GDP increases, so does the quantity of planned expenditure.

9. **c** The definition of autonomous expenditure is expenditure that is not affected by changes in real GDP.

10. **d** If unplanned inventories rise, aggregate planned expenditure is less than production, that is, is less than GDP. In response to the unplanned rise in inventories, firms reduce their level of production and real GDP decreases.

11. **b** If aggregate planned expenditure exceeds real GDP (aggregate production), inventories decline. In response, to rebuild their inventories, firms increase their production and GDP increases.

The Multiplier

12. **b** The multiplier here is 4.0 because 4.0 is the amount by which the change in autonomous spending is multiplied to give the change in equilibrium expenditure.

13. **d** Answer (d) is the formula for the multiplier.

14. **c** The multiplier is $\dfrac{1}{(1-MPC)}$, which means that, here, the multiplier equals 2.0.

15. **d** Comparing the answer to this question with the answer to the last question shows that as the MPC increases in magnitude, so does the multiplier.

16. **a** An increase in autonomous expenditure shifts the AE curve upward; a decrease shifts it downward.

17. **c** Income taxes reduce the effect a change in real GDP has on disposable income and thereby reduce the magnitude of the induced change in consumption expenditure.

18. **c** When autonomous expenditure decreases, firms' inventories pile up, so firms decrease production and real GDP decreases.

The Multiplier and the Price Level

19. **d** An increase in the price level decreases consumption expenditure, thereby shifting the AE curve downward and hence decreasing the equilibrium level of expenditure.

20. **c** The change in the price level causes a *shift* in the AE curve and a *movement along* the AD curve.

21. **a** The rightward shift in the AD curve equals the multiplied impact on equilibrium expenditure. In this case it is (2.0)($10 billion) = $20 billion, as illustrated in Figure 12.10 by the increase in the quantity of real GDP demanded from $50 billion to $70 billion.

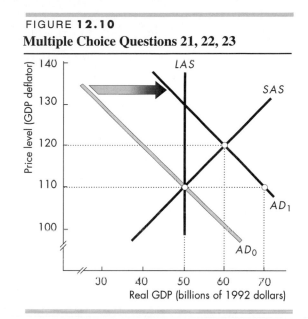

FIGURE **12.10**

Multiple Choice Questions 21, 22, 23

22. **c** Even though the AD curve shifts rightward by $20 billion, the SAS curve slopes upward. Hence in the short run, the increase in the equilibrium level of real GDP is less than $20 billion. Figure 12.10 illustrates this situation, where the $20 billion rightward shift in the AD curve creates only a $10 billion increase in equilibrium GDP.

23. **d** In the long run, real GDP returns to potential GDP without any long-run effect on real GDP. In Figure 12.10 in the long run real GDP returns to the potential GDP of $50 billion.

24. **d** The flatter the SAS curve, the less prices rise and the larger is the increase in equilibrium GDP and aggregate expenditure.

■ **Answers to Short Answer Problems**

1. Only two things can be done with a dollar change, say an increase, in disposable income: Spend all or part of it, or save all or part of it. The MPC, or marginal propensity to consume, indicates the fraction of the dollar change in disposable income that is spent on consumption, whereas the MPS, or marginal propensity to save, indicates the fraction of the dollar that is saved. Because consumption and saving are the only two uses to which the dollar can be put, the two fractions must sum to one.

2. Autonomous expenditure does not change when real GDP changes, whereas induced expenditure does change.

3. In the discussion of aggregate expenditure and equilibrium expenditure in this chapter, we assume that individual prices are fixed so that the price level is fixed. This "thought experiment" allows us to develop the economic model of the components of aggregate expenditure without worrying about the complication of price level changes. As a result, when we discuss how firms adjust to unwanted decreases in their inventories, we assume that firms respond by raising production, without prices changing. Hence when prices are fixed, equilibrium expenditure is attained by an increase in output.

However, in the *AS/AD* model, we relax this assumption and "allow" prices to change by reintroducing the aggregate supply curve. In the *AS/AD* model, we get the more realistic result that firms change both prices and production. In other words, in the short run, an increase in aggregate expenditure, which shifts the *AD* curve rightward, raises the price level *and* increases real GDP.

Short Answer Problem 4 (a) and (c)

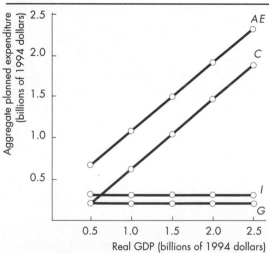

4. a. Figure 12.11 shows the consumption line, *C*, the investment line, *I*, and the government purchases line, *G*.

   b. Table 12.6 shows the schedule of aggregate expenditure. Aggregate expenditure equals the sum of consumption expenditure, investment, and government purchases. When GDP is, say, $1.0 billion, aggregate expenditure equals $0.6 billion + $0.3 billion + $0.2 billion, or $1.1 billion.

TABLE **12.6**

Aggregate Expenditure

Real GDP (billions of 1994 dollars)	Aggregate expenditure (billions of 1994 dollars)
0.5	0.7
1.0	1.1
1.5	1.5
2.0	1.9
2.5	2.3

FIGURE **12.12**

Short Answer Problem 4 (d)

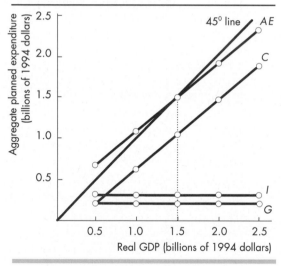

c. The aggregate expenditure curve, *AE*, is plotted in Figure 12.11. It is the vertical sum of the *C* + *I* + *G* curves in the figure.

d. Figure 12.12 shows the 45° line. The equilibrium level of expenditure equals $1.5 billion because the *AE* line crosses the 45° line at that point.

e. In Figure 12.12 the dotted line indicating the equilibrium level of expenditure shows that the equilibrium level of consumption expenditure is $1.0 billion, the equilibrium level of investment is $0.3 billion, and the equilibrium level of government purchases is $0.2 billion. Alternatively, in Table 12.1, the data in row 3, the row for which GDP is $1.5 billion, give the same answers for consumption expenditure, investment, and government purchases.

TABLE **12.7**

New Aggregate Expenditure

Real GDP (billions of 1994 dollars)	Aggregate expenditure (billions of 1994 dollars)
0.5	0.8
1.0	1.2
1.5	1.6
2.0	2.0
2.5	2.4

TABLE **12.8**

The *MPC*, *MPS*, and Multiplier

MPC	MPS	Multiplier
0.9	0.1	10.0
0.8	0.2	5.0
0.7	0.3	3.3
0.6	0.4	2.5
0.5	0.5	2.0

5. a. Table 12.7 shows the new schedule of aggregate expenditure. These expenditures are obtained in the same way as those in Table 12.6 in problem 4: At each level of real GDP, add consumption expenditure, investment, and government purchases.

b. The new equilibrium expenditure is $2.0 billion because that level of aggregate expenditure equals real GDP. The equilibrium level of consumption is $1.4 billion; investment, $0.4 billion; and government purchases, $0.2 billion.

c. Consumption expenditure increased by $0.4 billion, from $1.0 billion to $1.4 billion. Investment increased by $0.1 billion, from $0.3 billion to $0.4 billion. But government purchases did not change.

d. The multiplier is 5.0: The $0.1 billion increase in investment created a $0.5 billion increase in aggregate expenditure. The $0.5 billion increase in aggregate expenditure can be divided into a $0.1 billion (autonomous) increase in investment and a $0.4 billion (induced) increase in consumption expenditure.

6. Any initial increase in autonomous expenditure generates a direct increase in equilibrium expenditure. The basic idea of the multiplier is that this initial increase in aggregate expenditure generates *further* increases in aggregate expenditure as increases in consumption expenditure are induced. In each round of the multiplier process, the increase in spending, and thus the further increase in aggregate expenditure, are determined by the marginal propensity to consume. Because a larger marginal propensity to consume means a larger increase in aggregate expenditure at each round, the total increase in equilibrium expenditure is greater. Thus the multiplier is larger if the marginal propensity to consume is larger.

7. a. Table 12.8 completes Table 12.5. Because $MPC + MPS = 1.0$, $MPS = 1.0 - MPC$. Thus for the first row, $MPS = 1.0 - 0.9 = 0.1$. The multipliers can be calculated using either of two equivalent formulas, multiplier $= \dfrac{1}{(1 - MPC)} = \dfrac{1}{MPS}$.

b. As Table 12.8 shows, when the *MPC* falls in size, so too does the multiplier.

8. a. The multiplier in Wet is $\dfrac{1}{(1 - MPC)}$, or $\dfrac{1}{(1 - 0.75)} = 4.0$. Thus the change in equilibrium expenditure is $(4.0)($20 billion$)$, or $80 billion.

b. The aggregate demand curve shifts by an amount equal to the change in equilibrium expenditure. Equilibrium expenditure increases by $80 billion, so the aggregate demand curve shifts rightward by $80 billion.

c. If the marginal propensity to consume is 0.90, the multiplier is 10.0. Hence, in this case, equilibrium expenditure increases by $(10.0)($20 billion$) = $200 billion, and the aggregate demand curve shifts rightward by $200 billion.

d. When prices start to rise, the aggregate expenditure curve shifts downward. (The higher prices decrease consumption expenditure.) The downward shift in the aggregate expenditure curve reduces equilibrium expenditure. However, the aggregate demand curve does *not* shift. Instead, a movement occurs along the aggregate demand curve to a lower level of equilibrium real GDP.

9. The *AE* curve and the *AD* curve are different. The *AE* curve answers the question: For a given price level, how is equilibrium expenditure determined? When the price level rises, aggregate planned expenditure decreases so that the *AE* curve shifts downward and equilibrium expenditure decreases.

Aggregate demand is different: It relates the quantity of real GDP demanded to differing values of the price level. In other words, the *AD* curve uses the results derived using the *AE* curve to show how equilibrium expenditure changes when the price level changes.

10. a. Figure 12.13 shows the aggregate expenditure curve for price levels of 100 (AE_1) and 120 (AE_2). The equilibrium points are *b* and *c*, and the equilibrium levels of expenditure are $8 trillion and $4 trillion, respectively.

b. Figure 12.14 shows the three points on the *AD* curve. When the price level is 100, the aggregate quantity demanded is the equilibrium expenditure of $8 trillion (point *b*); when the price level is 110, the aggregate quantity demanded is the equilibrium expenditure of $6 trillion (point *a*); and when the price level is 120, the aggregate quantity demanded is $4 trillion (point *c*).

▣ You're the Teacher

1. "Wow, you're asking about a lot of stuff. Are you sure that I owe you *that* much? But, what the heck, let me go over this for you because it's bound to help me, too.

"Let's tackle your questions by thinking about the situation in which investment increases by $10 billion. Why did investment increase? I don't know; maybe because expectations of future profits increased; maybe because the interest rate dropped. Whatever the reason, though, it increased by $10 billion. Now, let's also say that the *MPC* equals 0.67.

"The first thing we can do is to calculate the multiplier. We know that the multiplier equals $\dfrac{1}{(1-MPC)}$, so in this case we get $\dfrac{1}{(1-0.67)} = 3.0$.

In other words, we know that the multiplier is 3.0 and that the $10 billion increase in investment leads to a (3.0)($10.0 billion) = $30.0 billion increase in equilibrium expenditure.

"Now I need to draw a figure; let's call it Figure 12.15 (on the next page). Check it out. Before investment increased, the economy was in equilibrium at point *a*. Here the initial aggregate demand curve, AD_0, crossed the short-run aggregate supply curve,

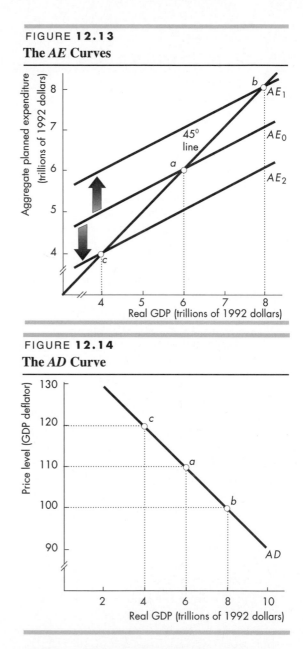

FIGURE 12.13

The *AE* Curves

FIGURE 12.14

The *AD* Curve

SAS_0, and the long-run aggregate supply curve, *LAS*. The equilibrium price level was 110 and the level of real GDP was $60 billion.

"Okay, now pay attention because here's where your questions start: The increase in investment shifts the *AD* curve rightward, and the size of the shift equals the change in equilibrium expenditure. In other words, the *AD* curve shifts rightward to AD_1, and the size of the shift equals $30 billion. The shift is the difference between point *b* and point *a* along the

FIGURE **12.15**

Short-Run Increase in Aggregate Demand

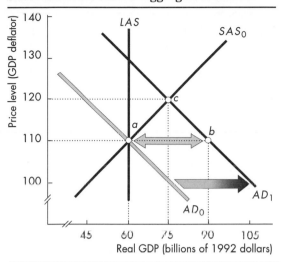

FIGURE **12.16**

Long-Run Increase in Aggregate Demand

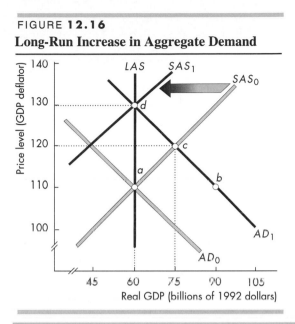

double headed arrow; this difference is $30 billion. So the AD curve shifts rightward by the multiplied impact on equilibrium expenditure.

"But a key point is that, in the short run, real GDP doesn't increase by all $30 billion. It would increase by the entire $30 billion only if prices did not change. But, in the short run, prices are going to start to change. And as they rise, people reduce their consumption expenditures, and the equilibrium amount of expenditure doesn't change by the entire $30 billion; it changes by something less. Figure 12.15 shows that the short-run equilibrium — where AD_1 crosses SAS_0 — is at point c. And at point c, real GDP increases by (only) $15 billion, to $75 billion. Why don't we go to point b? Because, in the short run, the price level has increased, from 110 to 120.

"But, look, point c can't be the end of the story. At point c, the price level has increased, but money wages haven't changed. As more time passes, workers negotiate higher wages, which take into account the higher prices. And as money wage rates rise, the short-run aggregate supply curve shifts leftward.

"The final part of the story is illustrated in Figure 12.16. Here the SAS curve has shifted leftward and the new, long-run equilibrium point is d, where the AD curve crosses the LAS curve and the SAS curve, SAS_1. Thus at point d, we've returned to the long-run equilibrium because prices *and* money wages have both adjusted: Real GDP has returned to its

TABLE **12.9**

Different Points

Point	Situation
a	Initial equilibrium
b	Price level constant, money wage constant
c	Price level increased, money wage constant
d	Price level increased, money wage increased

potential level ($60 billion) and the price level has increased to 130.

"I think Table 12.9 shows some results that can help you tie all these changes together. In it I've listed the four points shown in the figures I've drawn. Basically, we begin at point a. Then the increase in investment starts to move us to point b. If prices are sticky long enough, the multiplier process will have time to complete itself and we'll get to point b. But in the short run, prices rise and so we move to point c, where prices but not money wages have changed. And then, from point c, money wages start to adjust and we eventually move from point c to point d, where both prices and money wages have risen. Point d is the final, long-run equilibrium.

"Look, your question required a really long answer, so how about you springing for the pizza the next time we buy some?"

Chapter Quiz

1. Included in aggregate expenditure are
   a. consumption, saving, and government purchases.
   b. consumption expenditure, investment, and government purchases.
   c. investment, saving, and net exports.
   d. investment, government purchases, and disposable income.

2. When the consumption function lies above a 45° line,
   a. saving is positive.
   b. saving is negative.
   c. consumption expenditure is negative.
   d. disposable income is negative.

3. Expenditure that depends on the level of income is
   a. actual expenditure.
   b. induced expenditure.
   c. autonomous expenditure.
   d. equilibrium expenditure.

4. If the *MPS* = 0.1, the multiplier equals
   a. 10.0.
   b. 5.0.
   c. 1.0.
   d. None of the above.

5. If prices are fixed and the multiplier is 5, an increase in investment spending of $10 billion increases equilibrium expenditure by
   a. $50 billion.
   b. $10 billion.
   c. $5 billion.
   d. $2 billion.

6. If prices are fixed and the *MPC* is 0.80, a $5 billion increase in investment increases equilibrium expenditure by
   a. $25 billion.
   b. $15 billion.
   c. $10 billion.
   d. None of the above.

7. A decrease in the price level
   a. shifts the *AE* curve upward.
   b. shifts the *AE* curve downward.
   c. does not shift the *AE* curve.
   d. perhaps shifts the *AE* curve depending on whether the *MPC* is greater than or less than the *MPS*.

8. An increase in investment spending shifts the *AD* curve by a greater distance _____ whenever the *MPC* is _____.
   a. rightward; larger
   b. rightward; smaller
   c. leftward; larger
   d. leftward; smaller

9. In the long run, the multiplier
   a. is greater than 1.0 in value.
   b. equals 1.0 in value.
   c. is precisely twice the short-run multiplier.
   d. equals 0.

10. A change in _____ does not change autonomous expenditure.
    a. the price level.
    b. the interest rate.
    c. real GDP.
    d. any economic variable.

The answers for this Chapter Quiz are on page 328

13 FISCAL POLICY*

■ The Federal Budget

The **federal budget** is an annual statement of the government's expenditures and tax revenues. Using the federal budget to achieve macroeconomic goals such as full employment is **fiscal policy**.

The President proposes a budget to Congress, Congress passes budget acts, and the President vetoes or signs the acts. The **Employment Act of 1946** commits the government to strive for full employment. The **Council of Economic Advisers** is a group of economists who moni-tor the economy and keep the President informed.

♦ Tax revenues are received from four sources: personal income taxes, social insurance taxes, corporate income taxes, and indirect taxes.

♦ Expenditures are classified as transfer payments, purchases of goods and services, and interest payments on the debt.

The budget balance equals tax revenues minus expenditures.

♦ A **budget surplus** occurs if tax revenues exceed expenditures; a **budget deficit** occurs if tax revenues are less than expenditures; and a **balanced budget** occurs if tax revenues equal expenditures.

---

* This is Chapter 30 in *Economics*.

♦ The U.S. government had a budget deficit from 1970 to 1997. In 1998 the government had a budget surplus.

♦ **Government debt** is the total amount owed by the government. As a percentage of GDP, the debt declined after World War II until 1974, increased until the mid 1990s and has fallen since then.

♦ The U.S. is one of a few countries with a budget surplus; most nations have budget deficits.

■ Fiscal Policy Multipliers

Automatic fiscal policy is a change in fiscal policy caused by the state of the economy; **discretionary fiscal policy** is a policy action initiated by an act of Congress. **Lump-sum taxes** are taxes that do not change when real GDP changes.

♦ The **government purchases multiplier** is the magnification effect of a change in government purchases on equilibrium expenditure and real GDP; it is the amount by which a change in government purchases is multiplied to determine the change in equilibrium expenditure and real GDP.

♦ An increase in government purchases shifts the aggregate expenditure curve upward and increases equilibrium expenditure. Figure 13.1 (on the next page) illustrates this process, in which the AE curve shifts upward to AE_1 and the equilibrium expenditure rises from $6 trillion to $8 trillion.

♦ Without income taxes or imports, the government purchases multiplier is $\dfrac{1}{(1-MPC)}$.

FIGURE **13.1**
Increase in Government Purchases

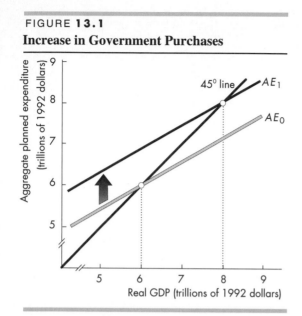

♦ An increase in lump-sum taxes shifts the aggregate expenditure curve downward and decreases equilibrium expenditure.

♦ The **lump-sum tax multiplier** is the amount by which a change in lump-sum taxes is multiplied to give the change in equilibrium expenditures.

♦ Without income taxes or imports, the lump-sum tax multiplier is $-\dfrac{MPC}{(1-MPC)}$.

♦ The lump-sum transfer payments multiplier is $\dfrac{MPC}{(1-MPC)}$.

Induced taxes change when GDP changes; **entitlement spending** is transfer payments that change when GDP changes. Both induced taxes and entitlement spending decrease the magnitude of the government purchases and lump-sum tax multipliers. The larger the *marginal tax rate*, the smaller the multipliers.

Import spending changes when GDP changes by an amount that depends on the *marginal propensity to import*. The larger the marginal propensity to import, the smaller the multipliers.

Automatic stabilizers are mechanisms that help stabilize GDP and operate without the need for explicit action.

The amount of the budget deficit changes with the business cycle. It increases just before, during, and just after a recession, and it decreases at other times.

The **structural surplus or deficit** is the budget balance that would occur if the economy were at full employment. The **cyclical deficit or surplus** is the actual deficit or surplus minus the structural surplus or deficit. It is not known if the current U.S. surplus is a structural surplus or a cyclical surplus.

■ Fiscal Policy Multipliers and the Price Level

♦ An **expansionary fiscal policy** is an increase in government purchases or decrease in tax revenues. Expansionary policy shifts the *AD* curve rightward.

♦ A **contractionary fiscal policy** is a decrease in government purchases or increase in tax revenues. Contractionary policy shifts the *AD* curve leftward.

♦ The horizontal amount by which the *AD* curve shifts is equal to the multiplied effect on equilibrium expenditure.

FIGURE **13.2**
Expansionary Fiscal Policy in the Short Run

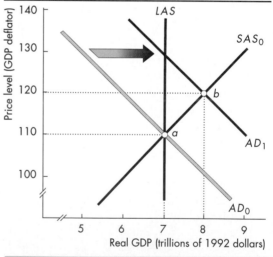

♦ The short-run effects of an expansionary fiscal policy are illustrated in Figure 13.2. Starting from an equilibrium in which GDP equals potential GDP, the *AD* curve shifts rightward by $2 trillion to AD_1 and the economy moves along SAS_0 from its initial equilibrium at point *a* to its new equilibrium at point *b*. The price level rises (from 110 to 120) and real GDP increases (from $7 trillion to $8 trillion). The rise in the price level decreases the size of the multiplier effect on real GDP.

FIGURE **13.3**
Expansionary Fiscal Policy in the Long Run

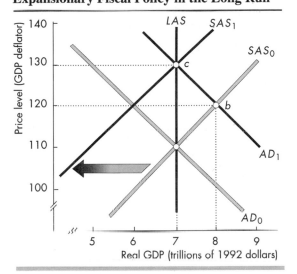

* The long-run effects of an expansionary policy are illustrated in Figure 13.3. The long-run equilibrium is at point *c*, and the economy has returned to its potential real GDP along its *LAS*. The price level rises (to 130 from its initial level of 110) and real GDP does not change (it starts and ends at potential GDP). The long-run multiplier is zero.

Limitations of fiscal policy include the following:

* Implementing fiscal policy is slow and so it is difficult to have the proper policy in place.

* At times it is difficult to determine if GDP is less than, equal to, or greater than potential GDP.

■ Fiscal Policy and Aggregate Supply

Fiscal policy may also affect aggregate supply. An income tax cut increases the quantities of labor and capital, so an income tax cut increases *both* aggregate demand and aggregate supply.

* Supply-side economists believe that the rightward shift in the *SAS* curve from a tax cut is large, so that a tax cut creates a large increase in GDP and only a small rise or even a fall in the price level.

* Most economists think that the effect on aggregate supply from a tax cut is less than that asserted by supply-siders.

A tax cut that strengthens incentives to supply resources increases GDP by more and is less inflationary than one that does not change these incentives.

HELPFUL HINTS

1. **MULTIPLIERS :** The previous chapter was the first that discussed the idea of the multiplier. This chapter continues the discussion by introducing additional multipliers, such as the government purchases multiplier. *All* multipliers exist for the same reason: An initial autonomous change that affects people's disposable income leads them to change their consumption expenditure. In turn, the consumption changes affect other people's income, which creates yet more induced changes in consumption expenditure.

2. **WHY DOES THE INVESTMENT MULTIPLIER EQUAL THE GOVERNMENT PURCHASES MULTIPLIER? :** The fact that the investment multiplier equals the government purchases multiplier occasionally leads to confusion among students who realize that an increase in investment spending will increase the nation's capital stock, but that an increase in government purchases may not affect the nation's capital stock. Remember, however, that multipliers calculate the amount by which the aggregate demand curve shifts when autonomous spending changes. The total demand for goods and services changes by the same amount regardless of whether the initial change in expenditure was by firms (for their investment) or by the government (for its purchases of goods and services). Hence the multiplier, which measures the size of this shift, is identical for investment and government spending.

An increase in investment spending will change the capital stock, whereas an increase in government purchases does not necessarily change the capital stock. And it is indeed the case that the aggregate supply curve(s) increases when the nation's capital stock increases. But even though the aggregate supply curve(s) might respond differently, ignoring any differences is convenient for two reasons. First, time is needed for the capital to be installed and come on-line. Thus, in the short run, the nation's capital stock does not change when investment increases and so, in the short run, the aggregate supply curve(s) does not shift. Second, even in the long run the change in investment spending creates only a minuscule fraction of a change in the nation's total capital stock. With the U.S. capital stock approaching $20 trillion, a $100 billion increase in investment creates only a 0.5 percent change in the capital stock. In the analysis of business cycle fluctuations in economic activity, that amount of change generally is ignored as too small to matter. Although important for the topic of long-term economic growth, for multiplier analysis a change in investment spending is treated the same as a change in government purchases.

Questions

■ True/False/Uncertain and Explain

The Federal Budget

1. The Council of Economic Advisers proposes the federal government's budget to Congress.

2. If tax revenues exceeds government expenditures, the government has a budget deficit.

3. The federal government has run small budget surpluses for most of the last two decades.

4. Most nations are running a government budget deficit.

Fiscal Policy Multipliers

5. The short run government purchases multiplier is greater than 1 because an increase in government purchases leads to an induced increase in consumption expenditure.

6. The larger the marginal propensity to consume, the larger the government purchases multiplier.

7. If the marginal propensity to consume is 0.8 and there are no income taxes nor imports, the government purchases multiplier is 5.0.

8. If the marginal propensity to consume is 0.8 and there are no income taxes nor imports, the lump-sum tax multiplier is –4.0.

9. Although an income tax reduces the magnitude of the government purchases multiplier, it has no effect on the magnitude of the lump-sum tax multiplier.

10. Changes in lump-sum taxes are an example of an automatic stabilizer.

11. By its definition, the structural surplus equals zero when the economy is at full employment.

Fiscal Policy Multipliers and the Price Level

12. A tax increase is an example of an expansionary fiscal policy.

13. In the short run, an increase in government purchases increases real GDP.

Fiscal Policy and Aggregate Supply

14. An increase in income taxes increases potential GDP.

15. The hallmark of supply-side economists is their belief that income taxes have a large effect on aggregate demand.

■ Multiple Choice

The Federal Budget

1. In the United States today, which of the following is the largest source of revenue for the federal government?
   a. Corporate income tax
   b. Personal income tax
   c. Indirect tax
   d. Government deficit

2. What is the largest component of federal government expenditures?
   a. Transfer payments
   b. Purchases of goods and services
   c. International purchases
   d. Interest on the debt

3. Suppose that the federal government's expenditures in a year are $1.5 trillion, and that its tax revenues for the year are $1.3 trillion. Hence the government is running a budget
   a. surplus of $1.3 trillion.
   b. surplus of $0.2 trillion.
   c. deficit of $0.2 trillion.
   d. deficit of $1.5 trillion.

4. Which of the following is largest?
   a. Federal government expenditures.
   b. Federal government tax revenues.
   c. The budget surplus.
   d. The federal government's public debt.

5. Currently the United States has a budget _____ and Japan has a budget _____.
   a. surplus; surplus
   b. surplus; deficit
   c. deficit; surplus
   d. deficit; deficit

Fiscal Policy Multipliers

Table 13.1 shows consumption expenditure, investment, and government purchases in a hypothetical nation that has no taxes and no foreign trade (so that both imports and exports equal zero). In Table 13.1 all the entries are in trillions of 1992 dollars. Use this table for the next five questions.

TABLE **13.1**

Aggregate Expenditure

Real GDP	Consumption expenditure	Investment	Government purchases
4.0	2.0	1.0	1.0
5.0	2.5	1.0	1.0
6.0	3.0	1.0	1.0
7.0	3.5	1.0	1.0
8.0	4.0	1.0	1.0

6. What is the aggregate expenditure when GDP equals $7.0 trillion?
   a. $7 trillion
   b. $5.5 trillion
   c. $3.5 trillion
   d. $1 trillion

7. What is the equilibrium level of expenditure?
   a. $7.0 trillion
   b. $6.0 trillion
   c. $5.0 trillion
   d. $4.0 trillion

8. What is the *MPC*?
   a. 1.00
   b. 0.90
   c. 0.50
   d. $4.0 trillion

9. What is the government purchases multiplier?
   a. 0.5
   b. 2.0
   c. 5.0
   d. 10.0

10. If government purchases increase by $1 trillion, before the price level changes, what is the new equilibrium level of expenditure?
    a. $7.0 trillion
    b. $6.0 trillion
    c. $5.0 trillion
    d. $4.0 trillion

For the next three questions, there are no income taxes and no foreign trade.

11. If the *MPC* is 0.9, what is the government purchases multiplier?
    a. 10.0
    b. 9.0
    c. −9.0
    d. −10.0

12. If the *MPC* is 0.8, what is the government purchases multiplier?
    a. 10.0
    b. 8.0
    c. 5.0
    d. −9.0

13. If the *MPC* is 0.9, what is the lump-sum tax multiplier?
    a. 10.0
    b. 9.0
    c. −9.0
    d. −10.0

14. Which of the following policies shifts the *AD* curve the farthest rightward?
    a. An increase in taxes of $10 billion
    b. A decrease in taxes of $10 billion
    c. An increase in government purchases of $10 billion
    d. An increase in lump-sum transfer payments of $10 billion

15. How do induced taxes, such as the income tax, affect the size of the government purchases multiplier?

    a. Income taxes increase the size of the multiplier.
    b. Income taxes have no effect on the size of the multiplier.
    c. Income taxes reduce the size of the multiplier.
    d. The answer depends on the presence or absence of lump-sum taxes in the economy in addition to income taxes.

16. Which of the following increases the multiplier?

    a. An increase in the marginal propensity to import
    b. An increase in the marginal tax rate
    c. An increase in the marginal propensity to save
    d. An increase in the marginal propensity to consume

17. Which of the following happens automatically if the economy goes into a recession?

    a. Government purchases of goods and services increase.
    b. Income taxes rise.
    c. A budget surplus falls.
    d. Lump-sum taxes fall.

18. If the federal government's budget is in deficit even when the economy is at full employment, the deficit is said to be

    a. persisting.
    b. non-cyclical.
    c. discretionary.
    d. structural.

Fiscal Policy Multipliers and the Price Level

19. Contractionary fiscal policy includes _____ government expenditures and _____ tax revenues.

    a. increasing; increasing
    b. increasing; decreasing
    c. decreasing; increasing
    d. decreasing; decreasing

20. Suppose that the government purchases multiplier is 2. Starting from potential GDP, if government purchases increase by $10 billion and prices do not change, equilibrium expenditure

    a. increases by $20 billion.
    b. increases by more than $20 billion.
    c. increases by less than $20 billion.
    d. is unaffected.

21. The government purchases multiplier is 2. Starting from potential GDP, if government purchases increase by $10 billion, in the short run, GDP

    a. increases by $20 billion.
    b. increases by more than $20 billion.
    c. increases by less than $20 billion.
    d. is unaffected.

22. The government purchases multiplier is 2. Starting from potential GDP, if government purchases increase by $10 billion and potential real GDP does not change, in the long run, GDP

    a. increases by $20 billion.
    b. increases by more than $20 billion.
    c. increases by less than $20 billion.
    d. is unaffected.

Fiscal Policy and Aggregate Supply

23. An increase in income taxes

    a. increases the quantity of labor employed.
    b. has no effect on the quantity of labor employed.
    c. increases the quantity of capital.
    d. decreases the quantity of capital.

24. Supply-side economists contend that a change in income taxes has

    a. a large effect on aggregate demand.
    b. a large effect on aggregate supply.
    c. no effect on aggregate demand.
    d. no effect on aggregate supply.

25. If supply-side economists are correct, an income tax cut has a _____ effect on GDP and a _____ effect on the price level than otherwise.

    a. larger; larger
    b. larger; smaller
    c. smaller; larger
    d. smaller; smaller

Short Answer Problems

1. Igor has been elected finance minister of Translyvania. Igor's first action is to hire a crack team of economists and to tell them that he wants a prediction of Translyvania's equilibrium expenditure for next year.

    a. The economists compiled their estimates of next year's real GDP, consumption expenditure, investment, and government purchases. These

TABLE 13.2

Expenditure in Translyvania

Real GDP	Consumption expenditure	Investment	Government purchases
1.0	0.8	0.3	0.1
1.5	1.2	0.3	0.1
2.0	1.6	0.3	0.1
2.5	2.0	0.3	0.1
3.0	2.4	0.3	0.1
3.5	2.8	0.3	0.1

TABLE 13.3

Aggregate Planned Expenditure in Translyvania

Real GDP (billions of 1992 stakes)	Aggregate planned expenditure (billions of 1992 stakes)
1.0	____
1.5	____
2.0	
2.5	____
3.0	____
3.5	____

data are shown in Table 13.2 in billions of 1992 stakes. (The "stake" is the unit of currency in Translyvania.) Translyvania has no foreign trade. Unfortunately, these economists lost their calculator and need your help to complete Table 13.3, which lists real GDP and aggregate expenditure.

b. Based on Table 13.3, what is equilibrium expenditure in Translyvania predicted to be?

2. After receiving the prediction for equilibrium expenditure in problem 1, Igor realizes that to be reelected, equilibrium expenditure needs to be 1 billion stakes higher. Igor once more summons his economists and tells them that he wants three policy proposals to raise equilibrium expenditure by $1 billion stakes. Recall that Translyvania has no foreign trade. All taxes and transfers are lump-sum. Further, the economists have found their calculator so they will be able to make recommendations.

a. What is the MPC in Translyvania?

b. What is the government purchases multiplier?

c. What is the lump-sum tax multiplier?

d. What is the lump-sum transfer multiplier?

e. Assuming that the price level does not change, what are three policies that can raise equilibrium expenditure by 1 billion stakes?

3. In problem 2, Igor had threatened his economists with exile to Canada if they erred, so he's satisfied that their proposals were accurate. Yet Igor finds to his dismay that after implementing one of the proposals, next year's equilibrium expenditure actually increased by less than 1 billion stakes. As Igor is sent packing back to his night job, he is wondering what went wrong. Explain to Igor why equilibrium expenditure increased by less than 1 billion stakes.

4. Briefly explain whether the following events will shift the AE curve and/or the AD curve. (For each case, assume that other variables remain constant.)

a. A rise in the price level.

b. A rise in expected future profits for businesses.

c. A tax cut.

d. An increase in government purchases.

5. Because of expectations that future profits will be lower, investment decreases.

a. Without any action on the part of the government, what is the effect on real GDP and the price level?

b. What fiscal policies might the government undertake to offset the effect of the decline in investment on real GDP and the price level?

6. Explain why the multiplier effect on real GDP from an expansionary fiscal policy is smaller when the aggregate supply curve is considered. If the expansionary policy has no incentive effects on aggregate supply, what is the long-run multiplier for real GDP?

7. The economy's aggregate expenditure curve is AE_0, as shown in Figure 13.4 (on the next page), and the aggregate demand curve is AD_0, as shown in Figure 13.5 (on the next page). The MPC is 0.75. The government lowers its lump-sum taxes by $2 billion. There are no income taxes and no imports.

a. In Figures 13.4 and 13.5 show the initial effect of the decrease in lump-sum taxes on the aggregate expenditure curve and aggregate demand curve. Draw your answers for the period of time over which the price level does not change.

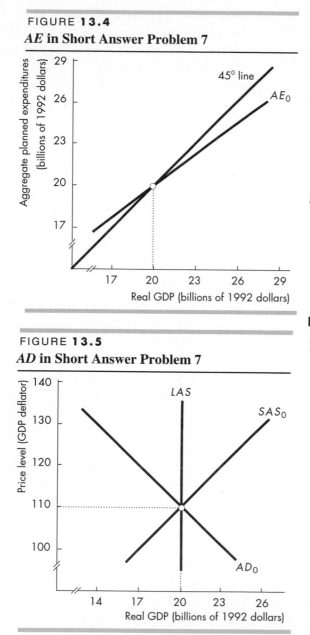

FIGURE **13.4**

AE **in Short Answer Problem 7**

FIGURE **13.5**

AD **in Short Answer Problem 7**

b. From Figure 13.5, what is the short-run effect on the price level and real GDP? Label the short equilibrium a. Without drawing it, explain the effect of the change in the price level on the *AE* curve in Figure 13.4.

c. In the long run, ignoring any incentive effects on the supply side, what is the effect on the price level? On real GDP? Without drawing it, what happens to the *AE* curve in Figure 13.4? Does the *AD* curve in Figure 13.5 shift as a result of the change in the price level?

8. Suppose that an income tax cut has incentive effects that increase aggregate supply. How does the effect on the price level and real GDP of this policy compare to that from a policy that has no supply side effects? What is the long-run multiplier when the policy has incentive effects?

■ You're the Teacher

1. "These multipliers are kind of cool, and I've studied them until I really understand them. But there's just one point that still puzzles me: How come the government can't use its fiscal policy to eliminate fluctuations in GDP caused by changes in investment? I'd think that this policy would be a good one for the government to follow!" Your friend has certainly hit on a good point; now what's a good answer?

Answers

■ True/False Answers

The Federal Budget

1. **F** The President proposes the budget to Congress. The Council of Economic Advisers helps the President by monitoring the economy and offering policy proposals.

2. **F** A budget deficit occurs when tax revenues fall short of government expenditures.

3. **F** The federal government ran a budget deficit each year from 1970 to 1997.

4. **T** The U.S. is one of a few governments that has a budget surplus rather than a budget deficit.

Fiscal Policy Multipliers

5. **T** The question presents the explanation of the multiplier.

6. **T** The larger the *MPC*, the more people change their consumption expenditure when their disposable income changes, which increases the government purchases multiplier.

7. **T** The government purchases multiplier is

$$\frac{1}{(1-MPC)}, \text{ or, in this case, } \frac{1}{(1-0.8)} = 5.0.$$

8. **T** The lump-sum tax multiplier is $-\dfrac{MPC}{(1-MPC)}$,

or $-\dfrac{0.8}{(1-0.8)} = -4.0.$

9. **F** An income tax reduces the magnitude of all multipliers.

10. **F** *Income* taxes are automatic stabilizers, falling when income decreases and rising when income increases.

11. **F** The structural surplus is the value of the surplus at full employment, but it is not necessarily equal to zero at full employment.

Fiscal Policy Multipliers and the Price Level

12. **F** An increase in taxes decreases consumption expenditure and so this policy is a contractionary one.

13. **T** An increase in government purchases shifts the *AD* curve rightward and, in the short run, increases real GDP.

Fiscal Policy and Aggregate Supply

14. **F** An increase in income taxes reduces the incentives to supply resources, thereby *decreasing* potential GDP.

15. **F** Supply-siders think that income taxes have a large effect on aggregate supply.

■ Multiple Choice Answers

The Federal Budget

1. **b** Personal income taxes are the largest source of revenue, closely followed by social insurance taxes.

2. **a** Transfer payments are by far the largest component of federal government spending.

3. **c** The government's deficit equals its expenditures, $1.5 trillion, minus its taxes, $1.3 trillion.

4. **d** The federal government's public debt is near $4 trillion, which dwarfs federal government expenditures (approximately $1.6 trillion), tax revenues (about $1.5 trillion), and the current surplus (about $100 billion).

5. **a** Unlike most other nations which have government budget deficits, the United States has a government budget surplus.

Fiscal Policy Multipliers

6. **b** Aggregate expenditure equals the sum of consumption expenditure, investment, and government purchases, so when real GDP equals $7.0 trillion, aggregate expenditure equals $3.5 trillion + $1.0 trillion + $1.0 trillion, or $5.5 trillion.

7. **d** Equilibrium expenditure is the level of aggregate expenditure that equals real GDP. In Table 13.1 when real GDP is $4.0 trillion, aggregate expenditure also equals $4.0 trillion, the level of equilibrium expenditure.

8. **c** The *MPC* equals $(\Delta C)/(\Delta YD)$. With no taxes, real GDP equals disposable income. Hence, when real GDP changes by $1 trillion, consumption expenditure changes by $0.5 trillion, so the *MPC* equals ($0.5 trillion)/($1 trillion), or 0.50.

9. **b** The government purchases multiplier is

$\dfrac{1}{(1-MPC)}$. Hence, with an *MPC* of 0.50, the

government purchases multiplier is 2.0.

10. **b** The equilibrium level of expenditures has increased by an amount equal to the government purchases multiplier times the change in government purchases, or (2)($1 trillion), so the new equilibrium is $2 trillion more than the old. Alternatively, $1 trillion can be added to the schedule of government purchases. Then the equilibrium expenditure becomes $6 trillion, the level of real GDP that creates a (new) level of aggregate expenditure equal to real GDP.

11. **a** The government purchases multiplier is $\dfrac{1}{(1-MPC)}$. When $MPC = 0.9$, this multiplier is $\dfrac{1}{(1-0.9)} = 10.0$.

12. **c** The answer to question 11 shows how to calculate the government spending multiplier. Comparing the answers to questions 11 and 12 shows that the smaller the MPC is, the smaller the government purchases multiplier.

13. **c** The lump-sum tax multiplier is $-\dfrac{MPC}{(1-MPC)}$, which equals $-\dfrac{0.9}{(1-0.9)} = -9.0$.

14. **c** The magnitude of the government purchases multiplier exceeds the magnitude of the lump-sum tax and transfer multipliers, so the increase in government expenditures shifts the AD curve the farthest rightward.

15. **c** Induced taxes, such as income taxes, reduce the change in disposable income that results from a change in GDP. Income taxes thus decrease the amount of induced consumption that results from a change in GDP. Hence income taxes reduce the size of the government purchases multiplier.

16. **d** When the marginal propensity to consume increases, each change in disposable income induces a larger change in consumption expenditure, so the multiplier is larger.

17. **c** During a recession, tax revenues fall and transfer expenditures rise, thereby decreasing the budget surplus.

18. **d** A structural deficit is a deficit that exists even when the economy is producing at its full employment.

Fiscal Policy Multipliers and the Price Level

19. **c** Both decreasing government expenditures and increasing tax revenues decrease aggregate demand.

20. **a** When the price level is constant, equilibrium expenditure (or, equivalently, the shift in the AD curve) equals the government purchases multiplier times the change in government purchases, or (2)($10 billion) = $20 billion.

21. **c** The AD curve shifts rightward by $20 billion and, in the short run, the equilibrium point moves along the upward sloping SAS curve so that the equilibrium level of real GDP increases by less than $20 billion.

22. **d** In the long run, the equilibrium returns to potential GDP, so, if potential GDP does not change, neither does real GDP.

Fiscal Policy and Aggregate Supply

23. **d** Increasing income taxes decreases the quantity of capital and the employment of labor, and thereby decreases potential GDP.

24. **b** Economists recognize that a change in income taxes affects aggregate supply, but most think that the effect is smaller than that proposed by supply-side economists.

25. **b** By increasing aggregate supply, the price level rises by less and GDP increases by more than otherwise.

■ Answers to Short Answer Problems

TABLE **13.4**

Aggregate Planned Expenditure in Translyvania

Real GDP (billions of 1992 stakes)	Aggregate planned expenditure (billions of 1992 stakes)
1.0	1.2
1.5	1.6
2.0	2.0
2.5	2.4
3.0	2.8
3.5	3.2

1. a. Table 13.4 shows the aggregate expenditure schedule in Transylvania. The schedule is computed by adding consumption expenditure, investment, and government purchases. For example, when real GDP is 3.5 billion stakes,

aggregate expenditure equals the sum of consumption expenditure (2.8 billion stakes) investment (0.3 billion stakes) and government purchases (0.1 billion stakes), 3.2 billion stakes.

b. Equilibrium expenditure is 2.0 billion stakes, because that level of real GDP equals aggregate expenditure.

2. a. The MPC equals $(\Delta C)/(\Delta YD)$, where Δ means "change in," C is consumption, and YD is disposable income. Because all taxes are lump sum, any change in income translates into an equal change in disposable income; that is, a 0.5 billion stake increase in GDP means that disposable income in Translyvania also increases by 0.5 billion stakes because taxes do not change. In the data, the MPC is the same at all levels of GDP. Hence the MPC between real GDP of 2.0 billion stakes and 2.5 billion stakes is equal to $(2.0 - 1.6)/(2.5 - 2.0) = (0.4)/(0.5) = 0.80$.

b. The government purchases multiplier is
$$\frac{1}{(1-MPC)} = \frac{1}{(1-0.8)} = 5.0.$$

c. The lump-sum tax multiplier is
$$-\frac{MPC}{(1-MPC)} = -\frac{0.8}{(1-0.8)} = -4.0.$$

d. The lump-sum transfer payments multiplier is
$$\frac{MPC}{(1-MPC)} = \frac{0.8}{(1-0.8)} = 4.0.$$

e. Three policies that can increase equilibrium expenditure by 1 billion stakes are to:

Increase government purchases by 0.2 billion stakes: The government purchases multiplier shows that this policy increases equilibrium expenditure by $(5.0)(0.2 \text{ billion}) = 1.0$ billion stakes.

Decrease lump-sum taxes by 0.25 billion stakes: The lump-sum tax multiplier shows that this policy increases equilibrium expenditure by $(-4.0)(-0.25 \text{ billion}) = 1.0$ billion stakes.

Increase lump-sum transfers by 0.25 billion stakes: The lump-sum tax transfers multiplier shows that this policy increases equilibrium expenditure by $(4.0)(0.25 \text{ billion}) = 1.0$ billion stakes.

3. Igor's error was relying upon the assumption that the price level does not change. All three of the policies described in problem 2 increase aggregate demand, thereby shifting the AD curve rightward. If the AD curve shifts rightward, the price level rises,

which lowers aggregate expenditure. In other words, Igor's policy shifted the AD curve rightward by 1.0 billion stakes, but the upward slope of the SAS curve implies that the equilibrium increase in real GDP — and hence the ultimate increase in equilibrium expenditure — is less than 1.0 billion stakes.

4. In general, any change that changes autonomous spending shifts the AE curve. Therefore all the changes shift the AE curve. And any change in autonomous expenditure not caused by a change in the price level shifts the AD curve. Therefore part (a) involves a movement along an AD curve and parts (b) through (d) create shifts in the AD curve.

a. The rise in the price level shifts the AE curve downward and creates a movement upward along the AD curve.

b. The rise in future expected profits increases investment, thereby shifting the AE curve upward and the AD curve rightward.

c. The decrease in taxes increases consumption expenditure and shifts the AE curve upward and the AD curve rightward.

d. An increase in government purchases shifts the AE curve upward and the AD curve rightward.

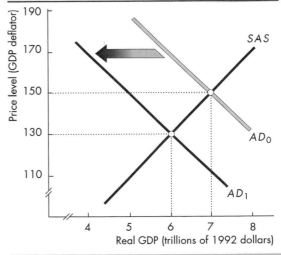

FIGURE **13.6**

Decrease in Aggregate Demand

5. a. The decrease in investment shifts the AD curve leftward, as shown in Figure 13.6. As a result, in the short run, real GDP decreases (in the figure, from \$7 to \$6 trillion) and the price level falls (in the figure, from 150 to 130).

b. In general terms, the government can undertake expansionary fiscal policy to offset the decline in investment. Such a policy would include increasing government purchases and/or government transfer payments, and/or lowering taxes. All of these actions shift the *AD* curve rightward.

6. The multiplier indicates the size of the change in real GDP relative to the size of an initial change in autonomous expenditure. The *AS* curve shows that the price level rises as aggregate demand increases. The rise in the price level lowers aggregate expenditure, leading to a smaller increase in real GDP than if the price level had remained constant. Indeed, in the long run, the economy returns to potential GDP. In the absence of effects on aggregate supply, the long-run multiplier is zero.

7. a. Figures 13.7 and 13.8 show the effect of the tax reduction on the *AE* and *AD* curves.

   In Figure 13.7 the $2 billion reduction in taxes raises disposable income by $2 billion. From the $2 billion increase, with the *MPC* equal to 0.75, (0.75)($2 billion), or $1.5 billion goes to increased consumption expenditure. Hence, as shown in Figure 13.7, the *AE* curve shifts upward (by $1.5 billion, the length of the small arrow) to AE_1. Figure 13.7 also shows that the increase in equilibrium expenditure is $6 billion, from $20 billion to $26 billion. Alternatively, the $6 billion increase in equilibrium expenditure equals the reduction in taxes, –$2 billion, multiplied by the lump-sum tax multiplier,

   $$-\frac{MPC}{(1-MPC)}, \text{ which is } -3.0.$$

   In Figure 13.8, the aggregate demand curve shifts rightward, from AD_0 to AD_1. As shown by the length of the double-headed arrow, the extent of the rightward shift is $6 billion, the increase in equilibrium expenditure.

   b. In Figure 13.8 the short-run equilibrium point is at *a*. The price level rises to 120, and real GDP increases to $23 billion. The increase in the price level from 110 to 120 decreases aggregate expenditure; that is, in Figure 13.7 the *AE* curve shifts downward from AE_1. Indeed, the *AE* curve shifts downward enough so that the equilibrium level of expenditure is $23 billion, the same level as real GDP in Figure 13.8.

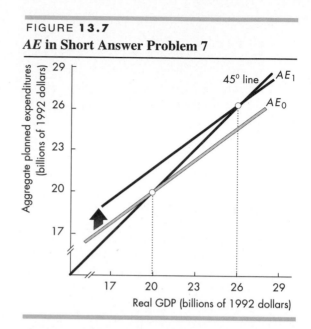

FIGURE **13.7**

AE in Short Answer Problem 7

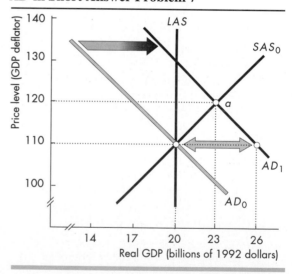

FIGURE **13.8**

AD in Short Answer Problem 7

c. In the long run, the economy returns to potential GDP. Hence, in the absence of any supply-side effects, as money wages rise and the *SAS* curve shifts leftward, the equilibrium eventually returns to the point where the *AD* curve crosses the *LAS* curve (point *b* in Figure 13.9 on the next page). In the long run, the price level equals 130 and real GDP equals $20 billion. The rise in the price level decreases aggregate expenditure, so the *AE* curve in Figure 13.7 continues to shift downward. Eventually, when the long-run

FIGURE **13.9**

The Long Run in Short Answer Problem 7

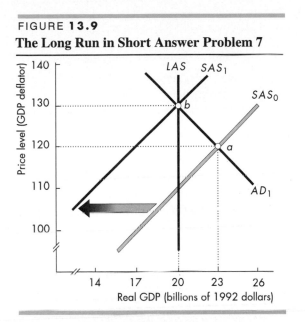

■ You're the Teacher

1. "Yeah, I think the multipliers are cool, too. I didn't have the foggiest idea about them until we started studying them in class.

"But look, let's talk about your question. I think the main deal here is that it's hard for the government to respond in a timely and appropriate fashion. One problem is the time required for the government to enact fiscal policy changes. As the text points out, the federal budget is proposed by the President early in the year and the final spending bills are signed by the President late in the year. It's got to take time to change the federal budget. I bet that one reason for the delay is the complexity of the budget and the budgeting process. Another reason is politics. You know how *we* disagree about who to vote for! Well, the political parties may agree that, say, tax cuts are needed, but disagree on precisely which taxes should be cut and by how much.

"Also, it can't be real easy to know what is the correct policy to pursue. Some observers may think that we are headed for a recession, and others believe that a strong expansion will occur over the next year or so. And who knows what potential GDP really is? I mean, it's a great concept for us to learn because it helps us get a lot of ideas straight, but in the real world it's got to be hard to know what potential GDP equals. So again I can see political parties squabbling — one thinking that we are below potential GDP and need expansionary policies to lower unemployment and the other thinking we are above potential GDP and need contractionary policies to limit inflation.

"So, I guess there are probably some reasons why the government doesn't use its fiscal policy to eliminate business cycles even though it would be great if the government could do so."

equilibrium is reached, the AE curve has shifted all the way back to AE_0. At this point, equilibrium expenditure is the same as initially, $20 billion, which also equals the level of potential GDP. The AD curve does *not* shift as a result of the higher price level.

8. If the tax cut has incentive effects that increase aggregate supply, the AD curve shifts rightward and so do the short-run and long-run aggregate supply curves. Because the aggregate supply curves shift rightward, the rise in the price level from a tax cut is less and the increase in real GDP is greater than when the aggregate supply curves do not shift. Indeed, if potential real GDP increases as a result of the incentive effects, the long-run multiplier exceeds zero because real GDP increases in the long run.

Chapter Quiz

1. A balanced budget occurs when the government's
   a. expenditures exceeds its tax revenues.
   b. expenditures equal its tax revenues.
   c. expenditures are less than its tax revenues.
   d. total debt equals zero.

2. As a fraction of GDP, the public debt
   a. has risen each year for the past 50 years.
   b. has fallen each year for the past 50 years.
   c. generally fell until about 1974 and today is higher than it was in 1974.
   d. generally rose until about 1974 and today is lower than it was in 1974.

3. Which of the following is <u>NOT</u> a problem with using fiscal policy to stabilize the economy?
   a. Implementing fiscal policy may be slow.
   b. At times it is difficult to determine if GDP is greater than or less than potential GDP.
   c. The government spending multiplier can change randomly.
   d. None of the above because they are all problems with using fiscal policy.

4. If the *MPC* is 0.80, the government spending multiplier equals
   a. 10.0.
   b. 8.0.
   c. 5.0.
   d. None of the above.

5. If the *MPC* is 0.80, the lump-sum tax multiplier equals
   a. −8.0.
   b. −5.0.
   c. −4.0.
   d. None of the above.

6. The presence of income taxes _____ the magnitude of the government spending multiplier and _____ the magnitude of the lump-sum tax multiplier.
   a. increases; increases
   b. increases; does not change
   c. decreases; does not change
   d. decreases; decreases

7. Income taxes and transfer payments
   a. act like economic shock absorbers and stabilize fluctuations in income.
   b. prevent the economy from moving toward equilibrium.
   c. increase the impact of changes in investment and net exports.
   d. increase the economy's growth rate.

8. In an economy with no income taxes nor imports, if the government increases its purchases by $10 billion and increases its lump-sum taxes by $10 billion, the *AD* curve
   a. shifts rightward by $100 billion.
   b. shifts rightward by $10 billion.
   c. shifts leftward by $90 billion.
   d. does not shift.

9. By definition, a discretionary fiscal policy
   a. requires action by the Congress.
   b. is triggered by the state of the economy.
   c. must involve changes in government purchases.
   d. must involve changes in taxes

10. Supply-side economists believe that a tax cut
    a. definitely increases GDP.
    b. definitely does not change GDP.
    c. definitely decreases GDP.
    d. maybe changes GDP, but the direction of the change is uncertain and depends on the size of the *MPC*.

The answers for this Chapter Quiz are on page 328

14 MONEY*

What is Money?

Money is anything generally acceptable as a **means of payment**, a method of settling a debt. It has three functions:

♦ Medium of exchange — money is accepted in exchange for goods and services. Without money, **barter** (exchanging one good for another) would be necessary.

♦ Unit of account — prices are measured in units of money.

♦ Store of value — money is exchangeable at a later date.

Money consists of currency plus deposits at banks and other financial institutions. The two major measures of money in the United States are:

♦ **M1** — currency outside of banks plus travelers checks plus checking deposits.

♦ **M2** — M1 plus saving and time deposits and money market mutual funds.

Liquidity means that an asset can be quickly converted into a means of payment with no loss of value. The assets in M2 that are not directly a means of payment are very liquid.

The deposits at financial institutions are money, but the checks transferring these deposits from one person to another are not money. Credit cards are not money; they are a way to get an instant loan.

Financial Intermediaries

A **financial intermediary** is a firm that takes deposits and then uses the deposits to make loans. Financial intermediaries include commercial banks, **thrift institutions** (savings and loan associations, savings banks, and credit unions) and money market mutual funds.

A balance sheet shows that a business's assets equal its liabilities plus its net worth. Banks divide their assets into two broad components:

♦ **Reserves** — cash in the bank's vault plus its deposits at Federal Reserve banks.

♦ Loans — liquid assets, investment securities, and loans.

Financial intermediaries provide four main economic services:

♦ Create liquidity — bank deposits are highly liquid, that is, easily convertible into money.

♦ Minimize cost of obtaining funds — borrowing from one bank is cheaper than borrowing from a variety of lenders.

♦ Minimize cost of monitoring borrowers — financial intermediaries specialize in monitoring borrowers.

♦ Pool risk — intermediaries reduce risk by making loans to many borrowers.

Financial Regulation, Deregulation, and Innovation

Financial intermediaries face two types of regulation:

♦ Deposit insurance — deposits at most intermediaries are insured by a federal agency.

---

* This is Chapter 31 in *Economics*.

♦ Balance sheet rules — intermediaries often face capital requirements, reserve requirements, deposit rules, and lending rules.

In the 1980s and 1990s, financial intermediaries were largely deregulated.

Developing new ways of borrowing and lending is called **financial innovation**. Financial innovation was rapid in the 1980s and 1990s. The extent of financial innovation depends on the economic environment, technology, and regulation.

■ How Banks Create Money

Banks (more generally, depository institutions) create money by making loans. The process by which they create money involves:

♦ The **reserve ratio** — the fraction of a bank's total deposits held as reserves.

♦ The **required reserve ratio** — the ratio of deposits to reserves that banks are required by regulation to have.

♦ **Excess reserves** — actual reserves minus required reserves.

If actual reserves exceed desired reserves, banks loan the excess reserves, increasing borrowers' deposits. This lending creates new deposits, that is, new money.

The extra lending creates a **deposit multiplier**, the amount by which a change in bank reserves is multiplied to give the change in bank deposits. A formula for the deposit multiplier is

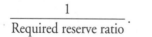

$$\frac{1}{\text{Required reserve ratio}}.$$

In the United States, the actual deposit multiplier is smaller than that calculated from the formula because banks hold excess reserves and people hold currency outside of banks.

■ Money, Real GDP, and the Price Level

♦ An increase in the quantity of money shifts the *AD* curve rightward, as illustrated in Figure 14.1.

♦ In the short run, the economy moves along the short-run aggregate supply curve SAS_0, the price level rises (to 120), and real GDP increases (to \$8 trillion).

♦ Money wage rates increase in the long run, and the short-run aggregate supply curve shifts from SAS_0

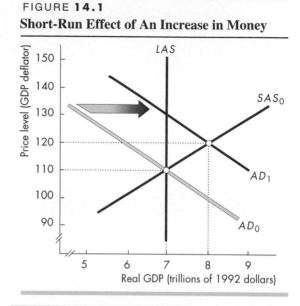

FIGURE **14.1**
Short-Run Effect of An Increase in Money

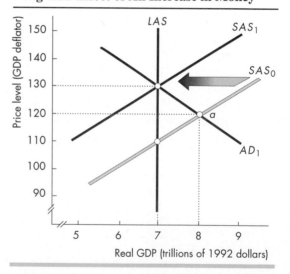

FIGURE **14.2**
Long-Run Effect of An Increase in Money

to SAS_1. This situation is illustrated in Figure 14.2, wherein real GDP returns to potential real GDP (\$7 trillion) and the price level rises still higher (to 130).

The **quantity theory of money** holds that, in the long run, an increase in the quantity of money causes an equal percentage increase in the price level.

The **velocity of circulation** is the average number of times a dollar of money is used in a year to buy goods and services in GDP. In terms of a formula, velocity of circulation, V, is given by $V = \dfrac{PY}{M}$, where P is the price level, Y is real GDP, and M is the quantity of money. The **equation of exchange** shows that the quantity of money multiplied by velocity equals (nominal) GDP, or

$$MV = PY.$$

The quantity theory makes two assumptions:

♦ Velocity is not affected by the quantity of money.

♦ Potential GDP is not affected by the quantity of money.

With these assumptions, the equation of exchange shows that $\dfrac{\Delta P}{P} = \dfrac{\Delta M}{M}$, which means that the percentage increase in the price level (the inflation rate) equals the percentage increase in the quantity of money.

The *AD/AS* model also predicts that, in the long run, an increase in the quantity of money causes the same percentage increase in the price level. However, the one-to-one relationship does not hold in the short run. Historical evidence from the United States and international evidence both show that in the long run, the money growth rate and inflation rate are positively related and that the year-to-year relationship is weaker.

Helpful Hints

1. **MONEY VERSUS INCOME :** Ordinary use of the term "money" does not make the important distinction that is made in economics. We often talk about income as the amount of money we earn, say, in a year. But this informal use of the term is not what is meant by the word in economics. In economics, "money" means M1 or M2. Informally, when we talk about the money we earn, actually we are talking about our "income." Keep this distinction in mind, that money means M1 or M2.

2. **THE DEPOSIT MULTIPLIER PROCESS :** One of the most important concepts presented in this chapter is the deposit multiplier process by which banks create money. There are two fundamental facts that allow banks to create money.

   First, one of the liabilities of banks is money: checking deposits. Banks create money by creating new checking deposits. Second, banks hold fractional reserves. That is, when a bank receives a de-

posit, it holds only part of it as reserves and loans the rest. When that loan is spent, part of the proceeds will likely be deposited in another bank, creating a new deposit (money).

The deposit multiplier process follows from this last point: Banks make loans when they receive new deposits; these loans are spent; and the proceeds are deposited in another bank, creating a new deposit. The process then repeats itself, adding more deposits (but in progressively smaller amounts) in each round. Practice going through examples until the process becomes clear to you.

3. **USE OF THE QUANTITY THEORY :** Analysts often use the quantity theory to help shape their thinking about the future inflation rate by using the rate of growth of the money supply to help predict whether the inflation rate is likely to rise or fall. Even though the relationship between the growth rate of the money supply and the inflation rate may not be one-to-one as suggested by the quantity theory, nonetheless the correlation between higher monetary growth rates and higher inflation rates is quite substantial.

You, too, can use this relationship to help predict the inflation rate. For instance, if you note that the growth rate of the money supply has jumped sharply higher, you should expect higher inflation rates to occur. Because interest rates tend to increase with the inflation rate, you would want to obtain loans with fixed (nominal) interest rates as quickly as possible. Conversely, you would not want to enter into long-term savings contracts with fixed interest rates.

Questions

■ True/False/Uncertain and Explain

What is Money?

1. Money is anything that is generally acceptable as a means of payment.

2. Checking accounts in banks are part of the M1 money supply.

3. The amount of M2 money is more than the amount of M1 money.

4. In modern economies, credit cards are money.

Financial Intermediaries

5. A bank's reserves consist of cash in its vault plus its deposits at Federal Reserve banks.

6. A savings and loan association is an example of a financial intermediary.

7. Financial intermediaries help minimize the cost of borrowing funds.

Financial Regulation, Deregulation, and Innovation

8. Financial intermediaries face regulations about their balance sheets.

9. Financial intermediaries have become more regulated in the 1980s and 1990s.

How Banks Create Money

10. If a depositor withdraws currency from a bank, that bank's total reserves decrease.

11. A bank helps create money by loaning excess reserves.

12. The deposit multiplier is equal to 1 divided by the required reserve ratio.

Money, Real GDP, and the Price Level

13. Since 1960, M2 velocity has increased more rapidly than M1 velocity has.

14. The quantity theory of money predicts that inflation is caused by rapidly growing velocity.

15. Almost surely, high inflation rates cause high monetary growth rates.

■ **Multiple Choice**

What is Money?

1. Which of the following is <u>NOT</u> a function of money?
   a. Medium of exchange
   b. Barter
   c. Unit of account
   d. Store of value

2. The fact that prices are quoted in terms of money reflects money's role as a
   a. cause of inflation.
   b. medium of exchange.
   c. unit of account.
   d. store of value.

3. Which is the largest component of the M1 money supply?
   a. Currency
   b. Traveler's checks
   c. Checking deposits
   d. Savings deposits

4. U.S. currency is
   a. part of M1 only.
   b. part of M2 only.
   c. part of M1 and M2.
   d. part of neither M1 nor M2.

5. Which of the following is a component of M2 but not of M1?
   a. Currency
   b. Checking accounts at banks
   c. Traveler's checks
   d. Savings accounts at banks

6. Which of the following is money?
   a. A check written for $200.
   b. A $200 checking deposit at a bank.
   c. A credit card with a $200 line of credit.
   d. All of the above.

Financial Intermediaries

7. Which of the following is a liability of a bank?
   a. Reserves
   b. Loans
   c. Securities
   d. Deposits

8. A bank's total reserves equal its
   a. total cash in its vaults.
   b. total cash in its vaults plus its deposits at the Federal Reserve banks.
   c. total cash in its vaults plus its total liquid deposits.
   d. total cash in its vaults plus its total liquid deposits plus its total deposits at the Federal Reserve banks.

9. Financial intermediaries do all the following <u>EXCEPT</u>
   a. minimize the cost of obtaining funds.
   b. create liquidity.
   c. pool risks.
   d. create required reserve ratios.

Financial Regulation, Deregulation, and Innovation

10. Which of the following statements is <u>FALSE</u>?
    a. Capital requirements determine the minimum amount of owners' funds that must be put into a financial intermediary.
    b. Banks are legally allowed to operate in only one state.
    c. Most deposits of financial intermediaries are insured by the Federal Deposit Insurance Corporation.
    d. A financial intermediary may be required to set aside a fraction of its deposits as reserves.

11. Of the following, which may create an incentive for financial innovation?
    a. Technological change
    b. Deregulation
    c. Low inflation and interest rates
    d. Liquidity creation.

How Banks Create Money

Table 14.1 presents the balance sheet of the "Fly By Night (FBN) Bank," one bank amongst the thousands in the United States. Use it for the next four questions.

TABLE 14.1

Balance Sheet of FBN Bank

Assets (millions of dollars)		Liabilities (millions of dollars)	
Reserves	$ 300	Deposits	$1,000
Loans	700		
Total	1,000	Total	1,000

12. If the required reserve ratio on deposits is 10 percent, the FBN Bank has required reserves of
    a. $300 million.
    b. $200 million.
    c. $100 million.
    d. $0.

13. If the required reserve ratio on deposits is 10 percent, the FBN Bank has excess reserves of
    a. $300 million.
    b. $200 million.
    c. $100 million.
    d. $0.

14. If the required reserve ratio on its deposits is 10 percent, then the FBN Bank can loan out a maximum of
    a. $300 million.
    b. $200 million.
    c. $100 million.
    d. $0.

15. After FBN Bank loans the maximum amount it can, the loans have been spent, and the proceeds deposited in other banks, FBN Bank has excess reserves of
    a. $300 million.
    b. $200 million.
    c. $100 million.
    d. $0.

16. When a bank helps create money, it does so by
    a. selling some of its investment securities.
    b. increasing its reserves.
    c. lending its excess reserves.
    d. printing more checks.

17. Suppose that banks hold no excess reserves and that people keep no currency outside the banking system. If the required reserve ratio is 10 percent, the deposit multiplier equals
    a. 10.0.
    b. 1.0.
    c. 0.1.
    d. none of the above.

Money, Real GDP, and the Price Level

18. In the short run, an increase in the quantity of money shifts the
    a. *AD* curve rightward.
    b. *SAS* curve rightward.
    c. *LAS* curve rightward.
    d. The answer is none of the above because an increase in the money supply does not shift the *AD*, *SAS*, or *LAS* curves.

19. In the short run, an increase in the quantity of money _____ the price level and _____ real GDP.
    a. raises; increases
    b. raises; does not change
    c. raises; decreases
    d. does not change; increases

20. In the long run, an increase in the money supply
____ the price level and ____ real GDP.

a. raises; increases
b. raises; does not change
c. raises; decreases
d. does not change; increases

21. The quantity theory of money is the idea that

a. the quantity of money is determined by banks.
b. the quantity of money serves as a good indicator of how well money functions as a store of value.
c. the quantity of money determines real GDP.
d. in the long run, an increase in the quantity of money causes an equal percentage increase in the price level.

22. The equation of exchange is

a. $MV = PY$.
b. $MP = VY$.
c. $MY = PV$.
d. $M/Y = PV$.

23. Velocity equals

a. YM/P.
b. PM/Y.
c. PY/M.
d. M/PY.

24. Nominal GDP, PY, is $6 trillion. The quantity of money is $2 trillion. Velocity is

a. 6 trillion.
b. 12.
c. 3.
d. 2.

25. Historical evidence shows that higher monetary growth rates are associated with

a. higher inflation rates.
b. no change in the inflation rate.
c. lower inflation rates.
d. higher growth rates of real GDP.

■ Short Answer Problems

1. Explain why credit cards are not money. Be sure to mention the role actually played by credit cards, that is, what they allow their owner to do.

2. Briefly explain how banks create money.

TABLE **14.2**

Initial Balance Sheet of HH Bank

Assets		Liabilities	
Reserves	$ 200	Deposits	$2,000
Loans	1,800		
Total	2,000	Total	2,000

TABLE **14.3**

HH Bank Balance Sheet

Assets		Liabilities	
Reserves	____	Deposits	____
Loans	____		
Total	____	Total	____

3. While digging in a local cemetery, Igor uncovers a musty chest containing $1,000 in currency. He rushes to deposit all $1,000 in his checking account at his bank, the "Helping Hand (HH) Bank." Before Igor made his deposit, the bank's balance sheet was as shown in Table 14.2.

a. Complete Table 14.3 to show the balance sheet of the HH Bank after Igor has deposited his $1,000 in currency but before any other actions have been taken.

b. The required reserve ratio is 10 percent. After Igor's deposit, what are the bank's actual reserves, required reserves, and excess reserves? What is the maximum amount that the bank can loan?

c. The bank loans the maximum it can to Drac, who wants to start a business. Complete Table 14.4 to show the balance sheet of the HH Bank after the loan has been made and Drac has withdrawn and spent the proceeds of the loan.

TABLE **14.4**

HH Bank Final Balance Sheet

Assets		Liabilities	
Reserves	____	Deposits	____
Loans	____		
Total	____	Total	____

TABLE **14.5**

A&L Bank Balance Sheet

Assets		Liabilities	
Reserves	___	Deposits	___
Loans	___		
Total	___	Total	___

TABLE **14.6**

A&L Bank Final Balance Sheet

Assets		Liabilities	
Reserves	___	Deposits	___
Loans	___		
Total	___	Total	___

4. Continuing problem 3, Drac uses the loan to buy supplies from Ula. Ula deposits the proceeds in her bank, the "Arm and Leg (A&L) Bank". Before the deposit, A&L Bank's balance sheet was the same as HH Bank's balance sheet shown in Table 14.2.

   a. In Table 14.5 show A&L Bank's balance sheet after Ula has deposited her funds.

   b. The required reserve ratio remains 10 percent. What are A&L Bank's actual reserves, required reserves, and excess reserves? What is the maximum amount that the bank can loan?

   c. The A&L Bank loans the maximum possible to Frank, who wants to repair his laboratory. After Frank has withdrawn his loan from the A&L Bank, complete Table 14.6 to show A&L Bank's final balance sheet.

TABLE **14.7**

HU Bank Balance Sheet

Assets		Liabilities	
Reserves	___	Deposits	___
Loans	___		
Total	___	Total	___

5. Continuing problem 4, Frank uses his loan to buy building material from Dr. Stein. Dr. Stein deposits the funds in the "Heads Up (HU) Bank". The HU Bank's balance sheet before Dr. Stein's deposit was the same as HH Bank's, shown in Table 14.2.

   a. In Table 14.7, show HU Bank's balance sheet after Dr. Stein has made the deposit.

   b. The required reserve ratio is still 10 percent. What are the bank's actual reserves, required reserves, and excess reserves? What is the maximum that the bank can loan?

TABLE **14.8**

Summary of Deposit Changes

Bank	Increase in deposit
Helping Hand	___
Arm and Leg	___
Heads Up	___

6. Table 14.8 collects the results from problems 3, 4, and 5 by showing the change in deposits at each of the three banks.

   a. Complete Table 14.8.

   b. At the end of the three rounds, by how much have deposits increased?

   c. What does the deposit multiplier equal? As the process of loaning and loaning again continues, what is the ultimate change in deposits?

FIGURE **14.3**

Effects of an Increase in the Money Supply

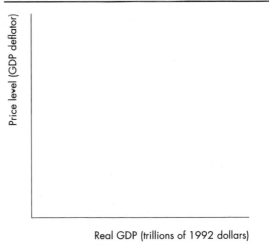

Real GDP (trillions of 1992 dollars)

7. In Figure 14.3 show how an increase in the money supply affects the price level and quantity of real GDP in the short run and the long run. Label the short-run equilibrium point *a* and the long-run equilibrium point *b*.

TABLE **14.9**

Quantity Theory

Money supply, M (billions of dollars)	Velocity, V	Price level, P	Real GDP, Y (trillions of dollars)
____	6	1.00	$6
$500	6	____	3
550	6	____	3
605	6	____	3

8. a. Complete Table 14.9.

    b. Between the second and third rows of Table 14.9, what is the percentage increase in the money supply? What is the inflation rate?

    c. Between the third and fourth rows of Table 14.9, what is the percentage increase in the money supply? What is the inflation rate?

    d. Comment on your answers to parts (b) and (c).

■ **You're the Teacher**

1. "I couldn't believe what I read in this chapter! Do you mean to tell me that when I deposit $100 in my checking account at my bank that the bank doesn't keep all $100? That should be illegal! I mean, how can this work? How can I ever get my money back?" Your friend has just discovered "fractional reserve banking." Your friend also has some strong opinions. Making sure to stay out of arm's reach — or at least, fist's reach — explain to your friend how fractional reserve banking works and how the $100 deposited in the bank will be there, awaiting your friend's withdrawal.

Answers

■ True/False Answers

What is Money?

1. **T** This is the general definition of money.
2. **T** Checking accounts are the largest component of M1.
3. **T** M2 equals M1 plus additional "savings" assets, so the amount of M2 must be larger than the amount of M1.
4. **F** Credit cards give their owners the ability to obtain a loan but are not money.

Financial Intermediaries

5. **T** This is the definition of bank reserves.
6. **T** Intermediaries, such as savings and loan associations, stand between — are intermediate to — savers and borrowers.
7. **T** Minimizing the cost of borrowing is a service provided by financial intermediaries.

Financial Regulation, Deregulation, and Innovation

8. **T** Balance sheet regulations include capital requirements, reserve requirements, deposit rules, and lending rules.
9. **F** Just the reverse: Financial intermediaries have become less regulated in recent years.

How Banks Create Money

10. **T** Part of the bank's reserves is its currency, so if a depositor withdraws currency, the bank loses reserves.
11. **T** The process of loaning (and then reloaning) excess reserves is the method by which banks create money.
12. **T** The deposit multiplier formula shows that an increase in the required reserve ratio reduces the size of the deposit multiplier.

Money, Real GDP, and the Price Level

13. **F** Since 1960, M2 velocity has not changed much, while M1 velocity has increased.
14. **F** The quantity theory predicts that inflation is caused by growth in the quantity of money.
15. **F** Almost surely, the reverse is true: High monetary growth rates cause high inflation rates.

■ Multiple Choice Answers

What is Money?

1. **b** Money eliminates the use of barter.
2. **c** A unit of account is the factor in which prices are given (e.g., 3 dollars per slice of pizza).
3. **c** Checking accounts comprise approximately 75 percent of M1.
4. **c** U.S. currency is part of M1 and M1 is part of M2.
5. **d** Savings accounts are not part of M1.
6. **b** Checking accounts, not the checks themselves, represent money. In addition, credit cards simply allow loans to be made quickly and are not money.

Financial Intermediaries

7. **d** Deposits are liabilities to banks because someone else owns the deposit, and, upon his or her request, the bank must return the funds to the owner.
8. **b** Answer (b) is the definition of a bank's reserves.
9. **d** Required reserve ratios are set by regulators, in particular, by the Federal Reserve.

Financial Regulation, Deregulation, and Innovation

10. **b** The Riegle-Neal Interstate Banking and Branching Efficiency Act was passed in 1994 and allows banks to operate in more than one state.
11. **a** Technological change can help foster innovation.

How Banks Create Money

12. **c** Required reserves equal 10 percent of deposits, or (0.10)($1,000 million) = $100 million.
13. **b** Excess reserves equal actual reserves ($300 million) minus required reserves ($100 million).
14. **b** A bank can loan all its excess reserves.
15. **d** After FBN Bank loaned all its excess reserves, it no longer has any excess reserves.
16. **c** By lending its reserves, the loan becomes deposits in another bank and, because deposits are part of the money supply, the loan has helped create money.
17. **a** The deposit multiplier equals 1/(required reserve ratio) or, in this case, 1/(0.10) = 10.0.

Money, Real GDP, and the Price Level

18. **a** An increase in the quantity of money increases aggregate demand, thereby shifting the *AD* curve rightward.

19. **a** The *AD* curve shifts rightward so in the short run the economy moves along an (upward sloping) *SAS* curve to a higher price level and increased real GDP.

20. **b** In the long run, the *AD* curve shifts rightward and the economy moves along its (vertical) *LAS* curve, so the price level rises but real GDP does not change.

21. **d** The quantity theory traces the cause of inflation to monetary growth.

22. **a** This answer is the definition of the equation of exchange.

23. **c** The equation of exchange, *MV = PY*, can be rearranged to show that velocity equals *PY/M*.

24. **c** The answer to this question can be calculated using the formula in the previous question. Intuitively, velocity equals the number of times an average dollar is spent on goods and services in GDP.

25. **a** Historical evidence thus supports the general thrust of the quantity theory.

■ Answers to Short Answer Problems

1. A credit card is not money, but a mechanism for borrowing money, which must be repaid. In other words, a credit card is merely a mechanism for rapidly arranging a loan. Repayment of the loan takes place when the credit card bill is repaid with money.

2. Banks create money by making new loans. When the loans are spent, the person receiving the funds deposits much of it in a bank, which is new money.

3. a. Table 14.10 shows the balance sheet at the Helping Hand (HH) Bank after Igor deposited his $1,000 in currency. The deposits increase by $1,000 and so do the bank's reserves. The bank's loans do not (initially) change.

   b. The HH Bank has $1,200 in total reserves; with the required reserve ratio of 10 percent, it must keep (0.1)($3,000), or $300 in required reserves; its excess reserves equal the difference between actual and required reserves, or $900. The maximum the bank can loan is its amount of excess reserves, or $900.

TABLE 14.10
HH Bank Balance Sheet

Assets		Liabilities	
Reserves	$1,200	Deposits	$3,000
Loans	1,800		
Total	3,000	Total	3,000

TABLE 14.11
HH Bank Final Balance Sheet

Assets		Liabilities	
Reserves	$ 300	Deposits	$3,000
Loans	2,700		
Total	3,000	Total	3,000

c. After HH Bank loans $900 and the $900 is spent, its new balance sheet is as presented in Table 14.11. Loans increase by $900, to $2,700. When Drac spends the proceeds of the loan, HH Bank's reserves fall by $900. Perhaps the easiest way to visualize the effect on the reserves is to envision Drac withdrawing the $900 in currency and then spending the currency. In this case, HH Bank's reserves immediately fall by $900. Alternatively, if Drac spends his loan by writing a check, HH Bank's reserves will fall when the check is cashed.

TABLE 14.12
A&L Bank Balance Sheet

Assets		Liabilities	
Reserves	$1,100	Deposits	$2,900
Loans	1,800		
Total	2,900	Total	2,900

4. a. Ula receives $900 from Drac. After Ula deposits the $900 in her deposit account at Arm and Leg (A&L) Bank, its balance sheet is as shown in Table 14.12. In this balance sheet, A&L Bank's deposits increase by $900 to $2,900 and its reserves also increase by $900, to $1,100.

   b. The A&L Bank's total reserves are $1,100; its required reserves are (0.10)($2,900), or $290; and its excess reserves are the difference between

TABLE **14.13**

A&L Bank Final Balance Sheet

Assets (millions of dollars)		Liabilities (millions of dollars)	
Reserves	$ 290	Deposits	$2,900
Loans	2,610		
Total	2,900	Total	2,900

actual reserves and required reserves, or $810. Thus A&L Bank can loan a maximum of $810.

  c. After Frank has spent his loan, A&L Bank's balance sheet is as shown in Table 14.13.

TABLE **14.14**

HU Bank Balance Sheet

Assets		Liabilities	
Reserves	$1,010	Deposits	$2,810
Loans	1,800		
Total	2,810	Total	2,810

5. a. After Dr. Stein deposits in the bank the $810 received from Frank, the balance sheet of Heads Up (HU) Bank is as shown in Table 14.14.

  b. The HU Bank has total reserves of $1,010; required reserves of (0.10)($2,810), or $281; and excess reserves of $1,010 − $281, or $729. The maximum loan that HU Bank can make is $729, the amount of its excess reserves.

TABLE **14.15**

Summary of Deposit Changes

Bank	Increase in deposit
Helping Hand	$1,000
Arm and Leg	900
Heads Up	810

6. a. Table 14.15 completes Table 14.8, showing the change in deposits at the three banks in problems 3, 4, and 5.

  b. At the end of the three rounds, deposits have increased by a total of $2,710.

  c. The deposit multiplier equals 1/(required reserve ratio). The required reserve ratio is 10 percent,

so the deposit multiplier equals 1/(0.10), or 10.0.

The ultimate change in deposits equals (deposit multiplier)(change in reserves). The change in reserves is Igor's initial $1,000 of currency. Thus deposits ultimately change by (10.0)($1,000), or $10,000.

FIGURE **14.4**

Effects of An Increase in the Money Supply

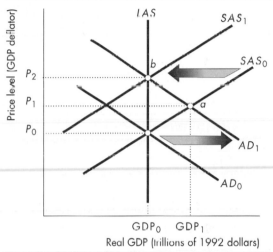

7. Figure 14.4 shows the short-run and long-run impacts of an increase in the money supply. The increase in the money supply shifts the *AD* curve rightward. In the short run, money wages do not change and the economy moves along SAS_0 to the new equilibrium point *a*. The price level rises (to P_1 from P_0), and real GDP increases (to GDP_1 from GDP_0). However, as time passes, money wages start to rise. This change shifts the *SAS* curve leftward until eventually the economy reaches its long-run equilibrium at point *b*. In the long run, the price level is (much) higher than initially (P_2 versus P_0), and the level of real GDP has returned to the initial level, potential GDP of GDP_0.

8. a. Table 14.16 (on the next page) completes Table 14.9. All the answers were calculated with the equation of exchange, $MV = PY$. For the first row, to calculate *M*, the equation of exchange was rearranged as $M = PY/V$ so that *M* equals $1,000 billion ($1 trillion). For the following rows, the equation of exchange was rearranged to show that $MV/Y = P$.

TABLE **14.16**

Quantity Theory

Money supply, M (billions of dollars)	Velocity, V	Price level, P	Real GDP, Y (trillions of dollars)
$1000	6	1.00	$6
500	6	1.00	3
550	6	1.10	3
605	6	1.21	3

b. Going from the second to the third row, the money supply grows by 10 percent, and (with constant velocity and real GDP) the price level grows by 10 percent, that is, the inflation rate is 10 percent.

c. Moving from the third to the fourth row shows that another 10 percent increase in the money supply results in another 10 percent growth in the price level.

d. The last three rows illustrate the quantity theory of money conclusion: A 10 percent increase in the money supply raises the price level by 10 percent.

■ **You're the Teacher**

1. "Look, don't worry. It's not illegal and you'll get your money back! Here's the deal: What you're talking about is called 'fractional reserve banking.' Banks have been doing this for a long time. Seventy or so years ago, some risk *was* involved in this procedure, but today it's safe. In fact, if it weren't for fractional banking and the banks lending out part of your deposits, they wouldn't be able to pay you interest on your account. Instead, they'd charge you for the cost of storing your money!

"Anyway, you're right that banks don't set aside the $100 you deposit with them. They do keep a fraction of the $100 in reserves but, just as you said, the majority of the deposit is loaned to people who want to borrow. But this isn't a problem for you when you want to get your cash back. On any day, banks have thousands of people who deposit cash and also thousands who want to withdraw it. And, on most days these amounts roughly balance. That is, the cash deposited will about equal the cash withdrawn. So, although you won't get back the exact same $100 you deposited with your bank, you will get back $100 that other customers have deposited.

"As I said, this process doesn't give a problem today. But I remember from my U.S. history class about the bank runs during the Great Depression. In those days, bank deposits weren't insured like they are today. Back then, if a bank failed, its depositors might lose all their deposits. So if depositors thought a bank was likely to fail, all the depositors would run to the bank to withdraw their money. When this sort of thing happened, the bank wouldn't have enough cash on hand because the amount deposited that day was a lot less than the amount that people wanted to withdraw. And because the bank didn't have the cash on hand, the bank would fail. Bank runs were a self-fulfilling prophecy: If people thought that a bank might fail, they would make a run on the bank, and the bank would fail. Today, the deposit insurance our book talks about prevents bank panics because depositors know that, even if their bank fails, they will get back their deposits. Today fractional reserve banking is safe, so you probably ought to worry more about your grade in our economics class than losing your money in the bank."

Chapter Quiz

1. The most direct way that money replaces barter is through money's use as a
   a. medium of exchange.
   b. store of value.
   c. unit of account.
   d. trade mechanism.

2. Juan takes $100 dollars from his checking account and transfers it to his saving account. As a result, M1 _____ and M2 _____.
   a. increases; increases
   b. decreases; does not change
   c. does not change; increases
   d. does not change; does not change

3. Juan takes $100 dollars from his wallet and deposits it in his checking account. As a result, M1 _____ and M2 _____.
   a. increases; increases
   b. increases; does not change
   c. does not change; increases
   d. does not change; does not change

4. Financial intermediaries create liquidity. Financial intermediaries pool risk.
   a. Both sentences are true.
   b. The first sentence is true and the second sentence is false.
   c. The first sentence is false and the second sentence is true.
   d. Both sentences are false.

5. The smaller the required reserve ratio,
   a. the larger the deposit multiplier.
   b. the smaller the deposit multiplier.
   c. the smaller M1 is relative to M2.
   d. None of the above.

6. Reserve requirements are rules setting
   a. the minimum percentage of deposits that must be kept as reserves.
   b. the minimum amount of the owners' wealth that must be invested in the financial intermediary.
   c. what sort of loans the financial intermediary can make.
   d. the types of assets a bank can purchase.

7. A bank's reserves include the _____ and the _____.
   a. deposits it has accepted; cash it keeps in its vault
   b. liquid loans it has made; deposits it keeps at the Federal Reserve
   c. liquid securities it has purchased; liquid loans it has made
   d. deposits it keeps at the Federal Reserve; cash it keeps in its vault

8. If the required reserve ratio is 20 percent, the deposit multiplier is
   a. 20.0.
   b. 10.0.
   c. 5.0.
   d. None of the above

9. Using data from different countries, it is apparent that a high growth rate of the money supply is associated with a
   a. high growth rate of real GDP.
   b. high inflation rate.
   c. low growth rate of velocity.
   d. low unemployment rates.

10. Velocity grows at 2 percent, the money supply at 6 percent and real GDP at 3 percent. Hence the inflation rate equals
    a. 11 percent.
    b. 7 percent.
    c. 5 percent.
    d. 3 percent.

The answers for this Chapter Quiz are on page 328

Chapter 15 MONETARY POLICY*

Key Concepts

■ The Federal Reserve System

The **Federal Reserve System** (or the Fed) is the central bank for the United States. A **central bank**, a bank for banks, regulates financial firms. The Fed is responsible for monetary policy. **Monetary policy** adjusts the quantity of money in circulation.

Three key players in the Fed are:

♦ The **Board of Governors** — seven members appointed by the President and confirmed by the Senate for 14-year terms. This group oversees operations of the Fed.

♦ The Federal Reserve Banks —12 regional banks, each of which has a president.

♦ The **Federal Open Market Committee** (FOMC) — the Fed's main policy-making group. Voting members are the Board of Governors, the president of the Federal Reserve Bank of New York and, on a rotating basis, presidents of four other regional Federal Reserve banks.

The Fed has three policy tools:

♦ **Required reserve ratio** — the Fed sets the required reserve ratio, the minimum percentage that depository institutions must hold as reserves.

♦ **Discount rate** — the interest rate the Fed charges banks which borrow reserves from it.

♦ **Open market operation** — the purchase or sale of government securities by the Fed.

The major assets on the Fed's balance sheet are gold and foreign exchange, U.S. government securities, and loans to banks. The major liabilities are Federal Reserve notes in circulation (currency) and banks' deposits (reserves). The **monetary base** is the sum of Federal Reserve notes, coins, and banks' deposits at the Fed.

■ Controlling the Money Supply

To increase the money supply, the Fed's three policy tools are used as follows:

♦ *Changes in the required reserve ratio:* A decrease in the required reserve ratio increases banks' lending and thus raises the money supply.

♦ *Changes in the discount rate:* A decrease in the discount rate raises banks' borrowing from the Fed, thereby increasing their reserves and hence increasing the money supply.

♦ *Open market operations:* When the Fed buys government securities, banks' reserves increase. (These reserves rise whether the Fed buys securities from a bank or from a member of the public.) The rise in banks' reserves causes them to increase their lending, so the money supply increases.

To decrease the money supply, the Fed reverses these policy actions, increasing the required reserve ratio, raising the discount rate, and selling government securities.

The **money multiplier** is the amount by which a change in the monetary base is multiplied to determine the change in the quantity of money. The money multiplier is greater than 1.0.

---

* This is Chapter 32 in *Economics*.

■ The Demand for Money

Four factors influence the demand for money:

♦ *The price level* — An increase in the price level increases the *nominal* demand for money.

♦ *The interest rate* — An increase in the interest rate raises the opportunity cost of holding money and decreases the quantity of real money demanded.

♦ *Real GDP* — An increase in real GDP increases the demand for money.

♦ *Financial innovation* — Innovations that lower the cost of switching between money and other assets decrease the demand for money.

FIGURE **15.1**
Money Demand

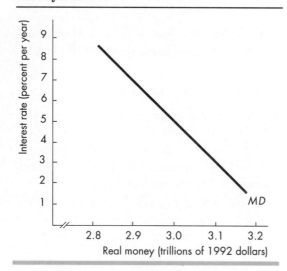

Figure 15.1 shows the demand for money curve (*MD*). The *real* quantity of money equals the nominal quantity divided by the price level. Changes in the interest rate create movements along the demand curve; changes in the other relevant factors shift the demand curve.

■ Interest Rate Determination

An interest rate is the percentage yield on a financial security; other variables being the same, the higher the price of the security, the lower is the interest rate.

The interest rate is determined by the equilibrium in the market for money, as illustrated in Figure 15.2. The real supply of money is $3.0 trillion, so the supply curve of money is *MS*. (The Fed sets the supply of

FIGURE **15.2**
The Equilibrium Interest Rate

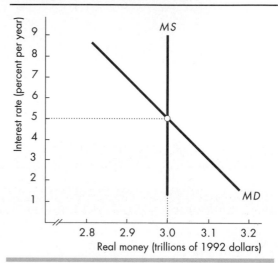

money.) The demand curve for money is *MD*, and the equilibrium interest rate is 5 percent.

♦ If the Fed increases the supply of money, the supply curve of money shifts rightward and the equilibrium interest rate falls.

♦ If the Fed decreases the supply of money, the supply curve of money shifts leftward and the equilibrium interest rate rises.

■ Monetary Policy

The data show that interest rates generally fall when the supply of money increases and generally rise when the supply of money decreases.

Paul Volcker: In 1979, when Volcker became chairman of the Fed, the inflation rate was high. The Fed slowed the growth rate of the money supply, interest rates rose, the inflation rate fell, and the economy went into a recession.

Alan Greenspan: Greenspan took over as chairman in 1987. From 1988 to 1990, the Fed slowed the monetary growth rate and forced interest rates higher. In 1990 a recession occurred, and the Fed responded by cutting interest rates and expanding the money supply. For the past years, the Fed has nudged along the expansion that started in 1992.

Economic agents can profit by predicting actions of the Fed, so interest rates may change before the money supply changes.

The Fed's actions ripple through the economy. Higher interest rates:

♦ Decrease consumption expenditure

♦ Decrease investment

♦ Increase the foreign exchange rate, which then decreases net exports

Data show that when the Fed raises short-term interest rates, generally after a year the growth of real GDP slows.

Helpful Hints

1. **OPEN MARKET OPERATIONS :** This activity is by far the Fed's most important policy tool. Open market operations occur every business day. The term "open market operation" refers to the Fed's purchase or sale of government securities. There is nothing mysterious about this process: All the Fed does is buy or sell government securities. Indeed, you could do the same thing; that is, you could go to a broker and buy, say, $5,000 of government securities or, if you already owned some, you could go to the broker and sell $5,000 of the securities you own.

However, even aside from the differences in scale, the economic impact of your purchase of a government security is different from that of the Fed's purchase. In particular, when you pay for your purchase, you use money that already exists in the economy. The total amount of money in the economy does not change. But when the Fed pays for a purchase of $5,000 of securities, the Fed introduces new money into the economy. If the Fed buys $5,000 of securities from a broker, it gives the broker a check drawn on the Fed. The broker presents the check to his or her bank. The bank increases the broker's account for $5,000 and then presents the check to the Fed. In turn, the Fed increases the bank's checking account at the Fed for $5,000. Because funds kept in the bank's checking account at the Fed are reserves for the bank, the bank gains reserves. You know that when banks gain reserves, they loan the excess reserves, causing the money supply to expand by a multiple of the initial increase in reserves. Thus the Fed's purchase of $5,000 of government securities will have a multiplier effect on the money supply.

2. **DOES AN OPEN MARKET OPERATION INCREASE OR DECREASE THE MONEY SUPPLY ?** Trying to keep track of whether an open market purchase of government securities by the Fed increases or decreases the money supply can be confusing. One way to remember their effects is to think of the following: "When the Fed buys government securities, it sells money; when the Fed sells government securities, it buys money." By associating the purchase of securities with the sale of money and vice versa, keeping track of whether a purchase or sale of government securities increases the money supply becomes straightforward.

Questions

■ True/False/Uncertain and Explain

The Federal Reserve System

1. The presidents of each of the Federal Reserve banks are nominated by the President of the United States and confirmed by the Senate.

2. As voting members, the FOMC comprises all the presidents of the Federal Reserve regional banks, the chairman of the Federal Reserve, and, on a rotating basis, four of the members of the Board of Governors.

3. The discount rate is the interest rate banks charge the Fed on the reserves the Fed borrows from banks.

Controlling the Money Supply

4. If the Fed lowers the required reserve ratio, the supply of money increases.

5. A purchase of government securities by the Fed reduces the supply of money.

6. If the Fed sells securities to a commercial bank, the money supply decreases but if the Fed sells securities to the public, the money supply does not change.

7. The higher the required reserve ratio, the larger the money multiplier.

The Demand for Money

8. The price level is the opportunity cost of holding money.

9. An increase in real GDP increases the demand for money.

Interest Rate Determination

10. If the Fed buys government securities, it lowers the interest rate.

11. If both the supply and demand for money increase, the interest rate definitely rises.

Monetary Policy

12. The data show that an increase in the supply of money lowers interest rates.

13. When a recession occurred in 1990, the Fed responded by raising interest rates.

14. An increase in the quantity of money increases aggregate demand.

15. Higher interest rates affect consumption expenditure, investment, and net exports.

■ Multiple Choice

The Federal Reserve System

1. Which group makes decisions about the course of the nation's monetary policy?
   a. The Fed's Board of Governors
   b. The FOMC
   c. The presidents of the Fed's regional banks
   d. The President and the Senate

2. The discount rate is the interest rate
   a. the Fed charges when it loans reserves to banks.
   b. banks charge their finest loan customers.
   c. banks pay on savings accounts.
   d. the Fed pays on reserves held by banks.

3. The purchase of $1 billion of government securities by the Fed is an example of
   a. the discount rate being affected.
   b. the multiple contraction of the money supply.
   c. an open market operation.
   d. a change in the required reserve ratio.

4. Of the following, which is a liability of the Federal Reserve?
   a. Government securities
   b. Loans to banks
   c. Banks' deposits at the Fed
   d. Foreign exchange

5. The monetary base equals the sum of
   a. checking accounts, coins, and currency.
   b. M1 plus savings accounts.
   c. banks' reserves plus checking accounts.
   d. Federal Reserve notes, coins, and banks' deposits at the Federal Reserve.

Controlling the Money Supply

6. Which of the following increases the money supply?
   a. A Fed purchase of government securities.
   b. An increase in the discount rate.
   c. An increase in the required reserve ratio.
   d. None of the above.

7. An increase in the required reserve ratio _____ the reserves that banks must hold and _____ the money supply.
   a. increases; increases
   b. increases; decreases
   c. decreases; increases
   d. decreases; decreases

8. The tool the Fed uses most often to change the money supply is
   a. changes in the discount rate.
   b. changes in the required reserve ratio.
   c. open market operations.
   d. changes in the demand for money.

9. An open market purchase of government securities by the Fed will
   a. increase the Fed's assets, but not increase its liabilities.
   b. increase its assets and its liabilities by the same amount.
   c. increase both its assets and its liabilities, but increase the assets by more.
   d. increase both its assets and its liabilities, but increase the liabilities by more.

10. Which of the following changes the size of the monetary base?
    a. A bank withdraws currency from the deposits it keeps at the Fed.
    b. A bank uses some of its reserves to make a loan.
    c. The Fed buys government securities from a bank.
    d. A firm deposits currency in its checking account at its bank.

11. If the money multiplier is 2.5, a $10 billion increase in the monetary base raises the quantity of money by
    a. $25 billion.
    b. $10 billion.
    c. $4.0 billion.
    d. $2.5 billion.

12. Which of the following actions best describes the correct sequence of events following an expansionary open market operation?
    a. The Fed sells government securities, which lowers bank reserves, leading to a drop in lending, leading to a reduction in the money supply.
    b. The Fed sells government securities, which lowers bank reserves, leading to a drop in lending, leading to an increase in the money supply.
    c. The Fed sells government securities, which lowers bank reserves, leading to an increase in lending, leading to an increase in the money supply.
    d. The Fed buys government securities, which increases bank reserves, leading to an rise in lending, leading to an increase in the money supply.

13. The monetary expansion process from an open market operation continues until
    a. required reserves are eliminated.
    b. the Fed eliminates required reserves.
    c. the discount rate is lower than other interest rates.
    d. excess reserves are eliminated.

The Demand for Money

14. An increase in _____ decreases the quantity of real money people want to hold.
    a. the price level
    b. real GDP
    c. the interest rate
    d. the supply of money

15. Which of the following does <u>NOT</u> directly shift the demand for money curve?
    a. A change in GDP.
    b. A change in the money supply.
    c. Financial innovation.
    d. None of the above because they all directly shift the demand for money curve.

16. Since 1976, in the United States the demand curve for M2 money has shifted
    a. rightward in almost all years.
    b. leftward in almost all years.
    c. rightward in most years until 1989 and then leftward in some years and rightward in others.
    d. leftward in most years until 1989 and then rightward in some years and leftward in others.

Interest Rate Determination

17. If the price of an asset rises and the amount paid on the asset does not change, what happens to the interest rate on the asset?
    a. It rises
    b. It does not change
    c. It falls
    d. The premise of the question is wrong because changes in the price of an asset have nothing to do with the interest rate paid on the asset.

18. Taken by itself, an increase in the supply of money
    a. raises the interest rate.
    b. does not change the interest rate.
    c. lowers the interest rate.
    d. perhaps raises or perhaps lowers the interest rate, depending on whether the demand curve for money has a negative or a positive slope.

19. If real GDP increases, the demand curve for real money will shift
    a. leftward and the interest rate will rise.
    b. leftward and the interest rate will fall.
    c. rightward and the interest rate will rise.
    d. rightward and the interest rate will fall.

Monetary Policy

20. The Federal Reserve directly controls which interest rate?
    a. The Federal Reserve directly controls the 3-month Treasury bill rate.
    b. The Federal Reserve directly controls the 6-month commercial bill rate.
    c. The Federal Reserve directly controls the discount rate.
    d. The Federal Reserve directly controls the federal funds rate.

21. In general,
    a. short-term interest rates move together.
    b. different short-term interest rates go their own separate ways.
    c. changes in the federal funds interest rate are very different from changes in other short-term interest rates.
    d. the discount rate is the most crucial short-term interest rate.

22. In 1979, to reduce the inflation rate, the Fed ____ interest rates and ____ growth in the money supply.
    a. raised; increased
    b. raised; decreased
    c. lowered; decreased
    d. lowered; increased

23. Before both the recession in 1981 and in 1990, the Federal Reserve
    a. raised interest rates.
    b. did not change interest rates.
    c. lowered interest rates.
    d. did none of the above because the Fed did not do the same thing before these two recessions.

24. When do interest rates change before the Fed takes an action to change them?
    a. When the demand for money is steep.
    b. When the demand for money is shallow.
    c. When the economy is emerging from a recession.
    d. When people are able to forecast the Fed's future actions.

25. A rise in short-term interest rates compared to long-term interest rates is associated with a(n)
    a. immediate decline in the growth rate of real GDP.
    b. immediate increase in the growth rate of real GDP.
    c. decline next year in the growth rate of real GDP.
    d. increase next year in the growth rate of real GDP.

■ **Short Answer Problems**

1. a. How does an increase in the required reserve ratio affect banks' excess reserves? The money supply?
   b. How does an increase in the discount rate affect banks' excess reserves? The money supply?

2. How does a purchase of government securities from a bank by the Fed lead to an increase in the banks' reserves?

TABLE **15.1**
Balance Sheet of the Federal Reserve

Assets (billions of dollars)		Liabilities (billions of dollars)	
Gold and foreign exchange	$19	Federal Reserve notes	$380
U.S. government securities	380	Banks' deposits	40
Loans to banks	1		
Other assets	20		
Total assets	$420	Total	$420

3. The Federal Reserve System's balance sheet is presented in Table 15.1. Suppose that the Fed buys $10 billion of government securities from a large bank and pays for the securities by increasing the bank's deposits at the Fed. In Table 15.2, show the effect of the purchase on the Fed's balance sheet. What is the change in the monetary base? If the money multiplier is 2.8, what is the resulting change in the money supply?

TABLE **15.2**
Short Answer Question 3

Assets (billions of dollars)		Liabilities (billions of dollars)	
Gold and foreign exchange	$___	Federal Reserve notes	$___
U.S. government securities	___	Banks' deposits	___
Loans to banks	___		
Other assets	___		
Total assets	$___	Total	$___

4. Return to the original balance sheet in Table 15.1. Suppose that the Fed sells $10 billion of government securities to a large bank and takes payment by decreasing the bank's deposit. Use Table 15.3 on the next page) to show the effect of the sale on the Fed's balance sheet. What is the resulting change in the monetary base? If the money multiplier is 2.8, by how much does the money supply change?

TABLE 15.3
Short Answer Question 4

Assets (billions of dollars)		Liabilities (billions of dollars)	
Gold and foreign exchange	$ __	Federal Reserve notes	$ __
U.S. government securities	__	Banks' deposits	__
Loans to banks	__		
Other assets	__		
Total assets	$ __	Total	$ __

5. Return to the original balance sheet in Table 15.1. Suppose that a bank withdraws $10 billion in Federal Reserve notes from its deposits at the Fed. Use Table 15.4 to show the effects of this withdrawal on the Fed's balance sheet. By how much does the monetary base change? If the money multiplier is 2.8, by how much does the money supply change?

TABLE 15.4
Short Answer Question 5

Assets (billions of dollars)		Liabilities (billions of dollars)	
Gold and foreign exchange	$ __	Federal Reserve notes	$ __
U.S. government securities	__	Banks' deposits	__
Loans to banks	__		
Other assets	__		
Total assets	$ __	Total	$ __

6. According to your answers to problems 3, 4, and 5, which had the larger effect on the supply of money: The actions of the Federal Reserve or the actions of commercial banks? What does your answer imply for the ability of the Federal Reserve to control the nation's money supply?

7. Initially, the market for money is in equilibrium, as illustrated in Figure 15.3. Then, the Fed increases the quantity of money by $100 billion.
   a. Draw this increase in Figure 15.3.
   b. What was the initial equilibrium interest rate? What happens to the equilibrium interest rate?
   c. Explain, in general, the adjustment process to the new equilibrium interest rate.

FIGURE 15.3
Short Answer Problem 7

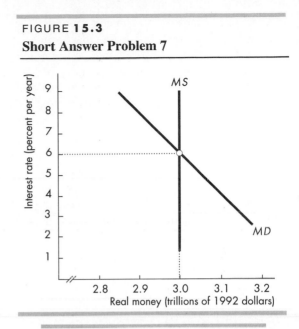

TABLE 15.5
The Demand For Money

Interest rate (percent per year)	Quantity of money demanded (billions of dollars)
3	$600
4	500
5	400
6	300

8. Table 15.5 gives data on the demand for money.
   a. Suppose that the equilibrium interest rate is 6 percent. What is the quantity of money?
   b. Suppose that the Fed wants to lower the interest rate to 4 percent. By how much must it change the money supply? If the money multiplier is 2.5, what magnitude of open market operation is necessary to lower the interest rate as desired? Is it an open market purchase or sale of government securities?

■ You're the Teacher

1. Your friend is talking: "Whenever the government runs a deficit and has to sell government securities, it automatically increases the money supply, right?" You realize that this comment actually is not "right"; in fact, it is wrong! Explain to your friend why it is wrong.

2. After your explanation, your friend responds, "Oh, okay, I see your point. But doesn't that mean, when the Treasury sells government securities, the Fed has to buy some?" Your friend's grasp of economics and the relationship between the Fed and Treasury is improving, but it's not yet perfect. This gives you the opportunity to help perfect it by answering this question.

3. Your friend has one last question about the Fed: "I can see a lot of what you're talking about. But there's one last thing that puzzles me. Let's see if I can lay it out. Now, the Fed buys a lot of government securities, and these securities all pay interest to the Fed. The Fed pays for them by printing Federal Reserve notes and increasing banks' reserves. But neither Federal Reserve notes nor banks' reserves pay any interest. So the Fed gets a lot of interest income and has no interest expense. It seems to me that this would be very profitable. Is it? And, if it is, what does the Fed do with the profit?" These are interesting questions; perhaps your friend thinks that the Fed spends its profits on the "mother of all parties" and would like to be invited. Tell your friend to forget about the party by explaining the profits and what happens to them.

Answers

■ True/False Answers

The Federal Reserve System

1. **F** The members of the Board of Governors are nominated by the President and confirmed by the Senate.

2. **F** As voting members, the FOMC comprises all the members of the Board of Governors, the president of the New York Federal Reserve Bank and, on a rotating basis, the presidents of four other regional Federal Reserve banks.

3. **F** The discount rate is the interest rate the Fed charges banks for the reserves that banks borrow from the Fed.

Controlling the Money Supply

4. **T** When the Fed lowers the required reserve ratio, banks have more excess reserves, which, through the process of loaning (and loaning again), increases the money supply.

5. **F** When the Fed purchases government securities, it pays for the purchases by increasing banks' reserves, which leads to an increase in the money supply.

6. **F** If the Fed sells securities to anyone, the money supply decreases.

7. **F** The higher the required reserve ratio, the less banks are able to loan from each deposit and so the smaller is the money multiplier.

The Demand for Money

8. **F** The interest rate is the opportunity cost of holding money.

9. **T** An increase in real GDP means that more transactions occur, which increases the demand for money.

Interest Rate Determination

10. **T** When the Fed buys government securities, the money supply increases which lowers the interest rate.

11. **F** If the increase in the demand for money is larger than the increase in the supply, the interest rate rises. On the other hand, if the increase in the supply exceeds the increase in demand, the interest rate falls.

Monetary Policy

12. **T** This fact is in accord with the theory.

13. **F** When the recession occurred, the Fed responded by increasing the money supply and lowering interest rates.

14. **T** Changing aggregate demand is part of the ripple effect of monetary policy.

15. **T** Higher interest rates ripple through the economy, thereby affecting economic activity in many sectors.

■ Multiple Choice Answers

The Federal Reserve System

1. **b** The FOMC is an important committee because it makes decisions about the nation's monetary policy.

2. **a** The discount rate is the interest rate that banks must pay when they borrow reserves from the Fed.

3. **c** An open market operation occurs whenever the Fed buys or sells government securities.

4. **c** Banks' deposits are a Fed liability because banks own the deposits, and the Fed must return the funds to a bank that wants to make a withdrawal from its deposit.

5. **d** Answer (d) defines the monetary base.

Controlling the Money Supply

6. **a** When the Fed buys government securities, the money supply increases; the other actions mentioned reduce the money supply.

7. **b** Because banks must hold more reserves, the increase in the required reserve ratio decreases the loans that banks make, which decreases the money supply.

8. **c** Open market operations are conducted every business day.

9. **b** An open market purchase of government securities increases the amount of government securities the Fed owns (a Fed asset) and also increases by the same amount either Federal Reserve notes or, more likely, banks' deposits at the Fed (both Fed liabilities).

10. **c** When buying a government security, the Fed pays for it either by increasing banks' deposits at the Fed or by issuing new Federal Reserve notes.

Both forms of payment increase the monetary base.

11. **a** The change in the quantity of money equals the money multiplier multiplied by the change in the monetary base or, in this case, (2.5)($10 billion) = $25 billion.

12. **d** Answers (a), (b), and (c) are incorrect because a Fed sale of government securities decreases the money supply. Answer (d) describes how the Fed's purchase of government securities increases the money supply.

13. **d** As long as banks have excess reserves, they increase their loans and hence increase the money supply.

The Demand for Money

14. **c** The interest rate is the opportunity cost of holding money, so an increase in the interest rate reduces the quantity of money demanded.

15. **b** Changes in the supply of money create movements along the demand for money curve; they do not shift the curve.

16. **c** Until about 1989, growth in real GDP generally increased the demand for M2. Since 1989, innovation has decreased the demand for M2 while GDP growth has increased it.

Interest Rate Determination

17. **c** There is an inverse relationship between the price of an asset and the interest rate paid on the asset.

18. **c** An increase in the money supply creates a surplus of money at the initial interest rate and, as people buy financial assets to be rid of the surplus, the price of financial assets rises, which drives down their interest rates.

19. **c** An increase in GDP increases the demand for money and, as the demand curve shifts rightward, the equilibrium interest rate rises.

Monetary Policy

20. **c** The Federal Reserve directly sets the discount rate, the interest rate banks pay when they borrow reserves from the Fed.

21. **a** Because short-term interest rates tend to move together, by affecting one short-term interest rate — the federal funds rate — the Fed can influence all short-term interest rates.

22. **b** By raising interest rates and slowing the growth rate of the money supply, the Fed restricted growth in aggregate demand and thereby reduced the inflation rate.

23. **a** Many observers think the Fed's actions helped create the recessions by raising interest rates.

24. **d** People forecast the Fed's policies because accurate forecasts can be profitable. For instance, if they can forecast when the Fed will lower the interest rate, they can buy securities that will rise in price when the interest rate falls and thereby make a quick profit.

25. **c** The rise in short-term interest rates reflects the Fed's policy of contracting the growth rate of the money supply, which ultimately has a contractionary effect on real GDP.

■ Answers to Short Answer Problems

1. a. An increase in the required reserve ratio means that for every dollar of deposits banks must keep more reserves either in their vault or at the Federal Reserve. As a result, banks' excess reserves — the reserves over and above the required reserves — fall because the total amount of required reserves increases. Because banks need to keep more reserves on hand for each dollar of deposits, they can make fewer loans. Then, with fewer loans, the supply of money decreases.

    b. An increase in the discount rate makes borrowing reserves from the Fed more expensive for banks. They respond by reducing the amount of reserves they borrow. As a result, their excess reserves decline. Then, similar to the answer in part (a), the decrease in banks' excess reserves leads to a decrease in the money supply.

2. An open market purchase of government securities by the Fed increases reserves by increasing one of its components, banks' deposits with the Federal Reserve. The process is direct: the Fed pays for the securities by increasing the bank's deposit at the Federal Reserve, which directly increases banks' reserves. Reserves expand by the amount of the open market purchase. (If the purchase is from the nonbank public, the Fed pays by writing checks on itself, which the sellers of the securities deposit in their banks. The banks increase the sellers' deposits at the bank, and, in turn, present the checks to the Federal Reserve. The Fed then increases the banks' deposits at the Fed.)

TABLE 15.6
Short Answer Question 3

Assets (billions of dollars)		Liabilities (billions of dollars)	
Gold and foreign exchange	$ 19	Federal Reserve notes	$380
U.S. government securities	390	Banks' deposits	50
Loans to banks	1		
Other assets	20		
Total assets	$430	Total	$430

3. Table 15.6 shows the effect of the Fed's purchase of $10 billion of government securities. Compared to the initial amounts shown in Table 15.1, government securities owned by the Fed have increased by $10 billion (from $380 to $390 billion) and the amount of banks' deposits at the Fed also has increased by $10 billion (from $40 to $50 billion). The monetary base equals the sum of Federal Reserve notes plus banks' deposits. Hence the monetary base has increased by $10 billion, from $420 billion initially to $430 billion after the purchase of government securities. If the money multiplier is 2.8, the money supply will increase by 2.8 times the change in the monetary base, or (2.8)($10 billion) = $28 billion.

TABLE 15.7
Short Answer Question 4

Assets (billions of dollars)		Liabilities (billions of dollars)	
Gold and foreign exchange	$ 19	Federal Reserve notes	$380
U.S. government securities	370	Banks' deposits	30
Loans to banks	1		
Other assets	20		
Total assets	$410	Total	$410

4. Table 15.7 shows the effect of the sale of $10 billion of government securities. The amount of government securities decreases by $10 billion, to $370 billion. As the bank pays for this purchase, the amount of its deposit — and hence the total amount of banks' deposits — decreases by $10 bil-

lion, to $30 billion. The monetary base, which equals the sum of Federal Reserve notes plus banks' deposits, falls from $420 to $410 billion, a decrease of $10 billion.

Finally, the change in the money supply equals the money multiplier, 2.8, times the change in the monetary base, –$10 billion, or (2.8)(–$10 billion) = –$28 billion; that is, the money supply declines by $28 billion.

TABLE 15.8
Short Answer Question 5

Assets (billions of dollars)		Liabilities (billions of dollars)	
Gold and foreign exchange	$ 19	Federal Reserve notes	$390
U.S. government securities	380	Banks' deposits	30
Loans to banks	1		
Other assets	20		
Total assets	$420	Total	$420

5. The effect of the banks' withdrawal of $10 billion from their deposits is presented in Table 15.8. The only effects are on the liability side of the balance sheet. The amount of Federal Reserve notes increases by $10 billion to $390 billion, and the amount of banks' deposits decreases by $10 billion to $30 billion. The monetary base equals the sum of Federal Reserve notes and banks' deposits. The key result in this question is that the effect on the monetary base is nil because the two changes offset each other. Thus neither the monetary base nor the money supply change.

6. Banks' withdrawals of currency from their deposits at the Fed has no effect on the supply of money. (Similarly, their deposit of Federal Reserve notes in their deposits at the Fed have no effect on the supply of money.)

   In general, setting aside when banks borrow reserves from the Fed (which is a relatively tiny amount of reserves), the quantity of money changes in reaction to the Federal Reserve's actions. Because the quantity of money changes whenever the Fed buys or sells government securities, the Fed can use the purchase or sale of government securities — which are open market operations — to control the nation's money supply.

FIGURE **15.4**
Short Answer Problem 7

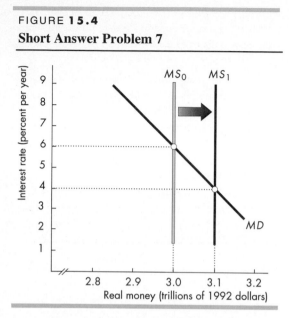

Real money (trillions of 1992 dollars)

7. a. Figure 15.4 shows the $100 billion increase in the quantity of money as the rightward shift from MS_0 to MS_1.
    b. The initial interest rate was 6 percent; after the increase in the money supply, the equilibrium interest rate fell, to 4 percent.
    c. An increase in the quantity of money means that, at the initial interest rate (6 percent), the quantity of money supplied is greater than the quantity of money demanded. Money holders want to reduce their money holdings and do so by buying financial assets. The increase in the demand for financial assets raises the price of financial assets and thus lowers their interest rate. As interest rates fall, the quantity of money demanded increases, which reduces the excess supply of money. This process continues until the interest rate has fallen sufficiently so that the quantity of money demanded is the same as the quantity of money supplied. The interest rate that sets the new quantity of money supplied equal to the quantity of money demanded is the (new) equilibrium interest rate.
8. a. When the interest rate is 6 percent, the quantity of money that people demand is $300 billion. Hence the quantity supplied also must be $300 billion.
    b. In order to reduce the interest rate to 4 percent, the Fed must increase the quantity of money

supplied to $500 billion. Thus the supply of money must increase by $200 billion. Because the money multiplier is 2.5, the monetary base must expand by $80 billion. (An additional $80 billion in the monetary base supply will cause a (2.5)($80 billion) = $200 billion increase in the money supply.) In order to increase the monetary base by $80 billion, the Fed must purchase $80 billion of government securities.

■ You're the Teacher

1. "Well, you're close but not quite right. Look, the deal is that you have to be careful to distinguish between the Fed and other branches of the government. Thus when the federal government runs a deficit, it's not the Fed that sells the government securities necessary to cover the deficit but the U.S. Treasury. And the Treasury sells the securities to anyone who will buy them, that is, to you, me, an insurance company, or whomever.

    "Since it was founded in 1913, the Federal Reserve has bought more than $450 billion of U.S. government securities. So, the Fed has a lot that it can sell if it wants. But, if you and I have bought some government securities in the past, we could sell them just like the Fed could sell the securities it holds. Of course, we probably can't sell as much as the Fed can.... Or, at least not until I hit the market with my Economics degree!

    "However, the amount isn't the key thing; it is that the Fed's securities are like ours in that they aren't newly issued securities. That is, unlike the Treasury selling *new* securities to finance the deficit, when the Fed sells its securities and when we sell ours, we aren't helping finance a new deficit. So when the federal government runs a deficit, it's the U.S. Treasury that sells securities to finance the deficit, not the Fed and not us!"

2. "Good question. There's no *legal* requirement that the Fed buy any of the securities. Indeed, as it happens, the Fed doesn't buy any directly from the Treasury; if the Fed wants to buy some of these newly issued securities, it lets a broker buy them from the Treasury, and then the Fed buys them from the broker. But, the fact that the Fed employs this sort of indirect purchase really shouldn't obscure the main issue: Whether it buys (indirectly) any of the Treasury's newly issued securities de-

pends mainly on what the Fed wants to do with its monetary policy. If the Fed wants to expand the money supply, it will buy some. If the Fed wants to contract the money supply, it won't buy any of the securities and, indeed, will sell some of its holdings.

"Now, I said that the Fed's decision depends *mainly* on its monetary policy. I talked with our teacher, and I learned that some economists think that the Fed will buy more securities when the government's deficit is larger because the Fed tries to help finance the government's spending.

"In this case, the money supply will expand more rapidly when the deficit is larger. But our teacher also said that this is an empirical question; that is, whether this more rapid expansion in the money supply actually occurs must be settled by careful testing of the data. And our teacher told me that this question is unresolved: some economists think

that the Fed does expand the money supply more rapidly when the deficit is larger; other economists disagree, claiming that the Fed is responding to other variables that influence its monetary policy."

3. "This is another great set of questions. Here are a couple of great answers! Sure, the Fed makes a lot of 'profit' and for exactly the reasons you stated: It earns a lot of interest income on its government securities and it pays no interest expense. But the Fed doesn't do anything wild and crazy with its profit: There's not a party to die for. Instead, the Fed pays its costs with its revenue. However, the amount of revenue easily covers those costs, so what happens to the extra? The Fed gives it back to the Treasury. That's right, the Fed sends the extra profit back to the U.S. Treasury so the Treasury can use it as revenue to help pay for the government's expenditures."

Chapter Quiz

1. The U.S. central bank is the
   a. Federal Central Bank.
   b. Federal Open Market Committee.
   c. Federal Reserve System.
   d. U.S. Treasury.

2. Open market operations are a policy tool of the Fed. Changing the tax rate imposed on interest paid by bonds is a policy tool of the Fed.
   a. Both sentences are true.
   b. The first sentence is true and the second sentence is false.
   c. The first sentence is false and the second sentence is true.
   d. Both sentences are false.

3. When the Fed changes the interest rate it charges banks for loans of reserves, the Fed has
   a. changed the required reserve ratio.
   b. changed the discount rate.
   c. changed the Treasury bill rate.
   d. conducted an open market operation.

4. The largest asset on the Fed's balance sheet is
   a. gold.
   b. loans to banks.
   c. government securities.
   d. None of the above.

5. When the Fed buys a government security, the monetary base _____ and the money supply _____.
   a. increases; increases
   b. increases; decreases
   c. decreases; increases
   d. decreases; decreases

6. An increase in the interest rate
   a. shifts the demand for money curve rightward.
   b. shifts the supply of money curve rightward.
   c. does not shift the demand for money curve.
   d. shifts the demand for money curve leftward.

7. If the demand for money increases by the same amount as the supply of money increases, the interest rate _____.
   a. rises
   b. does not change.
   c. falls
   d. probably changes, but without more information it is not possible to determine if it rises, falls, or does not change

8. If the Fed raises the required reserve ratio, the
   a. demand for money increases.
   b. demand for money decreases.
   c. supply of money increases.
   d. supply of money decreases.

9. If the Fed raises the required reserve ratio, the interest rate _____.
   a. rises
   b. does not change.
   c. falls
   d. probably changes, but without more information it is not possible to determine if it rises, falls, or does not change

10. If bond prices fall,
    a. interest rates rise.
    b. interest rates fall.
    c. banks' reserves increase.
    d. households increase the quantity of money they demand.

The answers for this Chapter Quiz are on page 328

Chapter 16 INFLATION*

Key Concepts

■ Inflation and the Price Level

Inflation is an ongoing process in which the price level is rising and money is losing value. Inflation is different than a rise in the price of one good or a one-time increase in the price level. The inflation rate equals

$$\frac{P_1 - P_0}{P_0} \times 100,$$ where P_1 is the current price level and

P_0 is last year's price level.

■ Demand-Pull Inflation

An inflation that starts from an initial increase in aggregate demand is a **demand-pull inflation**.

♦ Figure 16.1 illustrates the start of a demand-pull inflation. The increase in aggregate demand raises the price level from 110 to 120.

♦ With no further increase in aggregate demand, in the long run the price level rises to 130 and then stops. This process is a one-time change in the price level.

♦ For the inflation to become established, the rightward shift in the *AD* curve needs to continue. Persistent increases in the money supply are the cause of persistent rightward shifts in the *AD* curve, so monetary growth is the cause of demand-pull inflation.

The U.S. experienced demand-pull inflation through the middle of the 1970s, by which time the inflation rate was almost 10 percent per year.

FIGURE 16.1
Start of a Demand-Pull Inflation

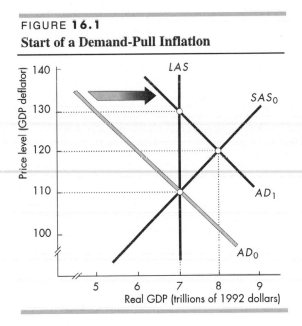

■ Cost-Push Inflation

A **cost-push inflation** starts as the result of an increase in costs. Money wage rates and the cost of raw materials are the main sources of cost-push inflation.

♦ The cost hike decreases short-run aggregate supply, raising the price level and decreasing GDP. The combination of a rising price level and decreasing GDP is called **stagflation**.

♦ If nothing else changes, in the long run money wages adjust and the price level stops rising. This process is a one-time increase in the price level.

♦ If in response to the short-run decline in GDP, the Fed increases the money supply, aggregate demand increases and prices rise still higher.

♦ The rise in the price level created by the increase in aggregate demand invites another cost hike. If it

---

* This is Chapter 33 in *Economics*.

occurs and aggregate demand increases again, a cost-push inflation results.

The U.S. experienced cost-push inflation in the late 1970s when OPEC hiked the price of oil higher and the Fed initially responded with an expansionary monetary policy.

■ Effects of Inflation

In the labor market, unanticipated inflation redistributes income between workers and employers. In addition, unanticipated inflation can hurt *both* workers and employers:

♦ Higher than expected inflation causes workers to quit their jobs to search for better paying positions. These workers have a period of unemployment and firms must incur costs to hire new workers.

♦ Lower than expected inflation lowers firms' profits, and they respond by laying off workers.

In the asset market, unanticipated inflation redistributes income between borrowers and lenders. When inflation is higher than expected, borrowers gain and lenders lose and vice versa when inflation is lower than expected. Additionally, unanticipated inflation causes *both* borrowers and lenders to be dissatisfied:

♦ Higher than expected inflation causes borrowers to want to have borrowed more and lenders to have loaned less.

♦ Lower than expected inflation makes borrowers want to have borrowed less and lenders want to have loaned more.

A **rational expectation** is a forecast based on all relevant information and it is the most accurate forecast possible. If people correctly anticipate the change that causes inflation, money wage rates adjust to reflect the higher price level. Figure 16.2 illustrates this case. The increase in aggregate demand to AD_1 is matched by higher wage rates that decrease short-run aggregate supply to SAS_1. Hence GDP stays at potential GDP and the anticipated inflation does not affect real GDP.

If aggregate demand increases more than people expect, unanticipated inflation occurs and real GDP exceeds potential GDP. If aggregate demand increases less than expected, the decrease in short-run aggregate supply exceeds the increase in aggregate demand. As a result, real GDP is less than potential GDP.

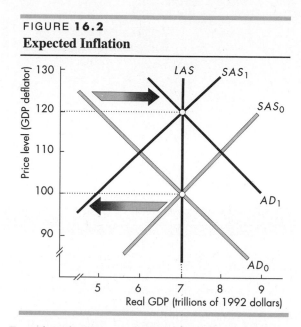

FIGURE **16.2**
Expected Inflation

Even though anticipated inflation does not affect real GDP, anticipated inflation still inflicts costs on the economy:

♦ *Transactions costs* — higher anticipated inflation causes people to use resources (e.g., boot leather) in order to spend their money more rapidly (by shopping more frequently). At still-higher anticipated inflation rates, people incur costs by using alternatives for money to conduct transactions.

♦ *Tax consequences* — anticipated inflation reduces the after-tax return from saving, which decreases saving and hence the capital stock. Long-run growth in GDP falls.

♦ *Increased uncertainty* — higher anticipated inflation causes people to spend time and resources avoiding losses from inflation, which reduces long-term economic growth.

■ Inflation and Unemployment: The Phillips Curve

A **Phillips curve** shows a relationship between inflation and unemployment. Moving along a short-run Phillips curve, expected inflation and the natural unemployment rate are constant.

The **short-run Phillips** curve shows a negative relationship between inflation and unemployment. Moving along the short-run Phillips curve, the expected inflation rate and natural rate of unemployment do not change.

FIGURE 16.3
Short-Run and Long-Run Phillips Curves

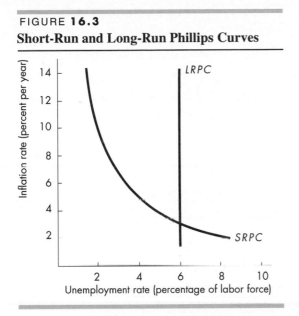

♦ Figure 16.3 shows a short-run Phillips curve, labeled *SRPC*. Along a short-run Phillips curve, higher inflation is associated with lower unemployment.

♦ The short-run Phillips curve is related to the short-run aggregate supply curve. A surprise increase in aggregate demand moves the economy upward along the *SAS* curve, leading to a higher price level — hence higher inflation — and an increase in real GDP — hence lower unemployment.

♦ A decrease in the expected inflation rate shifts the short-run Phillips curve downward by the amount of the decrease in expected inflation.

A **long-run Phillips curve** shows the relationship between the inflation rate and unemployment rate when the inflation rate equals the expected inflation rate.

♦ Figure 16.3 also shows a long-run Phillips curve, labeled *LRPC*. It is vertical at the natural rate of unemployment (6 percent in the figure).

♦ Both the short-run and long-run Phillips curves shift if the natural rate of unemployment changes. For instance, if the natural rate of unemployment increases by 1 percentage point, both the short-run and long-run Phillips curves shift rightward by 1 percentage point.

In the United States, changes in both the expected inflation rate and the natural rate of unemployment have shifted the Phillips curves.

■ Interest Rates and Inflation

The real interest rate is determined by saving supply and investment demand. The nominal interest rate is determined by the demand for money and the supply of money.

♦ The nominal interest rate equals the real interest rate plus the expected inflation rate.

♦ When inflation is anticipated, the nominal interest rate rises by the amount of expected inflation and the real interest rate does not change. The data show that higher inflation tends to be accompanied by higher nominal interest rates.

Helpful Hints

1. **RATIONAL EXPECTATIONS AND THE EFFECTS FROM A CHANGE IN THE MONEY SUPPLY :** An important implication of the rational expectations idea is that the consequences of a change in the money supply depend on expectations. The position of the short-run aggregate supply curve depends on the expected price level, which in turn depends on the expected change in the money supply. Hence an increase in the money supply can result in an increase in real GDP, no change in real GDP, or even a decrease in real GDP, depending on what was the expected change. Real GDP increases if the hike in aggregate demand is not anticipated or is underanticipated; real GDP does not change if the increase in aggregate demand is anticipated correctly; and real GDP decreases if the new aggregate demand is less than anticipated.

2. **LINKS BETWEEN AGGREGATE SUPPLY AND THE PHILLIPS CURVE :** Although the Phillips curve and the *AD/AS* model may appear different, actually the two are closely linked.

   Consider an unexpected increase in aggregate demand. In the short run, a movement occurs along the *SAS* curve. The price level rises, and real GDP increases above potential GDP. The rise in the price level means that inflation occurs, and the increase in GDP means that the unemployment rate falls. Hence the unexpected increase in aggregate demand has caused a movement along the short-run Phillips curve, with higher inflation and a fall in unemployment to below its natural rate.

GDP, in the long run, cannot remain greater than potential GDP. Tight conditions in the labor market (and other resource markets) cause money wage rates (and other resource prices) to rise to reflect the higher price level. Thus in the *AD/AS* model, the rise in money wage rates shifts the *SAS* curve leftward. Real GDP returns to the vertical *LAS* curve and equals potential GDP.

In terms of the Phillips curve, the unemployment rate cannot remain below its natural rate. Therefore as inflation continues and people come to expect it, the higher inflation rates are built into money wages (and the prices of other resources). The short-run Phillips curve shifts upward as people revise the amount of inflation they expect. The unemployment rate returns to the vertical long-run Phillips curve and equals the natural rate.

Note the strong links between the *AD/AS* model and the Phillips curve. In the short run, the increase in real GDP is associated with a drop in unemployment. In the long run, as real GDP returns to potential GDP in the *AD/AS* model, unemployment similarly returns to the natural rate in the Phillips curve model.

Questions

■ True/False/Uncertain and Explain

Inflation and the Price Level

1. If the price level at the beginning of 1999 is 120 and the price level at the beginning of 2000 is 130, the inflation rate is 8.3 percent.

2. Demand-pull inflation starts with an increase in aggregate demand.

3. An inflation that starts with an expansionary monetary policy is a cost-push inflation.

4. Cost-push inflation can cause stagflation.

5. By itself, a one-time increase in the price of oil creates an ongoing inflation.

Effects of Inflation

6. Inflation that is higher than expected redistributes income to savers.

7. A rational expectation is a forecast that always is correct.

8. If an increase in aggregate demand is anticipated correctly, inflation will not occur.

9. Higher anticipated inflation increases transaction costs.

Inflation and Unemployment: The Phillips Curve

10. The short-run Phillips curve shows that, if the inflation rate rises and the expected inflation rate does not change, the unemployment rate falls.

11. The long-run Phillips curve shows that higher inflation lowers unemployment.

12. An increase in the expected inflation rate shifts the short-run Phillips curve upward and the long-run Phillips curve rightward.

13. Data for the United States show that the short-run Phillips curve has not shifted during the last three decades.

Interest Rates and Inflation

14. During a period with zero expected inflation, the (nominal) interest rate is 5 percent. If the expected inflation rate rises to 6 percent, the nominal interest rate will rise to 11 percent.

15. Data for the United States show that higher inflation lowers the nominal interest rate.

■ Multiple Choice

Inflation and the Price Level

1. Which of the following is inflation?
   a. A one-time 25 percent rise in the price of a street hockey blade.
   b. A continuing rise of 4 percent per year in the price of a street hockey blade with no other prices changing.
   c. A one-time 25 percent rise in the prices of all goods.
   d. A continuing rise of 4 percent per year in the prices of all goods.

2. Of the following sequences of price levels, which correctly represents a 10 percent inflation rate?
   a. 100, 100, 100, 100
   b. 100, 110, 110, 110
   c. 100, 110, 120, 130
   d. 100, 110, 121, 133.1

Demand-Pull Inflation

3. Demand-pull inflation occurs when
   a. aggregate demand increases persistently.
   b. aggregate supply and aggregate demand decrease persistently.
   c. the government increases its purchases.
   d. oil prices increase substantially

4. In a demand-pull inflation, the *AD* curve shifts _____ and the *SAS* curve shifts _____.
   a. rightward; rightward
   b. rightward; leftward
   c. leftward; rightward
   d. leftward; leftward

5. Which of the following causes the aggregate demand curve to keep shifting rightward year after year?
   a. A one-time tax cut.
   b. A one-time increase in government purchases of goods and services.
   c. Inflation.
   d. Growth in the money supply.

Cost-Push Inflation

6. Cost-push inflation may start with
   a. a rise in money wage rates.
   b. an increase in government purchases.
   c. an increase in the money supply.
   d. a fall in the prices of raw materials.

7. A rise in the price level owing to an increase in the price of oil
   a. definitely triggers a cost-push inflation.
   b. definitely triggers a demand-pull inflation.
   c. may trigger a cost-push inflation.
   d. may trigger a demand-pull inflation.

8. Which of the following statements about a cost-push inflation is correct?
   a. Cost-push inflation starts when an increase in aggregate demand "pushes" costs higher.
   b. Cost-push inflation may start with a rise in the price of raw materials, but it requires increases in the money supply to persist.
   c. To persist, cost-push inflation needs a continual series of cost hikes with no change in aggregate demand.
   d. The United States has never experienced a cost-push inflation.

Effects of Inflation

9. As far as redistribution is concerned, if the inflation rate is lower than anticipated,
   a. lenders gain at the expense of borrowers and some workers gain at the expense of employers.
   b. borrowers gain at the expense of lenders and some workers gain at the expense of employers.
   c. lenders gain at the expense of borrowers and some employers gain at the expense of workers.
   d. borrowers gain at the expense of lenders and some employers gain at the expense of workers.

10. Which of the following is <u>NOT</u> true of a rational expectation forecast?
    a. It uses all available information.
    b. It is the best forecast possible.
    c. It always is correct.
    d. None of the above because they are all true.

11. A correctly anticipated increase in aggregate demand that causes a correctly anticipated increase in inflation leads to _____ in short-run aggregate supply and _____ in real GDP.
    a. an increase; an increase
    b. a decrease; an increase
    c. a decrease; no change
    d. a decrease; a decrease

12. If the aggregate demand curve shifts rightward less than expected,
    a. expectations could not be rational expectations.
    b. real GDP will be less than potential GDP.
    c. the real interest rate will be lower than expected.
    d. the real wage rate will be lower than expected.

13. Which of the following is <u>NOT</u> a cost of high anticipated inflation?
    a. Higher transactions costs.
    b. An unemployment rate that exceeds the natural rate.
    c. Increased uncertainty.
    d. A decrease in saving and investment.

14. Higher anticipated inflation
    a. increases economic growth.
    b. decreases economic growth.
    c. decreases unemployment.
    d. has no effect on economic growth or unemployment.

Inflation and Unemployment: The Phillips Curve

15. The short-run Phillips curve shows the relationship between
    a. the price level and real GDP in the short run.
    b. the price level and unemployment in the short run.
    c. inflation and unemployment when expected inflation equals the actual inflation.
    d. inflation and unemployment when expected inflation does not change.

16. The long-run Phillips curve shows the relationship between
    a. the price level and real GDP in the short run.
    b. the price level and unemployment in the short run.
    c. inflation and unemployment when expected inflation equals the actual inflation.
    d. inflation and unemployment when expected inflation does not change.

Use Figure 16.4 for the next four questions.

FIGURE **16.4**
Multiple Choice Questions 17, 18, 19, 20

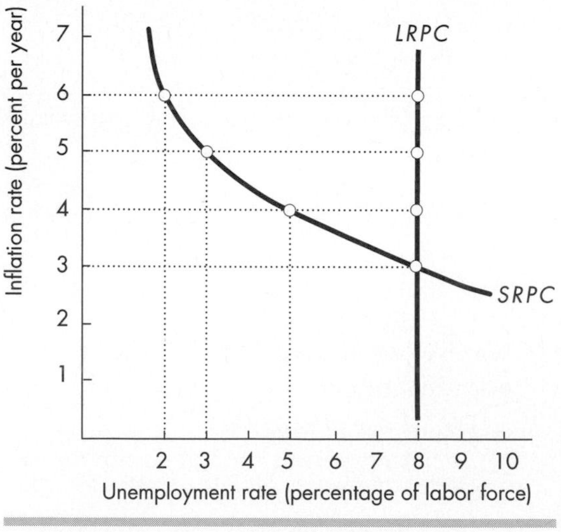

17. In the above figure, what is the natural rate of unemployment?
    a. 2 percent.
    b. 3 percent.
    c. 5 percent.
    d. 8 percent.

18. Based on Figure 16.4, what is the expected inflation rate?
    a. 3 percent.
    b. 4 percent.
    c. 5 percent.
    d. 6 percent.

19. If people's expected inflation rate does not change, for an inflation rate of 5 percent, what is the short-run unemployment rate?
    a. 2 percent.
    b. 3 percent.
    c. 5 percent.
    d. 8 percent.

20. After people's expected inflation rate completely adjusts, for an inflation rate of 5 percent, what is the long-run unemployment rate?
    a. 2 percent.
    b. 3 percent.
    c. 5 percent.
    d. 8 percent.

21. A rise in the expected inflation rate causes _____ in the long-run Phillips curve and _____ in the short-run Phillips curve.
    a. an upward shift; no shift
    b. a leftward shift; an upward shift
    c. no shift; no shift
    d. no shift; an upward shift

22. A rise in the natural rate of unemployment causes _____ in the long-run Phillips curve and _____ in the short-run Phillips curve.
    a. a rightward shift; no shift
    b. a leftward shift; a rightward shift
    c. a rightward shift; a rightward shift
    d. a leftward shift; a leftward shift

Interest Rates and Inflation

23. Suppose that, initially, the nominal interest rate is 8 percent and the expected inflation rate is 5 percent. If the expected inflation rate increases to 8 percent, what will be the new nominal interest rate?
    a. 8 percent
    b. 3 percent
    c. 13 percent
    d. 11 percent

24. U.S. data show that over the last 30 years, the real interest rate has _____, and that an increase in inflation is usually accompanied by _____ nominal interest rates.
    a. been constant; higher
    b. been constant; lower
    c. fluctuated; lower
    d. fluctuated; higher

■ **Short Answer Problems**

1. What will happen to the price level and real GDP if the money supply increases and the increase is not anticipated; that is, the price level is not expected to change? Be sure to tell what happens to the aggregate demand curve and short-run aggregate supply curve.

2. Explain how the events in problem 1 could lead to a demand-pull inflation spiral.

3. Explain the differences between the short-run Phillips curve and the long-run Phillips curve.

TABLE **16.1**

Phillips Curve

Inflation rate (percent per year)	Unemployment rate (percent of labor force)
3	7
4	6
5	5
6	4

4. Table 16.1 shows the Phillips curve when the expected inflation rate is 4 percent. The natural rate of unemployment is 6 percent, and the actual inflation rate is 4 percent.
    a. In Figure 16.5, draw the short-run Phillips curve (label it $SRPC_0$) and the long-run Phillips curve (label it $LRPC$).
    b. Suppose that the inflation rate rises to 6 percent and, immediately after the increase, the expected inflation rate does not change. What is the unemployment rate?

FIGURE **16.5**

Phillips Curves

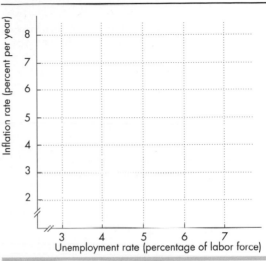

5. Continuing with the situation in part (b) of problem 4, when the inflation rate rises to 6 percent, suppose that after a year the expected inflation rate rises to 5 percent.
    a. In Figure 16.5, draw the new short-run Phillips curve that results from the change in the expected inflation rate. Label this Phillips curve $SRPC_1$.
    b. If the inflation rate remains at 6 percent, after inflation expectations have increased to 5 percent, what is the unemployment rate?

6. Continuing with the situation in Problem 4, suppose that, two years after the inflation rate increased to 6 percent, expected inflation rises to 6 percent.
    a. In Figure 16.5, draw the new short-run Phillips curve that results from the change in the expected inflation rate to 6 percent. Label this Phillips curve $SRPC_2$.
    b. If the inflation rate remains at 6 percent, after the expected inflation rate has increased to 6 percent, what is the unemployment rate?

7. What is the relationship between the expected inflation rate and the nominal interest rate?

TABLE **16.2**

Interest Rates and Inflation

Real interest rate (percent)	Inflation rate (percent)	Nominal interest rate (percent)
4	0	____
4	2	____
4	4	____
4	−2	____

8. Complete Table 16.2 to show the relationship between interest rates and the inflation rate.

9. When the inflation rate is expected to be zero, Jennifer wants to lend money if the interest rate is at least 4 percent, and Pat wants to borrow money if the interest rate is 4 percent or less. Thus they enter into a loan agreement at a 4 percent interest rate if they expect zero inflation.

   a. If they both expect an inflation rate of 2 percent over the period of the loan, what interest rate will they agree to?

   b. If they both expect a deflation rate of 2 percent over the period of the loan, what interest rate will they agree to?

   c. Suppose that Jennifer expects the inflation rate will be 4 percent, and Pat expects it will be 6 percent. Will they be able to work out a loan agreement? If so, what interest rate will they agree to?

   d. Suppose that Pat and Jennifer both expect inflation will be 2 percent, have agreed to the interest rate from your answer to part (a), and a loan of $100 for one year has been made. Instead of the expected inflation rate of 2 percent, the actual rate is 6 percent. Who gains, who loses, and how much?

■ **You're the Teacher**

1. "You know, I'm really glad that you talked me into taking this economics course because I've always wondered about inflation and, boy, this chapter sure helped me understand it better. One point still bothers me, though. I can see how monetary growth causes inflation because it makes the aggregate demand curve shift rightward. But what about government spending? Why can't it cause inflation, too?" Earn even more of your friend's gratitude by answering the question.

Answers

■ True/False Answers

Inflation and the Price Level

1. **T** The inflation rate is $\dfrac{130-120}{120}\times100 = 8.3$ percent.

2. **T** With the initial increase in aggregate demand, the price level starts to rise.

3. **F** An increase in the monetary growth rate increases aggregate demand and causes demand-pull inflation.

4. **T** When the short-run aggregate supply decreases, stagflation occurs: The price level rises and GDP decreases.

5. **F** Unless the Fed increases the money supply, a one-time increase in the price of oil creates a one-time increase in the price level.

Effects of Inflation

6. **F** Higher than expected inflation reduces the real value of loan payments, thereby harming savers by redistributing income to borrowers.

7. **F** Rational expectations are not always correct.

8. **F** If the increase in aggregate demand is anticipated, real GDP does not change but the price level rises so inflation occurs.

9. **T** As anticipated inflation rises, people take actions to hold less money by spending it more rapidly.

Inflation and Unemployment: The Phillips Curve

10. **T** Along the short-run Phillips curve, higher inflation rates lower the unemployment rate.

11. **F** The long-run Phillips curve is vertical, indicating that in the long run higher inflation does not lower unemployment.

12. **F** The increase in expected inflation does shift the short-run Phillips curve upward but does not shift the long-run Phillips curve.

13. **F** Data show several shifts in the Phillips curve because of changes in the expected inflation rate and in the natural rate of unemployment.

Interest Rates and Inflation

14. **T** With zero expected inflation, the nominal interest rate equals the real interest rate. Hence the real interest rate is 5 percent. Thus when the expected inflation rate is 6 percent, the nominal interest rate, which equals the real rate plus the expected inflation rate, is 5 percent plus 6 percent, or 11 percent.

15. **F** The data show that higher inflation is associated with higher nominal interest rates.

■ Multiple Choice Answers

Inflation and the Price Level

1. **d** Inflation is an on-going rise in the prices of all (or most) goods.

2. **d** The inflation rate is $\dfrac{P_1 - P_0}{P_0}\times100$, where P_1 is the current price level and P_0 is last year's price level. Of the price level sequences, only part (d) gives a persisting inflation rate of 10 percent.

Demand-Pull Inflation

3. **a** Demand-pull inflation results when the demand for goods increases, thereby "pulling up" the price level.

4. **b** Aggregate demand increases, which raises the price level. Hence money wages rise and aggregate supply decreases.

5. **d** Growth in the money supply means that the quantity of money in the economy continually increases, which persistently shifts the *AD* curve rightward.

Cost-Push Inflation

6. **a** Cost-push inflation starts with a factor that decreases aggregate supply.

7. **c** The oil price increase may trigger a cost-push inflation if the Fed responds by increasing the growth rate of the money supply.

8. **b** A rise in the price of a resource can kick off a cost-push inflation, but to persist the inflation needs ratification by persistent increases in the money supply.

Effects of Inflation

9. **a** Lenders gain because the real repayments on loans are higher than expected; some workers gain because real wages are higher than expected. (Not all workers gain because some workers are laid off and those workers are harmed.)

10. **c** Rational expectations are not always correct, but they are the best possible forecasts.

11. **c** The higher inflation causes higher money wages, which decrease short-run aggregate supply and results in no change in real GDP.

12. **b** If the *AD* curve shifts rightward less than expected, the price level is lower than expected, which means that real wages are higher than expected. Firms respond by cutting production so that real GDP is less than potential GDP.

13. **b** The other answers are all costs of anticipated inflation, which all increase dramatically when anticipated inflation rises to high levels.

14. **b** By lowering the nation's economic growth, anticipated inflation imposes a significant cost on a country.

Inflation and Unemployment: The Phillips Curve

15. **d** Answer (d) is the definition of the short-run Phillips curve.

16. **c** Answer (c) is the definition of the long-run Phillips curve. Comparing this question with question 15 shows the important role played by inflation expectations.

17. **d** The *LRPC* is vertical at the natural rate of unemployment, 8 percent.

18. **a** The *SRPC* crosses the *LRPC* at the level of expected inflation.

19. **b** In the short run, the economy moves along its *SRPC* so that the increase in the inflation rate reduces the unemployment rate to 3 percent.

20. **d** In the long run, the economy returns to the *LRPC* and unemployment returns to its natural rate, or 8 percent here.

21. **d** The long-run Phillips curve shifts only when the natural rate of unemployment changes; the short-run Phillips curve shifts when the natural unemployment rate changes and when the expected inflation rate changes.

22. **c** Both Phillips curves shift rightward by the amount of the increase in the natural rate of unemployment.

Interest Rates and Inflation

23. **d** Initially, the real interest rate is 3 percent, the 8 percent nominal interest rate minus the 5 percent expected inflation rate. Then, after the increase in expected inflation, the nominal interest rate equals the 3 percent real interest rate plus the 8 percent expected inflation rate.

24. **d** The real interest rate has averaged about 2.1 percent, but has fluctuated from one year to the next. And, a higher inflation rate is typically associated with higher nominal interest rates.

■ Answers to Short Answer Problems

1. An increase in the money supply shifts the aggregate demand curve rightward. If the price level is not expected to change, the short-run aggregate supply curve remains unchanged and the increase in aggregate demand causes a rise in the price level and an increase in real GDP.

2. The higher price level leads to demands for higher money wages, which push up the costs of production and shift the *SAS* curve leftward, leading to a further rise in the price level and a drop in real GDP. A demand-pull inflation spiral could result if the Federal Reserve again increases the money supply. In this case, the *AD* curve continues to shift rightward, triggering leftward shifts in the *SAS* curve and leading to an ongoing inflation.

3. The short-run Phillips curve applies when the expected inflation rate is constant. Therefore the short-run Phillips curve slopes downward so that if the inflation rate rises (and hence real wages fall) unemployment falls.

   The long-run Phillips curve applies when the expected inflation rate has fully adjusted to reflect changes in the actual inflation rate. In other words, along the long-run Phillips curve, the expected inflation rate equals the actual inflation rate. The long-run Phillips curve, therefore, is vertical at the natural rate of unemployment. Along the long-run Phillips curve, a rise in the actual inflation rate is matched by an equivalent rise in the expected inflation rate (so that the real wage rate is constant) and thus the unemployment rate remains constant at the natural rate.

4. a. Figure 16.6 (on the next page) shows the short-run and long-run Phillips curves.

   b. If the inflation rate rises to 6 percent and the expected inflation rate remains at 4 percent, the economy moves along the Phillips curve *SRPC*$_0$ to point *a* and the unemployment rate falls to 4 percent.

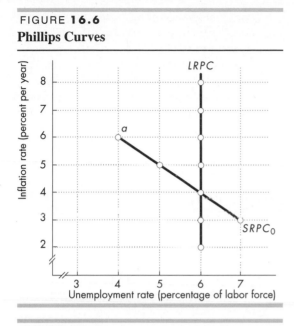

FIGURE **16.6**
Phillips Curves

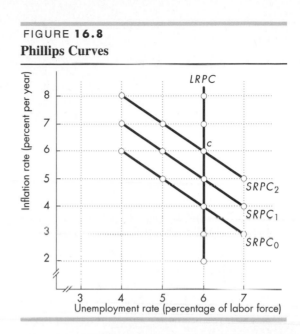

FIGURE **16.8**
Phillips Curves

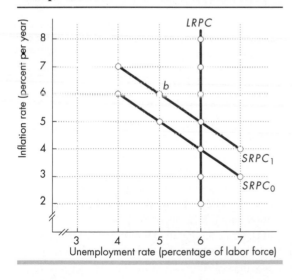

FIGURE **16.7**
Phillips Curves

5. a. When the expected inflation rate increases by 1 percentage point, the $SRPC$ shifts vertically upward by 1 percentage point. This shift is illustrated in Figure 16.7, where the short-run Phillips curve shifts from $SRPC_0$ to $SRPC_1$.

 b. When the expected inflation rate is 5 percent, the relevant Phillips curve is $SRPC_1$. Thus with the inflation rate (still) at 6 percent, the economy is at point b on $SRPC_1$, so the unemployment rate becomes 5 percent. Note that,

compared to the answer to part (b) of problem 4, when the inflation rate does not change, an increase in the expected inflation rate raises the unemployment rate.

6. a. The new $SRPC$ (when expected inflation is 6 percent) is in Figure 16.8 as $SRPC_2$.

 b. When the expected inflation rate rises to 6 percent, the unemployment rate is 6 percent. You can arrive at this answer in one of two ways. First, when the expected inflation rate is 6 percent, $SRPC_2$ is the relevant short-run Phillips curve. Hence when the inflation rate is 6 percent, the economy is at point c on $SRPC_2$. Alternatively, when the expected inflation rate is 6 percent *and* the actual inflation rate is 6 percent, the economy is on its long-run Phillips curve, $LRPC$, because the actual and expected inflation rates are equal. So with the inflation rate at 6 percent, the economy is at point c on $LRPC$.

7. When the expected inflation rate rises, the nominal interest rate rises to compensate for the increased rate at which the purchasing power of money is expected to erode. The point is that lenders and borrowers are interested in the quantity of goods and services that a unit of money will buy. With higher inflation, lenders insist on the higher interest rate, to compensate for the loss of purchasing power of money. Borrowers agree because they realize that repaying the loan will be easier when all prices, including their wages, have increased.

TABLE **16.3**

Interest Rates and Inflation

Real interest rate (percent)	Inflation rate (percent)	Nominal interest rate (percent)
4	0	<u>4</u>
4	2	<u>6</u>
4	4	<u>8</u>
4	−2	<u>2</u>

8. The nominal interest rate equals the real interest rate plus the inflation rate. Thus in the first row in Table 16.3, when the inflation rate is 0 percent, the nominal interest rate is 4 percent plus 0 percent, or 4 percent. Similarly, in the second row, when the inflation rate is 2 percent, the nominal interest rate is 4 percent plus 2 percent, or 6 percent.

Note that when inflation is zero, then (and only then) the real interest rate equals the nominal interest rate. Also note that for any real interest rate, the higher the inflation rate, the higher is the nominal interest rate.

9. a. Because both Jennifer and Pat expect the inflation rate to be 2 percent, they expect the value of money to decline by 2 percent. Thus they will agree to a 6 percent interest rate, with 2 percent offsetting the drop in the value of money, leaving a 4 percent real interest rate paid after accounting for inflation. (Note that this answer is the same as that shown in the second row in Table 16.3, for problem 8.)

b. If both Jennifer and Pat expect a deflation rate of 2 percent, they expect the value of money to increase by 2 percent. By the same logic as in part (a), they will agree to a 2 percent interest rate. (Again, note that this answer is the same result as in the fourth row in Table 16.3 in problem 8.)

c. If Jennifer expects a 4 percent inflation rate, she will want to lend only if the interest rate is at least 8 percent. Pat expects a 6 percent inflation rate and will borrow if the interest rate is 10 percent or less. As a result, Jennifer and Pat could agree on any interest rate between 8 and 10 percent.

d. From part (a), we know that in this situation they will agree to an interest rate of 6 percent, meaning that Pat repays $106. Jennifer expects a real gain of $4 (she can buy 4 percent more

goods), after accounting for the 2 percent inflation. However, the actual 6 percent inflation raises the price of goods by 6 percent, so her $106 after 1 year buys only the same amount of goods as the $100 did originally. She therefore has effectively lost $4, and Pat has gained the $4, owing to the real interest rate of zero. Therefore the higher-than-expected inflation rate has helped the borrower (Pat) and harmed the lender (Jennifer).

■ **You're the Teacher**

1. "This is a good question. The reason that monetary growth is the only factor that causes inflation involves two things: first, the difference between a one-time change in the price level and ongoing changes and second, what happens in reality.

"Let's start with the first point, the difference between a one-time change in the price level and ongoing changes. We both know by now that an increase in government purchases increases aggregate demand and that the increase in aggregate demand raises the price level. But to have an ongoing inflation, the price level must continue to rise. For government spending to be the source of inflation, then, it would need to expand year in and year out.

"Now let's get to the second point — what happens in the real world. In the real world, we know that GDP tends to grow by about 2 percent per year. So for government spending to contribute an extra increase to aggregate demand, it would need to grow more rapidly than everything else. I mean, if consumption expenditure, investment, net exports, and potential GDP all grow at the rate of, say, 2 percent, in order for aggregate demand to increase more rapidly than 2 percent — and consequently for government spending to cause the price level to rise more than otherwise — government spending would need to increase by more than 2 percent. But that hasn't happened. Indeed, as a fraction of GDP, government spending has been near 20 percent for about the last 40 years! So government spending has been increasing at about the same rate as everything else: It sure hasn't been increasing more rapidly and causing inflation!

"But the money supply has been growing more rapidly than everything else. Real GDP per person has grown by about 2 percent per year for the past half century, but the money supply has grown a lot more rapidly, by about 5 to 6 percent per year! As a result, year in and year out, the money supply grows so rapidly that it causes aggregate demand to increase faster than aggregate supply. So excessively rapid monetary growth is the source of inflation!"

Chapter Quiz

1. If this year's price level exceeds last year's price level,
   a. inflation occurred.
   b. inflation accelerated.
   c. deflation occurred.
   d. deflation accelerated.

2. A demand-pull inflation can be *started* by ____; a cost-push inflation can be *started* by ____.
   a. an increase in the price of oil; an increase in the price of oil
   b. a decrease in money wages; an increase in government spending
   c. an increase in the money supply; an increase in the price of oil
   d. an increase in the money supply; an increase in the money supply

3. To *continue*, a demand-pull inflation needs ____; to *continue*, a cost-push inflation needs ____.
   a. a continuing increase in the price of oil; a continuing increase in the price of oil
   b. a continuing decrease in money wages; a continuing decrease in money wages
   c. a continuing increase in the money supply; a continuing increase in the money supply
   d. a continuing increase in government spending; a continuing decrease in government spending

4. The relationship between unemployment and inflation is illustrated by
   a. the *AD* curve.
   b. the *LAS* curve.
   c. the *SAS* curve.
   d. the Phillips curves.

5. For a cost-push inflation to occur, higher oil prices must be accompanied by
   a. lower investment.
   b. higher tax rates.
   c. low government purchases.
   d. higher monetary growth.

6. If the inflation rate turns out to be lower than anticipated
   a. lenders can gain and borrowers can lose.
   b. lenders can lose and borrowers can gain.
   c. some workers can lose and some firms can gain.
   d. no one is harmed.

7. In a demand-pull inflation, money wages rise because a(n) ____ in aggregate demand creates a labor ____.
   a. increase; shortage
   b. increase; surplus
   c. decrease; shortage
   d. decrease; surplus

8. The short-run Philips curve crosses the long-run Phillips curve at the
   a. natural interest rate.
   b. nominal interest rate.
   c. actual inflation rate.
   d. expected inflation rate.

9. What influence shifts *both* the short-run and long-run Phillips curve rightward?
   a. An increase in the expected inflation rate equal to the increase in the actual inflation rate shifts both curves.
   b. A decrease in the expected inflation rate equal to the decrease in the actual inflation rate shifts both curves.
   c. An increase in the natural rate of unemployment shifts both curves.
   d. A decrease in the natural rate of unemployment shifts both curves.

10. Data show that higher inflation rates tend to be associated with
    a. higher real interest rates.
    b. lower real interest rates.
    c. higher nominal interest rates.
    d. lower nominal interest rates.

The answers for this Chapter Quiz are on page 328

Part Review 5 UNDERSTANDING AGGREGATE DEMAND AND INFLATION

FED LEAVES INTEREST RATES UNCHANGED

The Federal Reserve decided to leave benchmark interest rates unchanged, but said it is so "concerned about the potential for a buildup of inflationary imbalances" that it is leaning toward raising rates in the coming months for the first time in nearly a year.

The Fed suggested that demand in the U.S. economy is growing faster than the economy's ability to supply goods and services, despite gains in productivity.

The Fed's decision to adopt an end-of meeting statement, or directive, that says a rate increase is more likely than a rate cut doesn't mean that higher rates are a certainty. Rather, it is a clear statement that Fed officials at this moment see a much greater risk of accelerating inflation than of a worrisome slowdown in the economy.

The decision leaves the Fed's target for the federal funds interest rate at 4.75%, the level at which it has been since November. The Fed manipulates the fed-funds rate, at which banks lend to each other overnight, by buying and selling government securities. The Fed yesterday left unchanged the discount rate, at which it lends directly to banks.

When they met in early February, according to a summary of the meeting released subsequently, some Fed officials were already prepared to undo some of the rate cuts implemented last fall amid turmoil in the global economy and financial markets. Since then, the economy has proved much stronger than expected... .

"Against the background of already tight domestic labor markets and ongoing strength in demand in excess of productivity gains," the Fed statement said, "the Committee recognizes the need to be alert to developments over coming months that might indicate that financial conditions may no longer be consistent with containing inflation."

Richard Berner, chief U.S. economist at Morgan Stanley Dean Witter & Co., said the statement is the first step toward tighter monetary policy. "The basic point is that the inflation risks, while relatively small, are rising. Last fall's easing was put in place as we witnessed prospects for the global economy deteriorating." With those concerns abating, "it's appropriate for the Fed to take back some of the easing that they put in place last fall."

David Wessel, "Fed Leaves Interest Rates Unchanged," May 19, 1999, p. A2. Reprinted by permission of The Wall Street Journal, ©1999 Dow Jones & Co., Inc. All Rights Reserved Worldwide.

■ Analyze It

The FOMC meets every six weeks to determine the course of the nation's monetary policy. The article reports about its meeting in May, 1999. At this meeting the Federal Reserve did not change interest rates but the Fed announced that if interest rates were changed in the future, they likely would be increased.

1. Using an aggregate demand/aggregate supply diagram, illustrate what the Fed fears may occur.

2. The Fed worries that demand is growing faster than the economy's ability to supply goods and services. How does this worry relate to your aggregate demand/aggregate supply diagram?

3. What does the article suggest might be reasons why aggregate demand is growing rapidly?

4. Most observers believe that the Fed, under Alan Greenspan, has done a very good job of helping stabilize the economy. Does the Fed's recent performance mean that the policy favored by Greenspan is definitely the correct sort of policy for the Fed to follow? Why or why not?

Web Resources

For more information, browse the Parkin Web site to explore related links.

On the Top 10 list, visit the "Economic Report of the President - Making Fiscal Policy". Also on the top 10 list, visit "The Federal Reserve". As you visit this last site, ask yourself how much of the information there you would have understood before your class in economics. When you think about this question, you will gain a deeper appreciation for how much your class has increased your understanding of our world.

Mid-Term Examination

■ **Chapter 12**

1. On the 45° diagram, consumption expenditure is measured as
   a. a horizontal distance.
   b. a vertical distance.
   c. the area of a triangle.
   d. the area of a rectangle.

2. When the consumption function lies above the 45° line, households
   a. spend all of any increase in income on consumption.
   b. consume more than their disposable income.
   c. save some portion of their disposable income.
   d. save all of any increase in income.

3. Expenditure that depends on the level of income is
   a. spurious expenditure.
   b. equilibrium expenditure.
   c. induced expenditure.
   d. autonomous expenditure.

4. Suppose the MPC = 0.90, taxes do not depend on income, and there are no imports. Then a $100 increase in autonomous spending causes equilibrium expenditure to
   a. decrease by $100.
   b. increase by $100.
   c. increase by $900.
   d. increase by $1,000.

■ **Chapter 13**

5. The largest source of expenditure for the Federal government is
   a. government purchases of goods and services.
   b. transfer payments.
   c. corporate income taxes.
   d. interest on the debt.

6. In an economy with no international sector and no income taxes, if the MPC = 0.90, the lump-sum tax multiplier is
   a. −10.0.
   b. −9.0.
   c. −1.0.
   d. 10.0

7. Which of the following are expansionary fiscal policy?
   a. A cut in taxes and an increase in government purchases.
   b. An increase in taxes and a decrease in government purchases.
   c. An increase in taxes and an increase in government purchases.
   d. A cut in taxes and a decrease in government purchases.

8. Crowding out is a decrease in investment caused by
   a. contractionary monetary policy.
   b. expansionary monetary policy.
   c. expansionary fiscal policy.
   d. contractionary fiscal policy.

■ **Chapter 14**

9. If Daniel transfers $1,000 out of his checking account and places it in his savings account, instantly
   a. M1 and M2 fall.
   b. M1 falls and M2 rises.
   c. M1 and M2 rise.
   d. M1 falls and M2 does not change.

10. Your loan from a bank is
    a. an asset to you and a liability to your bank.
    b. a liability to you and asset to your bank.
    c. an asset to both you and your bank.
    d. a liability to both you and your bank.

11. A bank's reserves include
    a. the cash in its vault plus the value of its depositors' accounts.
    b. the cash in its vault plus any gold held for the bank at Fort Knox.
    c. the cash in its vault plus any deposits held at the Federal Reserve.
    d. its common stock holdings, the cash in its vault, and any deposits held at the Federal Reserve.

12. Banks are able to create money whenever they have excess
    a. reserves.
    b. deposits.
    c. loans.
    d. personnel.

■ **Chapter 15**

13. Which of the following is a policy tool of the Fed?
    a. Open market operations.
    b. The tax rate on interest income.
    c. Transfer payments.
    d. The government's deficit or surplus.

14. If the Fed buys government securities,
    a. banks' reserves and the money supply increase.
    b. banks' reserves decrease and the money supply increases.
    c. banks' reserves increase and the money supply decreases.
    d. banks' reserves and the money supply decrease.

15. If the money multiplier is 4 and the Fed sells $1 million in securities, the money supply will
    a. increase by $4 million.
    b. increase by $250,000.
    c. decrease by $2 million.
    d. decrease by $4 million.

16. If interest rates fall, then
    a. bond prices fall.
    b. bond prices rise.
    c. banks' reserves increase.
    d. households decrease their cash holdings.

■ **Chapter 16**

17. A cost-push inflation is <u>NOT</u> characterized by
    a. continuing increases in the money supply.
    b. continuing increases in money wage rates.
    c. a one-time increase in government purchases.
    d. All of the above are characteristics of cost-push inflation.

18. A demand-pull inflation requires persistent increases in
    a. tax rates.
    b. real wages.
    c. the money supply.
    d. government purchases.

19. If lenders and borrowers base their lending on an inflation forecast that turns out to be too low, with regard to income redistribution, borrowers
    a. are hurt and lenders are helped.
    b. are helped and lenders are hurt.
    c. and lenders are both hurt.
    d. and lenders are both helped.

20. The short-run Phillips curve ____; the long-run Phillips curve ____.
    a. slopes downward; slopes downward
    b. slopes upward; slopes upward
    c. is horizontal; is vertical
    d. slopes downward; is vertical

Answers

■ Reading Between the Lines

The Fed's fear is that aggregate demand increases so much that the price level rises substantially and inflation jumps higher. Figure 1 for 1999-2000 illustrates this fear. In the figure, long-run aggregate supply will increase from LAS_0 to LAS_1. Short-run aggregate supply will increase because of the increase in potential GDP but will decrease because money wage rates will rise. For simplicity, these two effects are assumed to be the same magnitude so that the short-run aggregate supply remains constant at SAS. The Fed is unsure by how much aggregate demand will increase. If it increases only a little, from AD_0 to AD_1, the price level will only rise from 110 to 115, for an inflation rate of about 4.4 percent. If, as the Fed fears, aggregate demand increases a lot, from AD_0 to AD_2, the price level will rise to 120 and the inflation rate will soar to approximately 8.7 percent.

The Federal Reserve is worried that demand is growing faster than the nation's ability to produce goods and services. The "ability to produce goods and services" refers to the nation's long-run aggregate supply curve. In terms of Figure 1, the Fed is concerned that the increase in aggregate demand (from AD_0 to AD_2) will be significantly greater than the increase in long-run aggregate supply (from LAS_0 to LAS_1).

The article mentions two possibilities why aggregate demand might be growing too rapidly. One possibility is the fact that the global economy has rebounded. As a result, U.S. exports may increase rapidly, thereby increasing U.S. aggregate demand. The other possibility, mentioned implicitly, is the Fed's policy in the fall. In the fall, the Fed cut interest rates because the Fed was concerned about the global economy. The decrease in interest rates may have spurred an increase in invest-

The Fed's Fear

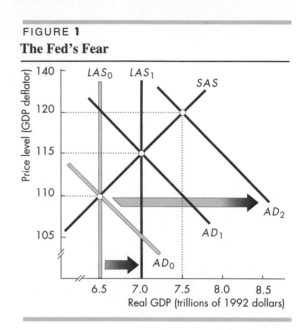

ment demand and consumption expenditure and be the cause of rapid increase in aggregate demand.

Most economists credit the Fed under Greenspan for helping stabilize the economy. However, this performance does *not* prove that the Fed's policies are always beneficial. First, some economists may assert that Greenspan's success has been the result of luck. Just as a flipped coin may show heads five — or more — times in a row, so, too, may Greenspan's guesses have been correct by random chance. Second, even if Greenspan is capable of accurately guiding the Fed, he is over seventy years old. There is no guarantee that his successor will be as good. Thus these economists argue that, on the average, the nation is better off if the Federal Reserve does not try to manage the economy using its monetary policy.

■ Mid-Term Exam Answers

1. b;   2. b;   3. c;   4. d;   5. b;   6. b;   7. a;   8. c;   9. d;   10. b;   11. c;   12. a;
13. a;   14. a;   15. d;   16. b;   17. c;   18. c;   19. b;   20. D.

Key Concepts

■ Cycle Patterns, Impulses, and Mechanisms

The *business cycle* is the irregular up-and-down movement of business activity. The average recession lasts a
bit more than one year, and GDP falls 6 percent from
peak to trough. The average expansion lasts almost four
years, and GDP rises 22 percent from trough to peak.

♦ Some cycles (e.g., tennis matches) require impulses
to start each cycle.

♦ Some cycles (e.g., sunrise and sunset) reflect the
design of the system.

♦ Some cycles (e.g., rocking horses) combine impulses and design.

Investment and capital accumulation play key roles in
the business cycle. Recessions occur when investment
decreases; expansions occur when investment increases.
Business cycles can be classified as aggregate demand
theories and real business cycle theory.

■ Aggregate Demand Theories of the Business Cycle

The **Keynesian theory of the business cycle** regards
volatile expectations as the cause of economic fluctuations.

♦ The Keynesian *impulse* is changes in firms' expectations about future sales and profits. This change
affects investment.

FIGURE **17.1**

Keynesian Theory

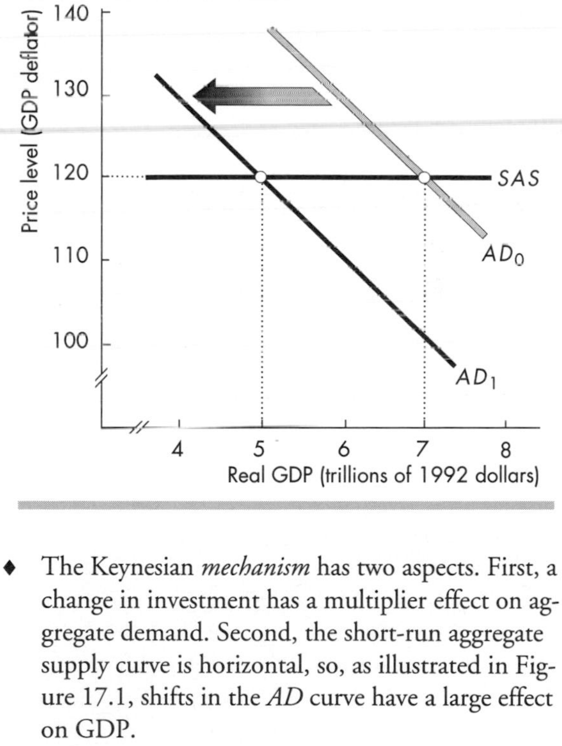

♦ The Keynesian *mechanism* has two aspects. First, a
change in investment has a multiplier effect on aggregate demand. Second, the short-run aggregate
supply curve is horizontal, so, as illustrated in Figure 17.1, shifts in the *AD* curve have a large effect
on GDP.

♦ The response of money wages is asymmetric; wages
do not fall in response to decreases in aggregate
demand but they do rise in response to increases in
aggregate demand. Hence the economy can remain
stuck in a recession.

---

* This is Chapter 34 in *Economics*.

FIGURE 17.2
Monetarist and Rational Expectations Theory

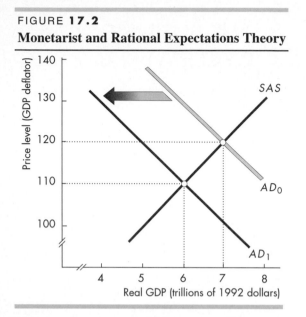

The **monetarist theory of the business cycle** regards fluctuations in the money stock as the main source of economic fluctuation.

♦ The *impulse* in the monetarist theory is changes in the growth rate of the quantity of money.

♦ The monetarist *mechanism* is changes in the growth rate of the money supply that shift the *AD* curve. The economy moves along an upward-sloping *SAS* curve, as is illustrated in Figure 17.2, for a decline in the monetary growth rate. Aggregate demand decreases from AD_0 to AD_1.

♦ Eventually, money wages respond to the change in the price level so that the *SAS* curve shifts and the economy returns to potential GDP.

A **rational expectation** is a forecast based on all available information. Rational expectations theories of business cycles focus on the rationally expected money wage rate. The two rational expectations theories are the **new classical theory** and **new Keynesian theory**.

♦ The *impulse* in the new classical theory is unanticipated changes in aggregate demand.

♦ The major *impulse* in the new Keynesian theory is unanticipated changes in aggregate demand, but anticipated changes also play a role.

♦ The rational expectations *mechanism* is an unexpected shift in the *AD* curve that moves the economy along its *SAS* curve as real wage rates change. Figure 17.2 illustrates the effect of an unexpected decrease in aggregate demand to AD_1. AD_0 is the

expected aggregate demand. The recession ends when aggregate demand increases back to expected aggregate demand.

♦ The new classical theory asserts that only unexpected changes in aggregate demand affect real wage rates and GDP.

♦ The new Keynesian theory holds that labor contracts allow money wages to change only slowly. A change in aggregate demand that was unanticipated *when* the labor contract was signed will affect real wages and GDP even if, when the event actually occurs, it has come to be anticipated.

■ Real Business Cycle Theory

The **real business cycle theory** (**RBC**) regards random fluctuations in productivity as the cause of business cycles.

♦ The *impulse* in RBC theory is technological changes that affect the growth rate of productivity.

♦ The RBC *mechanism* is a change in productivity that affects investment demand and labor demand. During a recession, both decrease. The decrease in investment demand lowers the real interest rate, so the *intertemporal substitution* effect decreases the supply of labor. Employment decreases, so, as illustrated in Figure 17.3, the *LAS* curve shifts leftward. The *AD* curve shifts leftward because of the decrease in investment. GDP decreases and the price level falls.

FIGURE 17.3
Real Business Cycle Theory

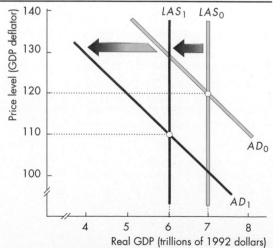

Criticisms of the RBC theory are that:

♦ Money wages are sticky.

♦ Intertemporal substitution is too weak to account for large fluctuations in employment.

♦ Technology shocks are implausible as an impulse that causes a business cycle.

♦ Productivity shocks, as measured, are correlated with factors that change aggregate demand.

Defenses of the RBC theory are that:

♦ It explains both business cycles and economic growth.

♦ It seems to be consistent with microeconomic data concerning labor supply, labor demand, and investment demand.

♦ Money is correlated with productivity shocks because changes in real GDP change the money supply.

♦ It suggests that efforts to smooth the business cycle may harm the economy.

■ Recessions and Expansions During the 1990s

The last U.S. recession in 1990–1991 was caused by higher oil prices and uncertainty, which slowed investment. The higher oil prices also decreased aggregate supply.

♦ Both the *AD* curve and the *SAS* curve shifted leftward. Real GDP fell and though the price level rose, it rose more slowly than in the previous year.

From 1991 through the end of 1998 the U.S. economy had 98 months of expansion. During this expansion, technological change, such as personal computers and biotechnology, created profit opportunities that required large amounts of investment.

♦ Increased investment and exports shifted the *AD* curve rightward. Capital accumulation increased potential GDP and labor productivity so the *LAS* curve shifted rightward. Real GDP increased significantly and the price level rose only modestly.

♦ The U.S. expansion is similar to what a real business model predicts, with technological change increasing investment, the demand for labor, and the supply of labor.

Between 1992 and 1998 Japanese real GDP increased only 6 percent (a growth rate of only 0.7 percent per year) and in 1999 real GDP in Japan was falling. Several factors contributed to the near decade long weak economic performance:

♦ Asset prices collapsed in 1990, which decreased consumption expenditure and investment.

♦ Fiscal policy was generally expansionary but there were times when it was contractionary.

♦ Monetary policy lowered the interest rate but investment did not increase.

♦ Japan's markets are plagued by structural distortions that limit competition and slow productivity growth.

■ The Great Depression

The Great Depression of the 1930s led to a decline in real GDP of 29 percent and an increase in the unemployment rate from 3.2 percent to 25 percent.

♦ The initial cause of the Great Depression was uncertainty and pessimism, which reduced investment and consumption expenditure on durable goods.

Economists disagree about why the initial recession turned into the Great Depression. Two hypotheses have been advanced:

♦ Aggregate demand continued to decrease because of uncertainty and pessimism.

♦ Bank failures and the collapse of the money supply caused aggregate demand to decrease.

The Great Depression is unlikely to occur again because of:

♦ Bank deposit insurance provided by the Federal Deposit Insurance Corporation (FDIC).

♦ The Federal Reserve's determination to act as the lender of last resort.

♦ The larger fraction of GDP that is accounted for by taxes and government spending.

♦ The increased number of families that have two (or more) wage earners.

Helpful Hints

1. **THE CHALLENGE OF THE REAL BUSINESS CYCLE THEORY :** RBC theory is based on the assumption that the economy is always producing on its long-run aggregate supply curve; that is, the economy is always at potential GDP. Because potential GDP is

also the full-employment level of GDP, the real business cycle theory asserts that, in the labor market, wages (or other mechanisms) are sufficiently flexible so that the economy is always at full employment. Thus the real business cycle theory view is that fluctuations in employment represent fluctuations in the level of full employment. The level of full employment changes when labor demand and/or labor supply changes. For instance, a decrease in labor demand decreases the level of full-employment equilibrium and actual employment in the economy decreases.

As the text indicates, the real business cycle theory of the economy is controversial. The assumptions underlying this approach seem extreme to many economists. Nonetheless, real business cycle theory has had a surprising amount of success in explaining various facts about business cycles, and a sizable minority of economists believe that the real business cycle theory is a good way to analyze the business cycle.

Which group of economists is correct? At this time, it is impossible to tell because the evidence on the real business cycle theory is still accumulating. But if this approach ultimately is accepted, it will represent a major change from the more conventional aggregate demand theories.

Questions

■ True/False/Uncertain and Explain

Cycle Patterns, Impulses, and Mechanisms

1. Recessions start when investment slows or decreases.

Aggregate Demand Theories of the Business Cycle

2. Keynesian, monetarist, and rational expectations theories of business cycles assert that fluctuations in aggregate demand are the cause of business cycles.

3. The impulse in the Keynesian theory of business cycles is a change in business' expectations of future sales and profits.

4. In the Keynesian theory, money wages do not fall in response to a decrease in aggregate demand.

5. According to the new classical rational expectations theory, an expected decrease in aggregate demand causes a recession.

6. The new Keynesian theory of the business cycle stresses intertemporal substitution.

Real Business Cycle Theory

7. According to the real business cycle theory, the cause of a recession is a slowdown in the growth rate of the quantity of money.

8. The real business cycle theory assumes that money wages are flexible and adjust quickly.

9. According to the real business cycle theory, the actual GDP always equals potential GDP.

Recessions and Expansions During the 1990s

10. The primary cause of the 1990–1991 recession was a dramatic slowdown in the growth of the money supply.

11. In the United States, between 1991 and 1998 both aggregate supply and aggregate demand have increased.

12. The Japanese slow growth experience of the 1990s was caused by very high interest rates.

The Great Depression

13. The stock market crash of 1929 was the cause of the Great Depression.

14. The existence of the Federal Deposit Insurance Corporation reduces the likelihood that a recession like the Great Depression could happen again.

15. One reason that a recession is unlikely to grow into another Great Depression is that the government sector today is much larger than it was during the 1930s.

■ Multiple Choice

Cycle Patterns, Impulses, and Mechanisms

1. An average recession lasts for about ____; an average expansion lasts for about ____.
   a. 1 year; 1 year
   b. 4 years; 1 year
   c. 1 year; 4 years
   d. 4 years; 4 years

2. In an average recession, real GDP falls by about
   _____; in an average expansion real GDP climbs by
   about _____.
   a. 6 percent; 6 percent
   b. 22 percent; 6 percent
   c. 6 percent; 22 percent
   d. 22 percent; 22 percent

3. Recessions begin when _____ decreases.
   a. consumption expenditure
   b. investment
   c. government purchases
   d. net exports

Aggregate Demand Theories of the Business Cycle

4. Which of the following is the impulse in the
   Keynesian business cycle theory?
   a. An unexpected change in aggregate demand.
   b. A change by the Fed in the growth rate of the
      quantity of money.
   c. A change in expectations about future sales and
      profits.
   d. A change in the growth rate of productivity.

5. Which theory of the business cycle has a mechanism
   that allows the economy to remain in a recession
   indefinitely?
   a. Keynesian
   b. Monetarist
   c. New classical
   d. New Keynesian

6. Which of the following is the impulse in the monetarist business cycle theory?
   a. An unexpected change in aggregate demand.
   b. A change by the Fed in the growth rate of the
      quantity of money.
   c. A change in expectations about future sales and
      profits.
   d. A change in the growth rate of productivity.

7. In the monetarist theory, a decrease in the growth
   rate of the quantity of money _____ decreases GDP
   and _____ decreases employment.
   a. temporarily; temporarily
   b. temporarily; permanently
   c. permanently; temporarily
   d. permanently; permanently

8. Which of the following is the impulse in the new
   classical business cycle theory?
   a. An unexpected change in aggregate demand.
   b. A change by the Fed in the growth rate of the
      quantity of money.
   c. A change in expectations about future sales and
      profits.
   d. A change in the growth rate of productivity.

9. According to the rational expectations theories, if
   the Federal Reserve unexpectedly reduces the money
   supply during a recession,
   a. nothing will happen because the recession is al-
      ready occurring.
   b. the recession will tend to deepen, as aggregate
      demand unexpectedly decreases.
   c. the recession will tend to end because aggregate
      supply unexpectedly increases.
   d. the recession will tend to end because aggregate
      demand unexpectedly increases.

Real Business Cycle Theory

10. Which of the following is the impulse in the real
    business cycle theory?
    a. An unexpected change in aggregate demand.
    b. A change by the Fed in the growth rate of the
       quantity of money.
    c. A change in expectations about future sales and
       profits.
    d. A change in the growth rate of productivity.

11. The intertemporal substitution effect refers to the
    idea that
    a. a higher real wage rate increases the quantity of
       labor supplied.
    b. a higher real wage rate decreases the quantity of
       labor supplied.
    c. a higher real interest rate increases the supply of
       labor.
    d. the demand for labor depends on the money
       wage rate, not the real wage rate although the
       supply of labor depends on the real wage rate.

12. By itself, an increase in aggregate demand increases
    GDP by the least amount in the _____.
    a. Keynesian theory
    b. monetarist theory
    c. new Keynesian theory
    d. real business cycle theory

13. According to the _____ theory of business cycles, a change in the monetary growth rate has no effect on real GDP.
    a. Keynesian
    b. monetarist
    c. new Keynesian
    d. real business cycle

14. Which of the following is <u>NOT</u> a criticism of the real business cycle theory?
    a. The impulse assumed for the real business cycle theory is implausible.
    b. The long-run aggregate supply curve is vertical.
    c. Money wages are sticky.
    d. The changes in productivity ascribed to technology actually are caused by aggregate demand.

Recessions and Expansions During the 1990s

15. The 1990–1991 recession in the United States was caused by a decrease in aggregate
    a. supply, accompanied by an increase in aggregate demand.
    b. supply and a decrease in aggregate demand.
    c. demand alone.
    d. demand, accompanied by an increase in aggregate supply.

16. The expansion in the U.S. during the 1990s most closely resembles the type of expansion predicted by the _____ theory.
    a. Keynesian
    b. monetarist
    c. new Keynesian
    d. real business cycle

17. From 1992 to 1998, U.S. economic growth was _____ Japan's economic growth.
    a. greater than
    b. equal to
    c. less than
    d. not comparable to

18. Which of the following is a cause of Japan's low GDP growth during the 1990s?
    a. Unexpectedly slow monetary growth.
    b. A soaring stock market that lead to more saving.
    c. Market distortions that have created low productivity growth.
    d. None of the above answers are correct.

The Great Depression

19. The Great Depression was the result of a _____ shift of the aggregate _____ curve.
    a. leftward; supply
    b. rightward; supply
    c. rightward; demand
    d. leftward; demand

20. According to monetarists such as Milton Friedman, the Great Depression was caused by
    a. the stock market crash of 1929.
    b. a massive contraction of the money supply, leading to large decreases in aggregate demand.
    c. an expansion of the money supply, leading to higher inflation.
    d. loss of business and consumer confidence.

21. In which episode was there a wave of bank failures?
    a. The Great Depression of the 1930s.
    b. The Japanese recession of the 1990s.
    c. The recession of 1990–1991.
    d. Both the Great Depression of the 1930s and the recession of 1990–1991.

22. The Federal Deposit Insurance Corporation (FDIC)
    a. keeps reserve requirements high so that banks can meet large withdrawals.
    b. loans reserves to banks.
    c. insures deposits, thereby reducing the incentive for depositors to make large withdrawals from banks expected to fail.
    d. insures banks against bad loans.

23. During the Great Depression, the Federal Reserve _____ the discount rate and allowed the money supply to _____.
    a. lowered; expand
    b. lowered; contract
    c. raised; expand
    d. raised; contract

24. Multi-income families reduce the probability of another Great Depression by
    a. reducing the probability of everyone in the family being simultaneously unemployed.
    b. investing more in the economy.
    c. paying more taxes.
    d. increasing fluctuations in consumption expenditure.

■ Short Answer Problems

FIGURE **17.4**

Short Answer Problem 1

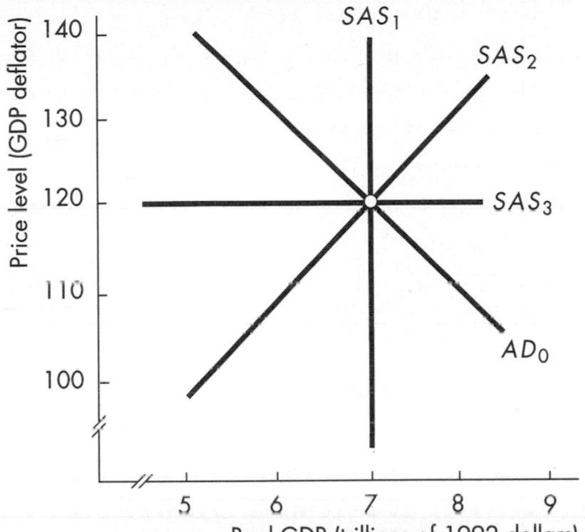

1. Figure 17.4 shows the initial aggregate demand curve, AD_0, and three aggregate supply curves.

   a. Which aggregate supply curve is consistent with Keynesian theory?

   b. Which aggregate supply curve is consistent with monetarist theory?

   c. Which aggregate supply curve is consistent with real business cycle theory?

2. Suppose that the aggregate demand curve in Figure 17.4 shifts leftward by $2 trillion.

   a. Draw this shift in Figure 17.4.

   b. Along which aggregate supply curve is the decrease in GDP the largest? The least?

   c. Relate your answers to part (b) to your answers to problem 1. For a decrease in aggregate demand, which theory predicts the largest decrease in GDP? The smallest decrease in GDP? The largest change in the price level? The smallest?

3. Suppose that the economy is in a recession. Further suppose that people *now* come to expect the Fed to respond by increasing the money supply.

   a. According to the new classical theory, what is the effect on real GDP and employment of the increase in the money supply?

   b. According to the new Keynesian theory, what is the effect on real GDP and employment of the increase in the money supply?

TABLE **17.1**

Theories and Impulses

Theory	Impulse
Keynesian	
Monetarist	
New classical	
New Keynesian	
Real business cycle	

4. Complete Table 17.1 by listing the impulse that each theory stresses as the primary cause of business cycles.

5. What is the basic controversy among economists about the behavior of the labor market during a recession? What is each theory's position in this controversy? Why is the controversy important in terms of designing an appropriate antirecessionary economic policy?

6. What caused the recession that became the Great Depression? What changed the recession into the Great Depression?

7. List four important features of the U.S. economy that make severe depression less likely today. Explain how each factor helps stabilize the economy.

8. How do government transfer payments help reduce the severity of a recession caused by an unexpected decrease in aggregate demand?

■ You're the Teacher

1. "Even before I read this chapter, I thought that business cycles were important. But one thing that I just can't understand is why economists can't figure out which theory of business cycles is correct. That's so important, I'd have thought they would know which theory is right! Are economists stupid or what?" Your friend has a rather jaundiced view of economists' intelligence. You would certainly like to set your friend straight about how bright economists are by explaining why the cause(s) of business cycles aren't totally known.

Answers

■ True/False Answers

Cycle Patterns, Impulses, and Mechanisms

1. **T** The data show that recessions start when investment slows and expansions begin when investment accelerates.

Aggregate Demand Theories of the Business Cycle

2. **T** The sole exception to the focus on aggregate demand is the real business cycle theory, which stresses fluctuations in aggregate supply as the source of business cycles.

3. **T** Because businesses' expectations about future profits can change so rapidly, Keynes called them "animal spirits."

4. **T** Because money wages do not fall, the economy remains stuck in a recession until aggregate demand increases.

5. **F** A decrease in aggregate demand causes a recession only if it is unexpected.

6. **F** The real business cycle theory stresses intertemporal substitution.

Real Business Cycle Theory

7. **F** Monetarists assign importance to a slowdown in the growth rate of the quantity of money. Real business cycle economists assert that changes in the quantity of money do not create business cycle fluctuations.

8. **T** With rapidly and efficiently adjusting money wages, the real business cycle theory asserts that the economy is always at full employment.

9. **T** According to real business cycle theory, technological change affects potential GDP, and it is fluctuations in potential GDP that cause business cycles.

Recessions and Expansions During the 1990s

10. **F** The primary causes were an increase in oil prices combined with an increase in uncertainty.

11. **T** Both aggregate demand and aggregate supply have increased. The increase in aggregate demand has exceeded that in aggregate supply, so the price level has risen.

12. **F** Japanese interest rates have been very low not very high.

The Great Depression

13. **F** The stock market crash may have increased uncertainty and helped spur the initial recession in 1929. However, it was not the sole cause of the Great Depression.

14. **T** By insuring deposits in banks, the FDIC relieves people of the worry that if their banks fail they might lose their funds.

15. **T** The government sector tends to stabilize the economy because government purchases do not decline in a recession.

■ Multiple Choice Answers

Cycle Patterns, Impulses, and Mechanisms

1. **c** Recessions are shorter than expansions.

2. **c** Generally, after each recession GDP climbs during the next expansion to new heights.

3. **b** A slowing of investment "kicks off" almost all recessions.

Aggregate Demand Theories of the Business Cycle

4. **c** The Keynesian theory emphasizes expectations of future sales and profits.

5. **a** Because money wages are assumed not to respond to decreases in aggregate demand, after a decrease in aggregate demand the economy remains mired in a recession until some other factor causes an increase in aggregate demand.

6. **b** Monetarists assert that the major impulse in creating business cycles is changes in the growth rate of the quantity of money.

7. **a** The decline in the growth rate of the quantity of money causes a recession, but then, as money wages adjust to the lower price level, the recession ends and the economy returns to full employment.

8. **a** The new classical theory point to unexpected changes in aggregate demand as the impulse that causes business cycles.

9. **b** According to the rational expectations theories, unexpected decreases in aggregate demand decrease GDP.

Real Business Cycle Theory

10. **d** The real business cycle theory asserts that the impulse leading to business cycles is changes in the growth rate of productivity.

11. **c** Basically, the higher real interest rate boosts the return from savings, so, in order to earn more and thus save more, people increase their supply of labor when the real interest rate rises.

12. **d** In the real business cycle theory, a change in aggregate demand by itself has no effect on real GDP; instead, it affects only the price level.

13. **d** Real business cycle theory asserts that only real factors can affect real GDP.

14 **b** The long-run aggregate supply is vertical in all theories because it reflects potential real GDP.

Recessions and Expansions During the 1990s

15. **b** The decrease in aggregate supply was caused by an increase in the price of oil; aggregate demand decreased because of greater uncertainty about future profits, which decreased investment.

16. **d** The expansion was created by increased productivity that has been the result of technological change, factors emphasized by the real business cycle theory.

17. **a** Between 1992 to 1998, U.S. economic growth was strong, with real GDP expanding by more than 20 percent. Japans' economic growth was much weaker, with real GDP expanding only 7 percent before heading into a severe recession in 1999.

18. **c** In part, Japan's low economic growth is the result of slow productivity growth.

The Great Depression

19. **d** Though which factors shifted the aggregate demand curve is controversial, the Great Depression reflected massive leftward shifts in the aggregate demand curve.

20. **b** Monetarists point to the Great Depression as evidence that changes in monetary growth are a major cause of business cycles.

21. **a** During the Great Depression the wave of bank failures dwarfed previous experience. Since the Great Depression, federal deposit insurance has eliminated bank failures as a major feature of recessions.

22. **c** By insuring deposits, the FDIC helps reduce the extent of bank failures.

23. **d** Economists generally agree that the Fed's policy during the Great Depression was the opposite of what it should have been.

24. **a** Because everyone in the family is not likely to be unemployed simultaneously, the family's income is much less likely to fall to zero. As a result, the family's consumption expenditures are more stable.

■ Answers to Short Answer Problems

1. a. Aggregate supply curve SAS_3 is consistent with the Keynesian view of a horizontal aggregate supply curve.

   b. Aggregate supply curve SAS_2 is a monetarist, upward-sloping aggregate supply curve.

   c. Real business cycle theory assets that the economy is always on its vertical long-run aggregate supply, so the real business cycle aggregate supply curve is SAS_1.

FIGURE **17.5**
Short Answer Problem 2

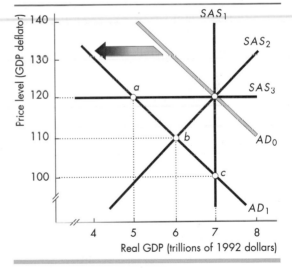

2. a. Figure 17.5 shows the $2 trillion decrease in aggregate demand.

   b. Along aggregate supply curve SAS_3 the new equilibrium is at point *a*. The price level has stayed constant (at 120), but GDP has declined by $2 trillion. The smallest change in GDP occurs with aggregate supply curve SAS_1. Along this aggregate supply curve, the new equilibrium is at point *c*, so the price level falls the most (from 120 to 100), but GDP does not change. It remains at $7 trillion.

c. Figure 17.5 shows that for a decrease in aggregate demand, the Keynesian theory (with its new equilibrium at point *a*) predicts the largest change in GDP and the smallest change in the price level. The real business cycle theory (with its new equilibrium at point *c*) predicts the largest change in the price level and the smallest change in GDP. Finally, the monetarist theory (with its new equilibrium at point *b*) is midway between the two extremes.

3. a. In the new classical theory only unexpected changes in aggregate demand affect real GDP and employment. If people expect the Federal Reserve to increase the money supply, they will expect the resulting increase in aggregate demand. Therefore the expected change in aggregate demand has no effect on GDP nor on employment.

   b. According to the new Keynesian theory, even though the increase in money supply is expected, it becomes expected only *after* some wage contracts have been signed. The increase in the money supply was unexpected when the contracts were signed. Hence the expected policy will still increase real GDP and employment.

TABLE **17.2**

Theories and Impulses

Theory	Impulse
Keynesian	Changes in expectations about future sales and profits
Monetarist	Changes in the monetary growth rate
New classical	Unexpected changes in aggregate demand
New Keynesian	Changes in aggregate demand that were unexpected when labor contracts were signed
Real business cycle	Changes in productivity growth

4. Table 17.2 shows the impulse that each theory stresses as the primary cause of business cycles. You may find this table a helpful summary of the different theories.

5. Economists disagree about the speed with which the money (and hence also the real) wage rate adjusts in the labor market.

Some economists (Keynesians and new Keynesians) believe that money wages are sticky and adjust only slowly to price level changes; indeed, Keynesian economists think that money wages do not adjust to decreases in aggregate demand. Monetarists also believe that money wages are sticky, but not as sticky as Keynesian and new Keynesian economists think. In particular, money wages will adjust to changes in the price level, but not immediately, in the monetarist view. New classical economists also may acknowledge some stickiness in money wages but less so than monetarists do. However, real business cycle economists think that the money wage is flexible and quickly adjusts to changes in the price level. As a result, the labor market always is in equilibrium and changes in employment reflect changes in full employment.

This issue has a significant implication for the design of an appropriate policy to respond to recession. If the Keynesians and new Keynesians are correct, expansionary monetary or fiscal policies may be useful in counteracting recessions because the decrease in employment is a sign that money wages are failing to adjust. However, if the real business cycle position is correct (so that the decline in employment during the recession is a sign that the level of full employment has fallen), expansionary monetary or fiscal policy will simply increase the rate of inflation and have no effect on real GDP or unemployment.

6. The major cause of the Great Depression was a decrease in aggregate demand, which was the consequence of reduced investment and consumer expenditure (especially on durable goods), owing to uncertainty and pessimism. However, these changes created only a "typical" recession, not the Great Depression. The reason(s) for the recession's worsening are controversial. Some economists contend that further decreases in aggregate demand caused by uncertainty led to the Great Depression. Other economists assert that the Federal Reserve failed to act in a timely and proper manner. In particular, these economists point to the massive contraction in the money supply and the waves of bank failures as the factors that converted a recession into the Great Depression.

7. Four important features of the U.S. economy that make severe depression less likely today are that:

   1. bank deposits are insured;

2. the Federal Reserve is better prepared to be the "lender of last resort";

3. taxes and government spending are a larger fraction of GDP; and

4. multi-income families are more economically secure.

The first two reasons make a collapse of the money supply and the banking system much less likely today. With deposit insurance, bank failures do not feed on each other; that is, if a bank fails today, its depositors are not afraid that they will lose all the deposits that have entrusted to the bank. Hence bank failures do not feed on each other. The fact that the Federal Reserve is more determined to play an active "lender of last resort" role means that, when banks need emergency funds, the Fed will loan them the funds rather than allow the bank to fail. Consequently, for both reasons, a massive wave of bank failures and contraction of the money supply, as occurred during the Great Depression, is unlikely.

The larger size of the government sector helps stabilize aggregate demand. Government purchases do not (automatically) decline during recessions, so aggregate demand may decrease less. As income falls during a recession, so too do income taxes, which helps moderate the drop in disposable income and thus stabilizes consumption expenditure.

Finally, the increased number of multi-income families also helps stabilize the economy. In a multi-income family, when one worker becomes unemployed during a recession, the family still has income from its other wage earner(s). Thus this family's consumption expenditures do not decrease as much during a recession and overall consumption expenditure — and hence aggregate demand — becomes more stable.

8. When a recession arises, unemployment increases and disposable income declines. Less disposable income leads to a reduction in consumption expenditure, which has a further multiplier effect (negatively) on aggregate demand. Transfer payments reduce the secondary effects of a recession by reducing the amount by which disposable income falls. As incomes fall and unemployment increases, government transfer payments increase in the form of higher unemployment benefits or other welfare payments. As a result, the decline in both disposable income and consumption are reduced.

■ You're the Teacher

1. "Look, economists really are smart. They're working on something that is *incredibly* complex. Let me give you an example: Economists would like to know how much a change in the money supply affects real GDP. Think of all the different possibilities. Man! Keynesians and monetarists say that changes in the money supply can have large effects. Rational expectations economists think that only unexpected changes can affect real GDP. And the real business cycle theory says that changes in the money supply have no effect. Just like you said, this range of answers sure covers all the bases!

"But, think about what we'd have to do to determine which answer is correct: Basically, we'd have to change the money supply and nothing else. That is, government spending couldn't change, the price of oil couldn't change, technology couldn't change — nothing could change. If any of these other things varied, real GDP might change because of that factor, not because of the change in the money supply. If we could conduct this type of 'controlled' experiment, we could figure out exactly how changes in the quantity of money affected real GDP. Do you think anyone will get to conduct this experiment? Of course not! So economists have to try to disentangle all the different things that affect real GDP and unemployment. All these things — taxes, government spending, technology, oil prices, interest rates, and the money supply — change every day, and each may have an impact on GDP. Isolating the effect of any one of them is nearly impossible.

"Economists do the best they can because they know the importance of figuring out which theory is right. And, you know, I think that working on this issue might actually be a real kick; I'm thinking about switching majors to economics! Becoming an economist can give me to chance to really help make a bunch of people's lives a lot better off. So, if I switch majors, you know that economists have to be really smart!"

Chapter Quiz

1. At the onset of a recession, _____ typically decreases.
   a. consumption expenditure
   b. investment
   c. government purchases
   d. net exports

2. Which theory assumes that money wages rates will not fall in a recession?
   a. The Keynesian theory.
   b. The monetarist theory.
   c. The new classical theory.
   d. The real business cycle theory.

3. Which theory assumes that the major cause of a business cycle expansion is an increase in the monetary growth rate?
   a. The Keynesian theory.
   b. The monetarist theory.
   c. The real business cycle theory.
   d. None of the above.

4. Which theory focuses on shifts in aggregate supply as the cause of business cycles?
   a. The Keynesian theory.
   b. The monetarist theory.
   c. The new classical theory.
   d. The real business cycle theory.

5. In which theory can a factor that was expected when a labor contract was signed have no effect on GDP?
   a. The Keynesian theory.
   b. The monetarist theory.
   c. The new Keynesian theory.
   d. None of the above.

6. In real business cycle models, business cycles exist because of
   a. repeated shocks to technology.
   b. policy errors by the Federal Reserve.
   c. repeated changes by Congress in tax rates.
   d. frequent changes in the public's labor supply.

7. In the 1990s, fiscal policy in Japan was
   a always expansionary.
   b. neutral.
   c. always contractionary.
   d. variable, during some times highly expansionary and at other times contractionary.

8. The Great Depression occurred in
   a. the 1930s.
   b. the 1940s.
   c. the 1970s.
   d. the 1980s.

9. During the Great Depression, GDP fell by approximately
   a. 2 percent.
   b. 11 percent.
   c. 19 percent.
   d. 29 percent.

10. Which of the following makes another Great Depression less likely?
    a. The fact that the *MPC* is lower in recent years.
    b. The fact that the *MPC* is higher in recent years.
    c. The existence of FDIC insurance for bank deposits.
    d. The fact that disposable income is higher in recent years.

The answers for this Chapter Quiz are on page 328

18 MACROECONOMIC POLICY CHALLENGES*

Key Concepts

■ Policy Goals

Four domestic macroeconomic policy goals are to:

♦ Achieve the highest sustainable rate of growth of potential real GDP.

♦ Smooth avoidable business cycle fluctuations.

♦ Maintain low unemployment.

♦ Maintain low inflation.

The first three goals are linked to the growth rate of real GDP. Hence the four policy goals can be defined in terms of two core targets — the growth rate of real GDP and the inflation rate.

■ Policy Tools and Performance

Fiscal policy is the use of the federal budget to achieve macroeconomic objectives; **monetary policy** is the adjustment of the quantity of money and interest rates to achieve macroeconomic goals.

Fiscal policy has ranged from mildly expansionary during the Kennedy years of the early 1960s to strongly expansionary during the Johnson years of the late 1960s to expansionary during the first Reagan term to somewhat contractionary during the Clinton years.

The money supply growth rate increased at the end of the 1960s and remained high throughout the 1970s before slowing after 1980. Monetary policy, whether measured by the growth rate of M2 or short-term interest rates, generally is expansionary before a presidential election and contractionary afterward. The two exceptions involved the failed reelection bids of Jimmy Carter and George Bush.

■ Long-Term Growth Policy

To increase the nation's long-term growth rate, a policy must increase one or more of the following:

♦ *National saving:* National saving equals government saving plus private saving. National saving can be increased either by increasing government saving, that is, by increasing the government budget surplus, or by enacting tax policies that raise the return from private saving, thereby increasing private saving.

♦ *Investment in human capital:* Policies that increase access to schooling and improve schools boost investment in human capital.

♦ *Investment in new technologies:* Policies, such as tax credits, that increase the return from developing new technologies, can raise investment in new technologies.

---

* This is Chapter 35 in *Economics*.

■ Business Cycle and Unemployment Policy

Policies fall into three categories:

♦ **Fixed-rule policies** — policies that are independent of the state of the economy.

♦ **Feedback-rule policies** — policies that respond to the economy.

♦ **Discretionary policies** — policies that respond to the state of the economy in a possibly unique way, depending on the policymaker's judgment. Discretionary policy essentially is a type of sophisticated feedback-rule policy.

Fixed and feedback rules react differently to aggregate demand shocks. In response to a decrease in aggregate demand:

♦ A **monetarist** fixed rule says, "Do nothing." (Monetarists are economists who think fluctuations in the money supply are the main cause of business cycle fluctuations.) This policy allows aggregate demand to decrease, causing a decrease in real GDP and a fall in the price level. If the decrease in aggregate demand is temporary, eventually it returns to its initial level and real GDP returns to potential GDP. If the decrease is permanent, eventually money wages fall so that short-run aggregate supply increases and real GDP returns to potential GDP.

♦ Feedback rules try to counter the swings in aggregate demand. When aggregate demand decreases, **Keynesian activists** advocate expansionary monetary and fiscal policy to offset the decrease. (Keynesians are economists who think fluctuations in aggregate demand combined with sticky money wages are the source of business cycles.) If the policy actions are handled correctly, real GDP remains at potential GDP.

In theory, feedback rules seem superior and the Fed apparently followed such rules from 1992-1998. But some economists argue that, in practice, feedback rules are flawed because they:

♦ Require knowledge of whether GDP is above or below potential GDP, information that may not be available.

♦ Operate with time lags that may be greater than the forecast horizon.

♦ Introduce unpredictability into long-term contracting by forcing people to try to forecast the policies.

A fourth argument against feedback rules is that they fail in the face of aggregate supply shocks. According to real business cycle theory, fluctuations in real GDP are the result of changes in long-run aggregate supply.

♦ With a fixed rule, a decrease in long-run aggregate supply decreases real GDP.

♦ With a feedback rule, a decrease in long-run aggregate supply decreases real GDP, which feeds back into an increase in aggregate demand. The increase in aggregate demand has no effect on real GDP, but can substantially raise the price level.

In reaction to these criticisms, one suggestion is **nominal GDP targeting** — keeping nominal GDP growth steady to avoid swings in inflation and real GDP.

To reduce the natural rate of unemployment, policies must change the incentives for unemployed job seekers or lower the minimum wage.

■ Inflation Policy

Inflation policy involves two issues: Avoiding cost-push inflation and slowing inflation.

Cost-push inflation results when the aggregate supply curve shifts leftward because of cost hikes. Success in avoiding cost-push inflation depends on the type of policy rule being followed:

♦ A monetarist fixed rule does not change aggregate demand in response to the decrease in GDP created by the decrease in aggregate supply. GDP falls and the price level rises, but sustained inflation does not result.

♦ A Keynesian feedback rule increases aggregate demand in response to the decrease in real GDP. The increase in aggregate demand pushes the price level even higher, and the cost increase may recur. A sustained cost-push inflation may break out.

Slowing inflation requires decreasing growth in aggregate demand.

♦ Surprise slowing of the inflation rate by unexpectedly decreasing growth in aggregate demand decreases real GDP and raises unemployment.

♦ A credible announced slowing of the inflation rate may be able to reduce inflation without decreasing GDP or raising unemployment.

♦ In practice, anti-inflationary policy generally causes recessions because economic agents do not believe announced anti-inflationary policies will be carried out.

Helpful Hints

1. **HOW SIGNIFICANT IS THIS CHAPTER?** It asks the most important macroeconomic policy question: Can the government and the Federal Reserve carry out successful policies to make the lives of individuals better?

   The answer makes a great deal of difference for everyone. For instance, if activist policies can be used to avoid business cycles, no college student need fear graduating just when a recession hits and no older worker need fear forced early retirement because of a recession. However, if activist policies actually worsen the severity of recessions, their use may condemn many students to search for work in the face of a severe recession and many older Americans to endure poverty. So the answer to the question of whether the government can carry out policies to improve our lives is tremendously important — and is currently unknown!

2. **DIFFERING VIEWS OF FIXED-RULE AND FEEDBACK-RULE PROPONENTS :** This chapter presents two opposing views of the usefulness of countercyclical policy. Aside from the "practical" problems discussed so clearly in the text, these differing views come partially from differing assumptions about one crucial factor: the speed with which the private sector reacts to macroeconomic shocks relative to the speed with which government reacts.

   The advocates of fixed rules believe that the private sector generally reacts quickly. People have rational expectations and process new information quickly because there are economic incentives to do so. For instance, wages should react quickly to changes in the price level. These advocates also believe that government reacts slowly because of lags in recognizing problems, developing policy, and implementing policy. Fixed-rule advocates conclude that feedback rules at best make no difference and at worst actually harm the economy.

   In contrast, advocates of feedback rules believe that the private sector reacts slowly — people sign long-term contracts that prevent wages from reacting quickly to changes in the price level. They also believe that the government can react more quickly than the private sector and therefore conclude that feedback rules can make the economy better off by speeding recovery from a recession.

Questions

■ True/False/Uncertain and Explain

Policy Goals

1. One of the goals of economic policy is to reduce the unemployment rate below its natural rate.

Policy Tools and Performance

2. In the United States, fiscal policy is implemented by the federal government.

3. The Federal Reserve conducts monetary policy.

Long-Term Growth Policy

4. Increasing national saving likely would increase the economic growth rate.

5. Decreasing the budget surplus will help increase the economy's long-term growth rate.

Business Cycle and Unemployment Policy

6. The statement, "allow the money supply to grow at the constant rate of 3 percent per year," is an example of a feedback-rule policy.

7. Discretionary policy can be characterized as a type of sophisticated feedback policy.

8. Economists agree that a feedback-rule policy is superior to a fixed-rule policy.

9. The less that is known about the natural rate of unemployment and the level of potential GDP, the stronger is the case for a fixed-rule policy.

10. The Fed strives to make its actions predictable and known to everyone as quickly as possible.

11. Feedback rule advocates assert that aggregate supply fluctuations are more frequent than fluctuations in aggregate demand.

12. Nominal GDP targeting is an example of a fixed-rule policy.

Inflation Policy

13. Cost-push inflation is particularly a problem for an economy if it follows monetarist fixed rules.

14. Reducing inflation usually leads to a recession.

15. If the Fed credibly announced its intention to slow the growth in aggregate demand, inflation would slow and GDP would remain equal to potential GDP.

■ Multiple Choice

Policy Goals

1. Which of the following is <u>NOT</u> a macroeconomic policy goal?
   a. Maintaining low inflation
   b. Maintaining low unemployment
   c. Limiting avoidable business cycle fluctuations
   d. Keeping GDP growing faster than potential GDP

2. Which of the following is one of the two core macroeconomic policy targets?
   a. Unemployment constant at 6 percent
   b. Steady growth in real GDP
   c. Steady growth in nominal GDP
   d. Inflation at the natural rate

Policy Tools and Performance

3. In the United States since 1960, fiscal policy has been
   a. persistently expansionary except during the Reagan years.
   b. persistently contractionary.
   c. neutral during the Reagan years and then expansionary during the Clinton years.
   d. expansionary during the Reagan years and then mildly contractionary during the Clinton administration.

4. The data show that in the United States, in the year before an election, monetary policy generally is ____, and in the year after an election, monetary policy generally is ____.
   a. expansionary; expansionary
   b. expansionary; contractionary
   c. contractionary; expansionary
   d. contractionary; contractionary

Long-Term Growth Policy

5. Since 1960, national saving in the United States has
   a. hovered around 20 percent of GDP.
   b. been approximately 5 percent of GDP.
   c. increased steadily and now is about 17 percent of GDP.
   d. averaged around 20 percent of GDP until 1982, after which it fell.

6. Tax changes that raise the return from private saving can be used to help
   a. reduce inflation.
   b. eliminate the business cycle.
   c. increase the rate of economic growth.
   d. increase the natural rate of unemployment.

7. Which of the following would help increase the nation's long-term growth rate?
   a. Raise the inflation rate.
   b. Provide tax incentives for research and development.
   c. Use a feedback rule to limit business cycle fluctuations.
   d. Make government policies more unpredictable.

Business Cycle and Unemployment Policy

8. Which of the following is an example of a fixed-rule policy?
   a. Wear your boots if it snows.
   b. Leave your boots home if it does not snow.
   c. Wear your boots every day.
   d. Listen to the weather forecast and then decide whether to wear your boots.

9. Expanding the money supply when the economy is in a recession is a policy that may
   a. reduce inflation.
   b. help stabilize the business cycle.
   c. increase the rate of economic growth.
   d. increase the natural rate of unemployment.

10. Suppose that a decline in aggregate demand occurs. The feedback rule being followed is: Increase the money supply whenever there is a decrease in aggregate demand. According to Keynesians, if there were no problems with feedback rules, the rule would result in
    a. an increase in real GDP to above potential GDP and a rise in the price level above its original value.
    b. a constant real GDP at potential GDP and a constant price level at its original value.
    c. an increase in real GDP, but not back to potential GDP, and no effect on the price level.
    d. a slow increase in real GDP back to potential GDP and no change in the price level.

11. Monetarists generally
    a. support the use of feedback rules.
    b. support the use of fixed rules.
    c. support nominal GDP targeting.
    d. are divided as to whether a feedback-rule policy or a fixed-rule policy is superior.

12. The rule, "Reduce taxes in a recession," is an example of a
    a. Keynesian fixed-rule policy.
    b. Keynesian feedback-rule policy.
    c. monetarist fixed-rule policy.
    d. monetarist feedback-rule policy.

13. Which type of economist believes that fluctuations in aggregate demand combined with very sticky money wages are the main source of business cycles and that activist feedback-rule policies should be followed?
    a. A Keynesian economist.
    b. A monetarist economist.
    c. A real business cycle economist.
    d. All economists.

14. Businesses become convinced that future profits from investment will be less than initially believed. This conviction causes a change in aggregate _____ and a _____ policy may be able to keep real GDP from falling below potential GDP.
    a. demand; fixed-rule
    b. demand; feedback-rule
    c. supply; feedback-rule
    d. supply; fixed-rule

15. Which of the following has been advanced to support the claim that feedback rules increase fluctuations in GDP?
    a. Policymakers use the wrong feedback rules to achieve their goals.
    b. Policymakers must take actions today that will not have their effects until well into the future.
    c. Policymakers do not really want to stabilize the economy.
    d. Policymakers have enough knowledge of the economy.

16. Economists who favor fixed-rule policies over feedback-rule policies argue that policy lags are
    a. shorter than the forecast horizon and that potential GDP is known reasonably well.
    b. shorter than the forecast horizon and that potential GDP is not known.
    c. longer than the forecast horizon and that potential GDP is known reasonably well.
    d. longer than the forecast horizon and that potential GDP is not known.

17. Which of the following is an argument in favor of a feedback rule?
    a. Feedback rules require greater knowledge of potential GDP than is available.
    b. Feedback rules make aggregate demand more variable than otherwise.
    c. Changes in aggregate supply cause most economic fluctuations.
    d. Changes in aggregate demand cause most economic fluctuations.

18. According to real business cycle theory,
    a. any decrease in real GDP is the result of a decrease in long-run aggregate supply.
    b. fluctuations in aggregate demand change potential real GDP.
    c. fluctuations in aggregate demand cannot affect the price level.
    d. feedback-rule policies are best.

19. According to real business cycle theories, if the Fed increases the money supply when real GDP declines, real GDP will
    a. increase, but only temporarily.
    b. increase permanently.
    c. not change and neither will the price level.
    d. not change but the price level will rise.

20. Nominal GDP targeting
    a. is an example of a fixed-rule policy.
    b. is an example of a feedback-rule policy.
    c. is an example of a discretionary policy.
    d. means carrying out an expansionary policy whenever the inflation rate is high.

Inflation Policy

21. A fixed-rule policy that sets the growth rate of the money supply at 4 percent per year
    a. ensures that cost-push inflation does not occur.
    b. counteracts temporary increases in aggregate demand.
    c. counteracts temporary decreases in real output.
    d. offsets aggregate supply fluctuations.

22. OPEC once again succeeds in drastically raising the price of oil. This price hike creates a change in aggregate ____, and a _____ policy runs the risk of creating a cost-push inflation.
    a. demand; fixed-rule
    b. demand; feedback-rule
    c. supply; feedback-rule
    d. supply; fixed-rule

23. If the Fed unexpectedly reduces the growth rate of the money supply, the short-run Phillips curve
    a. shifts leftward.
    b. shifts rightward.
    c. does not shift.
    d. becomes vertical.

24. The usual result when inflation is reduced is
    a. an immediate strong expansion.
    b. a recession.
    c. more rapid growth in aggregate demand.
    d. not known.

25. When might inflation be reduced without increasing unemployment?
    a. When the Fed unexpectedly reduces inflation.
    b. When the Fed announces that it will reduce inflation and people do not believe the Fed's announcement.
    c. When the Fed announces that it will reduce inflation and people believe the announcement.
    d. Never.

■ Short Answer Problems

1. Distinguish between a fixed-rule policy and a feedback-rule policy.

2. Assume the Fed knows exactly how much and when the aggregate demand curve will shift, both in the absence of monetary policy and when the Fed changes the money supply. Also assume that in 2000, a one-year decrease in aggregate demand occurs but in 2001 it returns to normal. Between 2000 and 2001, potential GDP does not grow.

    a. If the Fed follows the fixed rule, "Hold the money supply constant," in Figure 18.1 show how the temporary decrease in aggregate demand affects real GDP and the price level in 2000.

FIGURE **18.1**

Short Answer Problem 2 (a)

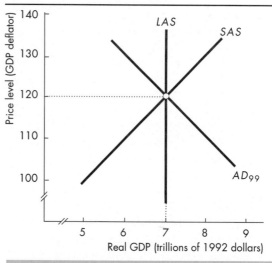

    b. The Fed continues to follow the fixed rule in part (a). In Figure 18.2 show the effect on real GDP and the price level in 2001.

FIGURE **18.2**

Short Answer Problem 2 (b)

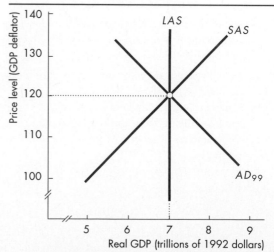

FIGURE **18.3**
Short Answer Problem 2 (c)

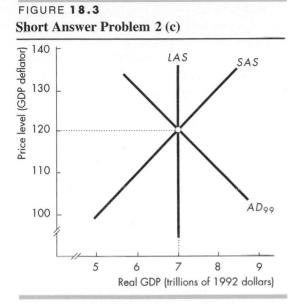

c. The Fed follows the feedback rule, "Raise the money supply whenever aggregate demand decreases and lower it whenever aggregate demand increases." The Fed's goal is to hold GDP equal to potential GDP. If there are no lags in the effect of monetary policy, in Figure 18.3 show the effect in 2000 of the temporary decrease in aggregate demand.

FIGURE **18.4**
Short Answer Problem 2 (d)

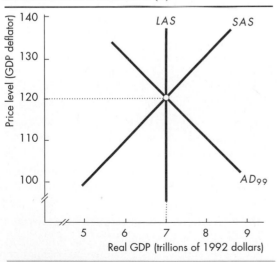

d. The Fed continues to follow the feedback rule in part (c). In Figure 18.4 show the effect of the

Fed's rule in 2001 on real GDP and the price level.

e. Assume that holding GDP as close as possible to potential GDP is a target for policymakers. Which policy — the fixed-rule policy or the feedback-rule policy — is best?

FIGURE **18.5**
Short Answer Problem 3 (a)

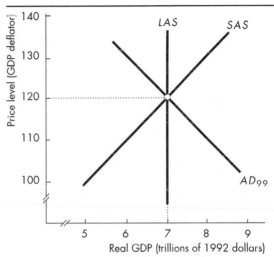

3. As in problem 2, the Fed knows exactly how much the aggregate demand curve will shift. In 2000 aggregate demand decreases but in 2001 it returns to normal. Between 2000 and 2001, potential GDP does not grow. But now assume that the Fed does not know when a change in the money supply will shift the aggregate demand curve.

a. Assume that the Fed follows the feedback rule, "Increase the money supply whenever aggregate demand decreases and decrease it whenever aggregate demand increases," and that the Fed's target is to hold real GDP equal to potential GDP. However, the Fed's policy of increasing the money supply does not have an effect for one year. In Figure 18.5, show the effect in 2000 of the temporary decrease in aggregate demand and policy response.

b. The Fed continues to follow the feedback rule. In Figure 18.6 (on the next page) show the effect in 2001 on real GDP and the price level. (Recall the policy undertaken in 2000.)

c. Has the Fed helped stabilize or destabilize the economy? Explain.

FIGURE **18.6**
Short Answer Problem 3 (b)

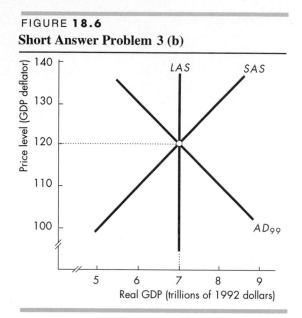

FIGURE **18.8**
Short Answer Problem 4 (b)

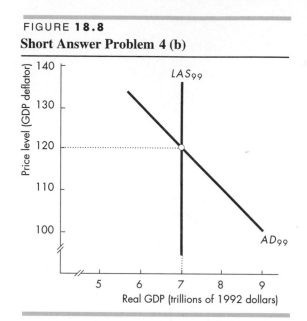

4. As in problem 2, suppose that the Fed knows exactly how much and when the aggregate demand curve will shift. However, unknown to the Fed, the economy operates according to the real business cycle theory; that is, the economy is always on its *LAS* curve. In 2000 a slowdown in productivity growth decreases long-run aggregate supply.

   a. If the Fed follows the fixed rule, "Hold the money supply constant," in Figure 18.7 show how the decrease in aggregate supply affects real GDP and the price level in 2000.

FIGURE **18.7**
Short Answer Problem 4 (a)

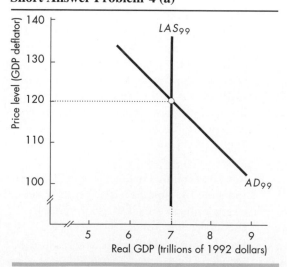

   b. Assume that the Federal Reserve follows the feedback rule, "Increase the money supply whenever real GDP decreases and decrease it whenever real GDP increases." If there are no lags in the effect of monetary policy, in Figure 18.8 show the combined effect in 2000 of the decrease in aggregate supply and the Fed's policy.

   c. Assume that holding GDP as close as possible to potential GDP is a target for policymakers. Which policy — the fixed-rule policy or the feedback-rule policy — is best? If keeping the inflation rate low is another target, which policy is best?

5. Summarize the results from problems 2, 3, and 4 by discussing when a feedback-rule policy and when a fixed-rule policy works best for society.

6. The very purpose of policy is to stabilize. How, then, can feedback rules result in even greater variability in aggregate demand?

7. What are the two core macroeconomic policy targets? How are they achieved theoretically with nominal GDP targeting?

8. If the Fed announced its intention to reduce the rate of inflation by lessening the rate of growth of the money supply, expected inflation would decline accordingly. Thus a reduction in the actual rate of inflation could be achieved without a recession. Why does this result not seem to be the case?

9. What is the relationship between policies designed to foster more rapid growth in potential GDP and policies designed to limit business cycle fluctuations in economic activity? Do any of these policies overlap? Explain. Is there a source of potential conflict between the policy goal of more rapid growth and the policy goal of limiting business cycles? If so, what is it?

■ You're the Teacher

1. Your friend is asking your opinion: "After reading this chapter, I'm confused. I don't know if the government should conduct activist, feedback-rule policies, or if it should stick to nonactivist, fixed-rule policies. What do you think?" Answer your friend's question.

Answers

True/False Answers

Policy Goals

1. **F** One of the goals is to hold the unemployment rate equal to the natural rate.

Policy Tools and Performance

2. **T** Fiscal policy refers to changes in federal government spending or taxing and so is under the control of the federal government.

3. **T** As Chapter 15 discussed, the Federal Reserve conducts the nation's monetary policy.

Long-Term Growth Policy

4. **T** By increasing the national saving rate, the nation can accumulate more capital, which would increase its economic growth rate.

5. **F** *Increasing* the government's budget surplus is a policy that would raise the growth rate.

Business Cycle and Unemployment Policy

6. **F** The statement in the question is a fixed rule because the monetary growth rate is fixed regardless of the current state of the economy.

7. **T** Discretionary policy means that policymakers respond to the current state of the economy, which is a form of feedback policy.

8. **F** The superiority of feedback rules or fixed rules is an issue that is still very clouded by much uncertainty.

9. **T** Uncertainty about the natural rate of unemployment and potential GDP means that incorrect policy actions are more likely, which strengthens the case for fixed rules.

10. **F** The Federal Reserve tries to keep many of its actions under wraps and does not necessarily strive to publicize its actions.

11. **F** Feedback rule proponents believe that most fluctuations come from aggregate demand.

12. **F** Nominal GDP targeting is a feedback rule because policy responds to current changes in nominal GDP.

Inflation Policy

13. **F** Fixed rules do not allow the money supply to react to cost changes, so fixed rules basically eliminate the possibility of cost-push inflation because aggregate demand does not respond to cost hikes.

14. **T** Reducing inflation most often leads to a recession.

15. **T** A credible announcement slows growth in money wages simultaneously with slowing the growth of prices, leaving real GDP equal to potential GDP.

Multiple Choice Answers

Policy Goals

1. **d** Achieving the highest sustainable growth in potential GDP is a goal.

2. **b** The other core macroeconomic policy target is keeping the inflation rate low.

Policy Tools and Performance

3. **d** Fiscal policy was expansionary during the Reagan years when taxes were cut and government purchases increased but contractionary during the years of the Clinton administration.

4. **b** The tendency for monetary policy to be expansionary before an election raises the possibility that monetary policy is conducted on the basis of politics rather than concern about taming the business cycle.

Long-Term Growth Policy

5. **d** The decline in national saving has led analysts to suggest policies designed to reverse the decline.

6. **c** By increasing the return from private saving, private saving will increase and the nation will accumulate more capital.

7. **b** By supporting research and development activities, the government can encourage the development of new technologies.

Business Cycle and Unemployment Policy

8. **c** Rule (c) is a fixed rule because it does not depend on the day's weather.

9. **b** By increasing aggregate demand, an expansionary monetary policy may reduce the high unemployment rate that occurs in a recession.

10. **b** The question demonstrates the situation wherein feedback rules help the economy by eliminating business cycle fluctuations in production and employment.

11. **b** Monetarists believe that feedback rules worsen economic performance, so they support fixed rules.

12. **b** The rule has taxes that depend on the state of the economy and thus is a feedback rule, the type of rule advocated by Keynesian economists.

13. **a** The impulse that causes business cycles in the Keynesian theory is fluctuations in aggregate demand caused by fluctuations in investment. Keynesians also recommend that these fluctuations be countered by activist feedback rules.

14. **b** A feedback-rule policy in this case increases aggregate demand. Such a policy offsets the initial decrease in aggregate demand and may keep production at potential real GDP.

15. **b** Lags may cause a policy to have an inappropriate effect when it finally impacts the economy.

16. **d** Both long lags and uncertainty about potential GDP increase the possibility that fixed rules would be superior to feedback rules.

17. **d** If changes in aggregate demand cause most of the fluctuations in GDP, feedback rules that shift aggregate demand in the opposite direction can offset the initial shock and help smooth the business cycle.

18. **a** Real business cycle theory asserts that the economy always produces on its long-run aggregate supply curve.

19. **d** In the real business cycle view, real GDP is determined solely by long-run aggregate supply, so monetary policy, which affects only aggregate demand, cannot change real GDP. Instead, monetary policy affects only the price level.

20. **b** Nominal GDP targeting makes policy depend on the rate of growth of nominal GDP.

Inflation Policy

21. **a** A major benefit of fixed rules that specify low rates of monetary growth is that they eliminate the possibility of high and persisting inflation.

22. **c** By decreasing aggregate supply, the increase in oil prices raises the price level and decreases real GDP. If the Fed's feedback rule conducts an expansionary monetary policy, the price level will rise still more, leading OPEC to again raise the price of oil, which creates a cost-push inflation.

23. **c** The unexpected change in the monetary growth rate cannot affect people's expectations about the

inflation rate, so the short-run Phillips curve does not shift.

24. **b** Reductions in inflation generally are accompanied by a recession.

25. **c** A credible, announced policy of reducing inflation may allow people's expectations to change so that inflation can be reduced without increasing unemployment.

■ **Answers to Short Answer Problems**

1. The difference between a fixed-rule policy and a feedback-rule policy is whether the specified action depends on the state of the economy. A fixed-rule policy specifies an action that will be pursued regardless of the state of the economy. For instance, a fixed-rule policy of increasing the money supply by 3 percent per year implies that the money supply will be increased by 3 percent regardless of whether the economy is expanding or contracting. In contrast, a feedback-rule policy of increasing the growth rate of the money supply if the economy is in a recession and decreasing the growth rate if the economy is in an expansion means that the growth rate of the money supply will change according to the state of the economy.

FIGURE **18.9**
Short Answer Problem 2 (a)

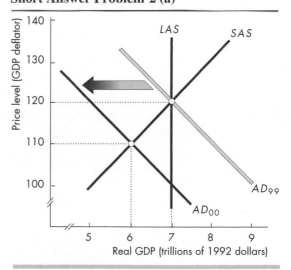

2. a. Figure 18.9 shows the effect. With a fixed rule, nothing offsets the decline in aggregate demand. Hence the decrease in aggregate demand decreases real GDP (from $7 trillion to $6 trillion) and the price level falls (from 120 to 110).

FIGURE **18.10**

Short Answer Problem 2 (b)

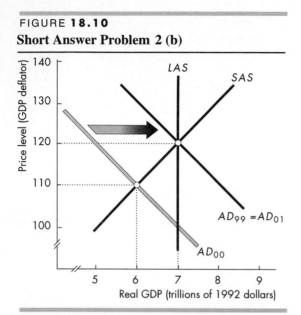

b. As Figure 18.10 shows, in 2001 the aggregate demand curve returns to its initial level of AD_{99}. Hence real GDP returns to its initial, full employment level of $7 trillion, and the price level returns to the initial level of 120.

FIGURE **18.11**

Short Answer Problem 2 (c)

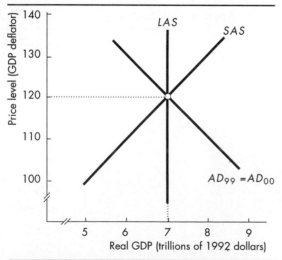

c. A feedback rule offsets the initial decrease in aggregate demand. The Fed's expansionary policy keeps aggregate demand stationary at AD_{99}. Figure 18.11 shows how real GDP remains at its full employment level ($7 trillion), with the price level remaining unchanged.

FIGURE **18.12**

Short Answer Problem 2 (d)

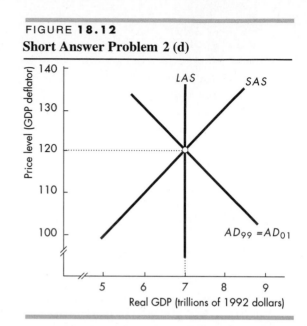

d. In 2001 aggregate demand returns to normal so the Fed terminates its expansionary policy. Aggregate demand thus does not change. Just as in Figure 18.12, real GDP equals potential GDP, $7 trillion, and the price level equals 120.

e. The feedback-rule policy was best for the economy because in neither year did real GDP deviate from potential GDP. With the fixed-rule policy, real GDP fell below potential GDP.

FIGURE **18.13**

Short Answer Problem 3 (a)

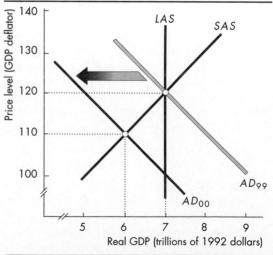

3. a. In 2000 the Fed conducts an expansionary policy, but because the policy does not take effect

until after a one-year lag, the policy has no effect in 2000. Hence as Figure 18.13 demonstrates, in 2000 aggregate demand decreases to AD_{00}, real GDP decreases to $6 trillion, and the price level falls to 110.

FIGURE **18.14**
Short Answer Problem 3 (b)

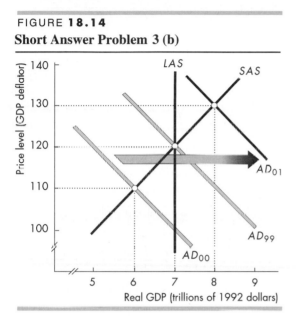

b. In 2001, with the increase in aggregate demand back to normal, the Fed's feedback rule causes it to end the expansionary policy. But in 2001, the expansionary policy that was conducted in 2000 affects the economy. Hence aggregate demand increases all the way to AD_{01}, as shown in Figure 18.14. Thus in 2001, real GDP exceeds potential GDP ($8 trillion instead of $7 trillion) and the price level is higher than otherwise (130 instead of 120).

c. The Fed's policy has destabilized the economy. In particular, business cycle fluctuations in economic activity have been made worse, not better. The Fed did nothing to offset the recession that occurred in 2000 and then, in 2001, the Fed's actions caused GDP to expand more than it otherwise would have.

4. a. Figure 18.15 shows the effect of the fixed rule in 2000. Long-run aggregate supply decreases, shifting the long-run aggregate supply curve from LAS_{99} to LAS_{00}. The fixed rule means that aggregate demand does not change. Hence real GDP decreases (to $6 trillion in the figure) and the price level rises (to 130 in the figure).

FIGURE **18.15**
Short Answer Problem 4 (a)

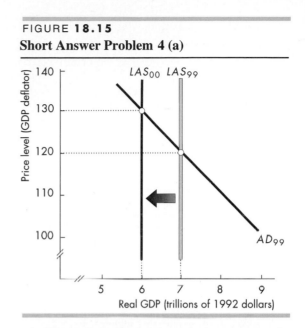

b. The Fed's feedback rule causes it to increase the money supply in 2000. As a result, aggregate demand in 2000 will increase, from AD_{99} in Figure 18.16 to AD_{00}. The long-run aggregate supply curve shifts to LAS_{00}. Hence real GDP decreases (to $6 trillion in the figure), and the price level rises (to 138 in the figure).

FIGURE **18.16**
Short Answer Problem 4 (b)

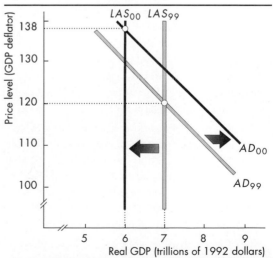

c. Neither rule was able to affect real GDP. Hence, as far as the first target is concerned, both policies have the same impact. However, the fixed rule delivers superior performance with respect to the inflation rate. In particular, with a fixed rule, the price level rose less than with the feedback rule (to 130 versus 138). Thus inflation during 2000 will be less with the fixed rule, so the fixed rule is better than the feedback rule on this count.

5. Problem 2 showed the effect of feedback rules at their best. The Fed's effective use of feedback rules was able to eliminate the pending recession and stabilize real GDP at potential GDP. The fixed rule allowed GDP to fall below potential GDP, which means that unemployment rises above the natural rate.

   However, problems 3 and 4 illustrated potential problems with feedback rules. In problem 3, the feedback rule did not save the economy from a recession in 2000. The lag until the feedback rule influenced aggregate demand allowed aggregate demand to decrease in 2000 and GDP to fall below potential GDP. In this respect, the feedback rule's effect in 2000 was identical to that of the fixed rule illustrated in problem 2 (a). However, in 2001 the feedback's effect was worse than that of the fixed rule. In particular, in 2001, problem 3 (b) showed that the feedback rule boosted GDP past potential GDP and raised the price level higher than it otherwise would have been. In effect, the feedback rule in 2001 created an unsustainable expansion and caused inflation in 2001 to be much higher than otherwise. The fixed rule, whose effect was demonstrated in problem 2 (b), did not have these drawbacks: The fixed rule allowed GDP to return to potential GDP and the price level to return to its initial level. Hence lags in the effect of feedback rules may make them undesirable relative to fixed rules.

   Problem 4 showed another drawback to feedback rules. Neither the fixed rule nor the feedback rule was able to keep GDP from decreasing. But the inflation with the feedback rule is higher than with the fixed rule. (Moreover, the feedback rule may create a sustained cost-push inflation, an effect that is absent from the fixed rule.)

   When feedback rules work well, as in problem 2, they definitely are superior to fixed rules. But when they fail, as in problems 3 and 4, fixed rules are optimal. Thus the ultimate question about policy rules may be: Which is more realistic, the situation described in problem 2 or those described in problems 3 and 4?

6. Policy actions affect aggregate demand only after a time lag. That means that a policy action taken today will have its intended effect sometime in the future. Therefore policymakers must forecast the state of the economy a year or two ahead to be confident that the effect of the policy action taken today will be appropriate when the effect occurs. Such forecasting is very difficult, both because the lags are long and because they are unpredictable. As a result, policymakers face the likelihood that the policy action taken today may have an inappropriate future effect. For instance, an expansionary monetary policy designed to counter a current recession may actually affect the economy two years later when the economy is already enjoying a robust expansion. Thus the expansionary policy may lead to accelerating inflation, which could destabilize rather than stabilize aggregate demand.

7. The two core macroeconomic policy targets are steady growth in real GDP at the maximum sustainable rate and keeping inflation low and predictable.

   Nominal GDP targeting uses feedback rules to try to keep nominal GDP at the target level. Supporters of nominal GDP targeting argue that, if nominal GDP falls below the target, it is the result of falling real GDP, and if nominal GDP rises above the target, it is the result of inflation. Hence conducting expansionary policy when nominal GDP growth is low will increase the growth rate of real GDP so that it moves closer to its maximum sustainable rate. Conducting contractionary policy when nominal GDP growth is high will reduce the inflation rate and keep it low. Achieving the target growth rate for nominal GDP will meet both core targets.

8. The problem is that expected inflation may not decline as a result of the Fed's announcement. A credibility problem may arise because expectations are much more strongly affected by the Fed's record of actions than by its announcements that it will take action. If people do not believe the Fed's announcement, they will not adjust expectations. Then, if the Fed carries out the policy, a recession will result despite the announcement. In addition, even if people did believe the announcement, sticky wages could slow the adjustment of the labor market. Thus even if the announcement was totally

credible, a recession might still be the result of the anti-inflation policy.

9. Policies designed to increase the long-term growth of potential GDP generally are quite different than ones designed to combat business cycle fluctuations in economic activity. To increase the growth rate of potential GDP, policies must be designed to increase national saving, to spur investment in human capital, and to increase research and investment in new technologies. Conversely, to reduce business cycle fluctuations, policies must be designed to off-set fluctuations in aggregate demand (if, indeed, fluctuations in aggregate demand are the source of the business cycle and if policies can successfully limit the fluctuations). Thus tax policies that increase the return from private saving, policies that increase the quality and access to schooling, and tax policies that increase the return from investment in new technologies may increase the rate of growth in potential GDP. They are quite different from the fiscal and monetary policies that might be used to limit business cycles.

However, one source of overlap and possible conflict may exist between the two sets of policies: To increase national saving and hence the growth rate of potential GDP, increasing the government's budget surplus is a potential policy. But to combat a recession, a tax cut and an increase in government spending are potential polices, and these policies decrease the government's budget surplus. Thus fiscal policy designed to stabilize the business cycle also may have an impact on the growth rate of potential GDP.

■ You're the Teacher

1. "I think that a lot of students (and policymakers!) fall into the trap of thinking that feedback rules must be better than fixed rules. I mean, before I read this chapter it seemed so obvious! I thought human intelligence and action must be better than doing nothing! I couldn't understand why we had recessions and slow economic growth because it seemed so clear that these were bad. Then, when I was studying earlier chapters, I thought that the government surely should be able to take actions to avoid recessions and to increase the rate of economic growth. Until I hit this chapter, although I didn't know the technical terms, I imagined that theoretically feedback rules should be able to avoid recessions and maybe even speed up growth. After all, it seemed like feedback rules could do everything fixed rules could, plus more.

"But this chapter was a real eye opener for me. I didn't know the problems with the actual implementation of feedback rules: like they require good knowledge of the economy, introduce unpredictability into the economy, can generate bigger fluctuations in aggregate demand because of lags, and do not work when aggregate supply changes. Once I thought about these things, it was clear that feedback rules aren't necessarily better than fixed rules.

"So, I guess I'm with you. I don't know the government should conduct an activist policy. And, you know, what the government should do is a serious question. In fact, I've been toying with the idea of taking more economics classes to get a better idea of what the answer to this question should be."

Chapter Quiz

1. Which of the following is a macroeconomic policy goal?
   a. Maintain a recessionary gap.
   b. Maintain an inflationary gap.
   c. Eliminate full employment GDP.
   d. Maintain low unemployment.

2. Use of government purchases and taxes for the purpose of stabilizing the economy is called
   a. macro policy.
   b. micro policy.
   c. monetary policy.
   d. fiscal policy.

3. To increase the economic growth rate, the government should NOT
   a. encourage research and development activities.
   b. tax saving.
   c. try to increase investment in new capital.
   d. try to increase investment in human capital.

4. A monetarist argues that the proper response of policy to changes in real GDP is to
   a. cut tax rates.
   b. increase monetary growth.
   c. decrease monetary growth.
   d. maintain constant monetary growth.

5. Under a feedback rule, if the economy is in a recession, an appropriate fiscal policy would be to
   a. decrease government purchases.
   b. not change government purchases or taxes.
   c. decrease taxes.
   d. increase the growth rate of the money supply.

6. Under a fixed rule, if the economy is in a recession, an appropriate fiscal policy would be to
   a. decrease government purchases.
   b. not change government purchases or taxes.
   c. decrease taxes.
   d. increase the growth rate of the money supply.

7. The rule "Always stop at a red light" is a
   a. fixed rule.
   b. feedback rule.
   c. discretionary rule.
   d. rational rule.

8. Advocates of feedback rules claim that
   a. a large amount of information is needed to pursue the correct policy.
   b. policymakers need time to recognize that a problem exists.
   c. the effects of policy take time to impact the economy.
   d. policymakers know enough to nudge the economy in the correct direction.

9. Cost-push inflation starts when
   a. aggregate demand increases.
   b. aggregate demand decreases.
   c. aggregate supply increases.
   d. aggregate supply decreases.

10. A cost-push inflation is least likely to occur when using
    a. a fixed rule.
    b. a feedback rule.
    c. discretionary policy.
    d. None of the above because no policy is able to stop a cost-push inflation from occurring.

The answers for this Chapter Quiz are on page 328

Part Review 6 UNDERSTANDING STABILIZATION PROBLEMS AND POLICIES

Reading Between the Lines

A REVOLUTION BY DEGREES FOR JAPAN

Since March, a number of Japanese companies have announced extensive overhauls, job cutbacks and internal realignments previously considered taboo in corporate Japan.

In the past, investors would have regarded the string of announcements as a bad April Fool's joke. Everyone regarded Japanese promises to restructure balance sheets and streamline operations as little more than lip service to gain a few more months of good will until the economy picked up and sales growth erased obvious problems.

Restructuring implied job cuts, whether outright, through attrition or by eliminating excess capacity, and job cuts were socially and politically unpalatable. Therefore, Japanese companies did not "risutora," or restructure.

Last week alone, however, more than 25,000 jobs were set for elimination at big corporations, and companies promised to reconsider their investments in money losing businesses and pare their notoriously bloated management hierarchies.

(Scott Hartz) cited the Government's extensive fiscal stimulus packages and the profitability crisis at corporations as reasons for enthusiasm. "I think these things do sow the seeds of change," Mr. Hartz said.

"The danger is that the gap between perception and reality is getting too wide too fast," said Tadashi Nakamae, a prominent economist. "That means another kind of minibubble is being created in the stock market - and we all know what happens to bubbles in the Japanese stock market."

Mr. Nakamae and others, including some Government officials, say that the Government is getting in the way of corporate overhaul, working to stimulate demand to support sales growth that will paper over problems like excess labor and capacity rather than force companies to address them.

The Government is doing everything it can to encourage its wary citizens and businesses to spend. It has started more large-scale public works programs, issued shopping coupons, cut taxes and increased its loan guarantee program.

The Bank of Japan has lowered short-term interest rates effectively to zero percent, which allows overextended corporate borrowers to maintain that condition rather than take radical steps to overhaul their balance sheets.

"The Government is trying to stop these restructuring programs from being too aggressive," said Craig Chudler, the equity strategist at Nikko Salomon Smith Barney in Tokyo. "These credit guarantees, the bank bailout, they're all an effort to get companies to survive rather than having them fail and making way for new types of business."

He and others say that the Government is simply unprepared for the social costs from unemployment …

Investors are nonetheless buying into the promises. Take Mitsubishi Electric's pledge to eliminate 14,500 jobs in three years …

Two-thirds of the cuts will be achieved by the time-honored Japanese practice of shifting workers to the company's affiliates and universities - in other words, by passing the problem on. "They're concentrating the profit in the part of the company that's visible and shoving the problems into the part that's not," said Scott Foster, who follows the company for ING Barings in Tokyo. "There's nothing wrong with that, but it's not what they're painting it to be."

Stephanie Strom, "A Revolution By Degrees For Japan," April 6, 1999, p. C1. Copyright ©1999 by The New York Times Company. Reprinted with permission.

■ Analyze It

After nearly a decade of slow or no growth, a number of Japanese firms announced that they would restructure in an effort to become more efficient. The firms promised to shed workers and unprofitable divisions. By restructuring, the companies promised to become more profitable and grow more rapidly. If these changes are carried out, a number of observers believe that the Japanese economy might turn the corner and resume its formally rapid pace of economic growth. Yet other observers believe that the companies are promising more than they plan to deliver.

1. What is the background to this 1999 article? In particular, what has been the record of the Japanese economy during the 1990s?

2. What are reasons why the Japanese economy has behaved so poorly during the 1990s? What problem do these announced restructurings aim, in part, to remedy?

3. Some analysts mention that the government may be opposed to the restructurings. Why might the government be opposed?

4. Do you think the announced changes are good for the Japanese economy? Why or why not?

Web Resources

For more information, browse the Parkin Web site to explore related links.

On the Top 10 list, visit the "Economic Report of the President" and also on the Top 10 list, visit "The Federal Reserve". If you looked at these sites before, take a moment to reflect on how the last two chapters in the textbook and your class lectures have continued to deepen your grasp of the world.

For an alternative, less day-to-day policy oriented site, look under "Methodology and History of Economic Thought — Collection" to click on "Keynes".

Mid-Term Examination

■ **Chapter 17**

1. In Keynesian business cycle theory, business cycles begin with changes in
   a. inflation expectations.
   b. consumer sentiment.
   c. business expectations about sales and profits.
   d. the public's expectations about Fed policies.

2. Monetarist business cycle theory asserts that increases in the growth rate of the money supply cause
   a. temporarily lower real wage rates.
   b. temporarily higher real wage rates.
   c. permanently higher real wage rates.
   d. no effect on real wages.

3. In a real business cycle model, labor supply decreases when the
   a. nominal interest rate rises.
   b. real interest rate rises.
   c. nominal interest rate falls.
   d. real interest rate falls.

4. The 1990-1991 recession was caused by
   a. only a large decrease in aggregate supply.
   b. only a large decrease aggregate demand shock.
   c. expansionary fiscal policy.
   d. decreases in both aggregate supply and aggregate demand.

■ **Chapter 18**

5. When the federal funds interest rate _____, the growth rate of M2 _____.
   a. falls; is constant
   b. rises; decreases
   c. rises; increases
   d. rises; is constant

6. If the government surplus rises, government saving
   a. increases.
   b. does not change.
   c. decreases.
   d. may increase, decrease, or not change depending on what happens to the amount of government purchases of goods and services.

7. Under a feedback-rule policy, if the economy goes into an expansion, the Fed
   a. decreases purchases of government securities.
   b. increases tax rates.
   c. decreases the amount of government purchases.
   d. All of the above.

8. Compared to the lags for fiscal policy, the lags for monetary policy are
    a. shorter, making fixed rules more likely to work well.
    b. shorter, making feedback rules more likely to work well.
    a. longer, making fixed rules more likely to work well.
    b. longer, making feedback rules more likely to work well.

Answers

■ Reading Between the Lines

The Japanese economy performed miserably in the 1990s. After entering this decade with the highest growth rate of any developed economy, it plunged to achieve one of the lowest growth rates of developed economies. As the text discusses, from 1992 to 1998 the Japanese economy grew at an annual rate of only 0.7 percent. And, in 1999 the economy plummeted into its most severe recession of the decade.

There are many possible reasons for the weak performance of the Japanese economy. On the macroeconomic level, inconsistent fiscal policy played a role. At some times, fiscal policy was strongly expansionary, with large increases in public spending and a huge budget deficit. At other times, though, fiscal policy was equally strongly contractionary, with taxes hiked and spending slashed. Monetary policy was rather consistently expansionary, but to no avail: As the article points out, the Bank of Japan lowered interest rates to almost 0 percent but neither investment nor consumption expenditure responded strongly. At a more micro level, the Japanese economy is riddled with inefficiencies. Firms are often protected by government regulations and, in response, firms are loath to lay off or fire workers. The Japanese nation has a strong tradition of "employment for life" once a worker is hired. These factors have been responsible for slow — or no — productivity growth during the 1990s. But in 1999 many Japanese firms decided to break with tradition and strive for efficiency. They announced restructurings designed to enhance their efficiency, in part by shedding unnecessary workers.

As Mr. Nakamae and Mr. Chudler point out, the Japanese government was opposed to these changes because they would increase the already high Japanese unemployment rate. In addition, the government worried that these changes may signal a profound change in Japanese culture so that employment was no longer "for life".

Most economists think that the proposed changes would help the economy move to more rapid growth, at least in the long run. In the short run, there would be some dislocations as unemployed workers searched for new jobs, but the long-run effects would be beneficial. These same economists, however, cautioned that the Japanese companies may be announcing more than they planned to do. As the article points out, some of the job cuts would not actually be cuts but instead would simply relocate workers from the parent company to subsidies. Economists argue that these sorts of paper change have little positive effect.

Whether or not the changes actually took place and, if they did, what the effect was upon the Japanese economy is not known as this answer is written. But, when you read this, some of the answers may be known. The Parkin web site is a good starting place to explore what has happened recently in Japan!

■ Mid-Term Exam Answers

1. c;   2. a;   3. d;   4. d;   5. b;   6. a;   7. a;   8. b

19 TRADING WITH THE WORLD*

■ Patterns and Trends in International Trade

The goods and services we buy from producers in other nations are our **imports**; the goods and services we sell to people in other nations are our **exports**. Most U.S. exports and imports are manufactured goods. Trade in goods accounts for most of U.S. international trade; trade in services (travel and transportation) accounts for the rest.

Trade has accounted for an increasingly large fraction of total output in the United States. The **balance of trade** is the value of exports minus the value of imports. In the United States the value of imports exceeded that of U.S. exports in 1998.

■ Opportunity Cost and Comparative Advantage

Comparative advantage is the factor that drives international trade. Countries can produce anywhere on their production possibility frontier (*PPF*) curve. Figure 19.1 shows a *PPF* for a nation producing at point *a*.

♦ The *PPF's* slope is (Δ bushels of grain)/(Δ cars), with Δ meaning "change in." The slope equals the opportunity cost of one more car at point *a*.

♦ A country has a **comparative advantage** in the production of the good if the country can produce it at a lower opportunity cost than any other country.

FIGURE 19.1
Slope of the *PPF* is the Opportunity Cost

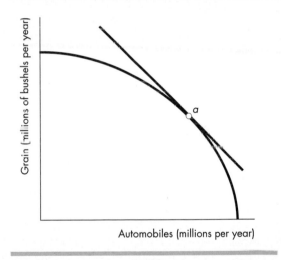

■ Gains from Trade

A country gains from trade by buying the goods from other nations that the nations produce at the lowest opportunity cost and selling to the other countries the goods it produces at the lowest opportunity cost.

♦ A nation gains by specializing in production of goods for which it has a comparative advantage and trading for other goods.

♦ With international trade, a nation receives a higher relative price for the goods it exports and pays a lower relative price for the goods it imports. The **terms of trade** is the price of a nation's imports.

*This is Chapter 36 in *Economics*.

♦ International trade allows all nations to consume *outside* their *PPFs*. The added consumption is the gains from trade.

■ Gains from Trade in Reality

Most trade can be explained by comparative advantage. However, some trade involves similar goods for two reasons:

♦ Diversified tastes — people demand many similar but slightly different products.

♦ Economies of scale — average total cost declines with output.

A nation can specialize in the production of one of the similar goods and capture economies of scale by trading the good throughout the world.

■ Trade Restrictions

Governments restrict trade to protect domestic industries. The main methods used to restrict trade are:

♦ **Tariffs** — taxes on imported goods.

♦ **Nontariff barrier** — any action other than a tariff that restricts international trade.

Today, U.S. tariffs are low compared to their historical levels. The **General Agreement on Tariffs and Trade** (GATT) is an international agreement designed to reduce tariffs and increase international trade. The **World Trade Organization**, to which the United States belongs, requires that nations more closely obey GATT rules. The **North American Free Trade Agreement** (NAFTA) is an agreement between the U.S., Canada, and Mexico that will remove most tariffs between these nations over a 15-year period.

Figure 19.2 illustrates the effects of a tariff.

♦ A tariff decreases the supply of the imported good. The new supply curve with the tariff lies above the old supply curve by the amount of the tariff (the length of the arrow).

♦ The price rises from P_0 to P_1 and the quantity decreases from Q_0 to Q_1. The government gains revenue as indicated in the figure. The tariff reduces the gains from trade and creates inefficiency.

♦ By decreasing imports to the domestic economy, foreigners can buy less from the domestic economy. Therefore the value of domestic exports decreases by an amount equal to the drop in the value of domestic imports.

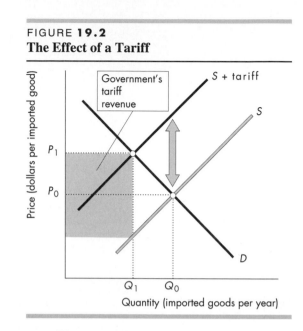

FIGURE **19.2**
The Effect of a Tariff

Nontariff barriers include quotas and voluntary export restraints.

♦ **Quota** — a quantitative restriction on the amount of a good that can be imported.

♦ **Voluntary export restraint** — an agreement between governments in which the exporting nation agrees to limit the volume of its exports.

Similar to tariffs, nontariff barriers raise the prices of imported goods and decrease the quantities imported. Unlike a tariff, the government gets no revenue from a nontariff barrier; the revenue from the higher price goes to importers in the case of quotas and to foreign exporters in the case of voluntary export restraints.

■ The Case Against Protection

Arguments in favor of protection are flawed. The arguments and their errors are:

♦ *National security* — the nation should protect industries that are necessary for its defense.
Error: Virtually every industry may be considered "vital" for defense; direct subsidies to targeted industries are more efficient than protection from international competition.

♦ **Infant-industry argument** — the nation should protect a young industry that will reap learning-by-doing gains in productivity and eventually be able to compete successfully in the world market.
Error: If the learning-by-doing benefits accrue only

to the firms in the industry, this argument fails because these firms can finance their own start-ups; direct subsidies are more efficient.

♦ **Dumping** — the nation should protect an industry from foreign competitors who sell goods below cost in order to gain a monopoly.
Error: Determining when a firm sells below cost is very difficult; only global natural monopolies are able to sustain a monopoly; if the firm is a natural monopoly, regulation is the more efficient way to restrain it.

♦ *Protection saves jobs* — imports cost U.S. jobs.
Error: Free trade costs jobs in importing industries, but it creates them in exporting industries; tariffs that protect jobs in import-competing industries do so at an exceedingly high cost.

♦ *Cheap foreign labor* — tariffs are necessary to compete with cheap foreign labor.
Error: U.S. labor is more productive than cheap foreign labor; U.S. firms can compete successfully in industries in which they have a comparative advantage because of their productivity relative to other nations.

♦ *Diversity and stability* — nations specialized in the production of one good may be subject to economic fluctuations.
Error: The United States is not specialized; nations that are specialized can gain by such specialization and then diversify by investing abroad.

♦ *Lax environmental standards* — protection is needed to compete against nations with weak environmental standards.
Error: Not all poor nations have weak standards; poor nations' concerns about the environment will increase when they grow richer through trade; currently poor nations may have a comparative advantage in pollution-intensive goods.

♦ *National culture* — protection is necessary to protect the nation's national culture.
Error: Those clamoring for protection are simply "rent-seekers" involved in the country's national media outlets; many "American" producers of media are from other nations.

♦ *Rich nations exploit developing countries* — protection prevents developed nations from forcing people in poor nations to work for slave wages.
Error: By allowing poor nations to trade with rich

ones, wages in poor nations rise because of the increased demand for labor.

■ **Why Is International Trade Restricted?**

♦ The government collects revenue from tariffs. This revenue source is important in developing nations.

♦ Some people are harmed by international trade and so they lobby politicians to limit free trade.

Helpful Hints

1. **DOES PROTECTION SAVE JOBS?** This argument is popular but incorrect. As you learned in this chapter, imposing a tariff on imports costs jobs in export industries. We lose jobs because foreigners, unable to sell as much to us, are thus unable to buy as much from us. Hence our export industries shrink, or fail to grow as much as otherwise.

   The claim that protection saves jobs continues to be made largely because the jobs saved by tariffs are highly visible, but the job losses are invisible. Factories that are in operation only because the goods they produce are favored with a tariff or other form of protection from foreign competition may be visited. However, it is impossible to visit a factory that would have been built had an exporting industry been able to expand. This asymmetry makes arguing that tariffs protect American jobs easy, but the argument is incorrect.

   Moreover, saving the jobs in the import-competing industry comes at a very high cost. For example, protection in the textile industry annually costs American residents $221,000 per job; in the automobile industry, $105,000 per job; in dairy products, $220,000 per job; and in steel, $750,000 per job. These costs greatly exceed the wages in these jobs. Just as it would be foolish to spend $221,000 to obtain $45,000, so, too, is it foolish for the nation to protect jobs when the cost of the protection exceeds the wages paid for the jobs! Hence protection winds up costing the country more than it benefits the nation.

2. **WHY DOES PROTECTION PERSIST?** Be sure that you understand the political economy point made in the last section of this chapter. Gains from free trade can be considerable, so why do countries im-

pose trade restrictions? The key is that, although free trade creates overall benefits to the economy as a whole, there are both winners and losers. The winners gain more in total than the losers lose, but the latter tend to be concentrated in a few industries. In other words, the gains from free trade are spread amongst many people — so the gain per person is small — while the costs are concentrated amongst only a few people— so the costs per person are large.

Because of this concentration, free trade is resisted. Even though trade restrictions benefit only a small minority while the overwhelming majority are harmed, implementation of trade barriers is not surprising. The cost of a particular trade restriction to each of the majority individually is quite small, but the benefit to each of the few individually large. Thus the minority has a strong incentive to have a restriction imposed, whereas the majority has little incentive to expend time and energy in resisting a trade barrier. The net result is that governments frequently wind up restricting free trade, even though the restrictions cost their nations more than they benefit it.

Questions

■ True/False/Uncertain and Explain

Patterns and Trends In International Trade

1. Nations can trade goods but not services.

2. The United States is a large importer and exporter of manufactured goods.

3. In 1998, the value of American imports exceeded the value of American exports.

Opportunity Cost and Comparative Advantage

4. Each nation's opportunity cost of producing any good or service is the same.

5. A nation has a comparative advantage in a good if it can produce the good at a lower opportunity cost than other nations.

Gains From Trade

6. Trade allows a nation to consume combinations of products that lie beyond its *PPF*.

7. Only the nation exporting a good gains from trade.

Gains From Trade in Reality

8. Nations do not trade similar goods.

9. Firms can capture economies of scale with international trade.

Trade Restrictions

10. Tariffs in the United States are at an all-time high.

11. Economists generally agree that high tariffs improve a nation's standard of living.

12. When governments impose tariffs, they increase their consumers' welfare.

13. A quota and a voluntary export restraint on an imported good both raise its price.

The Case Against Protection

14. The only argument for protection without any error is the infant-industry argument.

15. U.S. workers can compete with lower paid foreign workers in industries in which the U.S. has a comparative advantage.

16. International trade lowers wages in poor nations.

Why Is International Trade Restricted?

17. Free international trade benefits some citizens and harms others.

■ Multiple Choice Questions
Patterns and Trends In International Trade

1. Which of the following is a U.S. service export?
   a. A U.S. citizen buys dinner while traveling in Switzerland.
   b. A Canadian buys a dinner while traveling in Canada.
   c. A Swiss citizen buys a computer made in the United States.
   d. A Mexican citizen spends the night in a motel while visiting the United States.

2. In 1998
   a. trade in services accounted for about 50 percent of total U.S. exports.
   b. agricultural products accounted for over 50 percent of total U.S. exports.
   c. the U.S. government rejected the NAFTA treaty.
   d. U.S. imports were greater in value than U.S. exports.

Opportunity Cost and Comparative Advantage

Figures 19.3 and 19.4 show production in two nations, Solaris and Chaff. Production is taking place at point *a* in Solaris and at point *b* in Chaff. Use these figures for the next four questions.

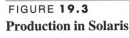

FIGURE **19.3**
Production in Solaris

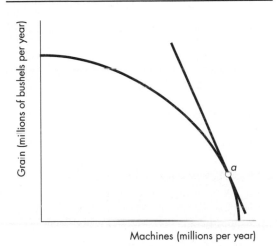

FIGURE **19.4**
Production in Chaff

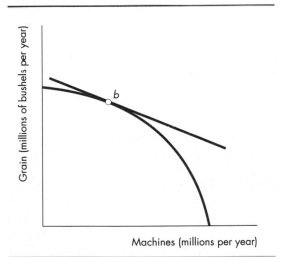

3. The slope of the *PPF* at point *a* in Solaris is 200 bushels of grain per machine; the slope of the *PPF* at point *b* in Chaff is 15 bushels of grain per machine. Without trade between the nations, what is the opportunity cost of a machine in Solaris?
   a. The cost is 200 bushels of grain.
   b. The cost is ¹/₂₀₀ bushels of grain.
   c. The cost is 15 bushels of grain.
   d. The cost is ¹/₁₅ bushel of grain.

4. Without trade between the nations, what is the opportunity cost of a machine in Chaff?
   a. The cost is 200 bushels of grain.
   b. The cost is ¹/₂₀₀ bushels of grain.
   c. The cost is 15 bushels of grain.
   d. The cost is ¹/₁₅ bushel of grain.

5. Solaris has a comparative advantage in ____, and Chaff has a comparative advantage in ____.
   a. machines; grain
   b. grain; machines
   c. machines and grain; neither good
   d. neither good; machines and grain.

6. Once Solaris and Chaff begin to trade, Solaris exports ____ to Chaff and Chaff exports ____ to Solaris.
   a. machines; grain
   b. grain; machines
   c. machines and grain; neither good
   d. neither good; machines and grain

Gains From Trade

7. Suppose that Musicland and Videoland produce two goods, CDs and videos. Musicland has a comparative advantage in the production of CDs if it is the case that in Musicland
   a. fewer videos must be given up to produce 1 CD than in Videoland.
   b. less labor is required to produce 1 CD than in Videoland.
   c. less capital is required to produce 1 CD than in Videoland.
   d. less labor and capital are required to produce 1 CD than in Videoland.

8. International trade allows a nation to
   a. produce and consume at a point beyond its *PPF*.
   b. produce at a point beyond its *PPF* but not consume at a point beyond its *PPF*.
   c. consume at a point beyond its *PPF* but not produce at a point beyond its *PPF*.
   d. neither produce nor consume at a point beyond its *PPF*.

9. International trade based on comparative advantage may allow each country to consume
   a. more of the goods it exports, but always less of the goods it imports.
   b. more of the goods it imports, but always less of the goods it exports.
   c. more of the goods it exports and imports.
   d. less of the goods it exports and imports.

10. The maximum gains from trade occur when
    a. there is no international trade.
    b. each nation produces according to its comparative advantage and trades with other nations.
    c. each nation uses tariffs rather than quotas.
    d. each nation uses quotas rather than tariffs.

Gains From Trade in Reality

11. The combination of diversified tastes and economies of scale can account for
    a. a nation importing and exporting similar products.
    b. why tariffs create inefficiency.
    c. specialization according to comparative advantage.
    d. the result that free trade allows nations to consume at points beyond their *PPF* even though they cannot produce at points beyond their *PPF*.

Trade Restrictions

12. A tariff is
    a. a government imposed limit on the amount of a good that can be exported from a nation.
    b. a government imposed barrier that sets a fixed limit on the amount of a good that can be imported into a nation.
    c. a tax on a good imported into a nation.
    d. an agreement between governments to limit exports from a nation.

13. Who benefits from a tariff on a good?
    a. Domestic consumers of the good
    b. Domestic producers of the good
    c. Foreign governments
    d. Foreign producers of the good

14. Suppose that the United States imports only textiles from Mexico and exports only computers to Mexico. If the United States imposes a tariff on Mexican textiles, the U.S. textile industry ____ and the U.S. computer industry ____.
    a. expands; expands
    b. expands; does not change
    c. expands; contracts
    d. contracts; expands

15. When does the government gain the most revenue?
    a. When it imposes a tariff.
    b. When it imposes a quota.
    c. When it negotiates a voluntary export restraint.
    d. The amount of revenue it gains is the same with a tariff and a voluntary export restraint.

The Case Against Protection

16. The (false) idea that an industry should be protected because of learning-by-doing until it is large enough to compete successfully in world markets is the ____ argument for protection.
    a. absolute advantage
    b. infant industry
    c. dumping
    d. diversity

17. Selling a product in a foreign nation at a price less than its cost of production is called
    a. infant industry exploitation.
    b. absolute advantage.
    c. dumping.
    d. net exporting.

18. When a rich nation buys a product made in a poor nation, in the poor nation the demand for labor ____ and the wage rate ____.
    a. increases; rises
    b. increases; falls
    c. decreases; rises
    d. decreases; falls

19. Which of the following is a valid reason for protecting an industry?

    a. The industry is unable to compete with low-wage foreign competitors.

    b. The industry is necessary to diversify the nation's production.

    c. Protection keeps richer nations from exploiting the workers of poorer countries.

    d. None of the above reasons is a valid reason for protection.

Why Is International Trade Restricted?

20. Which of the following statements about the gains from international trade is correct?

    a. Everyone gains from international trade.

    b. Some people gain from international trade and some lose, though overall the gains exceed the losses.

    c. Some people gain and some people lose from international trade; overall the losses exceed the gains.

    d. Everyone loses from international trade.

■ **Short Answer Problems**

FIGURE 19.5

Short Answer Problem 1

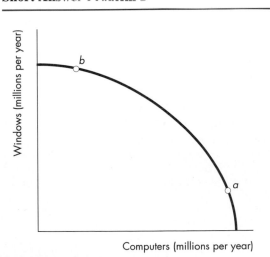

1. Two nations, Disc and Chip, have the same *PPF*. Both nations produce only two goods, windows and computers. Figure 19.5 shows their current production points: Disc at point *a* and Chip at point *b*.

    a. In which nation is the opportunity cost of a window lowest? In which is the opportunity cost of a computer lowest? Explain how you arrived at your answer.

    b. Which nation has a comparative advantage in producing windows? In producing computers? Why?

    c. If Disc and Chip trade, which nation would export windows? Which would export computers? Why?

2. A nation produces only wheat and computer chips. It has a comparative advantage in chips. Draw a production possibility frontier and use it to show how the nation specializes and the gains from trade.

3. How does a tariff on an imported good affect the domestic price of the good? The quantity of the good imported? The quantity of the good produced domestically?

4. How does a quota on an imported good affect the domestic price of the good, the quantity imported, and the quantity produced domestically?

5. How does a tariff on imports affect the exports of the country?

TABLE 19.1

Market for Watches in Norolex

Price (dollars per watch)	Quantity demanded (millions of watches)	Quantity supplied (millions of watches)
$20	65	15
25	60	20
30	55	25
35	50	30
40	45	35
45	40	40
50	35	45

6. Table 19.1 gives the domestic supply and demand schedules for watches for the nation of Norolex.

    a. Draw the supply and demand schedules in Figure 19.6. (On the next page.)

    b. What is the equilibrium price?

    c. How many watches are produced in Norolex? How many are purchased by consumers in Norolex?

FIGURE 19.6
Short Answer Problems 6 and 7

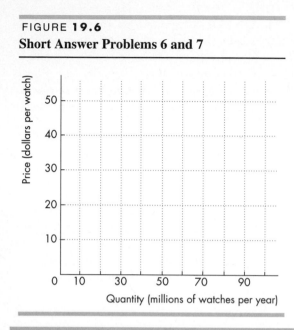

TABLE 19.2
Supply Schedule of Watches with Trade

Price (dollars per watch)	Quantity supplied in Norolex (millions of watches)	Quantity supplied by Switch (millions of watches)	Total quantity supplied (millions of watches)
$20	15	20	___
25	20	25	___
30	25	30	___
35	30	35	___
40	35	40	___
45	40	45	___
50	45	50	___

7. Norolex now trades with another nation, Switch. Switch exports watches to Norolex. Switch's export supply schedule is in Table 19.2 along with Norolex's domestic supply schedule.
   a. Complete Table 19.2 by determining the total supply schedule of watches.
   b. Graph the total supply schedule in Figure 19.6, which already contains the domestic supply and demand schedules you graphed from the previous question.
   c. What is the new equilibrium price of a watch?
   d. How many watches are produced in Norolex? How many are purchased by consumers in Norolex? How many are imported?

8. The watch industry in Norolex is unhappy with the situation after trade with Switch has occurred. The watch industry lobbies the government to impose a $15 per watch tariff on imports from Switch.
   a. Complete Table 19.3, which shows how the tariff affects imports from Switch.
   b. Using your answers from Table 19.3, complete Table 19.4, which shows the new total supply schedule after the tariff has been imposed.
   c. After the tariff is imposed, what is the equilibrium price of a watch in Norolex?
   d. How many watches are produced in Norolex? How many watches are purchased by consumers in Norolex? How many watches are imported?
   e. Relative to the situation in problem 6, explain who has gained from the tariff and who has lost. Explain why the gainers have gained and the losers have lost.

TABLE 19.3
Short Answer Problem 8 (a)

Price (dollars per watch)	Pre-tariff quantity supplied by Switch (millions of watches)	Post-tariff quantity supplied by Switch (millions of watches)
$20	20	5
25	25	10
30	30	15
35	35	___
40	40	___
45	45	___
50	50	___

TABLE 19.4
Short Answer Problem 8 (b)

Price (dollars per watch)	Quantity supplied in Norolex (millions of watches)	Quantity supplied by Switch (millions of watches)	Total quantity supplied (millions of watches)
$20	15	5	___
25	20	10	___
30	25	15	___
35	30	___	___
40	35	___	___
45	40	___	___
50	45	___	___

■ You're the Teacher

1. "I understand the stuff in this chapter about comparative advantage and it makes sense. But I still can't see how the United States can compete with nations like Mexico, where the wages are so low. I think the only way we can protect our high wages is to keep Mexican products out of our markets." Your friend may think that he or she understands comparative advantage, but your friend actually is missing the essential idea. Having informed friends is better than having ignorant ones, so help this one understand comparative advantage by explaining how American firms are able to compete with Mexican companies.

2. After you explain the error in question 1, your friend makes another mistake: "Well, thanks to you, now I can see how American firms can compete. But, still, international trade can't be good. After all, if this trade helps Mexico, we must lose. So I still think that international trade should be banned." Explain to your friend how international trade benefits both America and Mexico.

Answers

■ True/False Answers

Patterns and Trends In International Trade

1. **F** Services, such as travel abroad, transportation, and insurance, can be traded internationally.

2. **T** About 60 percent of U.S. imports and about 50 percent of U.S. exports are manufactured goods.

3. **T** In 1998, as throughout the 1980s and 1990s, the value of imports exceeded that of American exports.

Opportunity Cost and Comparative Advantage

4. **F** Because nations have different opportunity costs, international trade can raise the welfare of *each* nation.

5. **T** The question presents the definition of comparative advantage.

Gains From Trade

6. **T** By allowing consumption to occur beyond the limits expressed by the *PPF*, the nation gains from trade.

7. **F** All nations engaged in international trade gain from the trade.

Gains From Trade in Reality

8. **F** Diversity of tastes and economies of scale account for the considerable international trade that takes place in similar goods.

9. **T** Long production runs, which create economies of scale, can be sold internationally.

Trade Restrictions

10. **F** Tariffs in the United States are near an all-time low.

11. **F** Economists agree that tariffs reduce a nation's standard of living.

12. **F** By raising the price of imported goods, tariffs harm consumers.

13. **T** Tariffs, quotas, and voluntary export restraints all limit the quantity of imports and thus all raise the price of imports.

The Case Against Protection

14. **F** All arguments for protection are flawed.

15. **T** In industries with a comparative advantage, higher productivity more than offsets higher wages, so American firms can successfully compete.

16. **F** International trade *raises* wages in poor nations.

Why Is International Trade Restricted?

17. **T** Free trade benefits consumers and workers (and firms) in exporting industries. It harms workers (and firms) in import-competing industries.

■ Multiple Choice Answers

Patterns and Trends In International Trade

1. **d** The Mexican resident has purchased a service, lodging, from an American firm.

2. **d** The value of U.S. imports exceeded the value of U.S. exports in 1998 and in most recent years.

Opportunity Cost and Comparative Advantage

3. **a** The opportunity cost equals the slope of the *PPF* because the slope is the opportunity cost, in terms of grain, of producing 1 more machine.

4. **c** For the reason outlined in the answer to question 3, the opportunity cost of a machine in Chaff is 15 bushels of grain.

5. **b** The opportunity cost of grain is less in Solaris, and the opportunity cost of a machine is less in Chaff.

6. **b** Each nation exports the good in which it has a comparative advantage.

Gains From Trade

7. **a** The opportunity cost of a good is the number of other goods that must be foregone to increase production of the good.

8. **c** With or without international trade, producing at points beyond the *PPF* is impossible, but international trade allows consumption to occur at points beyond the *PPF*.

9. **c** By specializing in the products with a comparative advantage and trading with other nations, the nation may consume more of both the goods it imports and the goods it exports.

10. **b** Free trade with production taking place according to comparative advantage creates the maximum gains from trade.

Gains From Trade in Reality

11. **a** By specializing in the production of one good that is similar to another and then exporting the good, a firm can capture economies of scale and satisfy people's desires for its particular variation of the good.

Trade Restrictions

12. **c** Answer (c) is the definition of a tariff.

13. **b** Domestic producers gain because the price of the product rises.

14. **c** The textile industry gains from the tariff, and the computer industry loses.

15. **a** Unlike tariffs, the government gets no revenue from quotas and voluntary export restraints.

The Case Against Protection

16. **b** The description in the problem is the definition of the infant industry argument for protection.

17. **c** Although often alleged, dumping is difficult to prove because it is difficult to determine whether a firm is selling below its cost.

18. **a** By increasing the demand for the goods produced in the poor nation, the demand for labor increases, thereby raising the wage rate in that nation.

19. **d** All of the reasons offered for protection are faulty.

Why Is International Trade Restricted?

20. **b** Because the overall gains exceed the overall loses, in principle the losers from international trade can be compensated so that, on balance, everyone gains from the trade.

■ Answers to Short Answer Problems

1. a. The opportunity cost of a window is lowest in Disc. The opportunity cost of a computer is lowest in Chip.

   Figure 19.7 demonstrates these result. The opportunity cost of a computer equals the magnitude of the slope of the line tangent to the *PPF*. In Figure 19.7, the magnitude of the slope of the line tangent at point *b* is less than the magnitude of the line tangent at point *a*. Hence the opportunity cost of a computer is less at point *b*, which is where Chip produces. The opportunity cost of a window equals the inverse of the slopes

FIGURE **19.7**

Short Answer Problem 1

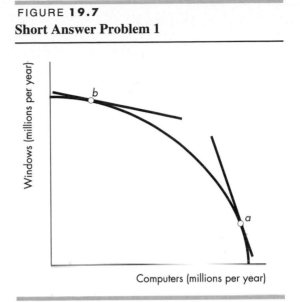

Computers (millions per year)

of these lines, so the opportunity cost of a window is less at point *a*, which is Disc's production point.

   b. Disc has a comparative advantage in producing windows because its opportunity cost of producing a window is less than Chip's opportunity cost. Similarly, Chip has a comparative advantage in producing computers.

   c. Disc would export windows and Chip would export computers because these are the goods for which each nation has a comparative advantage. Alternatively, windows are relatively cheaper in Disc, so Disc will export Windows. Computers are relatively less expensive in Chip, so Chip will export computers.

2. Figure 19.8 (on the next page) shows the situation in the nation. In the figure, before trade the nation initially produces and consumes *W* bushels of wheat and *C* chips. Without trade, the amount of wheat consumed equals the amount produced and the number of chips consumed equals the number produced. Once the nation trades, it changes its production of wheat and chips. With trade, the nation increases its production of computer chips and decreases its production of wheat. This change is illustrated in Figure 19.8, where the nation produces C_p chips and W_p bushels of wheat. However, the nation does not consume these amounts of chips and wheat. Instead, it exports chips and imports

FIGURE **19.8**

Short Answer Problem 2

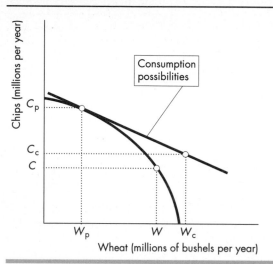

wheat so that it consumes (along its consumption possibilities line) C_c computer chips and W_c bushels of wheat. Note that the nation consumes fewer chips than it produces and more wheat than it grows.

The gains from trade are illustrated in Figure 19.8 because with trade the nation consumes more chips *and* more wheat than it consumed without trade. (Compare the initial consumption bundle of C chips and W bushels of wheat to the post-trade bundle of C_c chips and W_c bushels of wheat.) International trade has allowed this nation to increase its consumption of *all* goods, which makes its inhabitants better off.

3. A tariff on an imported good raises its price to domestic consumers because the foreign export supply decreases. As the domestic price of the good climbs, the quantity of the good demanded decreases, so the quantity imported decreases. The rise in the domestic price leads to an increase in the quantity of the good produced domestically.

4. The effect of a quota on the domestic price of the good, the quantity imported, and the quantity of the good produced domestically are exactly the same as the effects of a tariff discussed in the answer to short answer problem 3. The difference is that with a tariff the rise in the domestic price occurs because foreigners decrease their supply of the good at all prices (that is, the foreign supply curve with the tariff lies above the initial supply curve without the

tariff). A quota, however, forces the export supply curve to become vertical at the quota amount.

5. When a country imposes a tariff on its imports, the volume of its imports shrink, and the volume of its exports to other countries shrinks by the same amount. A tariff limits the amount of goods that other nations can sell to the first country and also lowers the price the other nations receive for their products. Thus when a nation limits its imports, foreign nations cannot afford to buy as many exports from the first country, so the tariff decreases the nation's exports.

FIGURE **19.9**

Short Answer Problem 6

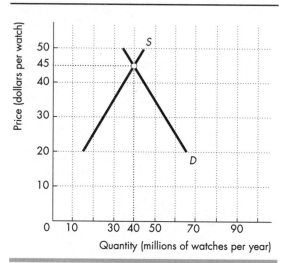

6. a. Figure 19.9 shows the demand and supply schedules.

   b. Either from Figure 19.9 or from the demand and supply schedules, the equilibrium price with no international trade is $45 because at this price the quantity demanded equals the quantity supplied.

   c. With no trade, forty million watches per year are produced domestically, and so 40 million watches per year are purchased by consumers in Norolex.

7. a. Table 19.5 (on the next page) shows the total supply schedule. At any price, the total quantity supplied in Norolex equals the sum of the quantity produced in Norolex plus the quantity supplied by Switch.

TABLE 19.5
Short Answer Problem 7 (a)

Price (dollars per watch)	Quantity supplied in Norolex (millions of watches)	Quantity supplied by Switch (millions of watches)	Total quantity supplied (millions of watches)
$20	15	20	35
25	20	25	45
30	25	30	55
35	30	35	65
40	35	40	75
45	40	45	85
50	45	50	95

FIGURE 19.10
Short Answer Problem 7

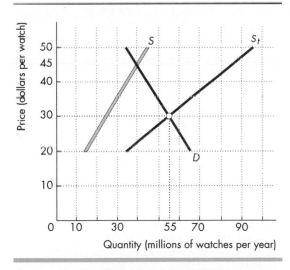

Quantity (millions of watches per year)

b. Figure 19.10 shows the total supply curve, S_t, the initial supply curve, and the demand curve.

c. The new equilibrium price of a watch is $30.

d. At the equilibrium price of $30, consumers in Norolex buy 55 million watches per year. At this price, watch firms in Norolex produce 25 million watches. The difference between the total quantity of watches purchased and the total quantity produced, 30 million watches per year, is imported from Switch.

8. a. Table 19.6 shows how the tariff affects the supply schedule of imports from Switch. A $15 per watch tariff lowers the receipts of the firms in Switch by $15 per watch. Hence when the price,

TABLE 19.6
Short Answer Problem 8 (a)

Price (dollars per watch)	Pre-tariff quantity supplied by Switch (millions of watches)	Post-tariff quantity supplied by Switch (millions of watches)
$20	20	5
25	25	10
30	30	15
35	35	20
40	40	25
45	45	30
50	50	35

TABLE 19.7
Short Answer Problem 8 (b)

Price (dollars per watch)	Quantity supplied in Norolex (millions of watches)	Quantity supplied by Switch (millions of watches)	Total quantity supplied (millions of watches)
$20	15	5	20
25	20	10	30
30	25	15	40
35	30	20	50
40	35	25	60
45	40	30	70
50	45	35	80

including the tariff, is $35 a watch, the watch companies receive only $20 per watch. As the initial supply schedule shows, when the Switch watch companies receive $20 per watch, they supply 20 million watches. The remainder of the supply schedule is calculated similarly.

b. The new total supply schedule equals the sum of the Norolex supply schedule plus the new, post-tariff Switch supply schedule. Table 19.7 shows the new total supply schedule.

c. The equilibrium price of a watch is $35.

d. At the price of $35, consumers buy 50 million watches per year. Firms in Norolex produce 30 million watches per year. Imports from Switch are 20 million watches per year.

e. The watch firms and their workers in Norolex have gained. With the tariff, they produce more watches and receive a higher price. The Norolex government also has gained because it obtains revenue from the tariff, $300 million. (The tariff revenue equals the tariff, $15 per watch, multiplied by the number of watches imported, 20 million.) Consumers in Norolex and the Switch watch manufacturing firms and their workers have lost. Consumers have lost because they must pay a higher price for a watch ($35 with the tariff compared to $30 without the tariff) and so respond by purchasing fewer watches. Switch firms and workers have lost because the lower price they receive for a watch leads them to produce fewer watches for export (20 million with the tariff versus 30 million without).

■ You're the Teacher

1. "Look, you don't have the main idea here. Let's use some numbers because they should help you catch on. Suppose that American wages are 10 times higher than Mexican wages. Now, it's also a fact that American workers are more productive than Mexican workers. Let's take two industries. In the first, call it industry A, suppose that American workers are 2 times as productive as Mexican ones; in the second, say, industry B, American workers are 20 times as productive. In industry A, American firms won't be able to compete with Mexican firms. Sure, our workers are twice as productive, but they are paid ten times as much. Therefore American firms will lose out in this industry. But in industry B, American companies firms will drive Mexican ones out of business. Even though our workers are paid 10 times as much as Mexican workers are paid, they produce 20 times as much as Mexican workers produce. So the per unit cost of the good is less in the United States, so American firms are going to be able to compete and compete successfully.

"The United States won't be able to compete successfully with Mexico in producing every type of good or service but the reason is that the United States does not (and cannot) have a comparative advantage in all goods and services even though it may well have an absolute advantage. But in the industry with the comparative advantage — industry B in my example — the United States is going to be able to compete and to win the competition."

2. "Well, I'm glad you're catching onto some of the ideas of this chapter, but you're missing another key point. The chapter explains how trade allows all nation to consume more goods and services than it can produce. Remember the diagrams showing how a nation can consume more of everything if it trades? Obviously, this fact has to make nations engaged in international trade better off.

"But there's also another a way to tackle this point. I read somewhere that 'trade is not a zero-sum game.' Here's what that means: If you and I voluntarily agree to a trade, like I'll trade my economics notes for your chemistry notes, the trade has to make us both better off. After all, if the trade didn't make me better off, I wouldn't agree to it and if it didn't make you better off, you wouldn't agree to it. This type of trade will enable both of us to raise our grades: me in chemistry and you in economics.

"Well, it's the same idea with trading between nations. Suppose that we import a VCR from Mexico and the Mexicans use the money we sent them to buy 50 bushels of wheat from Kansas. Essentially, we've traded the 50 bushels of wheat for the VCR. If this trade didn't make us better off, we wouldn't do it. So, too, for the Mexicans involved: If they didn't want the wheat more than the VCR, they won't agree to the transaction. And, as the chapter explained, if we specialize in wheat and Mexico in VCRs, we both will be able to consume more wheat and more VCRs than if we produced VCRs and wheat and Mexico produced VCRs and wheat.

"Or think about this more generally. For two potential trading partners to be willing to trade, they must have different comparative advantages, that is, different opportunity costs. Then they will trade and *both* parties will gain. If the countries do not trade, each faces and must pay its own opportunity costs. The price at which trade takes place will be somewhere between the opportunity costs of the two nations. With trade, the country with the lower opportunity cost of the good in question gains because it receives a price above its opportunity cost. Similarly, the country with the higher opportunity cost gains because it pays a price below its opportunity cost.

"You know, I think this is really cool. What it shows is that just as trade between us makes both of us better off, trade between nations makes both nations better off."

Chapter Quiz

1. It is ____ to import a service and it is ____ to export a service.
   a. possible; possible
   b. possible; not possible
   c. not possible; possible
   d. not possible; not possible

2. The U.S. balance of trade is the value of ____ and has been ____ in recent years.
   a. imports minus the value of exports; positive
   b. exports minus the value of imports; positive
   c. imports minus the value of exports; negative
   d. exports minus the value of imports; negative

3. A *PPF* has corn on the vertical axis and computers on the horizontal axis. The opportunity cost of an additional computer is the magnitude of the
   a. slope of a ray from the origin to the *PPF*.
   b. inverse of the slope of a ray from the origin to the *PPF*.
   c. slope of the *PPF*.
   d. inverse of the slope of the *PPF*.

4. Between two nations, to determine whether a nation has a comparative advantage in a product, it is necessary to compare the
   a. total amount produced in each nation.
   b. opportunity costs in the nations.
   c. total demand for the products in each nation.
   d. None of the above.

5. If a nation does *not* trade with the rest of the world, its consumption possibility frontier
   a. is identical to its *PPF*.
   b. lies outside its *PPF*.
   c. lies inside its *PPF*.
   d. has no particular relationship to its *PPF*.

6. The direct effect of a tariff is to restrict ____ and benefit ____.
   a. exports; producers
   b. exports; consumers
   c. imports; producers
   d. imports; consumers

7. The United States today imposes an average tariff of approximately
   a. 4 percent on imports.
   b. 4 percent on exports.
   c. 40 percent on imports.
   d. 40 percent on exports.

8. When a quota is imposed, the difference between the domestic price and the world price is collected by
   a. the domestic government.
   b. the foreign government.
   c. domestic consumers.
   d. domestic importers of the good.

9. It is possible for expensive U.S. labor to compete successfully against less expensive foreign labor because U.S. labor
   a. pays taxes in the United States.
   b. can travel abroad to produce the goods in other nations.
   c. frequently belongs to powerful labor unions that protect their interest.
   d. is more productive.

10. If a poor nation exports a good to a rich nation, in the poor nation wages in the export sector ____ and employment ____.
    a. rise; increases
    b. rise; decreases
    c. fall; decreases
    d. fall; increases

The answers for this Chapter Quiz are on page 328

20 INTERNATIONAL FINANCE*

Key Concepts

Financing International Trade

The **balance of payments accounts** measure international transactions.

♦ **Current account** — records exports, imports, net interest, and net transfers. The current account balance equals exports minus imports, net interest, and net transfers.

♦ **Capital account** — records foreign investment in the United States and U.S. investment abroad.

♦ **Official settlements account** — shows changes in **official U.S. reserves**, the nation's foreign exchange reserves.

The current account balance plus capital account balance plus official settlements account must sum to zero. In 1998 the United States had a current account deficit equal to its capital account surplus.

♦ A nation that is borrowing more from abroad than it is loaning abroad is a **net borrower**; a country that is loaning more abroad than it is borrowing is a **net lender**. The U.S. is a net borrower.

♦ A **debtor nation** owes more to foreigners than foreigners owe to it; a **creditor nation** has invested more in foreigners than foreigners have invested in it. The U.S. is a debtor nation.

National income accounting provides a framework for analyzing the current account. Combining the national income accounts result that GDP = $C + I + G + X - M$ and that GDP = $C + S + T$ gives:

$$X - M = (T - G) + (S - I),$$

where $X - M$ is the **net exports** balance, $T - G$ is the **government surplus or deficit**, and $S - I$ is the **private sector surplus or deficit**. In 1998, the government sector had a surplus of $70 billion, the private sector had a deficit of $222 billion, so net exports had a deficit of $152 billion.

In the United States, a government deficit increases the net export deficit after a lag. These deficits are called the **twin deficits**. Much U.S. borrowing from abroad is to finance investment.

The Exchange Rate

The **foreign exchange market** is the market in which the currency of one nation is traded for the currency of another. The price at which the currency exchanges is the **foreign exchange rate**.

♦ **Currency depreciation** — when a currency falls in value in terms of another currency.

♦ **Currency appreciation** — when a currency rises in value in terms of another currency.

As illustrated in Figure 20.1 (on the next page) the demand for U.S. dollars is inversely related to the U.S. exchange rate. There are two reasons for this relationship:

♦ Exports effect — when the exchange rate falls, the quantity of U.S. exports increases and so the quantity of dollars demanded increases.

---

* This is Chapter 37 in *Economics*.

FIGURE **20.1**

A Foreign Exchange Market

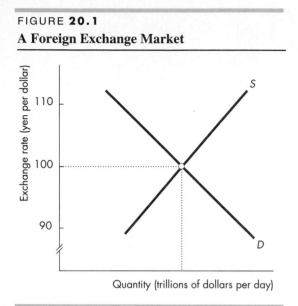

Quantity (trillions of dollars per day)

♦ Expected profit effect — for a given expected value of the U.S. exchange rate in the future, the higher the current exchange rate, the smaller the profit from holding U.S. dollars, so the quantity of dollars demanded decreases.

The demand for U.S. dollars shifts with changes in two factors:

♦ The **U.S. interest rate differential** — The U.S. interest rate differential equals the U.S. interest rate minus the foreign interest rate. A rise in the U.S. interest rate differential increases the demand for U.S. dollar assets, thus shifting the demand curve for U.S. dollars rightward.

♦ The expected future exchange rate — a rise in the expected future exchange rate increases the demand for U.S. dollars, thereby shifting the demand curve for U.S. dollars rightward.

People supply dollars when they buy other currencies to pay for U.S. imports or to buy foreign assets. As illustrated in Figure 20.1, the supply of U.S. dollars is positively related to the exchange rate, that is, the supply curve has a positive slope. There are two reasons for the positive relationship:

♦ Imports effect — when the exchange rate rises, the quantity of U.S. imports increases, which increases the quantity of U.S. dollars supplied.

♦ Expected profits effect — for a given value of the expected exchange rate in the future, the higher the current exchange rate, the greater the profit from

buying foreign currency, so the greater is the quantity of U.S. dollars supplied.

The U.S. dollar supply curve shifts with changes in two influences:

♦ The U.S. interest rate differential — an increase in this differential decreases the demand for foreign assets and thereby decreases the supply of U.S. dollars.

♦ The expected future exchange rate — a rise in the expected future exchange rate decreases the current supply of U.S. dollars as people hold the dollars to sell later at the higher exchange rate.

Figure 20.1 illustrates how demand and supply determine the equilibrium exchange rate, 100 yen in the figure. Changes in the demand and supply (shifts in the demand and supply curves) change the exchange rate.

FIGURE **20.2**

The Foreign Exchange Market in 1995-1998

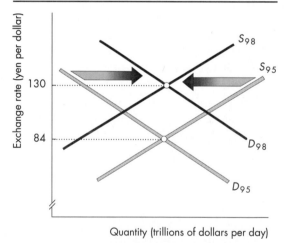

Quantity (trillions of dollars per day)

The exchange rate is volatile because the same factors affect both the demand for and supply of dollars. Figure 20.2 shows the foreign exchange market in 1995-1998.

♦ Interest rates rose in the U.S. and fell in Japan, increasing the U.S. interest rate differential.

♦ The expected future value of the yen fell, which means that the expected future value of the dollar rose.

Both changes increased the demand for dollars and decreased the supply, so the exchange rate jumped higher.

Two basic fundamentals help drive the foreign exchange market:

♦ **Purchasing power parity** — "equal value of money," that is, the exchange rate adjusts so that one currency can buy the same amount of goods and services as another currency.

♦ **Interest rate parity** — "equal interest rates," that is, the exchange rate adjusts so that the return from investing in assets in different nations is the same.

The Federal Reserve can intervene in the foreign exchange market by selling dollars — which drives the exchange rate lower — or by buying dollars — which drives the exchange rate higher.

Helpful Hints

1. **BASICS OF THE FOREIGN EXCHANGE MARKET :** There is an important difference between trade within a single country and trade between countries — currency. Individuals trading in the same country use the same currency and trade is straightforward. But international trade is complicated by the fact that individuals in different countries use different currencies. For example, a Japanese seller of goods will want payment in Japanese yen, but a U.S. buyer likely will be holding only U.S. dollars. This chapter addresses this trade complication by looking at the balance of payments for a country as well as the foreign exchange rate.

2. **DEMAND FOR U.S. DOLLARS :** The demand for U.S. dollars in the foreign exchange market arises from the desire on the part of foreigners to purchase U.S. goods and services (which requires dollars) and U.S. financial or real assets (which also requires dollars). Thus a Japanese importer of U.S. rice demands dollars to pay to U.S. rice farmers. And a Japanese investor who wants to buy a U.S. security also demands dollars to pay the current American owner.

    Foreign exchange rates are prices determined by supply and demand. Hence any factor that changes the demand for U.S. dollars will change the exchange rate. And, the influences that change the demand for U.S. dollars are the factors that change either the quantity of American goods (such as U.S. rice) or change the quantity of U.S. assets that foreigners buy.

Questions

■ True/False/Uncertain and Explain

Financing International Trade

1. The sum of the current account plus capital account plus official settlements account is positive for a nation that is a net lender.

2. A debtor nation must be a net borrower nation.

3. If investment is greater than saving, the private sector has a deficit.

4. $X - M$ equals $(T - G) + (S - I)$.

5. Throughout the 1990s, the United States has had both a current account deficit and a capital account deficit.

6. In the United States, a larger government sector deficit eventually leads to a larger net exports deficit.

The Exchange Rate

7. If the exchange rate between the U.S. dollar and the Japanese yen changes from 100 yen per dollar to 80 yen per dollar, the U.S. dollar has appreciated.

8. The lower the exchange rate, the cheaper foreigners find goods and services produced in America.

9. If the U.S. interest rate differential rises, the demand for U.S. dollars increases.

10. If the U.S. exchange rate is expected to appreciate in the future, the current supply of U.S. dollars decreases.

11. An increase in the U.S. interest rate differential raises the U.S. exchange rate.

12. The exchange rate is volatile because different factors influence the demand for and supply of dollars.

13. If the demand for U.S. dollars decreases and the supply increases, the exchange rate definitely falls.

14. Purchasing power parity means that if the U.S. dollar can buy more goods in Japan than in the United States, the U.S. exchange rate will fall.

15. If the Federal Reserve buys U.S. dollars, the exchange rate rises.

■ Multiple Choice

Financing International Trade

1. Which of the following is one of the balance of payments accounts?
   a. Current account
   b. Borrowing account
   c. Official lending account
   d. Net transfer interest account

2. Foreign investment in the United States and U.S. investment abroad are recorded in
   a. the current account.
   b. the capital account.
   c. the official settlements account.
   d. a balance of payments account that is not mentioned above.

3. Suppose the United States initially has no trade surplus or deficit. Then American firms increase their imports from Canada, financing that increase by borrowing from Canada. The United States now has a current account _____ and a capital account _____.
   a. surplus; surplus
   b. surplus; deficit
   c. deficit; surplus
   d. deficit; deficit

4. If the official settlements account is $0 and the United States has a current account deficit of $100 billion, then the
   a. capital account necessarily has a deficit of $100 billion.
   b. capital account necessarily has a surplus of $100 billion.
   c. government necessarily has a budget deficit of $100 billion.
   d. government necessarily has a budget surplus of $100 billion.

5. In recent years, the United States has been a _____ and a _____.
   a. net lender; creditor nation
   b. net lender; debtor nation
   c. net borrower; debtor nation
   d. net borrower; creditor nation

6. This year a nation is currently a net lender and is also a debtor nation. Which of the following statements accurately describes the nation's current situation?
   a. It has loaned more capital than it has borrowed abroad this year, but it has borrowed more than it has loaned during its history.
   b. It has borrowed more capital abroad than it has loaned this year and it also has borrowed more than it has loaned during its history.
   c. It has loaned more capital than it has borrowed abroad this year and it has loaned more than it has borrowed during its history.
   d. It has borrowed more capital abroad than it has loaned this year and it has loaned more than it has borrowed during its history.

Table 20.1 presents several national income accounts for a nation. Use the table for the next three questions.

TABLE 20.1

Multiple Choice Questions 7, 8, 9

Component	Billions of dollars
Government purchases, G	$600
Net taxes, T	500
Investment, I	250
Saving, S	400

7. What does the government's surplus equal?
   a. $600 billion
   b. $500 billion
   c. −$100 billion
   d. $0

8. What does the private sector surplus equal?
   a. $400 billion
   b. $250 billion
   c. $150 billion
   d. $0

9. What does the net exports balance equal?
   a. A deficit of $600 billion
   b. A deficit of $250 billion
   c. A surplus of $50 billion
   d. A surplus of $1,650 billion

10. The government sector deficit is $100 billion and the private sector deficit is $25 billion. Hence net exports equals
    a. –$125 billion.
    b. –$100 billion
    c. –$75 billion.
    d. $75 billion.

11. A decrease in the U.S. government budget deficit _____ the U.S. net exports deficit.
    a. increases
    b. does not change
    c. decreases
    d. perhaps decreases or increases the net exports deficit depending on whether the budget deficit is caused by an increase in government purchases or a decrease in taxes.

The Exchange Rate

12. Measured against the Japanese yen, over the last twenty years the U.S. dollar exchange rate
    a. generally has depreciated.
    b. generally has appreciated.
    c. depreciated for the first ten years and appreciated for the last ten years.
    d. appreciated for the first ten years and depreciated for the last ten years.

13. The foreign exchange rate changes from 140 yen per dollar to 130 yen per dollar. Then the yen has _____ against the dollar and the dollar has _____ against the yen.
    a. depreciated; appreciated
    b. depreciated; depreciated;
    c. appreciated; appreciated
    d. appreciated; depreciated

14. Foreigners demand U.S. dollars to
    a. sell the goods imported into the United States.
    b. buy the goods exported from the United States.
    c. take advantage of higher U.S. prices.
    d. for reasons that are not given in the previous answers.

Use Figure 20.3 for the next two questions.

FIGURE **20.3**

Multiple Choice Questions 15 and 16

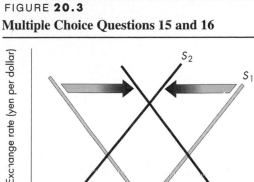

Quantity (trillions of dollars per day)

15. As illustrated in Figure 20.3, which influence might have shifted the demand curve?
    a. An increase in the U.S. exchange rate.
    b. An expectation that the U.S. dollar exchange rate will depreciate in the future.
    c. An increase in the U.S. interest rate differential.
    d. None of the above.

16. As illustrated in Figure 20.3, which influence might have shifted the supply curve?
    a. An increase in the U.S. exchange rate.
    b. An expectation that the U.S. dollar exchange rate will depreciate in the future.
    c. An increase in the U.S. interest rate differential.
    d. None of the above.

17. An increase in the expected future exchange rate shifts the demand curve for U.S. dollars _____ and the supply curve of U.S. dollars _____.
    a. rightward; rightward
    b. rightward; leftward
    c. leftward; rightward
    d. leftward; leftward

18. Which of the following increases the supply of U.S. dollars?
    a. A increase in foreigners' demand for goods and services made in the United States.
    b. An increase in the demand for U.S. assets by foreigners.
    c. The U.S. dollar is expected to appreciate in the future.
    d. The U.S. dollar is expected to depreciate in the future.

19. Of the following, when would the U.S. exchange rate fall the most?
    a. When the supply of and demand for U.S. dollars increase.
    b. When the supply of U.S. dollars increases and the demand for them decreases.
    c. When the supply of U.S. dollars decreases and the demand for them increases.
    d. When the supply of and demand for U.S. dollars decrease.

20. Which of the following would cause the dollar to depreciate against the yen?
    a. The Fed buys dollars.
    b. An increase in American interest rates.
    c. A decrease in interest rates in Japan.
    d. The dollar is expected to depreciate against the yen in the future.

21. Suppose the exchange rate between the U.S. dollar and the British pound is 0.5 pounds per dollar. If a radio sells for 38 pounds in Britain, what is the dollar price of the radio?
    a. $19
    b. $26
    c. $38
    d. $76

22. Purchasing power parity means
    a. that interest rates in different nations are the same.
    b. that interest rates in different nations adjusted by the expected change in the exchange rate are the same.
    c. that the purchasing power of different currencies is the same.
    d. something other than the answers given above.

23. Interest rate parity means that
    a. interest rates in two nations must be equal.
    b. interest rates in two nations can never be equal.
    c. a nation with a high interest rate has an exchange rate that is expected to depreciate.
    d. a nation with a high interest rate has an exchange rate that is expected to appreciate.

24. If the Fed buys U.S. dollars, the exchange rate
    a. rises.
    b. does not change.
    c. falls.
    d. changes, but the direction depends on whether the Fed's action affected the demand for dollars or the supply of dollars.

25. If the Fed buys U.S. dollars in the exchange market, it pays for the dollars with
    a. foreign currency.
    b. more U.S. dollars.
    c. imports.
    d. government securities.

■ **Short Answer Problems**

1. What is the relationship between a country's net exports deficit, its government budget deficit, and its private sector deficit?

TABLE **20.2**
Short Answer Problem 2

Component	Billions of dollars
Government purchases, G	$1,000
Net taxes, T	800
Investment, I	900
Saving, S	800

2. Table 20.2 shows data for a nation.
    a. What is the government surplus or deficit?
    b. What is the private sector surplus or deficit?
    c. What is the net exports balance?
    d. Suppose that the government decreased its net taxes by $100 billion and people responded by increasing their private saving by $100 billion. How do these changes affect the net exports balance?

TABLE **20.3**

International Lending and Borrowing

Year	Lending to foreigners (dollars)	Borrowing from abroad (dollars)
1996	$2,000	$3,000
1997	3,000	3,000
1998	5,000	1,000
1999	5,000	6,000

3. The nation of Sega is newly formed in 1996. Table 20.3 shows Sega's international borrowing and lending from 1996 through 1999.

   a. In 1996 was Sega a net borrower or lender? In 1997? In 1998? In 1999?

   b. At the end of 1996 was Sega a net creditor or debtor nation? At the end of 1997? At the end of 1998? At the end of 1999?

4. Igor has moved to Japan. He wants to buy 100 bats a year and can buy either American or Japanese bats. Igor thinks both are identical; hence he will buy the cheapest ones. The price of a bat in the United States is 5 dollars and in Japan is 500 yen.

   a. If the exchange rate between the U.S. and Japan is 110 yen per dollar, from where will Igor buy his bats — the United States or Japan? What is Igor's demand for U.S. dollars?

   b. If the exchange rate between the U.S. and Japan falls to 90 yen per dollar, from which country will Igor purchase his bats? What is Igor's demand for U.S. dollars?

   c. How does the quantity of U.S. dollars Igor demands change as the U.S. exchange rate falls from 110 yen per dollar to 90 yen per dollar?

5. Why does a rise in U.S. interest rates change the value of the exchange rate?

6. In Figure 20.4, show what happens to the demand for and supply of U.S. dollars if the U.S. exchange rate is expected to fall in the future. Does the current exchange rate rise or fall?

7. Table 20.4 presents the supply and demand schedules for U.S. dollars.

   a. Graph the supply and demand curves in Figure 20.5. What is the equilibrium exchange rate?

   b. Suppose that the Federal Reserve buys $200 billion of foreign securities. In Figure 20.5

FIGURE **20.4**

Short Answer Problem 6

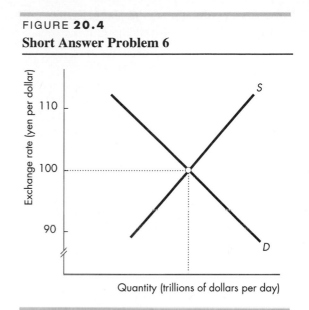

Quantity (trillions of dollars per day)

TABLE **20.4**

Supply and Demand of U.S. Dollars

U.S. exchange rate (yen per dollar)	Quantity of U.S. dollars demanded (trillions of dollars)	Quantity of U.S. dollars supplied (trillions of dollars)
130	$5.6	$6.0
120	5.7	5.9
110	5.8	5.8
100	5.9	5.7
90	6.0	5.6

FIGURE **20.5**

Short Answer Problem 7

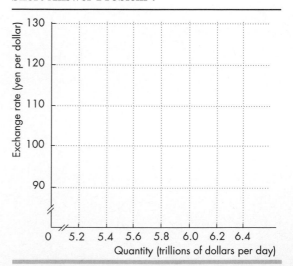

Quantity (trillions of dollars per day)

illustrate the effect of this increase in supply of U.S. dollars on the equilibrium foreign exchange rate.

c. Suppose that when the Federal Reserve purchased $200 billion of foreign securities, the U.S. interest rate fell. Further, suppose that the fall in the U.S. interest rate decreases the demand for U.S. dollars by $200 billion. Now illustrate the effect of the *combined* increase in supply and decrease in demand for U.S. dollars in Figure 20.5.

d. Is the change in the exchange rate larger when the supply alone changes, or when both the supply and demand change?

■ You're the Teacher

1. "Haven't I read somewhere that a current account deficit is called an 'unfavorable balance of trade'? Do you have any idea what this means, or why a current account deficit is called 'unfavorable'?" Your friend is indeed correct that a current account deficit is often called "unfavorable." Explain to your friend why you think a current account deficit has this name.

Answers

■ True/False Answers

Financing International Trade

1. **F** The sum of the current account, capital account, and official settlements account is *always* zero.

2. **F** A debtor nation may currently be a net loaner nation, which would thereby reduce its overall indebtedness.

3. **T** The private sector's surplus equals $S - I$, so if investment exceeds saving, the private sector has a deficit.

4. **T** The result that $X - M = (T - G) + (S - I)$ provides a framework for understanding what factors affect the net exports balance, $X - M$.

5. **F** Setting aside changes in official reserves, a current account deficit must be matched by an equal capital account surplus. Thus in the 1990s, the United States had a current account deficit and a capital account surplus.

6. **T** A larger budget deficit leads to a larger net exports deficit.

The Exchange Rate

7. **F** The fall in the exchange rate means that the U.S. dollar has depreciated. (The Japanese yen has appreciated.)

8. **T** The cheaper are U.S.-produced goods and services, the greater the quantity demanded by foreigners, so the greater the quantity demanded of U.S. dollars to buy the goods and services.

9. **T** An increase in the U.S. interest rate differential means that the interest rate paid on U.S. assets has risen relative to interest rates paid on foreign assets, which increases the demand for U.S. dollars.

10. **T** Suppliers want to hold — not sell — more U.S. dollars in order to reap the expected profit from the dollar's expected appreciation, so the current supply of dollars decreases.

11. **T** The demand for U.S. dollars increases and the supply decreases, both of which appreciate the U.S. exchange rate.

12. **F** The exchange rate is volatile precisely because the influences that change the demand for dollars also change the supply of dollars.

13. **T** The changes outlined in the question occurred in 1994-1995 when the U.S. dollar exchange rate depreciated.

14. **T** In the case outlined in the question, American residents will supply more dollars to buy yen, which thereby drives down the U.S. exchange rate.

15. **T** By buying U.S. dollars, the Fed increases the demand for dollars, thereby raising the U.S. exchange rate.

■ Multiple Choice Answers

Financing International Trade

1. **a** The current account records net exports, net transfers, and interest income from abroad minus interest payments to foreigners.

2. **b** The capital account records all investment accounts.

3. **c** The current account deficit reflects the excess of imports over exports while the capital account surplus reflects the excess of borrowing from foreigners over loaning to foreigners.

4. **b** With the official settlements account equal to zero, a current account deficit is balanced by an equal capital account surplus.

5. **c** Answer (c) correctly describes the recent situation with the United States.

6. **a** "Net lender" means that the nation is currently loaning more abroad than it is borrowing; "debtor" means that in the past the nation has borrowed more abroad than it has loaned. So, in total, the nation owes foreigners more than they owe it.

7. **c** The government surplus equals the difference between its net taxes and its spending, which in this case is –$100 billion. The negative sign indicates that the "surplus" is actually a deficit, so the government's deficit is $100 billion.

8. **c** The private sector surplus is the difference between the private sector's saving and investment.

9. **c** The net exports balance equals the sum of the government's (or public sector's) surplus, –$100 billion, plus the private sector's surplus, $150 billion, for a net exports surplus of $50 billion.

10. **a** Net exports equals the government sector deficit (the government budget deficit) plus the private sector deficit.

11. **c** Because of the tie between the government budget deficit and the net exports deficit, the two are sometimes called the "twin deficits."

The Exchange Rate

12. **a** Answer (a) accurately describes the history of the U.S. exchange rate.

13. **d** The yen has appreciated because it takes fewer yen to buy a dollar and the dollar has depreciated because a dollar buys fewer yen.

14. **b** The demand for U.S. dollars is derived from the demand from foreigners for U.S. goods and U.S. assets.

15. **c** The rise in the U.S. interest rate differential influences foreigners to demand more U.S. assets and fewer foreign assets, thereby increasing the demand for U.S. dollars.

16. **c** Similar to the previous answer, the rise in the U.S. interest rate differential influences U.S. residents to demand more U.S. assets and fewer foreign assets, thereby decreasing the supply of U.S. dollars.

17. **b** The increase in the future expected exchange rate raises the profit from owning U.S. dollars, which increases the demand and decreases the supply of dollars.

18. **d** This expectation increases the supply of dollars as people try to decrease the quantity of dollars they hold in order to limit their loss from the expected future depreciation.

19. **b** Both an increase in the supply of U.S. dollars and a decrease in the demand for U.S. dollars lower the U.S. exchange rate.

20. **d** This situation occurred in 1994-1995, and the dollar depreciated.

21. **d** It takes 2 dollars to purchase 1 pound, so the U.S. dollar cost of the British radio is (38 pounds)(2 dollars per pound) = 76 dollars.

22. **c** Answer (c) is essentially the definition of purchasing power parity.

23. **c** The expected depreciation "offsets" the higher interest rate.

24. **a** When the Fed buys dollars, it increases the demand for dollars, thereby raising the exchange rate.

25. **a** By purchasing dollars, the Fed must pay for the purchases with foreign currency. The Fed has only a certain amount of foreign currency, so

eventually the Fed would run out of foreign currency, at which time it would be forced to stop buying dollars.

■ Answers to Short Answer Problems

1. The national income accounting identities show that a country's net export deficit is equal to the sum of its government budget deficit and its private sector deficit. In particular, the relationship is $X - M = (T - G) + (S - I)$ where $X - M$ is the net exports balance, $T - G$ is the government surplus or deficit and $S - I$ is the private sector surplus or deficit.

2. a. The government surplus (or deficit) equals $T - G$. Hence, in the problem the government "surplus" is $800 billion minus $1,000 billion or $-$200 billion, that is, a government deficit of $200 billion.

   b. The private sector surplus (or deficit) is equal to $S - I$. Thus this formula yields a private sector "surplus" of $800 billion – $900 billion, that is, a deficit of $100 billion.

   c. The net exports balance, $X - M$, can be determined from the national income accounts formula $X - M = (T - G) + (S - I)$. Using the answers from parts (a) and (b) for the government deficit and private sector deficit gives the net exports balance equal to –$300 billion. That is, there is a deficit on the net exports balance of $300 billion.

   d. If taxes fall by $100 billion and private saving increases by $100 billion, using the formula $X - M = (T - G) + (S - I)$ shows that the net exports balance remains at $300 billion.

3. a. In 1996, Sega is a net borrower: its borrowing from the rest of world, $3,000, exceeds its lending to the rest of the world, $2,000. In 1997, Sega is neither a net borrower nor a net lender because its borrowing just equals its lending. In 1998 Sega is a net lender because its lending to the rest of the world, $5,000, exceeds its borrowing from the rest of the world, $1,000. In 1999 Sega is a net borrower.

   b. At the end of 1996, Sega is a debtor nation. It owed the rest of the world $3,000 (its borrowing to date), but the rest of the world owed Sega only $2,000 (its loans to the rest of the world to date). At the end of 1997 Sega is still a debtor nation: It owed the rest of the world a total of

$6,000 ($3,000 borrowed in 1996 plus $3,000 borrowed in 1997) and the rest of the world owed Sega only $5,000 ($2,000 loaned by Sega in 1996 plus $3,000 loaned in 1997). At the end of 1998, Sega is a creditor nation because the amount it owed the rest of the world, $7,000, is less than what the rest of the world owed Sega, $10,000. Even though in 1999 Sega is a net borrower, at the end of 1999 Sega is still a creditor nation because the amount it owed the rest of the world ($13,000) is less than the amount the rest of the world owed Sega ($15,000).

4. a. If Igor buys his bats from the United States, he will need 5 dollars per bat. With the exchange rate of 110 yen per dollar, a U.S. bat would cost 550 yen. A Japanese bat, however, costs only 500 yen. Hence Igor will buy from his Japanese supplier. Because Igor does not buy American bats, Igor's demand for U.S. dollars is zero.

   b. After the fall in the exchange rate, bats in the United States cost 450 yen. (5 dollars times 90 yen per dollar.) Thus bats are less expensive in the United States, so Igor buys from his American supplier. In order to pay this supplier, Igor demands 500 U.S. dollars.

   c. As the exchange rate fell, the quantity of U.S. dollars Igor demands increased. This result illustrates the downward slope of the demand curve for dollars: As the U.S. exchange rate falls, the quantity of U.S. dollars demanded increases.

5. A rise in U.S. interest rates changes the U.S. interest rate differential. More fundamentally, a rise in the U.S. interest rate increases the desirability of U.S. financial assets relative to foreign assets. In turn, this change affects the demand for U.S. dollars, which are necessary to buy American assets. In particular, foreigners increase their demand for U.S. dollars in order to buy more U.S. assets. The increase in the U.S. interest rate differential also decreases the supply of U.S. dollars because U.S. residents will buy fewer foreign assets. The increase in demand and decrease in supply both serve to raise the U.S. exchange rate.

6. If people expect that the U.S. exchange rate will fall in the future, they do not want to hold dollars because they will suffer a loss when the dollar falls in value. Hence the supply increases, as those people who currently own U.S. dollars try to sell them. And the demand decreases because buyers do not

FIGURE **20.6**
Short Answer Problem 6

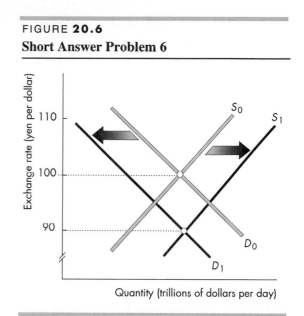

want to own the dollars when they fall in value. Figure 20.6 illustrates these responses. The demand curve shifts leftward, from D_0 to D_1 while the supply shifts rightward from S_0 to S_1. (Your figure does not need to be identical to Figure 20.6, but the direction of the shifts must be the same.) As Figure 20.6 shows, as a result of these changes the current exchange rate falls.

FIGURE **20.7**
Problem 7 (a)

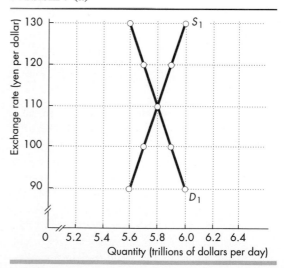

7. a. Figure 20.7 shows the demand and supply curves. The equilibrium exchange rate is 110 yen

FIGURE **20.8**
Short Answer Problem 7 (b)

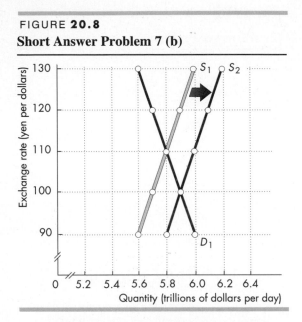

FIGURE **20.9**
Short Answer Problem 7 (c)

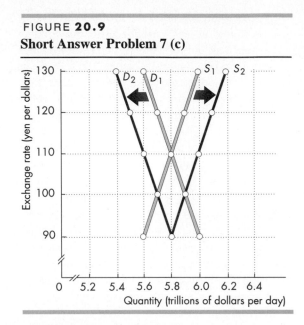

per dollar because this is the exchange rate at which the quantity of U.S. dollars demanded equals the quantity supplied.

b. When the Federal Reserve buys $200 billion of foreign securities, the quantity of U.S. dollars supplied increases by $200 billion. Thus, as illustrated in Figure 20.8, the supply curve of U.S. dollars shifts rightward by $200 billion. The increase in U.S. dollars depreciates the U.S. exchange rate to 100 yen per dollar.

c. Figure 20.9 illustrates the situation when the supply increases and demand decreases. The decrease in demand shifts the demand curve for U.S. dollars leftward by $200 billion, from D_1 to D_2. With both the shift in the supply and demand curves the exchange rate falls to 90 yen per dollar.

d. The exchange rate falls more when both the demand and supply curves shift. This result illustrates why exchange rates can be volatile: Factors that change the supply also affect the demand. In the case at hand, the Fed's actions affect *both* the supply for and demand of dollars. This situation is unlike that in most markets, in which the factors that influence the supply are generally different from those that affect the demand. Hence in the foreign exchange market, an increase in supply is often accompanied by a decrease in demand, driving the exchange rate sharply lower.

■ **You're the Teacher**

1. "You know, you're right, a current account deficit sometimes is called 'unfavorable.' I think there might be three reasons for this name. And actually all are rather silly!

"First, if we are running a current account deficit, it almost always means that the value of our imports exceeds the value of our exports; that is, the U.S. is importing more than it's exporting. Some observers claim that this situation costs us jobs in the United States. But look, we know from this chapter that this claim is wrong. I mean, we know that a current account deficit must be matched by a capital account surplus. So if our country runs a current account deficit, foreigners must be using the 'excess' funds to invest in the United States. Foreigners are buying U.S. financial assets, and that way they are keeping our interest rates lower than otherwise. And, by keeping U.S. interest rates lower, American businesses spend more on investment, which means that there are more people employed in industries that make investment goods, such as automobiles or machine tools. On net, a current account deficit doesn't seem likely to reduce jobs overall in the United States.

"Another reason that I can think of why a current account surplus is called 'unfavorable' is even sillier than the last. I bet some people think that foreigners actually keep the dollars abroad, that is, the U.S.

runs an official settlements surplus. Now, we know from this chapter that the official settlements balance is very small, so the idea that foreigners keep our money rather than use it to invest in the United States is *really* silly. But, if they did, I think this would be great! We'd get their goods in exchange for paper! Boy, I'd sure like to be able to buy the stuff I want and only have to give the stores paper on which I've scribbled some sort of design! If I could do this, I sure wouldn't call this situation 'unfavorable'!

"The last reason that comes to mind is the fact that if we're running a current account deficit, we must be running a capital account surplus. Thus foreigners are buying our assets. Some people think that when foreigners own enough of our assets, they can then control us and we'll be reduced to being some other nation's colony. Personally, I think this concern is also really silly, maybe the silliest of the bunch! First, there's no one nation that is buying up all our assets. Even if buying our assets could make us some sort of colony, what do you think the odds are that, say, Japan, Korea, France, Germany, South Africa, Poland, and all the other nations that own our assets can get together and agree to make us a colony? If you think this is likely, I have a large asset that extends over water in the city of Brooklyn that I'd love to sell to you! Second, even if a bunch of our assets are owned by someone else, so what? I mean, I owe a lot of money on my student loans, but the bank doesn't control me. And keep in mind that when these other nations buy our assets, they're basically at our mercy. For instance, suppose that Germany buys a lot of U.S. government securities. We could always decide that we simply wouldn't pay the Germans back! I mean, what are they going to do? Foreclose on the White House? Now, I don't think that we'll ever do this and I don't think that it's right, but come on. If we ever thought that foreigners were controlling us too much, we could take steps to end this control.

"So, I guess I can see why some people think that a current account deficit is 'unfavorable.' But I believe that what this claim actually shows is that the people making the claim haven't actually thought about the issue too deeply."

Chapter Quiz

1. The currency used to buy goods imported into a nation is generally

   a. gold.
   b. the currency of the nation importing the goods.
   c. the currency of the nation exporting the goods.
   d. None of the above.

2. A nation's balance of payments accounts include all of the following EXCEPT

   a. current account.
   b. national defense account.
   c. capital account.
   d. official settlements account.

3. A debtor nation is a country that

   a. currently borrows more than it lends.
   b. currently lends more than it borrows.
   c. owes foreigners more than foreigners owe to it.
   d. owes foreigners less than foreigners owe to it.

4. If the U.S. exchange rate changes from 120 yen per dollar to 105 yen per dollar, the dollar has

   a. appreciated.
   b. depreciated.
   c. become a net borrower.
   d. become a net lender.

5. If the expected future value of the U.S. exchange rate rises, the demand for dollars _____ and the supply of dollars _____.

   a. increases; increases
   b. increases; decreases
   c. decreases; increases
   d. decreases; decreases

6. If the expected future value of the U.S. exchange rate rises, the current U.S. exchange rate _____.

   a. rises
   b. does not change
   c. falls
   d. probably changes but in an ambiguous direction

7. An increase in the U.S. interest rate differential _____ the demand for U.S. dollars and the U.S. exchange rate _____.

   a. increases; rises
   b. increases; falls
   c. decreases; rises
   d. decreases; falls

8. An increase in the current U.S. exchange rate

   a. shifts the supply curve of U.S. dollars rightward.
   b. does not shift the supply curve of U.S. dollars either rightward or leftward.
   c. shifts the supply curve of U.S. dollars leftward.
   d. probably shifts the supply curve of U.S. dollars, but without more information it is impossible to determine the direction.

9. $X - M$ equals

   a. $(T - G) + (S - I)$.
   b. $(T - G) - (S - I)$.
   c. $(G - T) + (S - I)$.
   d. $(G - T) + (I - S)$.

10. The idea of "equal value for different currencies" is captured by

    a. interest rate parity.
    b. appreciation of all currencies.
    c. purchasing power parity.
    d. None of the above.

The answers for this Chapter Quiz are on page 328

UNDERSTANDING THE GLOBAL ECONOMY

WTO SUPPORTS U.S. IN DISPUTE OVER BANANAS

The World Trade Organization yesterday backed U.S. claims that the European Union's banana-import policies violate international rules, a significant American victory in an escalating series of trade disputes with the EU.

But the Geneva-based WTO arbitration panel rejected the U.S. estimate of how much damage the contentious EU banana policies cause American companies.

The WTO decision legitimized the U.S. decision to impose harsh retaliatory tariffs on a variety of EU goods. By setting the annual damage estimate at $191.4 million, however, the WTO forced the U.S. to pare down the list of European products-from Italian pecorino sheep cheese to British cashmere sweaters-it targeted for the 100% tariffs last month. The U.S. had estimated damages of $520 million a year.

The WTO "used much more conservative estimates than we did," said Peter Scher, the chief U.S. agricultural trade negotiator. "But any way you cut it, $200 million is a lot of money and, most importantly, this sends a very clear signal that they continue to violate their obligations."

It was the fifth time in six years that the WTO has ruled against the European banana policy, which favors bananas from former European colonies in Africa and the Caribbean over fruit from Central and South America. The U.S. says EU rules discriminate against banana distribution by two U.S. companies, Chiquita Brands International Inc. and Dole Foods Co.

The U.S. trade representative's office will announce the reduced list of retaliatory tariffs in the next few days. The tariffs effectively block imports of targeted items because they force up the prices to unreasonable levels.

"The U.S. has paid the cost of the EU's discrimination for six years-now the EU must pay the price," Mr. Scher said, adding that the U.S. remains open to a negotiated solution.

The banana dispute is at the heart of escalating trade tensions between the U.S. and the EU, with the U.S. charging that European import restrictions on a variety of goods are illegal. But in the past EU officials have blasted what they consider U.S. enthusiasm for taking unilateral action whenever it perceives its trade interests to be threatened.

■ Analyze It

The U.S./European Union dispute over bananas has raged for years. The European Union imposes higher tariffs and quotas on bananas imported from Central and South American. Most of the Central and South American bananas are shipped by two U.S. companies (Chiquita Brands International and Dole Foods Company). Thus the U.S. has filed complaints with the Word Trade Organization (WTO) that the European trade barriers violated international trade rules. The World Trade Organization agreed and, as reported in the article, estimated that the annual damage from the trade barriers was approximately $200 million.

1. Based on the WTO ruling, what is the United States allowed to do?

2. Use a supply and demand diagram to illustrate what the effect of the U.S. actions will be in the market for Italian pecorino sheep cheese.

3. The U.S. chief negotiator, Peter Scher, said that "The U.S. has paid the cost of the EU's discrimination for six years — now the EU must pay the price." Based on your supply and demand diagram in your answer to the previous question, who pays the price of the U.S.'s actions?

Web Resources

For more information, browse the Parkin Web site to explore related links.

Under "Economics Data," go to "Collections," then "On-Line Data," then "International". If your interests drive you in this direction, under "International," visit "International Trade".

Economic development is topic of incredible importance to billions of people in less developed nations. Explore this topic by looking under "Economic Development, Technological Change, and Growth," to visit "Economic Development" and then "Economic Development Institute and Global Environment".

Mid-Term Examination

■ **Chapter 19**

1. If the United States has an excess of exports over imports, the United States has
   a. a negative net exports balance that is financed by U.S. lending to foreigners.
   b. a negative net exports balance that is financed by U.S. borrowing from foreigners.
   c. a positive net exports balance that is financed by U.S. lending to foreigners.
   d. a positive net exports balance that is financed by U.S. borrowing from foreigners.

2. If an efficient country trades with the rest of the world, it produces at a point that lies
   a. inside its production possibility frontier.
   b. on its production possibility frontier.
   c. outside its production possibility frontier.
   d. either inside or outside its production possibility frontier.

3. When the full effects are considered, a reduction in tariffs would
   a. decrease imports and increase exports.
   b. increase imports and decrease exports.
   c. increase imports and exports.
   d. decrease imports and exports.

4. Which of the following earns revenue for the domestic government?
   a. Tariffs.
   b. Quotas.
   c. Voluntary export restraints.
   d. Subsidies.

■ **Chapter 20**

5. When selling exported goods, most often the seller wants
   a. gold.
   b. the currency of the seller's nation.
   c. the currency of the buyer's nation.
   d. bonds from the buyer's nation.

6. If a country has a current account surplus, that nation's quantity of net foreign assets is
   a. increasing
   b. decreasing.
   c. not affected.
   d. zero.

7. The demand curve for U.S. dollars
    a. is vertical.
    b. is horizontal.
    c. is positively sloped.
    d. is negatively sloped.

8. If the interest rate on Japanese yen assets rises, then the supply of dollars _____ and the demand for dollars _____.
    a. increases; increases
    b. increases; decreases
    c. decreases; increases
    d. decreases; decreases

Answers

■ Reading Between the Lines

Because the WTO ruled in favor of the U.S. complaint, the U.S. is allowed under international rules to impose retaliatory tariffs on products from the European Union. Retaliatory tariffs are extremely high tariffs (100 percent in this case) designed to eliminate specific products from being imported into the United States. The tariffs can be imposed as long as the offending party, the European Union in this case, continues its prohibited policies. If the policies are changed, the retaliatory tariffs must be removed.

Figure 1 shows the effect of this tariff in the market for Italian pecorino sheep cheese. In the figure, the initial (pre-tariff) supply curve S_1 and the price is (assumed to be) $4 per pound with 8,000 pounds imported per month. Because the cheese is Italian sheep cheese, the supply curve represents entirely cheese imported from Italian sources. Suppose that the United States imposes a 100 percent tariff on this cheese. The tariff means that at every quantity, the price of pecorino sheep cheese doubles, so that to have 8,000 pounds imported, the price would need to rise to $8 per pound. The retaliatory tariff shifts the supply curve to S_2. The demand curve is unaffected by the tariff and remains D. Along the supply curve S_2 to sell any cheese the minimum price sellers must receive is $6 per pound. But along demand curve D the maximum price consumers are willing to pay for pecorino sheep cheese is $5 per pound. Thus with the tariff, no cheese will be imported because the price is above the maximum demanders will pay and below the minimum suppliers must receive. The retaliatory tariff has eliminated imports of Italian pecorino sheep cheese.

FIGURE 1

The Pecorino Sheep Cheese Market

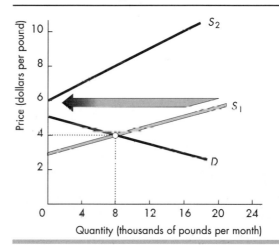

The figure points out that two groups pay the price of the tariff:

♦ Italian suppliers will find their U.S. market disappears because they will sell no cheese in the United States.

♦ In addition, however, U.S. consumers of pecorino sheep cheese pay a cost because they will no longer be able to consume this type of cheese.

Thus Peter Scher is incorrect when he suggests that only the EU "pays the price" of the tariff. A substantial group of losers from the tariff will be U.S. consumers of the products hit with the tariffs. So, just as the EU's policies keeping Central and South American bananas out of European markets harm European consumers, U.S. retaliatory tariffs harm U.S. consumers.

■ Mid-Term Exam Answers

1. c;   2. b;   3. c;   4. a;   5. b;   6. a;   7. d;   8. b

Final Exams

Exam I

1. Of the following, which would *not* be included in GDP?
   a. Your purchase of a haircut.
   b. Your purchase of a used textbook for this course.
   c. Your investment of $100 in a savings account at your bank.
   d. Neither b nor c would be included in GDP.

2. Which points in a production possibility frontier are both attainable and inefficient?
   a. Points beyond the frontier.
   b. Points on the frontier.
   c. Points within the frontier.
   d. Both points on and within the frontier.

3. Suppose a heat wave in the South causes millions of chickens to commit suicide. Keeping in mind that only live chickens can be sold to be processed into food, as a result of the heat the equilibrium relative price of a chicken dinner _____ and the equilibrium quantity _____.
   a. rises; increases
   b. probably changes, but in an ambiguous direction; decreases
   c. rises; probably changes, but in an ambiguous direction
   d. rises; decreases

4. If wages and prices were perfectly flexible so that the labor market is always in the equilibrium where the supply of labor equals the demand for it, then
   a. the *AS* curve is vertical.
   b. the *AS* curve is horizontal.
   c. the *AS* curve has a 45 degree slope.
   d. the *AD* curve is vertical.

5. According to the quantity theory, changes in the growth rate of the money supply cause changes in the inflation rate. Using the new classical (rational expectations) theory, if the public is aware of the Fed's monetary policy, then an increase in the growth rate of the money supply has no effect on the unemployment rate.
   a. Both sentences are true.
   b. The first sentence is true; the second sentence is false.
   c. The first sentence is false; the second sentence is true.
   d. Both sentences are false.

6. If the nominal interest rate is 10 percent and the real interest rate is 3 percent, the expected inflation rate is approximately
   a. 30 percent
   b. 13 percent
   c. 7 percent
   d. 3.3 percent

7. The stage of the business cycle during which output is falling is
   a. the recession.
   b. the expansion.
   c. the peak.
   d. the trough.

8. The supply curve for pizza is <u>NOT</u> directly shifted if there is a change in the
   a. number of sellers of pizza.
   b. technology used to produce pizza.
   c. price of pizza.
   d. price of resources (such as cheese) used to produce pizza.

9. If the government's tax revenues are $950 billion and its total expenditures are $900 billion, the government has a
   a. deficit of $50 billion
   b. surplus of $50 billion
   c. deficit of $900 billion
   d. surplus of $950 billion

10. An assumption of the neoclassical growth theory is that
    a. in the long run, people earn only a subsistence real wage.
    b. all technological advances are the result of people's deliberate actions.
    c. the economy-wide return to capital diminishes as more capital is accumulated.
    d. production can be replicated in identical firms.

11. Fiscal policy includes a change in
    a. the money supply.
    b. the price level.
    c. the unemployment rate.
    d. tax rates.

12. Suppose the MPC is 0.9 and there are no imports nor induced taxes. If investment falls by $20 billion and the government increases its purchases of goods and services by $50 billion, then the AD curve
    a. shifts rightward by $500 billion.
    b. shifts rightward by $300 billion.
    c. shifts rightward by $200 billion.
    d. shifts leftward.

13. As we move along a production possibility frontier producing more and more of a good, the opportunity cost of producing extra units of this good _____.
    a. falls
    b. does not change
    c. rises
    d. may rise, fall, or not change

14. GDP equals
    a. aggregate expenditure.
    b. aggregate income.
    c. the value of the aggregate production in a country during a given time period.
    d. all of the above

For the next two questions, suppose the government increased its purchases of goods, that is, G increases. In the short run, the economy moves along the short-run AS curve; in the long-run it moves along the long-run AS curve.

15. In the short run, the price level _____ and real GDP _____.
    a. rises; increases
    b. rises; does not change
    c. does not change; increases
    d. rises; decreases

16. In the long run, the price level _____ and real GDP _____.
    a. rises; increases
    b. rises; does not change
    c. does not change; increases
    d. rises; decreases

17. The discount rate is the interest rate that
    a. the Federal Reserve charges banks for loans from the Federal Reserve.
    b. banks charge the Federal Reserve for loans from the banks.
    c. banks charge each other for the loan of reserves.
    d. None of the above.

18. An increase in unemployment compensation payments means that the (total) cost to unemployed workers from searching for jobs has decreased. When the cost of searching for jobs decreases, unemployed workers will be more likely to accept job offers.
    a. Both sentences are true.
    b. The first sentence is true; the second sentence is false.
    c. The first sentence is false; the second sentence is true.
    d. Both sentences are false.

19. What type of unemployment would include a high school graduate who has just entered the labor force and is looking for a job?
    a. frictional
    b. structural
    c. cyclical
    d. excessive

20. Output is at its highest point at _____ and this is followed by _____.
    a. the recession; the trough.
    b. an expansion; a recession
    c. the peak; a recession.
    d. the peak; an expansion.

21. The most *common* way the Fed has of increasing the money supply is by
    a. raising the required reserve ratio.
    b. lowering the required reserve ratio.
    c. buying a government security.
    d. selling a government security.

22. According to the _____ theory of business cycles, a change in the monetary growth rate has no effect on real GDP.
    a. Keynesian
    b. monetarist
    c. new Keynesian
    d. real business cycle

23. Which of the following is included in the investment component of GDP?
    a. Microsoft's purchase of stock in IBM.
    b. GE's investment of $100,000 in a savings account at its bank.
    c. Ford Motor's purchase of a factory previously owned by GM.
    d. Leonardo's Pizza's (a local pizza restaurant) purchase of a new pizza oven.

24. The exchange rate changes from 100 yen per dollar to 130 yen per dollar. The yen has _____ against the dollar and the dollar has _____ against the yen.
    a. depreciated; appreciated
    b. depreciated; depreciated;
    c. appreciated; appreciated
    d. appreciated; depreciated

25. Which theory is characterized by the conclusion that people receive only a subsistence wage rate?
    a. The classical theory of growth.
    b. The Monetarist theory of business cycles.
    c. The Keynesian theory of business cycles.
    d. The neoclassical theory of growth.

26. A lot of trade between nations involves trading similar goods (that is, the U.S. both imports and exports automobiles to Japan). Which of the following is *not* a reason for trade in similar goods?
    a. Diversified tastes.
    b. Absolute advantage.
    c. Economies of scale.
    d. None of the above because they are all reasons for why nations trade similar goods..

27. A decrease in the expected future exchange rate shifts the demand curve for U.S. dollars _____ and the supply curve of U.S. dollars _____.
    a. rightward; rightward
    b. rightward; leftward
    c. leftward; rightward
    d. leftward; leftward

28. When the Federal Reserve buys a government security, banks' reserves will _____.
    a. increase
    b. not change
    c. decrease
    d. possibly change, depending on whether the Fed purchased the security from a bank or from another seller

29. Suppose that the growth rate of velocity is 1 percent, the growth rate of the money supply is 7 percent, and the growth rate of real GDP is 3 percent. Then the inflation rate is
    a. 8 percent.
    b. 6 percent.
    c. 5 percent.
    d. While the inflation rate can be calculated using the numbers given, none of the answers given above are correct.

30. The price of cheese used to produce pizza rises. As a result of the increase in cost, the equilibrium relative price of a pizza _____ and the equilibrium quantity produced _____.
    a. rises; increases
    b. rises; decreases
    c. falls; increases
    d. falls; decreases

Exam 2

1. If the *MPC* equals .9 and there are no imports nor induced taxes, in the *long-run* by how much does a $20 billion increase in government spending raise GDP?
   a. $0
   b. $20 billion
   c. $180 billion
   d. $200 billion

2. The situation of the price level rising and GDP falling — stagflation — could be caused by
   a. the *AD* curve shifting leftward.
   b. the *AD* curve shifting rightward.
   c. the *SAS* curve shifting leftward.
   d. the *SAS* curve shifting rightward.

3. Which of the following *shifts* the *SAS* leftward?
   a. an increase in the price level
   b. a decrease in the price level
   c. an increase in money wages
   d. a decrease in money wages

4. If the multiplier is 5, an increase of $20 billion in investment _____ equilibrium expenditures by _____.
   a. raises; $20 billion.
   b. lowers; $20 billion.
   c. raises; $100 billion.
   d. lowers; $100 billion.

5. In the *short-run*, an increase in the money supply _____ the price level and _____ real GDP.
   a. raises; increases
   b. raises; decreases
   c. does not change; increases
   d. raises; does not change

6. In the *long-run*, an increase in the money supply _____ the price level and _____ real GDP.
   a. raises; increases
   b. raises; decreases
   c. does not change; increases
   d. raises; does not change

7. Open-market operations are the purchase or sale of government securities by commercial banks.
   a. True
   b. False

8. An increase in consumers' income will cause the _____ curve for normal goods to shift _____.
   a. demand; leftward
   b. demand; rightward
   c. supply; leftward
   d. supply; rightward

9. Suppose that people decide eating pizza is stylish and simultaneously a new pizza oven is invented that lowers the cost of producing a pizza. The relative price of a pizza _____ and the quantity _____.
   a. rises; increases
   b. falls; increases
   c. probably changes, but in an ambiguous direction; increases
   d. rises; probably changes, but in an ambiguous direction

10. Which of the following factors does <u>NOT</u> *shift* the *AD* curve?
    a. a change in government purchases
    b. a change in the money supply
    c. a change in taxes
    d. a change in the price level

11. The most expansionary fiscal policy of the following is the one that
    a. lowers *G* and lowers taxes.
    b. raises *G* and lowers taxes.
    c. raises *G* and raises taxes even more.
    d. raises taxes.

12. According to monetarists, the Great Depression was caused by
    a. the stock market crash of 1929.
    b. a massive contraction of the money supply, leading to large decreases in aggregate demand.
    c. an expansion of the money supply, leading to higher inflation.
    d. a rise in business and consumer confidence.

13. When would the U.S. exchange rate rise the most?
    a. When the supply of and demand for U.S. dollars increase.
    b. When the supply of U.S. dollars increases and the demand for them decreases.
    c. When the supply of U.S. dollars decreases and the demand for them increases.
    d. When the supply of and demand for U.S. dollars decrease.

14. What type of unemployment would include an individual who is unemployed because of a general downturn in economic activity?
    a. Frictional unemployment
    b. Structural unemployment
    c. Cyclical unemployment
    d. Trough unemployment.

15. Along the path of the business cycle, real GDP rises during ____, then reaches ____, and then ____.
    a. a recession; a peak; an expansion
    b. an expansion; a peak; a recession
    c. a trough; an expansion; a peak
    d. a recession; a trough; an expansion

16. Which of the following is the impulse in the Keynesian business cycle theory?
    a. An unexpected change in aggregate demand.
    b. A change by the Fed in the growth rate of the money supply.
    c. A change in expectations about future sales and profits.
    d. An unexpected change in the growth rate of productivity.

17. What compensates a lender and charges a borrower for the amount of the loan *and* the fall in the value of money?
    a. The inflation rate.
    b. The nominal interest rate.
    c. The real interest rate.
    d. None of the above.

18. Which theory concludes that economic growth can continue indefinitely?
    a. The classical theory.
    b. The Keynesian theory.
    c. The new growth theory.
    d. The neoclassical theory.

19. The government sector deficit is $75 billion and the private sector deficit is $25 billion. Hence net exports equals
    a. −$100 billion.
    b. −$75 billion
    c. −$50 billion.
    d. −$25 billion.

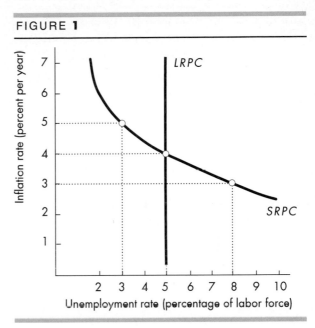

FIGURE 1

20. In the figure, the expected rate of inflation is
    a. 5 percent.
    b. 4 percent.
    c. 3 percent.
    d. None of the above

21. In the figure, the natural rate of unemployment is
    a. 3 percent.
    b. 5 percent.
    c. 8 percent.
    d. None of the above.

22. Which of the following is a fixed-rule policy?
    a. Increase government spending only if the unemployment rate exceeds 6 percent.
    b. Increase government spending in a recession.
    c. Have the money supply grow 3 percent per year each year.
    d. Decrease the growth rate of the money supply when the inflation rate becomes too high.

23. Along which curve does the price level change but not money wages?
    a. The *AD* curve.
    b. The *SAS* curve.
    c. The *LAS* curve.
    d. None of the above.

24. If the *MPC* = .9 and there are no imports nor induced taxes, what does the lump-sum tax multiplier equal?
    a. 10.0.
    b. 9.0.
    c. −10.0.
    d. −9.0.

25. If the price index last year is 200 and next year is 220, the inflation rate between the years is
    a. 220 percent
    b. 200 percent
    c. 20 percent
    d. 10 percent

26. A decrease in the required reserve ratio _____ excess reserves and _____ the money supply.
    a. increases; increases
    b. increases; decreases
    c. decreases; increases
    d. decreases; decreases

27. A nation's investment must be financed by
    a. national saving only.
    b. the government's budget deficit.
    c. borrowing from the rest of the world only.
    d. national saving plus borrowing from the rest of the world.

28. Suppose that capital per hour of work increases by 21 percent while real GDP per hour of work increases by 12 percent. The change in technology increased real GDP per hour of work by _____.
    a. 21 percent
    b. 17 percent
    c. 12 percent
    d. 5 percent

29. The maximum gains from international trade occur when
    a. there is no such trade.
    b. each nation produces according to its comparative advantage and trades with other nations.
    c. each nation uses tariffs rather than quotas to restrict trade.
    d. each nation uses quotas rather than tariffs to restrict trade.

30. In the United States, from 1960 to 1998, the demand for labor has
    a. increased more than the supply of labor has increased.
    b. increased less than the supply of labor increased.
    c. increased while the supply of labor has decreased.
    d. decreased while the supply of labor has increased by more.

Answers

■ Final Exam 1 Answers

1. d;   2. c;   3. d;   4. a;   5. a;   6. c;   7. a;   8. c;   9. b;   10. c;
11. d;   12. b;   13. c;   14. d;   15. a;   16. b;   17. a;   18. b;   19. a;   20. c;
21. c;   22. d;   23. d;   24. a;   25. a;   26. b;   27. c;   28. a;   29. c;   30. b.

■ Final Exam 2 Answers

1. a;   2. c;   3. c;   4. c;   5. a;   6. d;   7. b;   8. b;   9. c;   10. d;
11. b;   12. b;   13. c;   14. c;   15. b;   16. c;   17. b;   18. c;   19. a;   20. b;
21. b;   22. c;   23. b;   24. d;   25. d;   26. a;   27. d;   28. d;   29. b;   30. a.

Answers to Quizzes

Answers

Chapter 1
1. c;   2. b;   3. d;   4. c;   5. d;   6. a;   7. c;   8. c;   9. d;   10. d.

Chapter 2
1. c;   2. c;   3. a;   4. c;   5. c;   6. c;   7. c;   8. d;   9. b;   10. b.

Chapter 3
1. b;   2. d;   3. b;   4. d;   5. a;   6. a;   7. d;   8. b;   9. c;   10. d.

Chapter 4
1. d;   2. d;   3. b;   4. b;   5. c;   6. b;   7. c;   8. a;   9. b;   10. b.

Chapter 5
1. a;   2. c;   3. a;   4. a;   5. b;   6. c;   7. c;   8. c;   9. c;   10. d.

Chapter 6
1. b;   2. c;   3. a;   4. a;   5. a;   6. d;   7. b;   8. b;   9. b;   10. c.

Chapter 7
1. d;   2. a;   3. c;   4. a;   5. b;   6. c;   7. a;   8. c;   9. b;   10. d.

Chapter 8
1. c;   2. d;   3. b;   4. c;   5. d;   6. c;   7. c;   8. d;   9. b;   10. d.

Chapter 9
1. c;   2. d;   3. a;   4. b;   5. a;   6. a;   7. c;   8. c;   9. d;   10. c.

Chapter 10
1. c;   2. b;   3. b;   4. c;   5. d;   6. a;   7. b;   8. d;   9. b;   10. d.

Chapter 11
1. d;   2. d;   3. d;   4. d;   5. c;   6. c;   7. c;   8. b;   9. c;   10. b.

■ **Chapter 12**
1. b;   2. b;   3. b;   4. a;   5. a;   6. a;   7. a;   8. a;   9. d;   10. c.

Chapter 13
1. b;   2. c;   3. c;   4. c;   5. c;   6. d;   7. a;   8. b;   9. a;   10. a.

Chapter 14
1. a;   2. b;   3. d;   4. a;   5. a;   6. a;   7. d;   8. c;   9. b;   10. c.

Chapter 15
1. c;   2. b;   3. b;   4. c;   5. a;   6. c;   7. b;   8. d;   9. a;   10. a.

Chapter 16
1. a;   2. c;   3. c;   4. d;   5. d;   6. a;   7. a;   8. d;   9. c;   10. c.

Chapter 17
1. b;   2. a;   3. b;   4. d;   5. c;   6. a;   7. d;   8. a;   9. d;   10. c.

Chapter 18
1. d;   2. d;   3. b;   4. d;   5. c;   6. b;   7. a;   8. d;   9. d;   10. a.

Chapter 19
1. a;   2. d;   3. c;   4. b;   5. a;   6. c;   7. a;   8. d;   9. d;   10. a.

■ **Chapter 20**
1. c;   2. b;   3. c;   4. b;   5. b;   6. a;   7. a;   8. b;   9. a;   10. c.

Conclusion

SHOULD YOU MAJOR IN ECONOMICS?*

Should You Take More Economic Courses?

You have learned about supply and demand, utility and profit maximization, employment and unemployment, and Igor (at least in the study guide you learned about Igor!). Now, however, let's take a moment to look to the future.

♦ Should you take more classes or maybe even major in economics?

♦ What about graduate school in economics?

Economists generally assume that people try to make rational choices to maximize their own well-being. The purpose of this chapter is help you make that rational maximizing choice by providing low-cost information. Let us assess the benefits and see whether they outweigh the costs of studying economics.

Benefits from Studying Economics

■ Knowledge, Enlightenment, and Liberation

As John Maynard Keynes, a famous British economist, said, "The ideas of economists ... both when they are right and when they are wrong, are more powerful than is commonly understood. Indeed the world is ruled by little else. Practical men, who believe themselves to be quite exempt from any intellectual influences, are usually the slaves of some defunct economist." Studying economics is a liberating and enlightening experience. You don't want to be the slave of a defunct economist, do you? Liberate yourself. It's better to bring your ideas out in the open, to confront and understand them, rather than to leave them buried.

---

* This section was written by Robert Whaples of Wake Forest University.

■ Knowledge, Understanding, and Satisfaction

Many of the most important problems in the world are economic. Studying economics gives you a practical set of tools to understand and solve them. Every day, on television and in the newspapers, we hear and read about big issues such as economic growth, inflation, unemployment, health care reform, welfare reform, the environment, and the transition away from Communism. Your introduction to economics will let you watch the news or pick up a newspaper and better understand these issues. As an added bonus, economics helps you understand smaller, more immediate concerns, such as: How much Spam should I buy? Is skipping class today a good idea? Should I put my retirement funds in government bonds or in the stock market? After all, as George Bernard Shaw put it, "Economy is the art of making the most of life." Mick Jagger, who dropped out of the London School of Economics, complains that he "can't get no satisfaction." Maybe he should have studied more economics. The economic way of thinking will help you maximize your satisfaction.

■ Career Opportunities

All careers are not equal. While the wages in many occupations have not risen much lately, the wages of "symbolic analysts" who "solve, identify, and broker problems by manipulating symbols" are soaring.[1] These people "simplify reality into abstract images that can be rearranged, juggled, experimented with, communicated to other specialists, and then, eventually, transformed back into reality." Their wages have been rising as the globalization of the economy increases the demand for their insights and as technological developments (especially computers) have enhanced their productivity. Economists are the quintessential symbolic analysts as we manipulate ideas about abstractions such as supply and demand, cost and benefits, and equilibrium.

You can think of your training in economics as an exercise regimen, a workout for your brain.

You will use many of the concepts you will learn in introductory economics during your career, but it is the practice in abstract thinking that will really pay off. In fact, most economics majors do not go on to become economists. They enter fields that use their analytical abilities, including business, management, insurance, finance, real estate, marketing, law, education, policy analysis, consulting, government, planning, and even medicine, journalism, and the arts.

A recent survey of 100 former economics majors at my university included all of these careers. If you want to verify that economics majors graduate to successful and rewarding careers, just ask your professors or watch what happens to economics majors from your school as they graduate.

Statistics from the Bureau of the Census show that across the nation, economics majors earn more than most other majors (see Table 1).

TABLE **1**

Average Monthly Income of People Who Hold a Bachelor's Degree by Field of Study, Spring 1990

Engineering	$3,508
Agriculture and forestry	$3,273
Economics	$2,977
Mathematics and statistics	$2,947
Business and management	$2,780
Other	$2,639
Biology	$2,627
Physical and earth sciences	$2,559
Liberal arts and humanities	$2,239
Psychology	$2,196
Social sciences	$2,118
Nursing, pharmacy, health technologies	$2,056
English and journalism	$2,041
Education	$1,882

Source: U.S. Department of Commerce, Bureau of the Census, *Current Population Reports,* Series P-70, No. 32, "Educational Background and Economic Status: Spring 1990."

Other sources using data on entry-level wages verify these patterns. In 1993 the average annual starting salary of economics and finance majors was $28,584. While this is lower than the salaries for those with degrees in engineering, computer science, chemistry, and math, it is somewhat higher than salaries for those with degrees in business administration. Moreover, the entry-level salary of economics majors beats the entry-level salary of humanities majors by about $4,000, is almost $6,000 higher than the earnings for other social sciences (e.g., psychology, political science, anthropology, sociology), and tops the earnings of school teachers by even more. (*Source: Statistical Abstract of the United States,* 1994, Tables 246 and 289.) These numbers are updated annually, so feel free to look up the latest statistics. In addition, the employment rate of economics majors is higher than that of many other majors, such as those in the humanities and other social sciences. Finally, the supply of new economics majors has been falling lately (down about 10 percent since 1990). Since the demand has remained high, the future promises even brighter prospects for economics majors.

The Costs of Studying Economics

Since the "direct" costs of studying economics (tuition, books, supplies) aren't generally any higher or lower than the direct costs of other courses, indirect costs will be the most important of the costs to studying economics.

◼ Forgone Knowledge

If you study economics, you can't study something else. This forgone knowledge could be very valuable.

◼ Time and Energy

Economics is a fairly demanding major. Although economics courses do not generally take as much time as courses in English and history (in which you have to read a lot of long books) or anatomy and physiology (in which you have to spend hours in the lab and hours memorizing things), they do take a decent amount of time. In addition, some people find the material "tougher" than most subjects because memorizing is not the key. In economics (like physics), analyzing and solving are the keys.

■ Grades

As Table 2 shows, grades in introductory economics courses are generally a hair lower than grades in some other majors, including other social sciences and the humanities.[2] On the other hand, grades in economics are considerably higher than grades in the sciences and math.

TABLE 2

Average Grades and Grade Distribution by College Major

Department	Mean Grade	% Above B+	% Below B–
Music	3.16	44	21
English	3.12	27	12
Psychology	3.02	28	23
Philosophy	2.99	29	21
Art	2.95	29	24
Political science	2.95	24	23
Economics	2.81	20	31
Chemistry	2.66	17	44
Math	2.53	22	46

Caveat Emptor (Buyer Beware): Interpreting Your Grades Is Not Straight Forward

High grades provide direct satisfaction to most students, but they also act as a signal about the student's ability to learn the subject material. Unfortunately, because the grade distribution is not uniform across departments, you may be confused and misled by your grades. You may think that you are exceptionally good at a subject because of a high grade, when in fact nearly everyone gets a high grade in that subject. The important point here is that you should be informed about your own school's grade distribution. Just because you got a B in economics and an A in history does not necessarily mean that your comparative advantage is in learning history rather than economics. Everyone — or virtually everyone — may receive an A in history. Earning a B or a C in economics could mean that it is the best major for you because high grades are much harder to earn in economics. It is fun to have a high GPA in college, but maximizing GPA should not be your goal. Maximizing your overall well-being is probably your goal, and this might be obtained by trading off a tenth or so of your GPA for a more rewarding major — perhaps economics.

Potential Side Effects from Studying Economics

Studying economics has some potential side effects. I'm not sure whether they are costs or benefits and will let you decide.

■ Changing Ideas about What Is Fair

A recently completed study compared students at the beginning and end of the semester in an introductory economics course.[3] It found that by the end of the semester, significantly more of the students thought that the functioning of the market is "fair." This was especially true for female students. The results were consistent across a range of professors who fell across the ideological spectrum.

For example, the proportion of students who regarded it as unfair to increase the price of flowers on a holiday fell almost in half. The proportion that favored government control over flower prices, rather than market determination, fell by over 60 percent. The study argues that these responses do not reflect changes in deep values, but instead represent the discovery of previous inconsistencies and their modification in the light of new information learned during the semester.

■ Changing Behavior

Many people believe that the study of economics changes students' values and behavior. Some think that it changes them for the worse. Others disagree. In particular, it is argued that economics students become more self-interested and less likely to cooperate, perhaps because they spend so much time studying economic models, which often assume that people are self-interested. For example, one study reports experimental evidence that economics students are more likely than nonmajors to behave self-interestedly in prisoners' dilemma games and ultimatum bargaining games.[4]

This need not mean that studying economics will change you, however. Another study compares beginning freshmen and senior economics students and concludes that economics students "are already different when they begin their study of economics."[5] In other words, students signing up for economics courses are already different; studying economics doesn't change them. However, there are reasons to question both of these conclusions, because it is not clear whether these laboratory experiments using economic games reflect reality. One experiment asked students whether they would return money that had been lost. It found that economics students were more likely than others to say that they would keep the cash.

However, what people say and what they do are sometimes at odds. In a follow-up experiment, this theory was tested by dropping stamped, addressed envelopes containing $10 in cash in different campus classrooms. To return the cash, the students had only to seal the envelopes and mail them. The results were that 56 percent of the envelopes dropped in economics classes were returned, while only 31 percent of the envelopes dropped in history, psychology and business classes were sent in.[6] Perhaps economics students are less selfish than others!

Obviously, no firm conclusions have been reached about whether or how studying economics changes students behavior.

Costs versus Benefits

Suppose that you've weighed the costs and benefits of studying economics and you've decided that the benefits are greater than or equal to the costs. Obviously, then, you should continue to take economics courses. If you can't decide whether the benefits outweigh the costs, then you should probably collect more information — especially if it is good but inexpensive. In either case, read the rest of this section.

The Economics Major

The study of economics is like a tree. The introductory microeconomics and macroeconomics courses you begin with are the tree's roots. Most colleges and universities require that you master this material before you go on to any other courses. The way of thinking, the language, and the tools that you acquire in the introductory course are usually reinforced in intermediate microeconomics and macroeconomics courses before they are applied in more specialized courses that you take. The intermediate courses are the tree's trunk. Among the specialized courses that make up the branches of economics are econometrics (statistical eco-

nomics), financial economics, labor economics, resource economics, international trade, industrial organization, public finance, public choice, economic history, the history of economic thought, mathematical economics, current economic issues, and urban economics. The branches of the tree vary from department to department, but these are common. It will pay to check your college bulletin and discuss these courses with professors and other students.

Graduate School in Economics

■ Preparing for Graduate School in Economics

You can prepare for graduate school in economics by taking several math classes. This would probably include at least two years of calculus plus a couple of courses in probability and statistics and linear/matrix algebra. Ask your advisor about the particular courses to take at your college. In addition, the mathematical economics and econometrics courses in the economics department are essential. (*Helpful hint*: Even if you aren't going to graduate school, these mathematical courses can be valuable to you, just as more economics courses can be valuable for nonmajors.)

If your school offers graduate level economics courses, you might want to sit in on a few to get accustomed to the flavor of graduate school.

Most graduate programs require strong grades in economics, a good score on the Graduate Record Examination (GRE), and solid letters of recommendation. It is a good idea to get to know a few professors very well and to go above and beyond what is expected so that they can write glowing letters about you.

■ Financing Graduate School

Unlike some other graduate and professional degree programs, you probably won't need to pile up a massive amount of debt while pursuing a Ph.D. in economics. Most Ph.D. programs hire their economics graduate students as teaching or research assistants. Teaching assistants begin by grading papers and running review sessions and can advance to teaching classes on their own. Research assistants generally do data collection, statistical work, and library research for professors and often jointly write papers with them. Most assistantships will pay for tuition and provide you with enough money to live on.

▪ Where Should You Apply?

The best graduate school for you depends on a lot of things, especially your ability level, geographical location, areas of research interests, and, of course, financing. You should talk with your professors about ability level and areas of research. In addition, there are informative articles that give overall departmental rankings and rankings by subfield. See especially John Tschirhart, "Ranking Economics Department in Areas of Expertise," *Journal of Economic Education*, and David Colander, "Research on the Economic Profession," *Journal of Economic Perspectives*, Vol. 3, no. 4, Fall 1989, pp. 137–148. There will probably be more up-to-date rankings by the time you apply. Ask a professor or reference librarian to help you track them down. For smaller specialties (e.g., economic history, urban economics) it is especially important to get up-to-date information on any particular program.

▪ What You Will Do in Graduate School

Most graduate programs in economics begin with a year of theory courses in macroeconomics and microeconomics. After a year you will probably take a series of tests to show that you have mastered this core theory. If you pass these tests, in the second and third year of courses you will take more specialized subjects and perhaps take lengthy examinations in a couple of subfields. After this you will be required to write a dissertation —original research that will contribute new knowledge to one of the fields of economics. These stages are intertwined with work as a teaching and/or research assistant, and the dissertation stage can be quite drawn out. In the social sciences the median time that it takes for a student to complete the Ph.D. degree is about 7.5 years.[7] Be aware that a high percentage (roughly 50 percent) of students do not complete their doctoral degree.

▪ What Is Graduate School Like?

Graduate school in economics comes as a surprise to many students. The material and approach are distinctly different from what you will learn as an undergraduate. The textbooks and journal articles you will read in graduate school are often very theoretical and abstract. A good source of information is sitting in on courses or reading the reflections of recent students. See especially *The Making of an Economist* by Arjo Klamer and David Colander (Boulder, Colo.: Westview Press, 1990).

The Committee on Graduate Education in Economics (COGEE) undertook an important review of graduate education in economics and reported its findings in the September 1991 issue of the *Journal of Economic Literature*. COGEE asked faculty members, graduate students, and recent Ph.D.s to rank the most important skills needed to be successful in the study of graduate economics. At the top of the list were analytical skills and mathematics, followed by critical judgment, the ability to apply theory, and computational skills. At the bottom of the list were creativity and the ability to communicate. If you are interested in economic issues but do not have the characteristics required by graduate economics departments, there are other economics-related fields to consider, such as graduate school in public policy. Many economics majors go to business schools to obtain an MBA and are often better prepared than students who have undergraduate degrees in business.

Economics Reading

If decide to make studying economics part of your future, or if you're hungry for more economics, you should immediately begin reading the economic news and books by economists. Life is short. Why waste it watching TV?

The easiest way to get your daily recommended dose of economics is to keep up with current economic events. Here are a few sources to pick up at the newsstand, bookstore, or library over your summer or winter break.

▪ The *Wall Street Journal*

Many undergraduates subscribe to the *Wall Street Journal* (WSJ) at low student rates. Join them! Your professor will probably have student subscription forms. Not only is the WSJ a well-written business newspaper, but it also has articles on domestic and international news, politics, the arts, travel, and sports, as well as a lively editorial page (sorry, only one comic strip). Reading the WSJ is one of the best ways to tie the economics you are studying to the real world and to prepare for your career.

Magazines and Journals

The Economist, a weekly magazine published in England, is available at a student discount rate of $85/year. Pick up a copy at your school library and you will be hooked by its informative, sharp writing. *Business Week* is also well worth the read.

Also recommended are *Challenge* magazine and *The Public Interest*, two quarterlies that discuss economic policy. Finally, there is the *Journal of Economics Perspectives*, which is published by the American Economic Association and written to be accessible to undergraduate economics students.

Books by Economists

I recently asked a group of economics professors from across the country (members of the Teach-Econ computer discussion list) the following question: "A bright, enthusiastic student who has just completed introductory economics comes up to you, the professor, and asks you to recommend an economics book for reading over the summer. What do you suggest?"

Here is what they suggested that you, the bright, enthusiastic student, should read:

Top Choices

Milton Friedman, *Capitalism and Freedom.*

Robert Heilbroner, *The Worldly Philosophers: The Lives, Times, and Ideas of the Great Economic Thinkers.*

Steve Landsburg, *The Armchair Economist: Economics and Everyday Life.*

Other Good Choices

Alan Blinder, *Hard Heads, Soft Hearts: Tough-Minded Economics for a Just Society.*

Victor Fuchs, *How We Live.*

Paul Krugman, *Peddling Prosperity: Economic Sense and Nonsense in the Age of Diminished Expectations.*

Donald McCloskey, *If You're So Smart: The Narrative of Economic Expertise.*

Russell Roberts, *The Choice: A Parable of Free Trade and Protectionism.*

In addition, Adam Smith's *The Wealth of Nations* is a must read for every student of economics. Written in 1776, it is the most influential work of economics ever. Its insights are still valuable today.

Endnotes

1. This term is used by Robert Reich in *The Work of Nations*. The quote is from p. 178.

2. Richard Sabot and John Wakeman-Linn, "Grade Inflation and Course Choice," *Journal of Economic Perspectives*, Vol. 5, no. 1, Winter 1991, pp. 159–170.

3. Robert Whaples, "Changes in Attitudes about the Fairness of Free Markets among College Economics Students," *Journal of Economic Education*, Vol. 26, no. 4, Fall 1995.

4. Robert H. Frank, Thomas Gilovich, and Dennis T. Regan, "Does Studying Economics Inhibit Cooperation?" *Journal of Economic Perspectives*, Vol. 7, no. 2, Spring 1993, pp. 159–171.

5. John R. Carter and Michael D. Irons, "Are Economists Different, and If So, Why?" *Journal of Economic Perspectives*, Vol. 5, no. 2, Spring 1991, pp. 171–177.

6. "Economics Students Aren't Selfish, They're Just Not Entirely Honest," *Wall Street Journal*, January 18, 1995, B1.

7. See Ronald Ehrenberg, "The Flow of New Doctorates," *Journal of Economic Literature*, Vol. 30, June 1992, pp. 830–875. If breaks in school attendance are included, this climbs to 10.5 years. Of course, some students attend only part time, and most have some kind of employment while completing their degrees.